THE CRUSADES

READINGS IN MEDIEVAL CIVILIZATIONS AND
CULTURES: VIII
series editor: Paul Edward Dutton

THE CRUSADES

A READER

edited by

S.J. ALLEN AND EMILIE AMT

broadview press

National Library of Canada Cataloguing in Publication
The Crusades : a reader / edited by S.J. Allen and Emilie Amt.

(Readings in medieval civilizations and cultures)

Includes bibliographical references and index.
ISBN 1-55111-537-9

1. Crusades—Sources. I. Allen, S. J. (Susan Jane), 1959- II. Amt, Emilie, 1960- III. Series.
D151.C78 2003   909.07   C2003-902603-5

Broadview Press Ltd. is an independent, international publishing house, incorporated in 1985. Broadview believes in shared ownership, both with its employees and with the general public; since the year 2000 Broadview shares have traded publicly on the Toronto Venture Exchange under the symbol BDP.

We welcome comments and suggestions regarding any aspect of our publications—please feel free to contact us at the addresses below or at broadview@broadviewpress.com.

North America:

PO Box 1243, Peterborough, Ontario, Canada K9J 7H5

3576 California Road, Orchard Park, NY, USA 14127

Tel: (705) 743-8990; Fax: (705) 743-8353
E-mail: customerservice@broadviewpress.com

UK, Ireland, and continental Europe:

Plymbridge Distributors Ltd., Estover Road
Plymouth PL6 7PY UK

Tel: (01752) 202301;
Fax: (01752) 202333
E-mail: orders@plymbridge.com

Australia and New Zealand:

UNIREPS,
University of New South Wales
Sydney, NSW, 2052

Tel: 61 2 9664 0999;
Fax: 61 2 9664 5420
E-mail: info.press@unsw.edu.au

www.broadviewpress.com

This book is printed on acid-free paper containing 20% post-consumer fibre.

Text design and composition by George Kirkpatrick

PRINTED IN CANADA

For Edie Ross Dixson

CONTENTS

INTRODUCTION

The guardianship of Jerusalem, the most holy of cities for the Christian West, lay at the heart of a series of movements known today as the Crusades. In its strictest sense, a Crusade was a holy war called by the medieval papacy with the aim of gaining the Holy Land and, in particular, the city of Jerusalem. At the end of the eleventh century, when the Crusades began, Jerusalem and the surrounding territory were in the hands of Muslims, a people and religion little known in the West, save for the fact that they were not Christian. For Jerusalem did not belong solely, or even primarily, to Christianity. Its sacred role had been founded in Judaism, and, in the tradition of "people of the book," Islam too had ascribed a revered status to the city. Thus, each of these three great monotheistic religions laid claim to Jerusalem at the time of the Crusades, and each continues to do so today.

The evolution of the crusading ideal, however, went far beyond the restrictive definition given above. As will be evident from the primary sources provided here, crusading took on a much broader scope as it developed through the latter half of the Middle Ages and on into the early modern period. This development and its consequences form a central focus of this book. The crusading movement did not emerge out of a vacuum in 1095, nor did it end with the loss of the crusader states in the late thirteenth century. Moreover, the significance of these movements did not lie solely in battles and conquests. Just as important were the societies and institutions altered and created by the Crusades, as well as the legacy they left to both Europe and the Middle East.

The significance of Jerusalem and the Holy Land to western medieval culture is established in the first chapter, "Background and Origins." Here it can be seen how Christians of the West viewed the Middle East region, not simply with reverence, but with a sense of ownership that created a strong spiritual bond. A journey to the Holy Land was seen as the ultimate Christian pilgrimage (doc. 1), and although the vast majority of the medieval population never visited the region, the writings of those who had made the journey established it as a fundamental part of the West's religious heritage and birthright. This link was crucial to the ideology that would create the Crusades.

But Muslims also had a link to Jerusalem. The rise of Islam during the early Middle Ages had altered the religious and political face of the Middle East, North Africa, and Spain and set the stage for later struggles over these territories (doc. 4). Critical to the understanding of this change is a knowledge of both western and Islamic views of warfare. In the Quran (doc. 3) and the writings of churchmen such as Augustine (doc. 2), the origins of *jihad* and Christian holy war are evident. Important too are the attitudes each religion displayed toward those outside the faith. Documents such as the Pact of Omar (doc. 5), Ibnu Hayyan's accounts of Muslim and Christian conflicts in Spain

THE CRUSADES: A READER

(doc. 7), and even the Song of Roland (doc. 8) demonstrate the tolerance and tensions that could be found among Muslims, Jews, and Christians in the centuries prior to the First Crusade.

The Crusades were, however, a western European offensive, and their birth depended as much on conditions within Europe as on those in Spain or the Holy Land. The rise of popular piety, the violent struggles of the upper classes for land, and the ambitions of the papacy and church to strengthen ecclesiastical authority each played its part in the creation of the crusade mentality. Yet even all this was not enough to spark the crusading movement. The final element of the formula lay in eleventh-century conquests of parts of the Byzantine (Greek) Empire by the Seljuk Turks, and the subsequent pleas from the Byzantines to the West for aid. Pope Gregory VII's call for military aid against the Turks (doc. 11) in 1074 contained many elements of the ideology of holy war, including the horror of Christian places being in non-Christian hands, the demonizing of the Muslims, and sympathy for eastern Christians. The development of these ideas from the level of fraternal aid to that of a holy war, complete with both spiritual and material rewards, fell to Pope Urban II, who made the dream a reality at the Council of Clermont in 1095.

The second chapter, "The First Crusade," begins with Urban's call (doc. 12) and concludes with the fall of Jerusalem to the crusaders and reactions to the crusade's success. Many of the ideologies and strategies developed during the First Crusade would persist throughout the medieval period. In addition, the sources reveal attitudes and perceptions that would continue to direct crusading policy and action both in Europe and abroad. From Urban onward, the documents demonstrate the ethos and driving force of the crusading movement. Its motivation is particularly evident in the sources dealing with the Peasants' Crusade—an event that draws attention to the violence of the movement and its tendency toward intolerance and fanaticism (docs. 13-15). The massacres of European Jewish communities present the most obvious example of such extremism, which was further demonstrated in the atrocities committed by Peter the Hermit's crusade and the concluding slaughter of Jerusalem's inhabitants by the official crusading army (doc. 20). Also apparent are the political divisions between church and secular authorities, between the Byzantine Empire and the West, and among the crusade leaders themselves—divisions that undermined the progress of the First Crusade and the efforts of later campaigns. Despite these disturbing events and trends, the capture of Jerusalem was seen as a resounding triumph for the West, as Pope Paschal's letter (doc. 21) illustrates. Its impact upon the world of Islam, though recognized only slowly by the Muslim world, is represented here in the poet Abu l-Muzaffar Al-Abiwardi's lament for Jerusalem (doc. 22).

With the fall of Jerusalem, the crusaders' attention turned from warfare to control. Governance and society in the four crusader states—the county of

Edessa, the principality of Antioch, the county of Tripoli, and the kingdom of Jerusalem—are the subject of Chapter III, "The Crusader States." Whether defined as colonization or occupation, the establishment of Latin rule and a dominant western Christian community in Syria and Palestine had profound effects upon the Middle East, Byzantium, and Europe. Writers such as William of Tyre (doc. 23) and Fulcher of Chartres (doc. 24) tell of the difficulties in establishing a kingdom from scratch in a foreign land, while other sources highlight the day-to-day relations between the natives of Palestine and the European colonists. The Laws of the Kingdom of Jerusalem (doc. 26), the memoirs of Usamah Ibn Munqidh (doc. 30), and the writings of Burchard of Mount Sion (doc. 32) reveal the perceptions and misconceptions these groups had about one another and how native peoples were treated by the ruling Franks. As the establishment of the crusader states made pilgrimage easier and more attractive, the number of Christians traveling to the Holy Land increased. Travel accounts from Christian writers (docs. 27-28), along with writings by a Muslim and a Jewish traveler (docs. 29, 31), give vivid accounts of life in the crusader states and go some way toward explaining how a multi-cultural society functioned under western rule.

Yet the system was tenuous at best, held together not so much by the strength of the crusaders as by divisions among the Muslim emirs, who for forty years were more concerned with keeping one another in check than with ridding themselves of a foreign regime. The outnumbered crusaders were safe only so long as the Islamic emirates remained in such a fragmented state. The rise of Imad ad-Din Zengi upset the delicate balance and began to turn the tide in favor of the Muslims. The emergence of Zengi and his son and successor Nur ad-Din is chronicled in the first documents (33-34) of Chapter IV, "The Second and Third Crusades."

It was the fall of Edessa to Zengi in 1144 that prompted St. Bernard's call for the Second Crusade (doc. 35), a venture chronicled by Odo of Deuil, the chaplain of King Louis VII of France (doc. 36). The unexpected failure of the crusade resulted in widespread soul-searching and blame, here expressed in an anonymous, hostile view of the campaign from a German source and Bernard's own explanation of why things went wrong (doc. 38). This was the beginning of the end of Latin rule in the East.

Nur ad-Din died in 1174, and the mantle of Islamic leadership fell upon the shoulders of Salah al-Din Yusuf, known in the West as Saladin. The historian Baha ad-Din gives us a first-hand account of Saladin's life and character (doc. 39), while Saladin's secretary Imad ad-Din provides a poetic description of Saladin's greatest victory, the battle of Hattin (doc. 40), in which the crusader forces were decisively crushed. On October 2, 1187, Saladin accepted the surrender of Jerusalem. The anguish of this loss to western Christians is recorded in the writings of Roger of Wendover and Pope Gregory VIII (docs. 41-42), while the Muslim reaction is represented by a letter from Saladin himself (doc. 42). In each of these documents, the growing confidence of the Muslim forces is clear. The successes of Zengi, Nur ad-Din, and Saladin strengthened and defined *jihad*, in the same way the crusaders had defined Christian holy war.

Bowed but not beaten, the West prepared for the Third Crusade. Led by two European kings, Philip II "Augustus" of France and Richard I "the Lionheart" of England (a third ruler, Emperor Frederick "Barbarossa," drowned on his way to the East), this crusade was meticulously planned (doc. 43). The intrigues of European politics and the difficulties of Saladin's reign are also made apparent in the eyewitness accounts of the expedition (doc. 44). Ending in an unsatisfactory stalemate, the Third Crusade left the West with only a foothold in the Holy Land and Saladin with a weakened claim to authority.

Chapter V, "The Culture and Logistics of Crusading," leaves the chronology of the Crusades aside for the moment to examine the general issues of how a crusade was organized and the popular view of crusading. Taking the perspective of the individual crusader, rather than any major expedition, the chapter includes documents describing the preaching of crusades, the recruitment of soldiers (doc. 45), and the blessing of crusaders before their departure (doc. 48). To many potential soldiers, that first call to arms and the taking of vows marked the high point of their crusading careers. On the practical side, they had also to be concerned not only with spiritual benefits (the crusade indulgence, doc. 46) but also with the more practical crusader privileges that protected their property while they were gone and with making their own arrangements for their prolonged absence (docs. 46-47). To provide an overview of the conduct of a crusade on a larger scale, the chapter includes financial accounts of Louis IX's crusade (doc. 51) and excerpts from a guidebook for those planning military campaigns to the Holy Land (doc. 52).

One notable aspect of the culture of crusading was the ease with which military pursuits were merged with notions of Christian piety. Nowhere is this more marked than in the emergence of the military orders, most famously the Templars and the Hospitallers. Bernard of Clairvaux, the preacher of the Second Crusade, lent his support to the new institution in his treatise (doc. 49) on "the New Knighthood," or the Templars, which he idealistically viewed as superior to secular knights. A more practical approach is taken in the Templars' own Rule (doc. 50).

Chapter V also touches on the role of women in the crusading movement. Although women were often discouraged from direct participation, we do have records of their taking part in battles and sieges (doc. 54). On a more mundane level, women served the crusading soldiers as laundresses, companions, and prostitutes. It was the latter role that often earned them the blame for the failure of a crusade. Yet the risks and hardships of such women must have been as considerable as their male counterparts. Moreover, those women who said farewell to fathers and husbands and remained in Europe were by no means safe. Many faced domestic dangers with their male protectors away. One of the songs included at the end of the chapter (doc. 55) does not, however, dwell on these perils, but emphasizes, in true courtly love fashion, the longing and loneliness of a woman abandoned by her lover for the Crusades.

As the Crusades moved into the thirteenth century, the tone, direction, and purpose of the movement began to change. The prime instigator of this transformation was Pope Innocent III (1198-1216). One of the most gifted pontiffs of the medieval period, Innocent was a passionate supporter of the Crusades and was committed to overseeing their planning and execution. Chapter VI, "The Age of Innocent III," brings together documents relating to this innovative pope. His launching of a crusade against the heretic Albigensians (doc. 60), his extension of the ongoing crusades in Spain and the Baltic, and his legislative efforts to place the Crusades on a sound financial and strategic footing (doc. 56) redefined the movement and enabled it to adapt to the changing concerns and interests of the later Middle Ages. Notable trends in Innocent's reign were the growing emphasis on the economic aspect of crusading; the use of crusades in response to any threat against the church, secular or religious; and the tendency within eastern Europe to merge crusading with the conversion of non-Christian peoples. Innocent's endeavors were not always successful, the Fourth Crusade being a case in point, nor could he stem the tide of heresy or of popular movements such as the Children's Crusade (doc. 61). The Fifth Crusade came to grief in Egypt (doc. 63), despite a sound strategy aimed at the heart of Islamic wealth and power. Innocent's efforts were nonetheless far-reaching: among their results were the Fourth Lateran Council (doc.62) and the later rise of the Inquisition (doc. 59).

Innocent's involvement with crusading in northeastern Europe was part of a long-standing commitment by the church to bring Christianity to a largely pagan region. These efforts happened to coincide with the territorial ambitions of the kings and princes of the Holy Roman Empire, and it is the story of this conquest and of the crusading activities of the German emperors that is addressed in Chapter VII, "Crusades of the Holy Roman Empire." German incursions into eastern Europe took many forms. Pressures for land in the West led many to migrate eastwards, either settling into so-called wilderness areas or taking lands from the native inhabitants. The church too participated in this movement, as is demonstrated by works such as the Cistercian settlement poem (doc. 65) and Henry of Livonia's chronicle (doc. 68). But colonization and conversion were not always achieved peacefully. Wends, Slavs, Prussians, Lithuanians, and other eastern European peoples found themselves the object of crusading campaigns. The Teutonic Knights, a German military order founded in the Holy Land, were also brought in to conquer and settle the region. The sources associated with these crusades show not only how the church was redefining the crusade ideal, but also how mercantile interests were becoming entwined with crusading activity — interests that foreshadow the exploration, colonization, and economic exploitation characteristic of the early modern period. The sources are also important for what they reveal about the pagan peoples of eastern Europe. Although brimming with Christian bias, writers like Henry of Livonia, Helmold (doc. 67), and Nikolaus von Jeroschin (doc. 70) impart valuable information about indigenous customs, beliefs, and lifestyles. The crusades in eastern Europe did achieve their objectives. Brutal at times, they helped to establish Christianity in the region while developing strong economic and political ties to the West. The chapter concludes with the crusading exploits of the Holy Roman emperor Frederick II (1197-1250).

The Spanish crusades, like their eastern European counterparts, can also be counted as a victory for the medieval church and its secular allies. Chapter VIII, "Conflict and Coexistence in Spain," illustrates how the region was the site for both cultural interaction and religious and political conflict. Muslim Spain brought Europe into contact with the learning and scholarship preserved and expanded upon by the Islamic world. The coexistence of Muslims, Jews, and Christians under Islamic control created a community that, if not free of discrimination, did at least exhibit more tolerance and cooperation than what would follow under Christian rule: the documents detailing the final expulsion of Jews and Muslims from Christian Spain display a very different attitude from that found in the earlier Muslim laws.

Readers will find that the Spanish crusading texts exhibit much of the rhetoric and many of the customs of the larger crusading movement. In fact the long history of Muslim-Christian conflict on the Iberian Peninsula had created many of the very crusading traditions usually ascribed to the campaigns of the Holy Land. The establishment of specialized religious orders and the religious overtones in Christian war stories show how the West was able to equate these Spanish campaigns with the struggles in the Holy Land. They had the backing of the papacy and the spiritual recompense that accompanied such support. In addition, the Spanish crusades, being closer to home, offered a more assured opportunity for material rewards and perhaps the added satisfaction of providing aid to what was perceived as a palpable threat to Christian Europe.

Not that the Holy Land had been forgotten. The ideal of taking the cross to go to Jerusalem remained strong in the face of the crusading calamities of the thirteenth century. But the century that had begun with the reforms and crusading visions of Innocent III now found itself floundering amidst successive defeats and mounting criticism. Chapter IX, "Crusades at the Crossroads," documents this critical period. Beginning with the launch of the French king Louis IX's crusade in 1249 (doc. 84), the sources reflect, on the one hand, a desire to preserve the ideal of crusading and, on the other, a growing realization that the ideal was unobtainable in its time-honored form. Europe still longed to see and feel a part of a traditional crusade, yet the reality of the times did not allow for such activity. The crusade of the pious Louis IX came to nought. Popular movements such as the Shepherds' Crusade (doc. 85) continued to appear, though they were not endorsed by the church or secular authorities. Divisions among the crusading forces left in the Holy Land weakened their ability to defend themselves against the Muslim world, now led by the Mamluks. And both Franks and Muslims faced difficulties with the arrival from eastern Asia of the destructive Mongols.

The fall of Acre to the Muslims in May of 1291 and the subsequent loss of the last remnants of the crusader states triggered a number of European critiques and recovery schemes. The criticisms were directed primarily against the military orders, of which the Templars bore the brunt of Europe's disgust (docs. 93–94). Two of the recovery schemes, by Pierre Dubois (doc. 89) and Ramon Lull (doc. 91), are excerpted in Chapter IX. These reflect a new approach to what European thinkers still saw as the problem of Muslim rule in the Holy Land, emphasizing conversion over combat and colonization over occupation. Needless to say, these schemes did not yield their desired results. Conversion and colonization would become the central focus of Europe's attention as it moved into the Age of Discovery, but the recovery of Palestine would no longer be the object of these efforts.

The sources in the final chapter, "From Crusades to Colonization," confirm the development. John Mandeville's fanciful account of the Christian ruler Prester John demonstrates the West's growing awareness of a world beyond its borders and the opportunities such a world might afford. Rumors of the Mongols sparked curiosity among those who had not the misfortune of direct contact with these destructive nomads. The popes, in particular, saw the arrival of the Mongols as a golden opportunity to create an alliance that would once and for all rid the Holy Land of Islam. In this they were mistaken, as the correspondence between Pope Innocent IV and Guyuk Khan clearly shows (doc. 96). In time the invading Mongols would convert to Islam and be absorbed into eastern society. There would be no support from that quarter, and indeed the dream of a Latin Christian Jerusalem was dealt a further blow with the rise of a new Islamic dynasty, the Ottoman Turks.

The Ottomans expanded their empire right up to the borders of western Europe. But even the proximity of the threat did not spur the West into any unified action. Accounts of the Nicopolis Crusade of 1395 (doc. 98) detail a resounding defeat due in part to disagreements within the Christian leadership. Ineffective as it was, the crusade of Nicopolis would be the last help given by the West to its eastern Christian neighbors. Devastating internal wars, a major papal schism, and the struggle against heresy occupied the West and made any response to the Ottomans impossible. Fortunately for the West, the Turks suddenly found themselves under attack from the forces of the brutal Tamerlane, a Mongol who defeated the Ottomans in 1402 and thus perhaps kept them from moving into Europe. But with the death of Tamerlane in 1405, the Ottomans once more turned to the task of attacking Christian holdings; this time their efforts were focused on the long-sought prize of Constantinople. The Byzantine Empire had slowly weakened since the sack of the city by the Fourth Crusaders in 1204. In 1453 the great city fell to the Ottomans, and the eastern empire came to an end.

And what of crusading? While schemes for regaining Constantinople from the Ottomans and even the dream of recovering the Holy Land still floated about Europe, the final act of the Crusades was being played out by explorers and merchant ships headed for Africa, east Asia, and the Americas. These campaigners would seek souls and spices, not Jerusalem, and their actions would be motivated by economic gain and the promotion of God, king, and country. The European impulse for expansion had shifted from its narrow agenda of crusading to one that ultimately took it out of the realm of the Holy Land and into that of general conquest and colonization. Not that this was, in any way, a straightforward progression. The dream of a Christian Jerusalem remained a powerful image throughout the period, albeit alongside the more pragmatic goals of conquest and economic gain. As the documents of the final chapter illustrate, the growing commercial interests of the age, the rise of powerful European monarchies, and the difficulties of the church in dealing with secular and ecclesiastical problems led, in the end, to a new era, one that had neither the time nor the inclination for an old-style crusade.

The range of crusade sources is vast, and some readers may find that favorite topics have been omitted or favorite readings savagely abridged in the present volume. In the interests of providing a broad spectrum, difficult choices had to be made. We have endeavored to provide documents that demonstrate the variety of the crusading experience, a diversity of perspectives, the interaction of eastern and western society, and the transformation of the crusading agenda over time. No two historians define or teach the crusading period in quite the same way, but we hope that this collection will allow for a wide range of uses.

Our debts in compiling this reader have been many. We are grateful to Paul Dutton for his continuing encouragement and insightful guidance at every stage. Cynthia Feher's assistance in obtaining source materials has been absolutely invaluable, while Janet Sorrentino generously provided information on liturgical practice. Heidi Schnarr valiantly scanned an enormous amount of material onto disk and expertly proofread it; Stephen Bowden, Scott Pincikowski, Lauren Anderson, and Sarah Sponenberg also helped with technical aspects of the project. Hood College supported a portion of the work with a Summer Research Institute grant, and the Writing Group (you know who you are) helped by chivvying us along. Finally, we would like to recognize and encourage our students, whose interest in the history of religious warfare has been on the whole open-minded and unflagging, and who in the wake of the terrible events of September 2001 have shown a continuing desire to understand other cultures and to explore the history of conflicts that sadly persist today.

CHAPTER ONE:

BACKGROUND AND ORIGINS

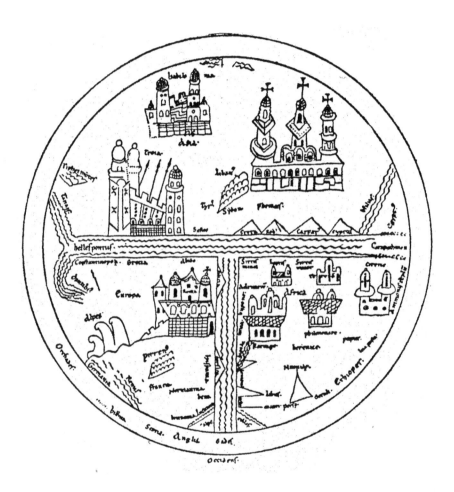

Fig. 1: A map of the world, produced in twelfth-century Europe. In this standard medieval representation, Asia occupies the top half of the circle, with Europe in the lower left quarter and Africa in the lower right quarter. Most such maps showed the city of Jerusalem at the center of the circle (here it has three cross-topped towers). From Theoderich, *Guide to the Holy Land*, ed. R.G. Musto (New York: Italica Press, 1986).

1. THE PILGRIMAGE OF ETHERIA

From early Christian times onward, European believers looked to the Holy Land, or Palestine, as their spiritual home. Much of the action of the Bible had taken place there, and Christianity had originated there. Many western Christians made special journeys, called pilgrimages, to the holy places which held, for them, a sacred meaning. In the second half of the fourth century, a Christian abbess named Etheria spent several years on such a pilgrimage from her home in Spain to the holy sites of the Middle East. She wrote about her travels in a letter to her nuns which survives only in part, and from which the following extracts are taken. The practice of pilgrimage to the Holy Land remained an ideal for devout medieval Christians into the period of the Crusades and beyond.

Source: trans. M.L. McClure and C.L. Feltoe, *The Pilgrimage of Etheria* (New York: The Macmillan Company, 1919), pp. 32-33, 41-44, 95-96; revised.

Edessa

...Departing [from Bathnae], we arrived at Edessa in the name of Christ our God, and, on our arrival, we straightway repaired to the church and memorial of St. Thomas. There, according to custom, prayers were made and the other things that were customary in the holy places were done; we read also some things concerning St. Thomas himself. The church there is very great, very beautiful and of new construction, well worthy to be the house of God, and as there was much that I desired to see, it was necessary for me to make a three days' stay there. Thus I saw in that city many memorials, together with holy monks, some dwelling at the memorials, while others had their cells in more secluded spots farther from the city.

Moreover, the holy bishop of the city, a truly devout man, both monk and confessor, received me willingly and said: "As I see, daughter, that for the sake of devotion you have undertaken so great a labor in coming to these places from far-distant lands, if you are willing, we will show you all the places that are pleasant to the sight of Christians." Then, first thanking God, I eagerly asked the bishop that he would deign to do as he said. He thereupon led me first to the palace of King Abgar, where he showed me a great marble statue of him—very much like him, as they said—having a sheen as if made of pearl. From the face of Abgar it seemed that he was a very wise and honorable man. Then the holy bishop said to me: "Behold King Abgar, who before he saw the Lord believed that he was in truth the Son of God." ... Then we entered the inner part of the palace, and there were fountains full of fish such as I never saw before, of so great size, so bright and of so good a flavor were they. The city has no water at all other than that which comes out of the palace, which is like a great silver river....

Antioch to Tarsus

When I had got back to Antioch, I stayed there for a week, while the things that were necessary for our journey were being prepared. Then, starting from Antioch and journeying through several stations, I came to the province called Cilicia, which has Tarsus for its metropolis. I had already been at Tarsus on my way to Jerusalem, but as the memorial of St. Thecla is at the third station from Tarsus, in Hisauria, it was very pleasant for me to go there, especially as it was so very near at hand.

Visit to St. Thecla's Church and Return to Constantinople

So, setting out from Tarsus, I came to a certain city on the sea, still in Cilicia, which is called Pompeiopolis. Thence I entered the borders of Hisauria and stayed in a city called Coricus, and on the third day I arrived at a city which is called Seleucia in Hisauria; on my arrival I went to the bishop, a truly holy man, formerly a monk, and in that city I saw a very beautiful church. And as the distance from there to [the church of] St. Thecla, which is situated outside the city on a low hill, was about fifteen hundred paces, I chose rather to go there in order to make the stay that I intended. There is nothing at the holy church in that place except numberless cells of men and of women. I found there a very dear friend of mine, to whose manner of life all in the East bore testimony, a holy deaconess named Marthana, whom I had known at Jerusalem, where she had come for the sake of prayer; she was ruling over the cells of *apotactitae* [that is, holy women] and virgins. And when she had seen me, how can I describe the extent of her joy or of mine? But to return to the matter in hand: there are very many cells on the hill and in the midst of it a great wall which encloses the church containing the very beautiful memorial. The wall was built to guard the church because of the Hisauri, who are very malicious and who frequently commit acts of robbery, to prevent them from making an attempt on the monastery which is established there. When I had arrived in the name of God, prayer was made at the memorial, and the whole of the acts of St. Thecla having been read, I gave endless thanks to Christ our God, who deigned to fulfill my desires in all things, unworthy and undeserving as I am.

Then, after a stay of two days, when I had seen the holy monks and *apotactitae* who were there, both men and women, and when I had prayed and made my communion, I returned to Tarsus and to my journey. From Tarsus, after a halt of three days, I set out on my journey in the name of God, and arriving on the same day at a station called Mansocrenae, which is under Mount Taurus, I stayed there. On the next day, going along the foot of Mount Taurus, and traveling by the route that was already known to me, through each province that I had traversed on my way out, to wit, Cappadocia, Galatia, and Bithynia, I arrived at Chalcedon, where I stayed for the sake of the very famous martyr memorial of St. Euphemia, which was already known to me from a former time.

On the next day, crossing the sea, I arrived at Constantinople, giving thanks to Christ our God who deigned to give me such grace, unworthy and undeserving as I am, for he had deigned to give me not only the will to go, but also the power of walking through the places that I desired, and of returning at last to Constantinople. When I had arrived there, I went through all the churches — that of the apostles and all the martyr-memorials, of which there are very many — and I ceased not to give thanks to Jesus our God, who had thus deigned to bestow his mercy upon me. From which place, ladies, light of my eyes, while I send these [letters] to your affection, I have already decided, in the name of Christ our God, to go to Ephesus in Asia, for the sake of prayer, because of the memorial of the holy and blessed apostle John. And if after this I am yet in the body, and am able to see any other places, I will either tell it to your affection in person, if God deigns to permit me this, or, if I have another project in mind, I will send you news of it in a letter. But do you, ladies, light of my eyes, deign to remember me, whether I am in the body or out of the body.

Jerusalem

...[The anniversaries of the] days when the holy church in Golgotha, which they call the martyrium, was consecrated to God are called "the days of dedication"; the holy church also which is at the Anastasis, that is, in the place where the Lord rose after his Passion [that is, his suffering and death], was consecrated to God on that day. The dedication of these holy churches is therefore celebrated with the highest honor, because the cross of the Lord was found on this same day. And it was so ordained that, when the holy churches above mentioned were first consecrated, that should be the day when the cross of the Lord had been found, in order that the whole celebration should be made together, with all rejoicing, on the self-same day. Moreover, it appears from the Holy Scriptures that this is also the day of dedication, when holy Solomon, having finished the house of God which he had built, stood before the altar of God and prayed, as it is written in the books of the Chronicles [2 Chron. 6, 7:8-10].

So when these days of dedication come, they are kept for eight days. And people begin to assemble from all parts many days before; not only monks and *apotactitae* from various provinces, from Mesopotamia and Syria, from Egypt and the Thebaid (where there are very many monks), and from every different place and province—for there is none who does not turn his steps to Jerusalem on that day for such rejoicing and for such high days—but lay people too in like manner, both men and women, with faithful minds, gather together in Jerusalem from every province on those days, for the sake of the holy day. And the bishops, even when they have been few, are present to the number of forty or fifty in Jerusalem on these days, and with them come many of their clergy. But why should I say more? For he who on these days has not been present at so solemn a feast thinks that he has committed a very great sin, unless some necessity, which keeps a man back from carrying out a good resolution, has hindered him. Now on these days of the dedication the adornment of all the churches is the same as at Easter and at Epiphany; also on each day the procession is made to the several holy places, as at Easter and at Epiphany. For on the first and second days it is to the greater church, which is called the martyrium. On the third day it is to Eleona, that is, the church which is on that mount from which the Lord ascended into heaven after his Passion, and in this church is the cave wherein the Lord used to teach his apostles on the Mount of Olives.

Questions: What was a pilgrim's experience like? What kinds of sites did Etheria visit and describe? What activities did she engage in? What sort of Christian presence existed in the places visited by Etheria? Etheria is from Spain; what is her attitude toward the Middle Eastern Christians? Is there any recognition in her narrative of a non-Christian population? For what audience was she writing, and what was her purpose?

2. AUGUSTINE OF HIPPO ON THE JUST WAR

Augustine of Hippo (d. 430) was one of the most influential early Christian theologians, helping to shape medieval thinking on a wide variety of topics. In the passages below, he discusses whether and when a Christian may rightly engage in violence. In the face of a strong pacifist strain in early Christian thought, Augustine was an important voice for the use of force. His arguments, though informed by Biblical examples and a Christian approach, are based on the ancient secular concept of the just war, which must meet certain objective criteria.

Source: trans. R. Stothert, in *Nicene and Post-Nicene Fathers*, First Series, Vol. 4, *Augustin: The Writings against the Manichaeans, and against the Donatists*, ed. P. Schaff (Buffalo: The Christian Literature Company, 1897), pp. 300–03; revised.

73. According to the eternal law, which requires the preservation of natural order, and forbids the transgression of it, some actions have an indifferent [that is, neutral] character, so that men are blamed for presumption if they do them without being called upon, while they are deservedly praised for doing them when required. The act, the agent, and the authority for the action are all of great importance in the order of nature. For Abraham to sacrifice his son of his own accord is shocking madness. His doing so at the command of God proves him faithful and submissive....

74. ...[The] account of the wars of Moses will not excite surprise or abhorrence, for in wars carried on by divine command, he showed not ferocity but obedience; and God, in giving the command, acted not in cruelty, but in righteous retribution, giving to all what they deserved, and warning those who needed warning. What is the evil in war? Is it the death of some who will soon die in any case, that others may live in peaceful subjection? This is mere cowardly dislike, not any religious feeling. The real evils in war are love of violence, revengeful cruelty, fierce and implacable enmity, wild resistance, and the lust of power, and such like; and it is generally to punish these things, when force is required to inflict the punishment, that, in obedience to God or some lawful authority, good men undertake wars, when they find themselves in such a position as regards the conduct of human affairs, that right conduct requires them to act, or to make others act, in this way. Otherwise John [the Baptist], when the soldiers who came to be baptized asked, "What shall we do?" would have replied, "Throw away your arms; give up the service; never strike, or wound, or disable anyone." But knowing that such actions in battle were not murderous, but authorized by law, and that the soldiers did not thus avenge themselves, but defended the public safety, he replied, "Do violence to no one, accuse no one falsely, and be content with your wages." ... Again, in the case of the centurion who said, "I am a man under authority, and have soldiers

under me: and I say to one, 'Go,' and he goes; and to another, 'Come,' and he comes; and to my servant, 'Do this,' and he does it," Christ gave due praise to his faith; he did not tell him to leave the service. But there is no need here to enter on the long discussion of just and unjust wars.

75. A great deal depends on the causes for which men undertake wars, and on the authority they have for doing so; for the natural order, which seeks the peace of humankind, ordains that the monarch should have the power of undertaking war if he thinks it advisable, and that the soldiers should perform their military duties in behalf of the peace and safety of the community. When war is undertaken in obedience to God, who would rebuke, or humble, or crush our human pride, it must be allowed to be a righteous war; for even the wars which arise from human passion cannot harm the eternal well-being of God, nor even hurt his saints; for in the trial of their patience, and the chastening of their spirit, and in bearing fatherly correction, they are rather benefited than injured. No one can have any power against them but what is given him from above. For there is no power but of God, who either orders or permits. Since, therefore, a righteous man, serving perhaps under an ungodly king, may do the duty belonging to his position in the state in fighting by the order of his sovereign—for in some cases it is plainly the will of God that he should fight, and in others, where this is not so plain, it may be an unrighteous command on the part of the king, while the soldier is innocent, because his position makes obedience a duty—how much more must the one be blameless who carries on war on the authority of God, of whom everyone who serves him knows that he can never require what is wrong?

76. If it is supposed that God could not enjoin warfare, because in after times it was said by the Lord Jesus Christ, "I say unto you, that you resist not evil: but if anyone strike you on the right cheek, turn to him the left also," the answer is that what is here required is not a bodily action but an inward disposition.... Thus the name martyrs, which means witnesses, was given to those who, by the will of God, bore this testimony, by their confessions, their sufferings, and their death. The number of such witnesses is so great that, if it pleased Christ ... to unite them all in one army, and to give them success in battle, as he gave to the Hebrews, what nation could withstand them? What kingdom would remain unsubdued? But as the doctrine of the New Testament is that we must serve God not for temporal happiness in this life, but for eternal felicity hereafter, this truth was most strikingly confirmed by the patient endurance of what is commonly called adversity for the sake of that felicity. So in the fullness of time the Son of God ... sends his disciples as sheep into the midst of wolves, and bids them not fear those that can kill the body, but cannot kill the soul, and promises that even the body will be entirely restored, so that not a hair shall be lost. Peter's sword he orders back into its

sheath, restoring, as it was before, the ear of his enemy that had been cut off. He says that he could obtain legions of angels to destroy his enemies, but that he must drink the cup which his Father's will had given him. He sets the example of drinking this cup, then hands it to his followers, manifesting thus, both in word and in deed, the grace of patience....

78. It is therefore mere groundless calumny to charge Moses with making war, for there would have been less harm in making war of his own accord, than in not doing it when God commanded him. And to dare to find fault with God himself for giving such a command, or not to believe that a just and good God did so, shows, to say the least, an inability to consider that in the view of divine providence, which pervades all things from the highest to the lowest, time can neither add anything nor take away; but all things go, or come, or remain according to the order of nature or what is deserved in each separate case, while in humans a right will is in union with the divine law, and ungoverned passion is restrained by the order of divine law; so that a good person wills only what is commanded, and a bad one can do only what he is permitted, at the same time that he is punished for what he wills to do unjustly. Thus, in all the things which appear shocking and terrible to human feebleness, the real evil is the injustice; the rest is only the result of natural properties or of moral demerit.... Still, we are sure that all these things are due either to the mercy or the judgment of God, while the measures and numbers and weights by which the Creator of all natural productions arranges all things are concealed from our view. For God is not the author, but he is the controller of sin; so that sinful actions, which are sinful because they are against nature, are judged and controlled, and assigned to their proper place and condition, in order that they may not bring discord and disgrace on universal nature. This being the case, and as the judgments of God and the movements of man's will contain the hidden reason why the same prosperous circumstances which some make a right use of are the ruin of others, and since our whole mortal life upon earth is a trial, who can tell whether it may be good or bad in any particular case — in time of peace, to reign or to serve, or to be at ease or to die — or in time of war, to command or to fight, to conquer or to be killed? At the same time, it remains true that whatever is good is so by the divine blessing, and whatever is bad is so by the divine judgment.

Questions: What criteria make war acceptable or "righteous"? What are the potential benefits of war? What are the dangers? How does Augustine answer the argument that Christ was a pacifist? How might Augustine's ideas about war be applied to a Christian offensive against non-Christians?

3. THE QURAN

The religion known as Islam was founded in the early seventh century by the prophet Mohammed, an Arab whose mystical visions led directly to the recording of the Quran (also spelled "Koran"), the holy book of Islam. Muslims believe the Quran is the word of Allah (the God of the Old Testament) as revealed directly to Mohammed. It occupies a place in Islam that is even more important than that of the Bible in Christianity. The following excerpts from the Quran discuss the Islamic view of war and interfaith relations.

Source: trans. R. Khalifa, *Quran: The Final Testament* (Tucson: Islamic Productions, 1989), pp. 29-30, 34, 42, 64, 76, 105, 110-11, 117, 119, 178, 550.

Sura 2

190. You shall fight in the cause of God against those who attack you, but do not aggress. God does not love the aggressors.

191. You may kill those who wage war against you, and you may evict them whence they evicted you, for oppression is worse than murder. Do not fight them at the sacred mosque, unless they attack you therein. If they attack you, you may kill them. This is the just retribution for such disbelievers.

192. If they refrain, then God is forgiver, most merciful.

193. You can also fight them to counter oppression, and to worship God freely. If they refrain, do not aggress, except against the aggressors.

194. Even during the sacred months, any aggression shall be met by an equivalent response. Thus, if they attack you, you may counter attack to inflict an equitable punishment. Observe God, and know that God is with the righteous.

195. You shall spend in the cause of God; do not throw yourselves with your own hands into destruction. You shall be charitable; God loves the charitable.

216. Fighting may be forced upon you, though you do not like it. But you may dislike something which is actually good for you, and you may like something which is actually bad for you. God knows while you do not know.

217. They ask you about fighting during the sacred months; say, "Fighting therein is a sacrilege. But repelling from the path of God, disbelieving in him and in the sanctity of the sacred mosque, and evicting its people therefrom are greater sacrileges in the sight of God. For oppression is worse than murder." They will continue to fight you in order to revert you from your religion, if they can. Those among you who revert from their religion, and die as disbelievers, have wasted all their works in this life and in the hereafter. These will

be dwellers of hell, wherein they abide forever.

256. There shall be no compulsion in religion: the right way is now distinguished from the wrong way. Thus, anyone who denounces the devil and believes in God, has gotten hold of the strongest bond that never breaks. God is hearer, omniscient.

Sura 3

113. They are not all the same; among the followers of the scripture [that is, Jews and Christians as well as Muslims], there are those who are righteous. They recite God's revelations through the night, and they fall prostrate.

114. They believe in God and the Last Day, they advocate righteousness and forbid evil, and they hasten to do righteous works. They are with the righteous.

115. Any good they do will not go unrewarded. God is fully aware of who the righteous are.

195. Their Lord responded to them [that is, the believers]: "I never fail to reward any worker among you for your work, be you male or female; you are equal to one another. Therefore, those who immigrate, and those who are evicted from their homes—those who are persecuted because of me—and those who fight and get killed, I will surely remit their sins and admit them into gardens with flowing streams." Such is the reward from God. God possesses the best reward.

196. Do not be impressed by the apparent success of the disbelievers.

197. They enjoy temporarily, then end up in hell, a miserable destiny.

198. But those who observe their Lord have deserved gardens with flowing streams; they abide therein forever. Such is their abode from God. What God possesses is far better for the righteous.

199. Surely, some followers of the previous scriptures [that is, Jews and Christians] do believe in God, and in what was revealed to them. They humble themselves before God, and they do not trade away God's revelations for a cheap price. These have deserved their recompense at their Lord. God is the most efficient in reckoning.

200. O you who believe, you shall be steadfast, you shall persevere, you shall be united, and you shall observe God, that you may succeed.

Sura 4

171. O people of the scripture, do not transgress the limits of your religion, and do not say about God other than the truth. The Messiah, Jesus, the son of Mary, was a messenger of God, and his word that he had sent to Mary, and a

spirit from him. Therefore, you shall believe in God and his messengers, and do not say, "Trinity." Stop, for your own good. God is only one god. [May he be] glorified, much too high to have a son. To him belongs everything in the heavens and everything on earth. God suffices as Lord and master.

Sura 5

14. Also those who said, "We are Christians," we took their covenant. But they disregarded some of the commandments given to them. Consequently, we condemned them to animosity and hatred among themselves, until the day of resurrection. God will then inform them of everything they had done.

15. O people of the scripture, our messenger has come to you to proclaim for you many things you have concealed in the scripture, while overlooking plenty more. A beacon has come to you from God, and a profound scripture.

16. With it, God guides those who seek his approval. He guides them to the paths of peace, leads them out of darkness into the light by his leave, and guides them in a straight path.

17. Pagans indeed are those who say that God is the Messiah, son of Mary. Say, "Who could prevent God if he willed to annihilate the Messiah, son of Mary, and his mother, and everyone on earth?" To God belongs the kingship of the heavens and the earth, and everything in between them. He creates whatever he wills. God is omnipotent.

18. The Jews and the Christians said, "We are God's children and his beloved." Say, "Why then does he punish you for your sins? You are no more than humans like the rest." He forgives whomever he wills and punishes whomever he wills. To God belongs the kingship of the heavens and the earth, and everything between them; to him is the final destiny.

51. O you who believe, do not take the Jews and the Christians as allies; they are allies of one another. Those among you who ally themselves with them belong with them. God does not guide the transgressors.

65. If only the people of the scripture believe and lead a righteous life, we will then remit their sins, and admit them into gardens of bliss.

66. If only they would uphold the Torah and the Gospel, and what is sent down to them herein [that is, in the Quran] from their Lord they would be blessed with provisions from above them and from beneath their feet. Some of them are righteous, but many of them are evildoers.

Sura 8

10. God provided you with this good news to strengthen your hearts. Victory comes only from God. God is almighty, most wise.

11. He causes peaceful slumber to overtake you and pacify you. He sends down water from the sky to clean you therewith. He removes from you the devil's curse, in order to assure your hearts and to strengthen your foothold.

12. Thus, your Lord inspired the angels: "I will be with you as you support those who believed. I will throw terror into the hearts of those who disbelieved. You may strike them above the necks; you may strike them everywhere."

13. This is because they actively fight against God and his messenger. For those who fight against God and his messenger, God's retribution is severe.

14. This is to punish the disbelievers; they have incurred the retribution of hell.

15. O you who believe, if you encounter the disbelievers who have mobilized against you, do not turn back and flee.

16. Anyone who turns back on that day, except to carry out a battle plan, or to join his group, has incurred wrath from God, and his abode is hell; what a miserable destiny!

Sura 60

8. God does not enjoin you from befriending those who do not fight you because of religion, and do not evict you from your homes. You may befriend them and be equitable towards them. God loves the equitable.

9. God enjoins you only from befriending those who fight you because of religion, evict you from your homes, and band together with others to banish you. You shall not befriend them. Those who befriend them are the transgressors.

Questions: What criteria make war acceptable? What are the limits placed on warfare? Compare these ideas with those of Augustine. What is the Quran's attitude toward Jews and Christians? How does it distinguish between Islam and Christianity? What values are emphasized in these extracts?

4. AL-BALADHURI ON EARLY MUSLIM CONQUESTS

In the century after Mohammed's revelation, Muslim Arabs conquered and converted lands from India in the east to Spain in the west. The historian Ahmad Ibn-Jabir al-Baladhuri lived in the ninth century, but the extracts below, from his history of an earlier era, describe some of the important Muslim conquests of the seventh century, namely in Palestine and Syria. One of the central figures of this early period was the great Muslim caliph Omar I.

Source: trans. P.K. Hitti, *The Origins of the Islamic State*, vol. I (New York: Columbia University, 1916), pp. 165-68, 186-91, 213-15; revised.

[The Muslim leader abu-Bakr as-Siddik] saw fit to direct his troops against Syria. To this effect he wrote to the people of Mecca, at-Ta'if, al-Yaman, and all the Arabs in Najd and al-Hijaz calling them for a holy war and arousing their desire for it and for the booty obtainable from the Greeks. Accordingly, people, including those actuated by greed as well as those actuated by the hope of divine remuneration, hastened to abu-Bakr from all quarters, and flocked to Medina. Abu-Bakr gave three banners to three men [that is, he appointed them commanders], namely: Khalid Ibn-Sa'id Ibn-al-'Asi Ibn-Umaiyah, Shurahbil Ibn-Hasanah, ... and 'Amr Ibn-al-'Asi ib-Wa'il as-Sahmi.... The tying of these banners took place on Thursday the first of Safar, year 13 [that is, 635], after the troops had camped at al-Jurf throughout the month of Muharram with abu-'Ubaidah Ibn-al-Jarrah leading their prayers. Abu-Bakr wanted to give a banner to abu-'Ubaidah; but the latter begged to be relieved. Others claim that he did give one to him, but that report is not confirmed. The fact is that when Omar became caliph, he conferred on him the governorship of all Syria....

Abu-Bakr instructed 'Amr Ibn-al-'Asi to [take] Palestine for his objective. Yazid he instructed to follow the way of Tabûk. To Shurahbil, he wrote to follow the way of Tabûk, too. At the outset each one of the commanders had 3,000 men under his leadership, but abu-Bakr kept on sending reinforcements until each one had 7,500. Later the total was increased to 24,000.

It is reported on the authority of al-Wakidi that abu-Bakr assigned 'Amr to Palestine, Shurahbil to the Jordan, and Yazid to Damascus, saying, "When you all fight together, your commander is the one in whose province you are fighting." It is also reported that to 'Amr he gave oral instructions to lead the prayers in case the armies were united, and to have each commander lead the prayer of his own army when the armies were separate. Abu-Bakr ordered the commanders to see that each tribe flew a banner of its own.

On his arrival in the first district of Palestine, 'Amr Ibn-al-Asi sent a message to abu-Bakr informing him of the great number of the enemy, their great armament, the wide extent of their land, and the enthusiasm of their troops. Abu-Bakr, thereupon, wrote to Khalid Ibn-al-Walid Ibn-al-Mughirah-l-Makhzûmi—who was at that time in Iraq—directing him to go to Syria. According to some, he thereby made him a commander over the commanders in the war. According to others, Khalid only commanded his men who accompanied him; but whenever the Muslims met for a battle, the commanders would choose him as their chief for his valor and strategy and the auspiciousness of his counsel.

The first conflict between the Muslims and the enemy took place in Dathin, one of the villages of Ghazzah, which lay on the way between the Muslims and the residence of the patrician [that is, military commander] of Ghazzah. Here the battle raged furiously, but at last Allah gave victory to his friends and defeat to his enemies whom he dispersed. All this took place before the arrival of Khalid Ibn-al-Walid in Syria....

When the Muslims were done with the fight against those who were gathered at al-Marj, they stayed there for fifteen days, at the end of which they returned to Damascus. This took place [in the] year 14. The Muslims took Al-Ghûtah and its churches by force. The inhabitants of Damascus took themselves to the fortifications and closed the gate of the city. Khalid Ibn-al-Walid, at the head of some 5,000 men whom abu-'Ubaidah had put under his command, camped at [the east gate]. Some assert that Khalid was the chief commander but was dismissed when Damascus was under siege. The convent by which Khalid camped was called Dair Khalid. 'Amr Ibn-al-Asi camped at the Tûma gate; Shurabil, at the Faradis gate, abu-'Ubaidah at the Jabiyah gate, and Yazid Ibn-abi-Sufyan from the Saghir gate to the one known as Kaisan gate. Abu-ad-Karda' appointed 'Uwaimir Ibn-'Amir al-Khazraji commander of a frontier garrison settled in the fortification at Barzah.

The bishop who had provided Khalid with food at the beginning of the siege was accustomed to stand on the wall. Once Khalid called him, and when he came, Khalid greeted him and talked with him. The bishop one day said to him, "Abu-Salaiman, your case is prospering and you have a promise to fulfill for me; let us make terms for this city." Thereupon, Khalid called for an inkhorn and parchment and wrote:

"In the name of Allah, the compassionate, the merciful. This is what Khalid would grant to the inhabitants of Damascus, if he enters therein: he promises to give them security for their lives, property, and churches. Their city-wall shall not be demolished; neither shall any Muslim be quartered in their houses. Thereunto we give to them the pact of Allah and the protection of his

Prophet, the caliphs and the believers. So long as they pay the poll-tax, nothing but good shall befall them."

One night, a friend of the bishop came to Khalid and informed him of the fact that it was the night of a feast for the inhabitants of the city, that they were all busy and that they had blocked the Sharki gate with stones and left it unguarded. He then suggested that Khalid should procure a ladder. Certain occupants of the convent, by which Khalid's army camped, brought him two ladders, on which some Muslims climbed to the highest part of the wall, and descended to the gate, which was guarded only by one or two men. The Muslims cooperated and opened the door. This took place at sunrise.

In the meantime, abu-'Ubaidah had managed to open the Jabiyah gate and sent certain Muslims over its wall. This made the Greek fighters pour to his side and lead a violent fight against the Muslims. At last, however, the Greeks took to flight. Then abu-'Ubaidah at the head of the Muslims opened the Jabiyah gate by force, and they made their entrance through it....

According to other reports, [the Muslims at the Jabiyah gate forced their way in first.] Seeing that abu-'Ubaidah was on the point of entering the city, the bishop hurried to Khalid and capitulated. He then opened the Sharki gate and entered with Khalid, with the statement which Khalid had written him unfolded in his hand. Regarding that, certain Muslims remarked, "By Allah, Khalid is not the commander. How could his terms then be binding?" To this, abu-'Ubaidah replied, "Even the lowest of the Muslims can make binding terms on their behalf." And sanctioning the [agreement] made by Khalid, he signed it, not taking into account the fact that a part of the city was taken by force. Thus all Damascus was considered as having capitulated. Abu-'Ubaidah wrote to Omar regarding that and forwarded the message. Then the gates of the city were opened and all the Muslims met within....

Al-Haitham Ibn-'Adi claimed that the people of Damascus capitulated agreeing to give up one-half of their homes and churches. Muhammed Ibn-Sa'd reported that abu-'Abdallah al-Wakidi said, "I have read the statement issued by Khalid Ibn-al-Walid to the people of Damascus and found no mention in it of 'half the homes and churches.' I do not know where the one who reported it got his information. The fact is that when Damascus was taken possession of, a great number of its inhabitants fled to Heraclius, who was then at Antioch, leaving many vacant dwellings behind that were later occupied by the Muslims." ...

As 'Amr was besieging Jerusalem in the year 16 [that is, 638], abu-'Ubaidah ... came to him and, according to a report, sent him from Jerusalem to Antioch, whose people had violated the covenant. 'Amr reduced the city and returned [to Jerusalem]. Only two or three days after his return, the inhabitants of Jerusalem asked to capitulate to abu-'Ubaidah on the same terms as those of the cities of Syria as regards tax and *kharaj* [that is, land tax], and to have the same treatment as their equals elsewhere, provided the one to make the contract be Omar Ibn-al-Khattab in person. Abu-'Ubaidah communicated this in writing to Omar, who came first to al-Jabiyah in Damascus and then to Jerusalem. He made the terms of capitulation with the people of Jerusalem to take effect and gave them a written statement. The conquest of Jerusalem took place in the year 17....

[An eyewitness reported the following:] I was one of those who went with abu-'Ubaidah to meet Omar as he was coming to Syria. As Omar was passing, he was met by the singers and tambourine players of the inhabitants of Adhri'at with swords and myrtle. Seeing that, Omar shouted, "Keep still! Stop them!" But abu-'Ubaidah replied, "This is their custom (or some other word like it), commander of the believers, and if you should stop them from doing it, they would take that as indicating your intention to violate their covenant." "Well, then," said Omar, "let them go on."

Questions: What motivations for conquest are cited here? What kinds of campaign arrangements were made? What were the expectations of the conquered peoples? How were they treated? How does al-Baladhuri use and evaluate his historical sources? Compare the actions described in this narrative with those approved by the Quran.

5. THE PACT OF OMAR

The early agreements described in the previous document became the basis for similar arrangements across the Islamic world, surviving in later texts such as the one below, which dates from around the ninth century but is still known as the Pact of Omar. The terms dictated by the Muslim conquerors were not entirely new even in the seventh century; some provisions were virtually identical to those that Christians had previously imposed on their non-Christian subjects.

Source: trans. J.R. Marcus, *The Jew in the Medieval World, A Source Book: 315-1791* (Cincinnati: Union of American Hebrew Congregations, 1938), pp. 13-15.

In the name of God, the merciful, the compassionate!

This is a writing to Omar from the Christians of such and such a city. When you [Muslims] marched against us [Christians], we asked of you protection for ourselves, our posterity, our possessions, and our co-religionists; and we made this stipulation with you, that we will not erect in our city or the suburbs any new monastery, church, cell, or hermitage; that we will not repair any of such buildings that may fall into ruins, or renew those that may be situated in the Muslim quarters of the town; that we will not refuse the Muslims entry into our churches either by night or by day; that we will open the gates wide to passengers and travelers; that we will receive any Muslim traveler into our houses and give him food and lodging for three nights; that we will not harbor any spy in our churches or houses, or conceal any enemy of the Muslims.

That we will not teach our children the Quran; that we will not make a show of the Christian religion nor invite anyone to embrace it; that we will not prevent any of our kinsmen from embracing Islam, if they so desire. That we will honor the Muslims and rise up in our assemblies when they wish to take their seats; that we will not imitate them in our dress, either in the cap, turban, sandals, or parting of the hair; that we will not make use of their expressions of speech, nor adopt their surnames; that we will not ride on saddles, or gird with swords, or take to ourselves arms or wear them, or engrave Arabic inscriptions on our rings; that we will not sell wine; that we will shave the front of our heads; that we will wear girdles [that is, belts] round our waists.

That we will not display the cross upon our churches or display our crosses or our sacred books in the streets of the Muslims, or in their market-places; that we will strike the clappers in our churches lightly; that we will not recite our services in a loud voice when a Muslim is present; that we will not carry palm-branches [on Palm Sunday] or our [saints'] images in procession in the streets; that at the burial of our dead we will not chant loudly or carry lighted candles in the streets of the Muslims or their market-places; that we will not take any slaves that have already been in the possession of Muslims, nor spy into their houses; and that we will not strike any Muslim.

All this we promise to observe, on behalf of ourselves and our co-religionists, and receive protection from you in exchange; and if we violate any of the conditions of this agreement, then we forfeit your protection and you are at liberty to treat us as enemies and rebels.

Questions: How is the subordinate status of the Christians expressed in the terms of this document? Why do the Muslims want the Christians to promise not to teach the Quran, dress like Muslims, or adopt Muslim customs? What are the long-term implications of the prohibition on repairing churches? How does this form of agreement compare with the pact made with the Christians of Damascus?

6. EARLY INDULGENCES

As the Muslims began to spread through the Iberian peninsula and to venture across the Pyrenees, they encountered the armies of the Franks, the Germanic people who controlled much of western Europe from 500 to 900 and whose core territory would later be known as France. Frankish leaders, who were allied with the papacy, sometimes emphasized the religious aspect of their struggle against the Muslims in Spain. In the documents below, two different popes describe how fighting against the Muslims affected the fate of the individual Frankish soul. The context of this theology of "indulgence" is the sacrament of penance, whereby a Christian must sincerely confess his or her sins and do penance in order to receive God's forgiveness and, after death, eternal life in heaven.

Source: trans. O.J. Thatcher and E.H. McNeal, *A Source Book for Mediaeval History* (New York: Charles Scribner's Sons, 1905), pp. 511-12.

Pope Leo IV (847-55) to the Franks

Now we hope that none of you will be slain, but we wish you to know that the kingdom of heaven will be given as a reward to those who shall be killed in this war. For [God] the omnipotent knows that they lost their lives fighting

Fig. 2: A. An eleventh-century French censer, used to spread the smoke of burning incense during Christian church services, representing a church in Jerusalem and reminding European worshipers of the holy city. From P. Lacroix, *The Arts in the Middle Ages* (London: Chapman and Hall, 1870).

for the truth of the faith, for the preservation of their country, and the defense of the Christians. And therefore God will give them the reward which we have named.

Pope John II, 878

John II to the bishops in the realm of Louis II [the Stammerer]. You have modestly expressed a desire to know whether those who have recently died in war, fighting in the defense of the church of God and for the preservation of the Christian religion and of the state, or those who may in the future fall in the same cause, may obtain indulgence for their sins. We confidently reply that those who, out of love to the Christian religion, shall die in battle fighting bravely against pagans or unbelievers, shall receive eternal life. For the Lord has said through his prophet: "In whatever hour a sinner shall be converted, I will remember his sins no longer." By the intercession of St. Peter, who has the power of binding and loosing in heaven and on the earth, we absolve, as far as is permissible, all such and commend them by our prayers to the Lord.

Questions: Which soldiers, specifically, are said here to have earned a heavenly reward? How do the popes justify the assertion that these men will go to heaven? Are there any limits on the "indulgences" granted here?

7. IBNU HAYYAN ON WARFARE IN SPAIN

Early indulgences like the ones in the previous selection most often conferred their benefits on those who fought against the Moors, or Muslims of Spain. In the following passage, the respected eleventh-century Muslim historian Ibnu Hayyan, from Cordoba, describes some of this warfare. The events in this selection begin in 1064.

Source: trans. P. de Gayangos, *The History of the Mohammedan Dynasties in Spain* (London: The Oriental Translation Fund, 1843), vol. II, pp. 265-70; revised.

The army of Al-ardemelis encamped before Barbastro and besieged it. Yusuf Ibn Suleyman Ibn Hud [at that time king of Saragossa], instead of hastening, as he ought to have done, to the relief of the city, left the inhabitants to defend themselves as they best could; and the consequence was that the enemy got possession of it, as we will presently relate. The Christians besieged it for forty consecutive days without gaining any advantage, until, having received intelligence that the garrison were divided and had quarreled among themselves, owing to the scarcity of provisions, they pressed their attacks with increased vigor, and succeeded in introducing 5,000 of their best men at arms into the suburbs. The Muslims were astounded, and betook themselves to the inner city, where they fortified themselves. Great battles then ensued between the two hosts, in which no less than 500 Franks fell. At last it happened that the subterranean aqueduct, by means of which the city was supplied with water from the river, fell out of repair; several large stones having fallen into and choked the course, the progress of the water was arrested, and the supply cut off from the river. Upon which the inhabitants of Barbastro, despairing of their lives, hastened to the camp of the enemy, and bought security for their persons and property at the price of certain sums of money, and a number of slaves, which they immediately delivered into the conqueror's hands. No sooner, however, had the Christian king received the money and other articles stipulated in the convention, than he violated it; and, falling on the poor inhabitants, slaughtered the whole of them, with the exception of the kayed Ibnu-t-tawil, and the qadi Ibn 'Isa, who, with a few more of the principal inhabitants of the place, contrived to escape from the general massacre. The spoil made by the Christians on this occasion, in money, furniture, and apparel, exceeds all computation, since we are assured that the share of one of their chiefs only, who was the general of the cavalry, amounted to about 1,500 young maidens, besides 500 loads of merchandise, dresses, ornaments, and every description of property, the whole of which he carried to his stronghold. The number of Muslims who perished or were made captives on this occasion amounted to 100,000 souls; although other [reports] reduce that number to about one-half....

The reason which induced the Christian king to order the massacre of the inhabitants was this. They say that when he entered Barbastro and saw the numbers of the population, fear lodged in his heart, and he became apprehensive lest the Muslims of the neighboring districts should come to their assistance, and help them to regain possession of their city. He therefore decided on exterminating them all, if he could, and ordered a general slaughter; which lasted until upwards of 6,000 Muslims fell by the swords of the Christians. At last the king ordered the massacre to cease, and commanded that such of the inhabitants as remained should be spared, and allowed to quit the city. When the order was made public, the rush of the people to the gate [of the city] was such that a considerable number of them lost their lives by suffocation. Others were wiser and let themselves down from the walls by means of ropes; all, however, ran to the river in order to quench their thirst. About 700 of the principal inhabitants of the place, fearing for their lives, waited until their fate should be known. When the massacre had ceased, and the Christians had taken as many captives as they wanted, and the remainder had either fled through the gates, or let themselves down from the walls, or perished in the pressure, it was announced by the public crier that the slaughter had ended, and that every citizen might return in safety to his dwelling; they then left their place of concealment and hastened home to their families. No sooner, however, had they arrived there, than, by the command of their king, the Franks (may the curses of God fall upon their heads!) summoned them out of their houses, and led them all into captivity with their wives and children. May the Almighty save us from similar calamity!...

We will put an end to this afflicting and heart-rending narrative by recording an anecdote which will of itself convey a sufficient idea of the manifold sufferings of the Muslims on this occasion. Some time after this catastrophe, a Jewish merchant went to Barbastro for the purpose of redeeming the daughter of one of the principal [Muslim] inhabitants, who had escaped from the massacre. At the division of the spoil, the maiden had fallen to the lot of a [Christian] count, whom the Jew well knew, one of those left in charge of the city [after the king's departure]. The Jew went to the count's residence, and, causing himself to be announced by the servants, was admitted into his presence. He there found the Christian occupying the part of the house where its late Muslim proprietor usually sat, reclining on his very couch, and clothed in his most valuable robes. The room, however, with its carpets, cushions, and hangings, was in the same state as when its owner left it on the fatal day; and nothing had been changed or touched of its [Moorish] paintings and ornaments. His female slaves, with their hair tied, were all standing by his bedside, ready to obey his will.

"The count," said the Jew, "welcomed me, and inquired the object of my visit; which I told him plainly and without disguise, pointing to the many maidens who were in the room, and in whose number was the one I came to redeem. The count smiled, and said to me, in the language of his nation, 'Be quick, then, and if the girl you seek is among these, point her out to me; if not, you may go to my castle, where you will find many more among my prisoners and captives; look for the person you mean — we will then come to terms.'

"I replied, 'I need not repair to your castle. The person in search of whom I have come is among yonder maidens; if you consent to part with her, I am ready to meet your demands.'

"'And what have you brought to tempt me?' said the count.

"'I have brought you fine gold in great quantity, and costly and new merchandise,' was my answer.

"'And no doubt you flatter yourself that you have brought things to tempt me, and which I do not possess already. O Bahjah!' said he, addressing one of his female slaves, 'take some of your fellow servants with you, and bring here the large chest, so that I may show him some of my own property.'

"The chest was brought into the room, and Bahjah proceeded to take out, first, a bag containing 10,000 gold dinars [that is, coins]; next, several bags full of dirhems [that is, another kind of coin]; lastly, many trays covered with gold ornaments, and jewels in such profusion, that, when displayed before the Christian, there were enough to cover him completely and conceal him [from my view]. The count then said to Bajah, 'Bring yonder wardrobe closer,' which she did, taking out such a profusion of costly silken and cotton robes, as well as gold and silver brocades, of every color and pattern, that I was actually bewildered, and say plainly that I had brought nothing with me to be compared with the least valuable of the articles exhibited before me. But what was my astonishment when the Christian told me that what I saw was but a small portion of the treasures which he possessed, and that he had so many other precious articles of all sorts, that nothing could be produced which was either new or desirable to him.

"He then swore, by his God, that had he possessed none of the valuable objects [exhibited] before me, and had I come for the express purpose of offering them to him as a ransom for the fair captive, he would still not part with her; and he added, 'This maiden is the daughter of the late owner of this house, who, if I am rightly informed, was a man of rank and influence among his fellow citizens; and for this reason I intend to keep her in my service, as the people of her nation were accustomed to do with our women, whenever they fell into their hands, at the time that they were all-powerful in this country. Now that the scales are turned, and that we have the superiority over them, we do as they did; nay, we do still more.

"Do you see yonder that youthful and delicate maiden over there (pointing to one who stood in a corner of the room with a lute in her hand)? She is actually trembling from fear of my anger. Take your lute,' he said to her in his barbarous jargon, 'and sing to this visitor of ours in your plaintive strain.' The maid took the lute, as she was commanded, and sat down to tune it; and I saw the tears rolling down her fair cheeks; but, with the Christian casting upon her a look of anger, she attempted to sing some verses which I did not understand any more than her Christian master did; although, strange to say, he kept drinking drafts of liquor he had before him, and giving signs of mirth [as if he understood the meaning of them].

"At last, seeing that I could not gain my object, I took leave of the count, and went elsewhere [about the city] to dispose of my goods, where I saw in the hands of the commonest Christians such amount of plunder and captives as left me completely bewildered."

About the end of Jumada, the first of the ensuing year, the news came to Cordoba that Barbastro had been retaken by the Muslims. This happened thus: Ahmed Al-muktadir Ibn Hud, through whose criminal negligence that city had been lost (since, in order to revenge himself upon the inhabitants who had gone over to his brother, he had allowed them to become the prey of the

Christians), wishing to silence those who spoke ill of him, to wash out the indelible spot cast upon his character, and to atone for a sin which nothing short of the immense forgiveness of God can obliterate, marched to Barbastro at the head of his own troops and the reinforcements which his ally 'Abbad had sent him. Having there attacked the unbelievers, Ahmed displayed so much courage and performed such feats of arms, that even the coward [in his army] hesitated, and felt an inclination to behave well. (May God pour his favor on the brave!) The Muslims and the unbelievers fought with renewed fury, until, at last, God was pleased to grant the victory to the former, and to disperse their enemies, who turned their backs in confusion, and ran tumultuously towards the city gates, followed by the Muslims, who entered along with them, and slaughtered the whole of the garrison with the exception of a few, who fled the field of battle [in another direction], of a few children whom compassion saved from death, and of those among their principal men who redeemed themselves by the payment of heavy ransoms. All the rest were either put to death or made slaves, together with their wives and children.

In this manner was the city of Barbastro restored to the Muslims by the will of the creator of all things, with the loss of about fifty of the bravest Muslims only, who fell martyrs to the faith, and whose names God immediately wrote down, to give them entrance into Paradise. The loss of the unbelievers was very considerable, since it amounted to 1,000 horsemen and 500 foot. The city was purified from the filth of idolatry, and cleansed from the stains of infidelity and polytheism.

Questions: How might a Christian writer have described Al-mansur's campaign against Santiago? How did the hostilities come to escalate over time? How were non-combatants affected by the warfare described here? What does the author mean by polytheism?

8. THE SONG OF ROLAND

In the eleventh century, the knights of western Europe were entertained by poetic tales of heroic deeds; the most famous surviving such text is the anonymous poem The Song of Roland, *a story set in the late eighth century (though not written down until the eleventh century). Roland, the hero, is a commander in the army of his uncle, King Charles (Charlemagne), engaged in fighting against the Moors, or Spanish Muslims. The poem has little value as an account of the eighth-century wars, but as a window on Christian military culture, knightly ideals, and European views of Muslims on the eve of the Crusades it is highly informative. It was influential as an expression of the crusading ethos and as incitement for Christians to engage Muslims in warfare.*

Source: trans. I. Butler, *The Song of Roland* (Boston: Houghton Mifflin Company, 1904), pp. 79-94; revised.

Count Roland never loved the cowardly, or the proud, or the wicked, or any knight who was not a good vassal, and now he calls to Archbishop Turpin, saying: "Lord, you are on foot and I on horseback; for your love I would make halt, and together we will take the good and the ill; I will not leave you for any living man; the blows of [our swords] Almace and Durendal shall give back this assault to the pagan [Muslims]." Then says the archbishop: "A traitor is he who does not smite; Charles is returning, and well will he avenge us."

"In an evil hour," say the pagans, "were we born; woeful is the day that has dawned for us! We have lost our lords and our peers. Charles the valiant comes hither again with his great host; we hear the clear trumpets of those of France, and great is the noise of their cry 'Mountjoy!' Count Roland is of such might he cannot be vanquished by mortal man. Let us hurl our missiles upon him, and then leave him." Even so they did; and cast upon him many a dart and javelin, and spears and lances and feathered arrows. They broke and rent the shield of Roland, tore open and unmailed his hauberk, but did not pierce his body: but [his horse] Veillantif was wounded in thirty places, and fell from under the count, dead. Then the pagans flee, and leave him; Count Roland is left alone and on foot.

The pagans flee in anger and wrath, and in all haste they fare toward Spain. Count Roland did not pursue after them, for he has lost his horse Veillantif, and whether he wishes or not, is left on foot. He went to the aid of Archbishop Turpin, and unlaced his golden helm from his head, and took off his white hauberk of fine mail, and he tore his tunic into strips and with the pieces bound his great wounds. Then he gathers him in his arms, and lays him down full softly upon the green grass, and gently he beseeches him: "O gracious baron, I pray your leave. Our comrades whom we so loved are slain, and it is not right to leave them thus. I would go seek and find them, and range them before you."

Fig. 3: Charlemagne. This eleventh- or twelfth-century French statue portrays the great ninth-century Frankish emperor featured in *The Song of Roland*. From P. Lacroix, *Military and Religious Life in the Middle Ages* (London, Chapman and Hall, 1874).

"Go and return again," says the archbishop. "Thank God, this field is yours and mine."

Roland turns away and fares on alone through the field; he searches the valleys and the hills; and there he found Ivon and Ivory, and Gerin, and Gerier his comrade, and he found Engelier the Gascon, and Berengier, and Oton, and he found Anseïs and Samson, and Gerard the old of Rousillon. One by one he has taken up the barons, and has come with them unto the archbishop, and places them in rank before him. The archbishop cannot help but weep; he raises his hand and gives them benediction, and thereafter says: "Alas for ye, lords! May God the glorious receive your souls, and bring them into paradise among the blessed flowers. And now my own death torments me sore; never again shall I see the great emperor." ...

Now Roland feels that death is near him, and his brains flow out at his ears; he prays to the Lord God for his peers that he will receive them, and he prays to the angel Gabriel for himself. That he may be free from all reproach, he takes his horn of ivory in one hand, and Durendal, his sword, in the other, and farther than a crossbow can cast an arrow, through a cornfield he goes on towards Spain. At the crest of a hill, beneath two fair trees, are four stairs of marble; there he falls down on the green grass in a swoon, for death is close upon him....

Now Roland feels that his sight is gone from him. With much striving he gets upon his feet; the color has gone from his face; before him lies a brown stone, and in his sorrow and wrath he smites ten blows upon it. The sword grates upon the rock, but neither breaks nor splinters; and the count says: "Holy Mary, help me now! Ah, Durendal, alas for your goodness! Now am I near to death, and have no more need of you. Many a fight in the field have I won with you, many a wide land have I conquered with you, lands now ruled by Charles with the white beard. May the man who would flee before another never possess you. For many a day have you been held by a right good lord, never will there be such another in France the free." ...

And again Roland smote upon the brown stone and beyond all telling shattered it; the sword grates, but springs back again into the air and is neither dinted nor broken. And when the count sees he may in no way break it, he laments, saying: "O Durendal, how fair and holy a thing you are! In your golden hilt is many a relic — a tooth of St. Peter, and some of the blood of St. Basil, and hairs from the head of my lord, St. Denis, and a bit of the raiment of the Virgin Mary. It is not right that you fall into the hands of the pagans; only Christians should wield you. May no coward ever possess you! Many wide lands have I conquered with you, lands which Charles of the white beard rules; and thereby is the emperor great and mighty."

Now Roland feels that death has come upon him, and that it creeps down from his head to his heart. In all haste he fares under a pine tree, and has cast himself down upon his face on the green grass. Under him he laid his sword and his horn of ivory; and he turned his face toward the pagan folk, for he wanted Charles and all his men to say that the gentle count had died a conqueror. Speedily and full often he confesses his sins, and in atonement he offers his glove to God....

Count Roland lay under the pine tree; he has turned his face towards Spain, and he begins to call many things to remembrance — all the lands he had won by his valor, and sweet France, and the men of his lineage, and

Charles, his liege lord, who had brought him up in his household; and he cannot help but weep. But he would not wholly forget himself, and again he confesses his sins and begs forgiveness of God: "Our Father, who art truth, who raised up Lazarus from the dead, and who defended Daniel from the lions, save thou my soul from the perils to which it is brought through the sins I wrought in my life days." With his right hand he offers his glove to God, and St. Gabriel has taken it from his hand. Then his head sinks on his arm, and with clasped hands he has gone to his end. And God sent him his cherubim, and St. Michael of the seas, and with them went St. Gabriel, and they carried the soul of the count into paradise.

Questions: What are the qualities of the ideal knight, Roland? What is considered proper conduct in and after battle? What attitudes toward warfare are held by the characters in this text? Compare these with the ideas of Augustine. What is the role of religion in warfare?

9. DECLARATION OF THE TRUCE OF GOD

The eleventh century saw a peace movement in Europe whereby the church attempted to restrain internal violence and warfare by a series of decrees. In 1027 the first "Truce of God" forbade fighting on Sundays and during the holy seasons of Lent and Advent; later the times of truce were extended. The truce was supplemented by various declarations of the "Peace of God," which prohibited harming certain individuals. The decree reprinted here was issued by the bishop of Cologne in Germany in 1083.

Source: trans. D.C. Munro, *Translations and Reprints from the Original Sources of European History*, series I, vol. I (Philadelphia: University of Pennsylvania Department of History, 1902), no. 2, pp. 9–12; revised.

Inasmuch as in our own times the church, through its members, has been extraordinarily afflicted by tribulations and difficulties, so that tranquility and peace were wholly despaired of, we have endeavored by God's help to aid it, suffering so many burdens and perils. And by the advice of our faithful subjects we have at length provided this remedy, so that we might to some extent re-establish, on certain days at least, the peace which, because of our sins, we could not make enduring. Accordingly we have enacted and set forth the following: having called together our parishioners to a legally summoned council, which was held at Cologne, the chief city of our province, in the church of St. Peter, in the 1083rd year of our Lord's incarnation, ... after arranging other business, we have caused to be read in public what we proposed to do in this matter. After this had been for some time fully discussed "pro and con" by all, it was unanimously agreed upon, both the clergy and the people consenting, and we declared in what manner and during what parts of the year it ought to be observed:

Namely, that from the first day of the Advent of our Lord through Epiphany, and from the beginning of Septuagesima to the eighth day after Pentecost and through that whole day, and throughout the year on every Sunday, Friday, and Saturday, and on the fast days of the four seasons, and on the eve and the day of all the apostles, and on all days canonically set apart — or which shall in the future be set apart — for fasts or feasts, this decree of peace shall be observed, so that both those who travel and those who remain at home may enjoy security and the most entire peace, so that no one may commit murder, arson, robbery, or assault, no one may injure another with a sword, club, or any kind of weapon, and so that no one irritated by any wrong, from the Advent of our Lord to the eighth day after Epiphany, and from Septuagesima to the eighth day after Pentecost, may presume to carry arms, shield, sword, or lance, or moreover any kind of armor. On the remaining days indeed, that is on Sundays, Fridays, apostles' days, and the vigils of the apostles, and on every day set aside, or to be set aside, for fasts or feasts, bearing arms shall be legal, but on this condition, that no injury shall be done in any way to anyone. If it shall be necessary for anyone in the time of the decreed peace — i.e., from the Advent of our Lord to the eighth day after Epiphany, and from Septuagesima to the eighth day after Pentecost — to go from one bishopric into another in which the peace is not observed, he may bear arms, but on the condition that he shall not injure anyone, except in self-defense if he is attacked; and when he returns into our diocese he shall immediately lay aside his arms. If it shall happen that any castle is besieged during the days which are included in the peace, the besiegers shall cease from attack unless they are set upon by the besieged and compelled to beat the latter back.

And in order that this statute of peace should not be violated by anyone rashly or with impunity, a penalty was fixed by the common consent of all; if a free man or noble violates it, i.e., commits homicide or wounds anyone or is at fault in any manner whatsoever, he shall be expelled from our territory, without any indulgence on account of the payment of money or the intercession of friends, and his heirs shall take all his property; if he holds a fief, the lord to whom it belongs shall receive it again. Moreover, if it is learned that his heirs after his expulsion have furnished him any support or aid, and if they are convicted of it, the estate shall be taken from them and given to the king. But if they wish to clear themselves of the charge against them, they shall take an oath with twelve men who are equally free or equally noble. If a slave kills a man, he shall be beheaded; if he wounds a man, he shall lose a hand; if he does an injury in any other way with his fist or a club, or by striking with a stone, he shall be shorn and flogged. If, however, he is accused and wishes to prove his innocence, he shall clear himself by the ordeal of cold water, but he must himself be put into the water and no one else in his place; if, however, fearing the sentence decreed against him, he flees, he shall be under a perpetual excommunication; and if he is known to be in any place, letters shall be sent thither, in which it shall be announced to all that he is excommunicate, and that it is unlawful for anyone to associate with him. In the case of boys who have not yet completed their twelfth year, the hand ought not to be cut off; but only in the case of those who are twelve years or more of age. Nevertheless if boys fight, they shall be whipped and deterred from fighting.

It is not an infringement of the peace if anyone orders his delinquent slave, pupil, or anyone in any way under his charge to be chastised with rods or cudgels. It is also an exception to this constitution of peace, if the lord king publicly orders an expedition to attack the enemies of the kingdom or is pleased to hold a council to judge the enemies of justice. The peace is not violated if, during the time, the duke or other counts, advocates, or their substitutes hold courts and inflict punishment legally on thieves, robbers, or other criminals.

The statute of this imperial peace is especially enacted for the security of those engaged in feuds; but after the end of the peace, they are not to dare to rob and plunder in the villages and houses, because the laws and penalties enacted before the institution of the peace are still legally valid to restrain them from crime, moreover because robbers and highwaymen are excluded from this divine peace or indeed from any peace.

If anyone attempts to oppose this pious institution and is unwilling to promise peace to God ... or to observe it, no priest in our diocese shall presume to say a mass for him or shall take any care for his salvation; if he is sick, no Christian shall dare to visit him; on his deathbed he shall not receive the Eucharist, unless he repents. The supreme authority of the peace promised to God and commonly extolled by all will be so great that it will be observed not only in our times, but forever among our posterity, because if anyone shall presume to infringe, destroy, or violate it, either now or ages hence, at the end of the world, he is irrevocably excommunicated by us.

The infliction of the above-mentioned penalties on the violators of the peace is no more in the power of the counts, centenaries, or officials, than in that of the whole people in common; and they are to be especially careful not to show friendship or hatred or to do anything contrary to justice in punishing, and not to conceal the crimes, if they can be hidden, but to bring them to light. No one is to receive money for the release of those taken in fault, or to attempt to aid the guilty by any favor of any kind, because whoever does this incurs the intolerable damnation of his soul; and all the faithful ought to remember that this peace has not been promised to men, but to God, and therefore must be observed all the more rigidly and firmly. Wherefore we exhort all in Christ to guard inviolably this necessary contract of peace, and if anyone hereafter presumes to violate it, let him be damned by the ban of irrevocable excommunication and by the anathema of eternal perdition.

In the churches, however, and in the cemeteries of the churches, honor and reverence are to be paid to God, so that if any robber or thief flees thither, he is by no means to be killed or seized, but he is to remain there until by urgent hunger he is compelled to surrender. If any person presumes to furnish arms or food to the criminal or to aid him in flight, the same penalty shall be inflicted on him as on the criminal. Moreover, by our ban we interdict laymen from punishing the transgressions of the clergy and those living under this order; but if seized in open crime, they shall be handed over to their bishop. In cases in which laymen are to be mutilated, the clergy are to be suspended from office, and with the consent of the laymen they are to suffer frequent fasts and floggings until they atone.

Questions: How violent was medieval European society? What does the decree reveal about problems of law and order? What does it reveal about the position and ambitions of the church? How likely was it that the Truce of God would noticeably reduce violence? What forms of violence were still permissible?

10. MATTHEW OF EDESSA ON THE SELJUK CONQUESTS

The crisis that prompted the first calls for crusades began with the invasion of parts of the Middle East by the Seljuk Turks. In the following account, an early twelfth-century Armenian historian, Matthew of Edessa, gives a Middle Eastern Christian view of the Seljuks' arrival, as well as an Armenian view of the Greek rulers of the Byzantine empire, of which Armenia was a part.

Source: trans. A.E. Dostourian, *Armenia and the Crusades, Tenth to Twelfth Centuries: The Chronicle of Matthew of Edessa* (Lanham and New York: University Press of America, 1993), pp. 44, 130, 132-35.

...When the year 467 of the Armenian era [that is, 1018-1019] began, the divine-rebuking wrath of God was awakened against all the Christian peoples and against those worshipping the holy cross, for a fatal dragon with deadly fires rose up and struck those faithful to the holy Trinity. In this period the very foundations of the apostles and prophets were shaken, because winged serpents came forth and were intent on spreading like fire over all the lands of the Christian faithful. This was the first appearance of the bloodthirsty beasts. During these times the savage nation of infidels called [Seljuk] Turks gathered together their forces. Then they came and entered Armenia in the province of Vaspurakan and mercilessly slaughtered the Christian faithful with the edge of the sword.... Until that time the Armenians had never seen Turkish cavalry forces. When they encountered these Turks, armed with bows and having flowing hair like women, they found them strange-looking....

In [1070-1071] ... Alp Arslan, the brother [and successor] of the [late Turkish] sultan Tughrul, rose up and went forth like a torrential stream; with a tremendous number of troops he marched forth and arrived in Armenia like a cloud filled with murky darkness, bringing with him much destruction and bloodshed. Descending upon [Manzikert], he captured the town in one day since there was no garrison there, for its Roman [that is, Greek] guardians had fled. Alp Arslan slaughtered all the inhabitants of the town because of the insult directed at his brother, the sultan Tughrul, by these same inhabitants at a previous time; for this insult had not as yet been avenged at the time of Tughrul's death....

When the Greek emperor Diogenes heard the news of this recent calamity [that is, the Turkish invasion of Armenia], roaring like a lion he commanded all his numerous forces be collected; so edicts were issued and heralds sent forth throughout all the [western parts of the Byzantine Empire]. Thus a very great and formidable number of troops was gathered together from the entire country of the Goths, from all the Bulgars, from all the distant islands, from Cappadocia and all of Bithynia, from Cilicia and Antioch, from Trebizond, and from Armenia—whose remnants of very courageous soldiers still existed; moreover, Diogenes had mercenaries from the infidels of Khuzistan brought, and thus the emperor gathered together a formidable army, as numerous as the sands of the sea....

Going forth with a tremendous number of troops, Diogenes went to the East, to Armenia, and, descending upon the town of [Manzikert], captured it. The forces of the [Turkish] sultan who were in the town fled, and when the emperor captured them, he slaughtered them. The news of all this reached Alp Arslan, who was before the city of Aleppo; and so he started back for the East, since he was told that the Roman [that is, Greek] emperor was marching in the direction of Persia at the head of a very formidable army.... As he was returning, a letter written by perfidious Romans [that is, Greeks] from Diogenes' army reached Alp Arslan, and it read as follows: "Do not flee, for the greater part of our forces is with you." Hearing this, the sultan immediately stopped. Then he wrote a very amicable letter to the emperor Diogenes concerning the establishment of peace and harmony between both sides; each side was to remain in peace with the other, neither one ever harming the other; moreover, the Christians would be looked upon as friends, and thus there would be a perpetual peace and alliance between the [Turks] and the [Greeks].

When Diogenes heard these things, not only did he become arrogant and refuse to accept the sultan's offer, but he became even more bellicose than ever. Then the aforementioned malicious and perfidious men approached Diogenes and said: "O emperor, no one is able to stand against your innumerable forces. Your troops are going forth from the camp to procure victuals; send them away regiment by regiment [to forage for themselves], so that they might not go hungry before the day of battle." So the emperor had the emir Ktrich' return to Constantinople and had Tarkhaniat go against Khlat' with thirty thousand men; moreover, he sent 12,000 men to the Abkhazes, and thus because of the emperor all the [Greek] forces became scattered. Now Alp Arslan was informed of all these treacherous machinations. So, when the sultan saw Diogenes's inflexible and stubborn attitude, he went into battle against the [Greek] forces, leading on the whole army of Khurasan with the fervor of a lion cub. When Diogenes learned of the advance of the Persian army against him, he ordered the battle trumpet sounded and had all the [Greek] forces drawn up in orderly fashion. He appointed as commanders of his troops Khatap and Vasilak, Armenian nobles who were brave and were regarded as great warriors. A very violent battle took place the greater part of the day, and the [Greek] forces were defeated. Khatap and Vasilak were killed, and all the [Greek] troops were put to flight, being forced to fall back on the imperial camp. When Diogenes saw this, he ordered all his forces to regroup, but there was no one to heed his summons, for Tarkhaniat and the other [Greek] magnates had returned to Constantinople with their troops. When the emperor learned of this, he realized the treachery of his own [Greeks]. So the battle continued the next day. In the morning hours the battle trumpet was sounded, and heralds went forth and proclaimed the wishes of the emperor Diogenes; he promised honors, high positions, and jurisdiction over the towns and districts to all those who would courageously fight against the [Turkish] forces. Soon the sultan, very well organized, advanced into battle against the [Greek] troops. At that point the emperor Diogenes went forth and reached a place of battle near [Manzikert], called Toghotap'. There he placed the Uz and Pecheneg mercenaries on his right and left flanks and the other troops on his van and rear. When the battle grew intense, the Uzes and Pechenegs went over to the side of the sultan.

At that point all the [Greek] troops were defeated and turned in complete flight. Countless [Greek] troops were slaughtered and many captives were taken. The emperor Diogenes himself was taken prisoner and brought into the presence of the sultan in chains, together with countless and innumerable captives. After a short while the sultan made an alliance of peace and friendship with the [Greek] emperor. Then the sultan adopted Diogenes as his blood brother and took an oath to God as a guarantee of his sincerity; moreover, with a solemn oath he pledged that there would be perpetual friendship and harmony between the [Turks] and the [Greeks]. After all this with great pomp Alp Arslan sent the emperor back to Constantinople, to his imperial throne.

When Diogenes reached Sebastia, news came to him that Michael, the son of Ducas, occupied the imperial throne. At this all the emperor's troops abandoned him and fled, and so he was forced to take refuge in the city of Adana. The emperor Michael's forces gathered against him. Diogenes, in turn, because of the danger in which he found himself, put on the garments of an *abeghay* [that is, a monk] and, going to the [Greek] general who was the brother of Ducas, said: "You no longer need to worry about me, for henceforth I intend to live in a monastery; let Michael be emperor and may God be with him." Notwithstanding all this, on that same day the [Greek] nation once again crucified God as had the Jews, for they tore out the eyes of Diogenes, their very own sovereign, who then died from the intense pain [of the blinding]. When Alp Arslan heard this, he wept bitterly and regretted the death of Diogenes. Then the sultan said: "The [Greek] nation has no God, so this day the oath of peace and friendship taken by both the [Turks] and the [Greeks] is nullified; henceforth I shall consume with the sword all those people who venerate the cross, and all the lands of the Christians shall be enslaved."

Questions: What sense of historical causation is evident in this text? What tensions within the Byzantine Empire are revealed? How does the Armenian Christian viewpoint influence the content of the account? Compare this story with the extracts from Song of Roland (doc. 8).

11. GREGORY VII'S CALL FOR ASSISTANCE TO THE GREEKS

The second capture of Manzikert by the Seljuks, described in the preceding narrative by Matthew of Edessa, led directly to the following document, issued in 1074. In it, Pope Gregory VII urges European Christians to intervene against the Seljuk Turks on behalf of the Byzantine Greeks. His call was largely ignored.

Source: trans. O.J. Thatcher and E.H. McNeal, *A Sourcebook for Medieval History, Selected Documents Illustrating the History of Europe in the Middle Ages* (New York: Charles Scribner's Sons, 1905), pp. 512–13.

Gregory, bishop, servant of the servants of God, to all who are willing to defend the Christian faith, greeting and apostolic benediction.

We hereby inform you that the bearer of this letter, on his recent return from across the sea [that is, from Palestine], came to Rome to visit us. He repeated what we had heard from many others, that a pagan race had over-come the Christians and, with horrible cruelty, had devastated everything almost to the walls of Constantinople, and were now governing the conquered lands with tyrannical violence, and that they had slain many thousands of Christians as if they were but sheep. If we love God and wish to be recognized as Christians, we should be filled with grief at the misfortune of this great [Greek] empire and the murder of so many Christians. But simply to grieve is not our whole duty. The example of our Redeemer and the bond of fraternal love demand that we should lay down our lives to liberate them. "Because he laid down his life for us: and we ought to lay down our lives for the brethren" [I John 3:16]. Know, therefore, that we are trusting in the mercy of God and in the power of his might and that we are striving in all possible ways and making preparations to render aid to the Christian [Greek] Empire as quickly as possi-ble. Therefore, we beseech you by the faith in which you are united through Christ in the adoption of the sons of God, and by the authority of St. Peter, prince of apostles, we admonish you that you be moved to proper compassion by the wounds and blood of your brethren and the danger of the aforesaid empire and that, for the sake of Christ, you undertake the difficult task of bear-ing aid to your brethren [the Greeks]. Send messengers to us at once to inform us what God may inspire you to do in this matter.

Questions: What exactly does Gregory ask for in this document? How does he justify the call? Who is his intended audience? How does he try to appeal to that audience? How does this letter meet the criteria laid out in Augustine's discussion of justifiable war?

CHAPTER TWO:

THE FIRST CRUSADE

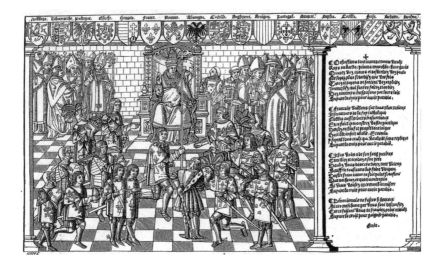

Fig. 4: The Council of Clermont, 1095, in a fifteenth-century woodcut. Pope Urban II preaches the First Crusade to an assembly of churchmen and knights. From P. Lacroix, *Military and Religious Life in the Middle Ages* (London, Chapman and Hall, 1874).

12. URBAN II'S CALL FOR A CRUSADE

In March 1095, envoys from the Byzantine emperor Alexius II addressed Pope Urban II at a church council at Piacenza, describing Constantinople's urgent need for soldiers to supplement his existing mercenaries and home guard in the fight against the Turks. The envoys' words are not recorded, but it is clear that they wanted the pope to recruit European soldiers to serve in Alexius's army.

A few months later, in November, the crusading movement was launched at the close of a general church council at Clermont in France, when Urban delivered a sermon which responded to Alexius's plea by calling upon European Christians to rescue the Holy Land from Muslim occupation. Below are four accounts of this address, all by churchmen, and all written after the conclusion of the First Crusade. Fulcher of Chartres, Robert the Monk, and Baldric of Dol are each believed to have been present at the council. Evidence also suggests that some if not all of these accounts were based on earlier records of this event.

Sources: Fulcher and Robert: trans. O.J. Thatcher and E.H. McNeal, *A Source Book for Medieval History: Selected Documents Illustrating the History of Europe in the Middle Ages* (New York: Charles Scribner's Sons, 1905), pp. 514, 516-21, revised; Baldric and Guibert: trans. A.C. Krey, *The First Crusade: The Accounts of Eye-witnesses and Participants* (Princeton: Princeton University Press, 1921), pp. 33-40.

Fulcher of Chartres

"Most beloved brethren: Urged by necessity, I, Urban, by the permission of God chief bishop and prelate over the whole world, have come into these parts as an ambassador with a divine admonition to you, the servants of God....

"Although, O sons of God, you have promised more firmly than ever to keep the peace among yourselves and to preserve the rights of the church, there remains still an important work for you to do. Freshly quickened by the divine correction, you must apply the strength of your righteousness to another matter which concerns you as well as God. For your brethren who live in the east are in urgent need of your help, and you must hasten to give them the aid which has often been promised them. For, as most of you have heard, the Turks and Arabs have attacked them and have conquered the territory of Romania [that is, the Greek empire] as far west as the shore of the Mediterranean and the Hellespont, which is called the Arm of St. George. They have occupied more and more of the lands of those Christians, and have overcome them in seven battles. They have killed and captured many, and have destroyed the churches and devastated the empire. If you permit them to continue thus for a while with impunity, the faithful of God will be much more widely attacked by them. On this account I, or rather the Lord, beseech you as

Christ's heralds to publish this everywhere and to persuade all people of whatever rank, footsoldiers and knights, poor and rich, to carry aid promptly to those Christians and to destroy that vile race from the lands of our friends. I say this to those who are present, but it is meant also for those who are absent. Moreover, Christ commands it.

"All who die by the way, whether by land or by sea, or in battle against the pagans, shall have immediate remission of sins. This I grant them through the power of God with which I am invested. O what a disgrace, if such a despised and base race, which worships demons, should conquer a people which has the faith of omnipotent God and is made glorious with the name of Christ! With what reproaches will the Lord overwhelm us if you do not aid those who, with us, profess the Christian religion! Let those who have been accustomed to wage unjust private warfare against the faithful now go against the infidels and end with victory this war which should have been begun long ago. Let those who for a long time have been robbers now become knights. Let those who have been fighting against their brothers and relatives now fight in a proper way against the barbarians. Let those who have been serving as mercenaries for small pay now obtain the eternal reward. Let those who have been wearing themselves out in both body and soul now work for a double honor. Behold! on this side will be the sorrowful and poor, on that, the rich; on this side, the enemies of the Lord, on that, his friends. Let those who go not put off the journey, but rent their lands and collect money for their expenses; and as soon as winter is over and spring comes, let them eagerly set out on the way with God as their guide."

Robert the Monk

In 1095 a great council was held at Auvergne, in the city of Clermont. Pope Urban II, accompanied by cardinals and bishops, presided over it. It was made famous by the presence of many bishops and princes from France and Germany. After the council had attended to ecclesiastical matters, the pope went out into a public square, because no house was able to hold the people, and addressed them in a very persuasive speech, as follows:

"O race of Franks, O people who live beyond the mountains [that is, from Rome], O people loved and chosen by God, as is clear from your many deeds, distinguished over all other nations by the situation of your land, your catholic faith, and your regard for the holy church, we have a special message and exhortation for you. For we wish you to know what a grave matter has brought us to your country. The sad news has come from Jerusalem and Constantinople that the people of Persia, an accursed and foreign race, enemies of God, 'a generation that set not their heart aright, and whose spirit was not steadfast with God' [Ps. 78:8], have invaded the lands of those Christians and devastated them with the sword, rapine, and fire. Some of the Christians they have carried away as slaves; others they have put to death. The churches they have either destroyed or turned into mosques. They desecrate and overthrow the altars. They circumcise the Christians and pour the blood from the circumcision on the altars or in the baptismal fonts. Some they kill in a horrible way by cutting open the abdomen, taking out a part of the entrails and tying them to a stake; they then beat them and compel them to walk until all their entrails are drawn out and they fall to the ground. Some they use as targets for their arrows. They compel some to stretch out their necks, and then they try to see whether they can cut off their heads with one stroke of the sword. It is better to say nothing of their horrible treatment of the women. They have taken from the Greek empire a tract of land so large that it takes more than two months to walk through it. Whose duty is it to avenge this and recover that land, if not yours? For to you more than to other nations the Lord has given the military spirit, courage, agile bodies, and the bravery to strike down those who resist you. Let your minds be stirred to bravery by the deeds of your forefathers, and by the efficiency and greatness of Charles the Great, and of Louis his son, and of the other kings who have destroyed Turkish kingdoms and established Christianity in their lands. You should be moved especially by the holy grave of our Lord and Savior which is now held by unclean peoples, and by the holy places which are treated with dishonor and irreverently befouled with their uncleanness.

"O bravest knights, descendants of unconquered ancestors, do not be weaker than they, but remember their courage. If you are kept back by your love for your children, relatives, and wives, remember what the Lord says in the Gospel: 'He that loveth father or mother more than me is not worthy of me' [Matt. 10:37]; 'and everyone that hath forsaken houses, or brothers, or sisters, or father, or mother, or wife, or children, or lands for my name's sake shall receive a hundredfold and shall inherit everlasting life' [Matt. 19:29]. Let no possessions keep you back, no solicitude for your property. Your land is shut in on all sides by the sea and mountains and is too thickly populated. There is not much wealth here and the soil scarcely yields enough to support you. On this account you kill and devour each other, and carry on war and mutually destroy each other. Let your hatred and quarrels cease, your civil wars come to an end, and all your dissensions stop. Set out on the road to the holy sepulcher, take the land from that wicked people and make it your own. That land which, as the scripture says, is flowing with milk and honey, God gave to the children of Israel. Jerusalem is the best of all lands, more fruitful than all others, as it were a second paradise of delights. This land our Savior made illustrious by his birth, beautiful with his life, and sacred with his suffering; he redeemed it with his death and glorified it with his tomb. This royal city is now held captive by her enemies, and made pagan by those who know not God. She asks and longs to be liberated and does not cease to beg you to come to her aid. She asks aid especially from you because, as I have said, God has given more of the military spirit to you than to other nations. Set out on this journey and you will obtain the remission of your sins and be sure of the incorruptible glory of the kingdom of heaven."

When Pope Urban had said this and much more of the same sort, all who were present were moved to cry out with one accord, "It is the will of God, it is the will of God." When the pope heard this he raised his eyes to heaven and gave thanks to God, and, commanding silence with a gesture of his hand, he said: "My dear brethren, today there is fulfilled in you that which the Lord says in the Gospel, 'Where two or three are gathered together in my name, there I am in the midst' [Matt. 18:20]. For unless the Lord God had been in your minds you would not all have said the same thing. For although you spoke with many voices, nevertheless, it was one and the same thing that made you speak. So I say unto you, God, who put those words into your hearts, has caused you to utter them. Therefore let these words be your battle cry, because God caused you to speak them. Whenever you meet the enemy in battle, you shall all cry out, 'It is the will of God, it is the will of God.' And we do not command the old or weak to go, or those who cannot bear arms. No women shall go without their husbands, or brothers, or proper companions, for such would be a hindrance rather than a help, a burden rather than an advantage. Let the rich aid the poor and equip them for fighting and take them with them. Clergymen shall not go without the consent of their bishop, for otherwise the journey would be of no value to them. Nor will this pilgrimage be of any benefit to a layman if he goes without the blessing of his priest. Whoever therefore shall determine to make this journey and shall make a vow to God and shall offer himself as a living sacrifice, holy, acceptable to God [Rom. 12:1], shall wear a cross on his brow or on his breast. And when he returns after having fulfilled his vow he shall wear the cross on his back. In this way he will obey the command of the Lord, 'Whosoever doth not bear his cross and come after me is not worthy of me'" [Luke 14:27].

When these things had been done, while all prostrated themselves on the earth and beat their breasts, one of the cardinals, named Gregory, made confession for them, and they were given absolution for all their sins. After the absolution, they received the benediction and permission to go home.

Baldric of Dol

"We have heard, most beloved brethren, and you have heard what we cannot recount without deep sorrow — how, with great hurt and dire sufferings, our Christian brothers, members in Christ, are scourged, oppressed, and injured in Jerusalem, in Antioch, and the other cities of the East. Your own blood-brothers, your companions, your associates (for you are sons of the same Christ and the same church) are either subjected in their inherited homes to other masters, or are driven from them, or they come as beggars among us; or, which is far worse, they are flogged and exiled as slaves for sale in their own land. Christian blood, redeemed by the blood of Christ, has been shed, and Christian flesh, akin to the flesh of Christ, has been subjected to unspeakable degradation and servitude. Everywhere in those cities there is sorrow, everywhere misery, everywhere groaning (I say it with a sigh). The churches in which divine mysteries were celebrated in olden times are now, to our sorrow, used as stables for the animals of these people! Holy men do not possess those cities; nay, base and bastard Turks hold sway over our brothers. The blessed Peter first presided as bishop at Antioch; behold, in his own church the gentiles [that is, the non-Christians] have established their superstitions, and the Christian religion, which they ought rather to cherish, they have basely shut out from the hall dedicated to God! The estates given for the support of the saints and the patrimony of nobles set aside for the sustenance of the poor are subject to pagan tyranny, while cruel masters abuse for their own purposes the returns from these lands. The priesthood of God has been ground down into the dust. The sanctuary of God (unspeakable shame!) is everywhere profaned. Whatever Christians still remain in hiding there are sought out with unheard of tortures.

"Of holy Jerusalem, brethren, we dare not speak, for we are exceedingly afraid and ashamed to speak of it. This very city, in which, as you all know, Christ himself suffered for us, because our sins demanded it, has been reduced to the pollution of paganism and, I say it to our disgrace, withdrawn from the service of God. Such is the heap of reproach upon us who have so much deserved it! Who now serves the church of the blessed Mary in the valley of Josaphat, in which church she herself was buried in body? But why do we pass over the Temple of Solomon, nay of the Lord, in which the barbarous nations placed their idols contrary to law, human and divine? Of the Lord's Sepulcher we have refrained from speaking, since some of you with your own eyes have seen to what abominations it has been given over. The Turks violently took from it the offerings which you brought there for alms in such vast amounts, and, in addition, they scoffed much and often at your religion. And yet in that place (I say only what you already know) rested the Lord; there he died for us; there he was buried. How precious would be the longed-for, incomparable place of the Lord's burial, even if God failed there to perform the yearly miracle! For in the days of his passion all the lights in the Sepulcher and round about in the church, which have been extinguished, are re-lighted by divine command. Whose heart is so stony, brethren, that it is not touched by so great a miracle? Believe me, that man is bestial and senseless whose heart such divinely manifest grace does not move to faith! And yet the gentiles see this in common with the Christians and are not turned from their ways! They are, indeed, afraid, but they are not converted to the faith; nor is it to be wondered at, for a blindness of mind rules over them. With what afflictions they wronged you who have returned and are now present, you yourselves know too well, you who there sacrificed your substance and your blood for God....

"What are we saying? Listen and learn! You, girt about with the badge of knighthood, are arrogant with great pride; you rage against your brothers and cut each other in pieces. This is not the [true] soldiery of Christ which rends asunder the sheep-fold of the Redeemer. The holy church has reserved a soldiery for herself to help her people, but you debase her wickedly to her hurt. Let us confess the truth, whose heralds we ought to be; truly, you are not holding to the way which leads to life. You, the oppressors of children, plunderers of widows; you, guilty of homicide, of sacrilege, robbers of another's rights; you who await the pay of thieves for the shedding of Christian blood—as vultures smell fetid corpses, so do you sense battles from afar and rush to them eagerly. Verily, this is the worst way, for it is utterly removed from God! If, forsooth, you wish to be mindful of your souls, either lay down the girdle of such knighthood, or advance boldly, as knights of Christ, and rush as quickly as you can to the defense of the eastern church. For she it is from whom the joys of your whole salvation have come forth, who poured into your mouths the milk of divine wisdom, who set before you the holy teachings of the Gospels. We say this, brethren, that you may restrain your murderous hands from the destruction of your brothers, and in behalf of your relatives in the faith oppose yourselves to the gentiles. Under Jesus Christ, our leader, may you struggle for your Jerusalem, in Christian battle-line, most invincible line, even more successfully than did the sons of Jacob of old—struggle, that you may assail and drive out the Turks, more execrable than the Jebusites, who are in this land, and may you deem it a beautiful thing to die for Christ in that city in which he died for us. But if it befall you to die this side of it, be sure that to have died on the way is of equal value, if Christ shall find you in his army. God pays with the same shilling, whether at the first or eleventh hour. You should shudder, brethren, you should shudder at raising a violent hand against Christians; it is less wicked to brandish your sword against Saracens. It is the only warfare that is righteous, for it is charity to risk your life for your brothers. That you may not be troubled about the concerns of tomorrow, know that those who fear God want nothing, nor those who cherish him in truth. The possessions of the enemy, too, will be yours, since you will make spoil of their treasures and return victorious to your own; or empurpled with our own blood, you will have gained everlasting glory. For such a commander you ought to fight, for one who lacks neither might nor wealth with which to reward you. Short is the way, little the labor, which, nevertheless, will repay you with the crown that fades not away. Accordingly, we speak with the authority of the prophet: 'Gird thy sword upon thy thigh, O mighty one.' Gird yourselves, every one of you, I say, and be valiant sons; for it is better for you to die in battle than to behold the sorrows of your race and of your holy places. Let neither property nor the alluring charms of your wives entice you from going; nor let the trials that are to be borne so deter you that you remain here."

And turning to the bishops, he said, "You, brothers and fellow bishops; you, fellow priests and sharers with us in Christ, make this same announcement through the churches committed to you, and with your whole soul vigorously preach the journey to Jerusalem. When they have confessed the disgrace of their sins, do you, secure in Christ, grant them speedy pardon. Moreover, you who are to go shall have us praying for you; we shall have you fighting for God's people. It is our duty to pray, yours to fight against the Amalekites [that is, biblical enemies of the Hebrews]. With Moses, we shall extend unwearied hands in prayer to heaven, while you go forth and brandish the sword, like dauntless warriors, against Amalek."

As those present were thus clearly informed by these and other words of this kind from the apostolic lord, the eyes of some were bathed in tears; some trembled, and yet others discussed the matter. However, in the presence of all at that same council, and as we looked on, the bishop of Puy, a man of great renown and of highest ability, went to the pope with joyful countenance and on bended knee sought and entreated blessing and permission to go. Over and above this, he won from the pope the command that all should obey him, and that he should hold sway over all the army in behalf of the pope, since all knew him to be a prelate of unusual energy and industry.

Guibert of Nogent

"… Most beloved brethren, if you reverence the source of that holiness and glory, if you cherish these shrines which are the marks of his footprints on earth, if you seek [the way], God leading you, God fighting in your behalf, you should strive with your utmost efforts to cleanse the holy city and the glory of the Sepulcher, now polluted by the concourse of the gentiles, as much as is in their power.

"If in olden times the Maccabees attained to the highest praise of piety because they fought for the ceremonies and the Temple, it is also justly granted you, Christian soldiers, to defend the liberty of your country by armed endeavor. If you, likewise, consider that the abode of the holy apostles and any other saints should be striven for with such effort, why do you refuse to rescue the cross, the blood, the tomb? Why do you refuse to visit them, to spend the price of your lives in rescuing them? You have thus far waged unjust wars, at one time and another; you have brandished mad weapons to your mutual destruction, for no other reason than covetousness and pride, as a result of which you have deserved eternal death and sure damnation. We now hold out to you wars which contain the glorious reward of martyrdom, which will retain that title of praise now and forever....

"And you ought, furthermore, to consider with the utmost deliberation, if by your labors, God working through you, it should occur that the mother of churches should flourish anew to the worship of Christianity, whether, perchance, he may not wish other regions of the East to be restored to the faith against the approaching time of the Antichrist. For it is clear that Antichrist is to do battle not with the Jews, not with the Gentiles; but, according to the etymology of his name, he will attack Christians. And if Antichrist finds there no Christians (just as at present when scarcely any dwell there), no one will be there to oppose him, or whom he may rightly overcome....

"If neither the words of the scriptures arouse you, nor our admonitions penetrate your minds, at least let the great suffering of those who desired to go to the holy places stir you up. Think of those who made the pilgrimage across the sea! Even if they were more wealthy, consider what taxes, what violence they underwent, since they were forced to make payments and tributes almost every mile, to purchase release at every gate of the city, at the entrance of the churches and temples, at every side-journey from place to place: also, if any accusation whatsoever were made against them, they were compelled to purchase their release; but if they refused to pay money, the prefects of the gentiles, according to their custom, urged them fiercely with blows. What shall we say of those who took up the journey without anything more than trust in their barren poverty, since they seemed to have nothing except their bodies to lose? They not only demanded money of them, which is not an unendurable punishment, but also examined the calluses of their heels, cutting them open and folding the skin back, lest, perchance, they had sewed something there. Their unspeakable cruelty was carried on even to the point of giving them scammony [that is, a purge] to drink until they vomited, or even burst their bowels, because they thought the wretches had swallowed gold or silver; or, horrible to say, they cut their bowels open with a sword and, spreading out the folds of the intestines, with frightful mutilation disclosed whatever nature held there in secret. Remember, I pray, the thousands who have perished vile deaths, and strive for the holy places from which the beginnings of your faith have come. Before you engage in his battles, believe without question that Christ will be your standard-bearer and inseparable forerunner."

The most excellent man concluded his oration and by the power of the blessed Peter absolved all who vowed to go and confirmed those acts with apostolic blessing. He instituted a sign well suited to so honorable a profession by making the figure of the cross, the stigma of the Lord's passion, the emblem of the soldiery, or rather, of what was to be the soldiery of God. This, made of any kind of cloth, he ordered to be sewed upon the shirts, cloaks, and *byrra* [that is, a type of cloak] of those who were about to go. He commanded that if anyone, after receiving this emblem, or after taking openly this vow, should shrink from his good intent through base change of heart, or any affection for his parents, he should be regarded an outlaw forever, unless he repented and again undertook whatever of his pledge he had omitted. Furthermore, the pope condemned with a fearful anathema all those who dared to molest the wives, children, and possessions of these who were going on this journey for God.

Questions: What reasons does the pope give for calling on Europeans to go to the East? What do these accounts tell us of the aims and ambitions of the papacy and the church at this time? What rewards, both material and spiritual, does the pope offer to those who go on crusade? How does the papal view of warfare compare with that of Augustine (doc. 2)? How and why do the four accounts differ from each other? Of the four accounts of Urban's speech, which do you believe to be the most accurate? Why?

13. ALBERT OF AACHEN ON THE PEASANTS' CRUSADE

While the army of the First Crusade was assembling, there arose a number of popular crusading movements led by a variety of charismatic preachers. Unorganized and often violent, these groups exhibited a fanatical belief in the justness of their cause—a belief that resulted in the slaughter of Jewish communities in Europe and hostile encounters with fellow Christians in both eastern Europe and Byzantium as the "armies" made their way toward Jerusalem during 1096. Most medieval accounts of these popular crusaders are critical of their actions and motives, and it is certainly true that politics and personal gain were as much a part of the movement as religious feeling. Although not accepted by higher church authorities, leaders such as Peter the Hermit gained a great following, demonstrating the intensity of popular piety within Europe at this time. Despite the criticism, every major medieval crusade would be accompanied by pogroms against the Jews of Europe, and hostility between western and eastern Christians would continue to be a prominent feature of the crusading movement. Albert of Aachen, a twelfth-century historian, was not a crusader, but his account of the Peasants' Crusade is believed to be based on the reports of an eyewitness or participant.

Source: trans. A.C. Krey, *The First Crusade: The Accounts of Eye-witnesses and Participants* (Princeton: Princeton University Press, 1921), pp. 48-52, 54-56, revised.

There was a priest, Peter by name, formerly a hermit. He was born in the city of Amiens, which is in the western part of the kingdom of the Franks, and he was appointed preacher in Berri in the aforesaid kingdom. In every admonition and sermon, with all the persuasion of which he was capable, he urged setting out on the journey as soon as possible. In response to his constant admonition and call, bishops, abbots, clerics, and monks set out; next, most noble laymen, and princes of the different kingdoms; then, all the common people, the chaste as well as the sinful, adulterers, homicides, thieves, perjurers, and robbers; indeed, every class of the Christian profession, nay, also, women and those influenced by the spirit of penance—all joyfully entered upon this expedition....

In the year of the incarnation of the Lord 1096, ... in the reign of Pope Urban II, formerly Odoard, on the eighth day of March, Walter, surnamed the Penniless, a well-known soldier, set out, as a result of the preaching of Peter the Hermit, with a great company of Frankish foot soldiers and only about eight knights. On the beginning of the journey to Jerusalem he entered into the kingdom of Hungary. When his intention and the reason for his taking this journey became known to Lord Coloman, most Christian king of Hungary, he was kindly received and was given peaceful transit across the entire realm, with permission to trade. And so without giving offense, and without being attacked, he set out even to Belgrade, a Bulgarian city, passing over to Malevilla, where the realm of the king of Hungary ends. Thence he peacefully crossed the Morava river.

But sixteen of Walter's company remained in Malevilla, that they might purchase arms. Of this Walter was ignorant, for he had crossed long before. Then some of the Hungarians of perverse mind, seeing the absence of Walter and his army, laid hands upon those sixteen and robbed them of arms, garments, gold, and silver, and so let them depart, naked and empty-handed. Then these distressed pilgrims, deprived of arms and other things, hastened on their way to Belgrade, which has been mentioned before, where Walter with all his band had pitched tents for camp. They reported to him the misfortune which had befallen them, but Walter heard this with equanimity, because it would take too long to return for vengeance.

On the very night when those comrades, naked and empty-handed, were received, Walter sought to buy the necessities of life from a chief of the Bulgarians and the magistrate of the city; but these men, thinking it a pretense, and regarding them as spies, forbade the sale of anything to them. Wherefore, Walter and his companions, greatly angered, began forcibly to seize and lead away the herds of cattle and sheep, which were wandering here and there through the fields in search of pasture. As a result, serious strife arose between the Bulgarians and the pilgrims who were driving away the flocks, and they came to blows. However, while the strength of the Bulgarians was growing even to 140, some of the pilgrim army, cut off from the multitude of their companions, arrived in flight at a chapel. But the Bulgarians, their army growing in number, while the band of Walter was weakening and his entire company scattered, besieged the chapel and burned sixty who were within; on most of the others, who escaped from the enemy and the chapel in defense of their lives, the Bulgarians inflicted grave wounds.

After this calamity and the loss of his people, and after he had passed eight days as a fugitive in the forests of Bulgaria, Walter, leaving his men scattered everywhere, withdrew to Nish, a very wealthy city in the midst of the Bulgarian realm. There he found the duke and prince of the land and reported to him the injury and damage which had been done him. From the duke he obtained justice for all; nay, more, for in reconciliation the duke bestowed upon him arms and money, and the same lord of the land gave him peaceful conduct through the cities of Bulgaria, Sofia, Philippopolis, and Adrianople, and also license to trade.

[Walter] went down with all his band, even to the imperial city, Constantinople, which is the capital of the entire Greek empire. And when he arrived there, with all possible earnestness and most humble petition he implored from the lord emperor himself permission to delay peacefully in his kingdom, with license to buy the necessities of life, until he should have as his companion Peter the Hermit, upon whose admonition and persuasion he had begun this journey. And he also begged that, when the troops were united, they might cross in ships over the arm of the sea called the Strait of St. George, and thus they would be able to resist more safely the squadrons of the Turks and the gentiles [that is, non-Christians]. The outcome was that the requests made of the lord emperor, Alexius by name, were granted.

Not long after these events, Peter and his large army, innumerable as the sands of the sea—an army which he had brought together from the various realms of the nations of the Franks, Swabians, Bavarians, and Lotharingians—were making their way to Jerusalem. Descending on that march into the kingdom of Hungary, he and his army pitched their tents before the gate of Oedenburg....

Peter heard [of the events at Malevilla] and, because the Hungarians and Bulgarians were fellow Christians, absolutely refused to believe so great a crime of them, until his men, coming to Malevilla, saw hanging from the walls the arms and spoils of the sixteen companions of Walter who had stayed behind a short time before, and whom the Hungarians had treacherously presumed to rob. But when Peter recognized the injury to his brethren, at the sight of their arms and spoils, he urged his companions to avenge their wrongs.

These sounded the trumpet loudly, and with upraised banners they rushed to the walls and attacked the enemy with a hail of arrows. In such quick succession and in such incredible numbers did they hurl them in the face of those standing on the walls that the Hungarians, in no wise able to resist the force of the besieging Franks, left the walls, hoping that within the city they might be able to withstand the strength of the Gauls. Godfrey, surnamed Burel—a native of the city of Etampes, master and standard-bearer of 200 footsoldiers, himself a footsoldier, and a man of great strength—seeing the flight of the Hungarians away from the walls, then quickly crossed over the walls by means of a ladder he chanced to find there. Reinald of Broyes, a distinguished knight, clad in helmet and coat of mail, ascended just after Godfrey; soon all the knights, as well as the footsoldiers, hastened to enter the city. The Hungarians, seeing their own imminent peril, gathered 7,000 strong for defense; and, having passed out through another gate which looked toward the east, they stationed themselves on the summit of a lofty crag, beyond which flowed the Danube, where they were invincibly fortified. A very large part of these were unable to escape quickly through the narrow passage, and they fell before the gate. Some who hoped to find refuge on the top of the mountain were cut down by the pursuing pilgrims; still others, thrown headlong from the summit of the mountain, were buried in the waves of the Danube, but many escaped by boat. About 4,000 Hungarians fell there, but only a hundred pilgrims, not counting the wounded, were killed at that same place.

This victory won, Peter remained with all his followers in the same citadel five days, for he found there an abundance of grain, flocks of sheep, herds of cattle, a plentiful supply of wine, and an infinite number of horses....

When Peter learned of the wrath of the king [of Hungary] and his very formidable gathering of troops, he deserted Malevilla with all his followers and planned to cross the Morava with all spoils and flocks and herds of horses. But on the whole bank he found very few boats, only 150, in which the great multitude must pass quickly over and escape, lest the king should overtake them with a great force. Hence many who were unable to cross in boats tried to cross on rafts made by fastening poles together with twigs. But driven hither and thither in these rafts without rudders, and at times separated from their companions, many perished, pierced with arrows from the bows of the Patzinaks, who inhabited Bulgaria. As Peter saw the drowning and destruction which was befalling his men, he commanded the Bavarians, the Alemanni, and the other Teutons, by their promise of obedience, to come to the aid of their Frankish brethren. They were carried to that place by seven rafts; then they sank seven small boats of the Patzinaks with their occupants, but took only seven men captive. They led these seven captives into the presence of Peter and killed them by his order.

When he had thus avenged his men, Peter crossed the Morava river and entered the large and spacious forests of the Bulgarians with supplies of food, with every necessity, and with the spoils from Belgrade. And after a delay of eight days in those vast woods and pastures, he and his followers approached Nish, a city very strongly fortified with walls. After crossing the river before the city by a stone bridge, they occupied the field, pleasing in its verdure and extent, and pitched their tents on the banks of the river....

Peter, obedient to the mandate of the emperor, advanced from the city of Sofia and withdrew with all his people to the city Philippopolis. When he had related the entire story of his misfortune in the hearing of all the Greek citizens, he received, in the name of Jesus and in fear of God, very many gifts for him. Next, the third day after, he withdrew to Adrianople, cheerful and joyful in the abundance of all necessary things. There he tarried in camp outside the walls of the city only two days, and then withdrew after sunrise on the third day. A second message of the emperor was urging him to hasten his march to Constantinople, for, on account of the reports about him, the emperor was burning with desire to see this same Peter. When they had come to Constantinople, the army of Peter was ordered to encamp at a distance from the city, and license to trade was fully granted....

At the beginning of summer in the same year in which Peter and Gottschalk, after collecting an army, had set out, there assembled in like fashion a large and innumerable host of Christians from diverse kingdoms and lands; namely, from the realms of France, England, Flanders, and Lorraine.... I know not whether by a judgment of the Lord, or by some error of mind, they rose in a spirit of cruelty against the Jewish people scattered throughout these cities and slaughtered them without mercy, especially in the kingdom of Lorraine, asserting it to be the beginning of their expedition and their duty against the enemies of the Christian faith. This slaughter of Jews was done first by citizens of Cologne. These suddenly fell upon a small band of Jews and severely wounded and killed many; they destroyed the houses and synagogues of the Jews and divided among themselves a very large amount of money. When the Jews saw this cruelty, about 200 in the silence of the night began flight by boat to Neuss. The pilgrims and crusaders discovered them, and after taking away all their possessions, inflicted on them similar slaughter, leaving not even one alive.

Not long after this, they started upon their journey, as they had vowed, and arrived in a great multitude at the city of Mainz. There Count Emico, a nobleman, a very mighty man in this region, was awaiting, with a large band of Teutons, the arrival of the pilgrims who were coming thither from diverse lands by the king's highway.

The Jews of this city, knowing of the slaughter of their brethren, and that they themselves could not escape the hands of so many, fled in hope of safety to Bishop Rothard. They put an infinite treasure in his guard and trust, having much faith in his protection, because he was bishop of the city. Then that excellent bishop of the city cautiously set aside the incredible amount of money received from them. He placed the Jews in the very spacious hall of his own house, away from the sight of Count Emico and his followers, that they might remain safe and sound in a very secure and strong place.

But Emico and the rest of his band held a council and, after sunrise, attacked the Jews in the hall with arrows and lances. Breaking the bolts and doors, they killed the Jews, about 700 in number, who in vain resisted the force and attack of so many thousands. They killed the women, also, and with their swords pierced tender children of whatever age and sex. The Jews, seeing that their Christian enemies were attacking them and their children, and that they were sparing no age, likewise fell upon one another, brother, children, wives, and sisters, and thus they perished at each other's hands. Horrible to say, mothers cut the throats of nursing children with knives and stabbed others, preferring them to perish thus by their own hands rather than to be killed by the weapons of the uncircumcised.

From this cruel slaughter of the Jews a few escaped; and a few because of fear, rather than because of love of the Christian faith, were baptized. With very great spoils taken from these people, Count Emico, Clarebold, Thomas, and all that intolerable company of men and women then continued on their way to Jerusalem, directing their course towards the kingdom of Hungary, where passage along the royal highway was usually not denied the pilgrims. But on arriving at Wieselburg, the fortress of the king, which the rivers Danube and Leytha protect with marshes, the bridge and gate of the fortress were found closed by command of the king of Hungary, for great fear had entered all the Hungarians because of the slaughter which had happened to their brethren....

But while almost everything had turned out favorably for the Christians, and while they had penetrated the walls with great openings, by some chance or misfortune, I know not what, such great fear entered the whole army that they turned in flight, just as sheep are scattered and alarmed when wolves rush upon them. And seeking a refuge here and there, they forgot their companions...

Emico and some of his followers continued their flight along the way by which they had come. Thomas, Clarebold, and several of their men escaped in flight towards Carinthia and Italy. So the hand of the Lord is believed to have been against the pilgrim who had sinned by excessive impurity and fornication, and who had slaughtered the exiled Jews through greed of money, rather than for the sake of God's justice, although the Jews were opposed to Christ. The Lord is a just judge and orders no one unwillingly, or under compulsion, to come under the yoke of the Catholic faith.

There was another detestable crime in this assemblage of wayfaring people, who were foolish and insanely fickle. That the crime was hateful to the Lord and incredible to the faithful is not to be doubted. They asserted that a certain goose was inspired by the Holy Spirit, and that a she goat was not less filled by the same Spirit. These they made their guides on this holy journey to Jerusalem: these they worshipped excessively; and most of the people following them, like beasts, believed with their whole minds that this was the true course. May the hearts of the faithful be free from the thought that the Lord Jesus wished the sepulcher of his most sacred body to be visited by brutish and insensate animals, or that he wished these to become the guides of Christian souls, which by the price of his own blood he deigned to redeem from the filth of idols!

Questions: How did the leaders and members of the Peasant's Crusade view their role with regard to Urban II's call? How did they justify their actions? What do these documents say about the church's influence and authority over the European population at the time of the First Crusade? What were the motivations behind the attacks on European Jewish communities? Were Christian attitudes toward the Jews uniform? What is Albert's opinion of the murderers of the Jews?

Fig. 5: The massacre of the Jews of Cologne in 1096, as shown in a fifteenth-century woodcut. From P. Lacroix, *Manners, Customs, and Dress during the Middle Ages* (London: Chapman and Hall, 1874).

14. SOLOMON BAR SAMSON ON THE MASSACRES OF JEWS

Jewish writers also recorded the terrible events of 1096. In the following account, written in Hebrew in the mid-twelfth century, the historian Solomon bar Samson provides a different perspective on the massacres at Mainz described by Albert of Aachen in the previous document.

Source: trans. J.R. Marcus, *The Jew in the Medieval World* (New York: Harper and Row Publishers, 1938), pp. 115-18; revised.

It was on the third of Siwan ... at noon [on May 2], that Emico the wicked, the enemy of the Jews, came with his whole army against the city gate [of Mainz], and the citizens opened it up for him. Then the enemies of the Lord said to each other: "Look! They have opened up the gate for us. Now let us avenge the blood of 'the hanged one' [that is, Jesus]."

The children of the holy covenant [that is, the Jews] who were there, martyrs who feared the most high, although they saw the great multitude, an army numerous as the sand on the shore of the sea, still clung to their creator. Then young and old donned their armor and girded on their weapons, and at their head was Rabbi Kalonymus ben Meshullam, the chief of the community. Yet because of the many troubles and the fasts which they had observed they had no strength to stand up against the enemy. Then came gangs and bands, sweeping through like a flood, until Mainz was filled from end to end.

The foe Emico proclaimed in the hearing of the community that the enemy be driven from the city and be put to flight. Panic was great in the town. Each Jew in the inner court of the bishop girded on his weapons, and all moved towards the palace gate to fight the crusaders and the citizens. They fought each other up to the very gate, but the sins of the Jews brought it about that the enemy overcame them and took the gate.

The hand of the Lord was heavy against his people. All the gentiles [that is, non-Jews] were gathered together against the Jews in the courtyard to blot out their name, and the strength of our people weakened when they saw the wicked Edomites [that is, in this case, Christians] overpowering them. The bishop's men, who had promised to help them, were the very first to flee, thus delivering the Jews into the hands of the enemy. They were indeed a poor support; even the bishop himself fled from his church, for it was thought to kill him also because he had spoken good things of the Jews....

When the children of the holy covenant saw that the heavenly decree of death had been issued and that the enemy had conquered them and had entered the courtyard, then all of them—old men and young, virgins and children, servants and maids—cried out together to their Father in heaven and, weeping for themselves and for their lives, accepted as just the sentence of God. One to another they said: "Let us be strong and let us bear the yoke of the holy religion, for only in this world can the enemy kill us—and the easiest of the four [means of] death is by the sword. But we, our souls in paradise, shall continue to live eternally, in the great shining reflection."

With a whole heart and with a willing soul they then spoke: "After all it is not right to criticize the acts of God—blessed be he and blessed be his name—who has given to us his Torah and a command to put ourselves to death, to kill ourselves for the unity of his holy name. Happy are we if we do his will. Happy is anyone who is killed or slaughtered, who dies for the unity of [God's] name, so that he is ready to enter the world to come, to dwell in the heavenly camp with the righteous—with Rabbi Akiba [that is, a second-century Jewish martyr] and his companions, the pillars of the universe, who were killed for his name's sake. Not only this; but he exchanges the world of darkness for the world of light, the world of trouble for the world of joy, and the world that passes away for the world that lasts for all eternity." Then all of them, to a man, cried out with a loud voice: "Now we must delay no longer, for the enemy are already upon us. Let us hasten and offer ourselves as a sacrifice to the Lord. Let him who has a knife examine it that it not be nicked, and let him come and slaughter us for the sanctification of the only One, the everlasting, and then let him cut his own throat or plunge the knife into his own body."

As soon as the enemy came into the courtyard they found some of the very pious there with our brilliant master, Isaac ben Moses. He stretched out his neck, and his head they cut off first. The others, wrapped in their fringed praying-shawls, sat by themselves in the courtyard, eager to do the will of their creator. They did not care to flee into the chamber to save themselves for this temporal life, but out of love they received upon themselves the sentence of God. The enemy showered stones and arrows upon them, but they did not care to flee; and [Esther 9:5] "with the stroke of the sword, and with slaughter, and destruction" the foe killed all of those whom they found there. When those in the chambers saw the deed of these righteous ones, how the enemy had already come upon them, they then cried out, all of them: "There is nothing better than for us to offer our lives as a sacrifice."

The women there girded their loins with strength and slew their sons and their daughters and then themselves. Many men, too, plucked up courage and killed their wives, their sons, their infants. The tender and delicate mother slaughtered the babe she had played with; all of them, men and women, arose and slaughtered one another. The maidens and the young brides and grooms looked out of the windows and in a loud voice cried: "Look and see, O our God, what we do for the sanctification of thy great name in order not to exchange you for a hanged and crucified one...."

Thus were the precious children of Zion, the Jews of Mainz, tried with ten trials like Abraham, our father, and like Hananiah, Mishael, and Azariah [Daniel 3:21]. They tied their sons as Abraham tied Isaac his son, and they received upon themselves with a willing soul the yoke of the fear of God, the king of the kings of kings, the holy one, blessed be he, rather than deny and exchange the religion of our king for [Isaiah 14:19] "an abhorred offshoot [that is, Jesus]...." They stretched out their necks to the slaughter and they delivered their pure souls to their Father in heaven. Righteous and pious women bared their throats to each other, offering to be sacrificed for the unity of [God's] name. A father turning to his son or brother, a brother to his sister, a woman to her son or daughter, a neighbor to a neighbor or a friend, a groom to a bride, a fiancé to a fiancée, would kill and would be killed, and blood touched blood. The blood of the men mingled with their wives', the blood of the fathers with their children's, the blood of the brothers with their sisters', the blood of the teachers with their disciples', the blood of the grooms with their brides', the blood of the leaders with their cantors', the blood of the judges with their scribes', and the blood of infants and sucklings with their mothers'. For the unity of the honored and awe-inspiring name were they killed and slaughtered.

The ears of him who hears these things will tingle, for who has ever heard anything like this? Inquire now and look about: was there ever such an abundant sacrifice as this since the days of the primeval Adam? Were there ever 1,100 offerings on one day, each one of them like the sacrifice of Isaac, the son of Abraham?

For the sake of Isaac who was ready to be sacrificed on Mount Moriah, the world shook, as it is said [Isaiah 33:7]: "Behold their valiant ones cry without;" and [Jeremiah 4:28] "the heavens grow dark." Yet see what these martyrs did! Why did the heavens not grow dark and the stars not withdraw their brightness? Why did not the moon and the sun grow dark in their heavens when on one day, on the third of Siwan, on a Tuesday, 1,100 souls were killed and slaughtered, among them so many infants and sucklings who had not transgressed nor sinned, so many poor, innocent souls?

Wilt thou, despite this, still restrain thyself, O Lord? For thy sake it was that these numberless souls were killed. Avenge quickly the blood of thy servants which was spilt in our days and in our sight. Amen.

Questions: Compare Solomon bar Samson's account with Albert of Aachen's. Why did the Jews react as they did to the coming attack? How did they interpret the massacre? What Jewish values are evident in this account?

15. ANNA COMNENA'S *ALEXIAD*

Anna Comnena (1083-1148) was the daughter of the Byzantine emperor Alexius I. Her book, The Alexiad, a biography of her father, is an important source for the First Crusade, offering a Byzantine Greek view of the western Crusaders. Here she describes the fate of the Peasant's Crusade (the size of which she greatly overestimates) and the arrival of Urban's official crusading force in the winter and spring of 1096-97 and the spring of 1097. Bohemond of Taranto was a member of the Norman Hauteville family of Sicily—a family that had been engaged in warfare against the Byzantine Empire before the First Crusade.

Source: trans. A.C. Krey, *The First Crusade: The Accounts of Eye-witnesses and Participants* (Princeton: Princeton University Press, 1921), pp. 70-71, 76-78, 94-97.

...[Emperor] Alexius was not yet, or very slightly, rested from his labors when he heard rumors of the arrival of innumerable Frankish armies. He feared the incursions of these people, for he had already experienced the savage fury of their attack, their fickleness of mind, and their readiness to approach anything with violence....

And finally, he kept ever in mind this information, which was often repeated and most true—that they were known to be always immoderately covetous of anything they strove after and to break very easily, for any reason whatsoever, treaties which they had made. Accordingly, he did not indulge in any rest, but made ready his forces in every way, so that when occasion should demand he would be ready for battle. For it was a matter greater and more terrible than famine which was then reported. Forsooth, the whole West, and as much of the land of barbarian peoples as lies beyond the Adriatic Sea...— all this, changing its seat, was bursting forth into Asia in a solid mass, with all its belongings, taking its march through the intervening portion of Europe.

A certain Gaul [that is, a Frank, or person from France], Peter by name, surnamed Kuku-Peter, had set out from his home to adore the Holy Sepulcher. After suffering many dangers and wrongs from the Turks and Saracens, who were devastating all Asia, he returned to his own country most sorrowfully. He could not bear to see himself thus cut off from his proposed pilgrimage and intended to undertake the expedition a second time....

After Peter had promoted the expedition, he, with 80,000 footsoldiers and 100,000 knights, was the first of all to cross the Lombard strait. Then passing through the territory of Hungary, he arrived at the queenly city. For, as anyone may conjecture from the outcome, the race of the Gauls is not only very passionate and impetuous in other ways, but, also, when urged on by an impulse, cannot thereafter be checked. Our emperor, aware of what Peter had suffered from the Turks before, urged him to await the arrival of the other counts....

But relying on the multitude of those who followed him, Peter did not heed the warning and, after crossing the strait, pitched camp at a little town called Helenopolis.

But since there were also Normans in his army, estimated at about 10,000 men, these, separating themselves from the rest of the body, devastated the region lying around the [Christian] city of Nicaea, rioting most cruelly in every way. For they tore some of the children apart limb from limb and, piercing others through with wooden stakes, roasted them in fire; likewise, upon those advanced in years they inflicted every kind of torture. When those in the city saw this being done, they opened the gates and went out against them. As a result, a fierce battle took place, in which, since the Normans fought ferociously, the citizens were hurled back into the fortress. The Normans, after gathering up all the plunder, again returned to Helenopolis. There a quarrel arose between themselves and the other pilgrims who had not gone off with them, a thing which usually happens in an affair of this kind, envy inflaming the wrath of those left behind, and a riotous fight followed the quarrel. The fierce Normans again separated [from the others] and captured Xerogord on their way at the first attack.

When this was learned, the [Turkish] sultan sent Elchanes against them with a suitable number of troops. When he reached them, he recaptured Xerogord, killed some of the Normans with the sword, and carried off the rest as captives, planning at the same time, also, an attack upon those who had remained with Kuku-Peter. And he set ambushes at opportune places into which, when they left for Nicaea, they would unexpectedly fall and be killed. But knowing also of the avarice of the Gauls, he had summoned two men of bold spirit and ordered them to go to the camp of Kuku-Peter to announce that the Normans had captured Nicaea and were now sacking it to the utmost. This report, brought to the camp of Peter, excited all violently; for when the mention of plunder and riches was heard, they straightway set out in tumult on the road which leads to Nicaea, forgetful of their military training and of observing discipline in going out to battle. For the Latins are not only most fond of riches, as we said above, but when they give themselves to raiding any region for plunder, are also no longer obedient to reason, or any other check. Accordingly, since they were neither keeping order nor forming into lines, they fell into the ambush of the Turks around Draco and were wretchedly cut to pieces. Indeed, so great a multitude of Gauls and Normans were cut down by the Ishmaelite [that is, Arab] sword that when the dead bodies of the killed, which were lying all about in the place, were brought together, they made a very great mound, or hill, or look-out place, lofty as a mountain, and occupying a space very conspicuous for its width and depth. So high did that mound of bones tower, that some barbarians of the same race as the killed later used the bones of the slain instead of stones in constructing a wall, thus making that fortress a sort of sepulcher for them. It stands to this day, an enclosure of walls built with mixed rocks and bones.

And thus, after all had been wiped out in the slaughter, Peter returned with only a few to Helenopolis. The Turks, in their desire to get him into their power, again beset him with an ambush. But when the emperor heard of the whole affair and learned how great was the slaughter of men, he held it very wrong that Peter should also be taken. Immediately, therefore, he summoned Catacalon Constantine Euphorbenus, of whom mention has often been made in this history, and sent him with suitable forces on war-vessels across the sea as a succor to Peter. When the Turks saw him approach, they fled....

[After the demise of Peter's force, there followed the official Crusade army, one of whose leaders was Bohemond of Taranto.]

But when Bohemond had arrived at Apri with his companions, realizing both that he was not of noble birth, and that for lack of money he had not brought with him a large enough army, he hastened, with only ten Gauls, ahead of the other counts and arrived at Constantinople. He did this to win the favor of the emperor for himself, and to conceal more safely the plans which he was concocting against him. Indeed, the emperor, to whom the schemes of the man were known, for he had long since become acquainted with the hidden and deceitful dealings of this same Bohemond, took great pains to arrange it so that before the other counts should come he would speak with him alone. Thus having heard what Bohemond had to say, he hoped to persuade him to cross before the others came, lest, joined with them after their coming, he might pervert their minds.

When Bohemond had come to him, the emperor greeted him with gladness and inquired anxiously about the journey and where he had left his companions. Bohemond responded to all these things as he thought best for his own interests, affably and in a friendly way, while the emperor recalled in a familiar talk his bold undertakings long ago around Durazzo and Larissa and the hostilities between them at that time. Bohemond answered, "Then I confess I was your enemy; then I was hostile. But, behold I now stand before you like a deserter to the ranks of the enemy! I am a friend of your majesty." The emperor proceeded to scrutinize the man, considering him cautiously and carefully and drawing out what was in his mind. As soon as he saw that Bohemond was ready to consent to swear an oath of fealty to him, he said, "You must be tired from the journey and should retire to rest. We will talk tomorrow about anything else."

So Bohemond departed to Cosmidion, where hospitality was prepared for him, and he found a table richly laden with an abundance of food and condiments of all kinds. Then the cooks came and showed him the uncooked flesh of animals and birds, saying: "We have prepared this food which you see on the table according to our skill and the custom of this region; but if, perchance, these please you less, here is food, still uncooked, which can be prepared just as you order." The emperor, because of his almost incredible tact in handling men, had commanded that this be done and said by them. For, since he was especially expert in penetrating the secrets of minds and in discovering the disposition of a man, he very readily understood that Bohemond was of a shrewd and suspicious nature; and he foresaw what happened. For, lest Bohemond should conceive any suspicion against him, the emperor had ordered that raw meats be placed before him, together with the cooked, thus easily removing suspicion. Neither did his conjecture fail, for the very shrewd Bohemond took the prepared food without even touching it with the tips of his fingers, or tasting it, and immediately turned around, concealing, nevertheless, the suspicion which occurred to him by the following ostentatious show of liberality. For under the pretext of courtesy he distributed all the food to those standing around; in reality, if one understood rightly, he was dividing the cup of death among them. Nor did he conceal his cunning, so much did he hold his subjects in contempt; for he this day used the raw meat which had been offered to him and had it prepared by his own cooks after the manner of his country. On the next day he asked his men whether they were well. Upon their answering in the affirmative, that they were indeed very well, that not even one felt even the least indisposed, he disclosed his secret in his reply: "Remembering a war, once carried on by me against the emperor, and that strife, I feared lest perchance he had intended to kill me by putting deadly poison in my food."

Such a man was Bohemond. Never, indeed, have I seen a man so dishonest. In everything, in his words as well as in his deeds, he never chose the right path; and when anyone deviates from the moderation of virtue, it makes little difference to whatsoever extreme he goes, for he is always far from honesty.

For the rest, the emperor then summoned Bohemond and exacted from him the usual oath of the Latins. The latter, knowing well his own resources, and realizing that he was neither of noble birth nor well supplied by fortune with wealth, for he had no great force, but only a moderate number of Gauls with him, and being, besides, dishonest in character, readily submitted himself to the will of the emperor....

Moreover, the emperor, who understood fully his wicked intention and perverse mind, skillfully managed carefully to remove whatever might further Bohemond's ambitious designs. Wherefore, Bohemond, seeking a home for himself in the East and using Cretan scheming against Cretans, did not obtain it. For the emperor feared lest, after obtaining power, he would use it to place the Latin counts under obligation to him, finally thus accomplishing easily what he wished. But since he did not want Bohemond to surmise that he was already discovered, the emperor misled him by this hope: "Not yet," he said, "has the time come for the thing which you say; but after a little it shall come about by your fortitude and trust in me."

After the emperor had bestowed upon the Gauls promises, gifts, and honors of every kind, the next day he solemnly took his seat on the imperial throne. Summoning Bohemond and all the counts, he talked about the things which would happen to them on the journey. He wanted, likewise, to show what methods and means of warfare the Turks were wont to employ, and to give directions how the line of battle should be drawn up against them, how ambushes should be set, and how they ought not to follow the fleeing Turks too far. And so, both by gifts of money and by flattering speeches, he soothed the rude nature of the people, and, after giving useful advice, he persuaded them to pass over the sea.

Questions: What was the Byzantine reaction to the Peasants' Crusade? Why did this venture fail? What did the Byzantines think of the official crusaders? What accounts for the mistrust and misunderstanding between the Byzantines and the westerners? What did Alexius want? What is his daughter's intent in writing her book?

16. THE DEEDS OF THE FRANKS

The Deeds of the Franks is an anonymous work believed to have been written by a crusader in the service of Bohemond of Taranto. Written sometime between 1100 and 1103, it demonstrates a clear bias toward Bohemond and a strong distrust of Byzantium and its emperor. Below is a passage on the same meeting of Bohemond and the eastern emperor described by Anna Comnena in the previous document.

The leaders of the First Crusade did not all arrive in Constantinople at the same time, traveling, as they did, from different parts of Europe. Fearing the collective strength of the crusaders, the Byzantine emperor was eager to deal with each of these nobles in turn and then send them quickly on their way across the Hellespont into Asia Minor. Once across, the crusaders faced many hardships, some of which are described below in a later section from The Deeds.

Source: trans. A.C. Krey, *The First Crusade: The Accounts of Eye-witnesses and Participants* (Princeton: Princeton University Press, 1921), pp. 93-94, 118-19.

When the emperor heard that the most honorable man, Bohemond, had come to him, he commanded that he be received with honor and carefully lodged outside the city. When he had been so lodged, the evil emperor sent for him to come to speak with him in secret. Thither, also, came Duke Godfrey [of Bouillon] with his brother [Baldwin of Boulogne], and at length [Raymond] the count of St. Gilles approached the city. Then the emperor in anxious and fervid rage was pondering some way by which they might seize these knights of Christ adroitly and by fraud. But divine grace disclosing [his plans], neither time nor place was found by him, or his men, to do them ill. At last, all the noble [Greek] leaders who were at Constantinople were assembled. Fearing lest they should be deprived of their country, they decided in their counsels and ingenious calculations that our dukes, counts, or all the leaders, ought to make an oath of fealty to the emperor. These absolutely refused and said: "It is indeed unworthy of us, and, furthermore, it seems to us unjust to swear an oath to him." Perchance we shall yet often be deceived by our leaders. In the end, what were they to do? They say that under the force of necessity they humiliated themselves, willy-nilly, to the will of the most unjust emperor. To that most mighty man Bohemond, however, whom he greatly feared because in times past he [that is, Bohemond] had often driven him from the field with his army, the emperor said that, if he willingly took the oath to him, he would give him in return land in extent from Antioch fifteen days' journey and eight in width. And he [that is, the emperor] swore to him in such wise that, if he loyally observed that oath, he would never pass beyond his own land. Knights, so brave and so sturdy, why did they do this? For the reason that they were constrained by much necessity. The emperor also gave to all our men a pledge of security. He likewise took oath that he, together with his army, would come with us, by land and by sea; that he would afford us faithfully a market by land and sea, and that he would diligently make good our losses; in addition, that he did not wish, and would not permit, any of our pilgrims to be disturbed or come to grief on their way to the Holy Sepulcher....

[The crusaders then moved on from Constantinople into Asia Minor.]

Then we went on pursuing the most iniquitous Turks, who daily fled before us. But they went to all the fortified towns or cities, deceiving and deluding the inhabitants of those lands, saying: "We have conquered all the Christians and have so overcome them that no one of them will ever dare to arise before us; only let us come in." They destroyed the churches, homes, and everything else, upon entering, and carried off with them the horses, asses, mules, gold, and silver, and whatever they could find. In addition, also, they carried off the children of Christians with them and burned and devastated everything that was convenient or useful, fleeing, greatly frightened, before our faces. Accordingly, we were following them through deserts, and dry and uninhabitable land, from which we scarcely escaped and came out alive. Hunger and thirst pinched us on all sides, and there was absolutely nothing for us to eat, unless, by chance, tearing and grinding grain with our hands, we continued to exist on such food as wretchedly as possible. There most of our cavalry ceased to exist, because (thereafter) many of these became footsoldiers. For want of horses, our men used oxen in place of cavalry horses, and because of the very great need, goats, sheep, and dogs served as beasts of burden.

Meanwhile we began to enter the best land, filled with bodily nourishment, delicacies, and goods of all kinds, and then we approached Iconium. The inhabitants of that land persuaded and advised us to take along skins filled with water, because there is the greatest lack of water about one day's march from there. We accordingly did so, until we came to a certain river, and there we lodged for two days. However, our scouts began to go on ahead until they came to Heraclea, in which town there was a very large gathering of Turks, waiting and plotting how they could harm and put to grief the knights of Christ. The knights of almighty God found and boldly attacked these Turks. And thus our enemy was overcome on that day, and they fled as swiftly as an arrow flies when discharged with a mighty pull of string and bow. Our men, accordingly, entered the city immediately and remained there for four days.

Questions: Compare this account with that of Anna Comnena, above. What is your estimate of Bohemond's character? How did the crusaders view the Greek Christians? Why was the oath of fealty so controversial? In what ways were the crusaders unprepared for warfare in the East?

17. LETTER OF STEPHEN OF BLOIS

After some successes in Asia Minor in 1097, the crusaders entered Syria. Here Baldwin of Boulogne and his force left the main army and struck out for the city of Edessa in northern Mesopotamia, where a native Christian population was at odds with its ruler. In the spring of 1098, Baldwin established the "county" of Edessa as the first of the crusader states. Meanwhile, in the autumn of 1097, the main army had begun the siege of Antioch, in northern Syria, which would last some nine months and prove a turning point of the crusade. The following letter was written by Stephen, count of Blois, to his wife Adela from outside Antioch on March 29, 1098. Despite its confident tone, Stephen himself deserted the campaign and returned to Europe just prior to the crusaders' capture of the city. Contrary to his claim here, he was not the leader of the whole crusading army.

Source: trans. D.C. Munro, *Translations and Reprints from the Original Sources of European History*, Series I, Vol. I (Philadelphia: University of Pennsylvania Department of History, 1895), no. 4, pp. 5–8; revised.

Count Stephen to Adela, his sweetest and most amiable wife, to his dear children, and to all his vassals of all ranks—his greeting and blessing.

You may be very sure, dearest, that the messenger whom I sent to give you pleasure, left me before Antioch safe and unharmed, and through God's grace in the greatest prosperity. And already at that time, together with all the chosen army of Christ, endowed with great valor by him, we had been continuously advancing for twenty-three weeks toward the home of our Lord Jesus. You may know for certain, my beloved, that of gold, silver and many other kind of riches I now have twice as much as your love had assigned to me when I left you. For all our princes, with the common consent of the whole army, against my own wishes, have made me up to the present time the leader, chief and director of their whole expedition.

You have certainly heard that after the capture of the city of Nicaea we fought a great battle with the perfidious Turks and by God's aid conquered them. Next we conquered for the Lord all Romania and afterwards Cappadocia. And we learned that there was a certain Turkish prince Assam, dwelling in Cappadocia; thither we directed our course. All his castles we conquered by force and compelled him to flee to a certain very strong castle situated on a high rock. We also gave the land of that Assam to one of our chiefs and in order that he might conquer the above-mentioned Assam, we left there with him many soldiers of Christ. Thence, continually following the wicked Turks, we drove them through the midst of Armenia, as far as the great river Euphrates. Having left all their baggage and beasts of burden on the bank, they fled across the river into Arabia.

The bolder of the Turkish soldiers, indeed, entering Syria, hastened by forced marches night and day, in order to be able to enter the royal city of Antioch before our approach. The whole army of God, learning this, gave due praise and thanks to the omnipotent Lord. Hastening with great joy to the aforesaid chief city of Antioch, we besieged it and very often had many conflicts there with the Turks; and seven times with the citizens of Antioch and with the innumerable troops coming to its aid, whom we rushed to meet, we fought with the fiercest courage, under the leadership of Christ. And in all these seven battles, by the aid of the Lord God, we conquered and most assuredly killed an innumerable host of them. In those battles, indeed, and in very many attacks made upon the city, many of our brethren and followers were killed and their souls were borne to the joys of paradise.

We found the city of Antioch very extensive, fortified with incredible strength and almost impregnable. In addition, more than 5,000 bold Turkish soldiers had entered the city, not counting the Saracens, Publicans, Arabs, Turcopolitans, Syrians, Armenians and other different races of whom an infinite multitude had gathered together there. In fighting against these enemies of God and of our own we have, by God's grace, endured many sufferings and innumerable evils up to the present time. Many also have already exhausted all their resources in this very holy passion. Very many of our Franks, indeed, would have met a temporal death from starvation, if the clemency of God and our money had not succored them. Before the above-mentioned city of Antioch indeed, throughout the whole winter we suffered for our Lord Christ from excessive cold and enormous torrents of rain. What some say about the impossibility of bearing the heat of the sun throughout Syria is untrue, for the winter there is very similar to our winter in the west.

When truly Caspian [Bagi Seian], the emir of Antioch — that is, prince and lord — perceived that he was hard pressed by us, he sent his son Sensodolo [Chems Eddaulah] by name, to the prince who holds Jerusalem, and to the prince of Calep, Rodoam [Rodoanus], and to Docap [Deccacus Ibn Toutousch], prince of Damascus. He also sent into Arabia to Bolianuth and to Carathania to Hamelnuth. These five emirs with 12,000 picked Turkish horsemen suddenly came to aid the inhabitants of Antioch. We, indeed, ignorant of all this, had sent many of our soldiers away to the cities and fortresses. For there are 165 cities and fortresses throughout Syria which are in our power. But a little before they reached the city, we attacked them at three leagues' distance with 700 soldiers, on a certain plain near the "Iron Bridge." God, however, fought for us, his faithful, against them. For on that day, fighting in the strength that God gives, we conquered them and killed an innumerable multitude — God continually fighting for us — and we also carried back to the army more than two hundred of their heads, in order that the people might rejoice on that account. The emperor of Babylon also sent Saracen messengers to our army with letters, and through these he established peace and concord with us.

I love to tell you, dearest, what happened to us during Lent. Our princes had caused a fortress to be built before a certain gate which was between our camp and the sea. For the Turks, daily issuing from this gate, killed some of our men on their way to the sea. The city of Antioch is about five leagues' distance from the sea. For this reason they sent the excellent Bohemond and Raymond, count of St. Gilles, to the sea with only sixty horse-men, in order that they might bring mariners to aid in this work. When, however, they were returning to us with those mariners, the Turks collected an army, fell suddenly upon our two leaders and forced them to a perilous flight. In that unexpected flight we lost more than 500 of our footsoldiers — to the glory of God. Of our horsemen, however, we lost only two, for certain.

On that same day truly, in order to receive our brethren with joy, and ignorant of their misfortunes, we went out to meet them. When, however, we approached the above-mentioned gate of the city, a mob of horsemen and footsoldiers from Antioch, elated by the victory which they had won, rushed upon us in the same manner. Seeing these, our leaders sent to the camp of the Christians to order all to be ready to follow us into battle. In the meantime our men gathered together and the scattered leaders, namely, Bohemond and Raymond, with the remainder of their army came up and narrated the great misfortune which they had suffered.

Our men, full of fury at these most evil tidings, prepared to die for Christ and, deeply grieved for their brethren, rushed upon the sacrilegious Turks. They, the enemies of God and of us, hastily fled before us and attempted to enter their city. But by God's grace the affair turned out very differently; for, when they wanted to cross a bridge built over the great river Moscholum, we followed them as closely as possible, killed many before they reached the bridge, forced many into the river, all of whom were killed, and we also slew many upon the bridge and very many at the narrow entrance to the gate. I am telling you the truth, my beloved, and you may be very certain that in this battle we killed thirty emirs, that is princes, and, three hundred other Turkish nobles, not counting the remaining Turks and pagans. Indeed, the number of Turks and Saracens killed is reckoned at 1,230, but of ours we did not lose a single man.

While on the following day (Easter) my chaplain Alexander was writing this letter in great haste, a party of our men, lying in wait for the Turks, fought a successful battle with them and killed sixty horsemen, whose heads they brought to the army.

These which I write to you are only a few things, dearest, of the many which we have done, and because I am not able to tell you, dearest, what is in my mind, I charge you to do right, to carefully watch over your land, to do your duty as you ought to your children and your vassals. You will certainly see me just as soon as I can possibly return to you. Farewell.

Questions: What does the letter tell us about siege warfare and tactics? How does Stephen view his role within the crusading army? How does he view the crusading enterprise? What are his concerns? Does the fact of his subsequent desertion cast a different light on his account?

18. ANSELM OF RIBEMONT ON EVENTS AT ANTIOCH

The city of Antioch finally fell to the crusaders in early June, 1098, but the fortress still withstood them, and a Muslim army in turn quickly besieged the crusaders in the city. The situation is described in the following document by Anselm of Ribemont, a friend and patron of the church and a devout crusader. Here he is writing to the archbishop of Rheims in northern France. He also recounts the discovery of a significant relic, the holy lance.

Source: trans. A.C. Krey, *The First Crusade: The Accounts of Eye-witnesses and Participants* (Princeton: Princeton University Press, 1921), pp. 189–91.

But on the following day Corbara approached with the king of Damascus, Duke Baldach, the king of Jerusalem, and very many others [that is, Muslims] and laid siege to the city. Accordingly, we were both besieged by them, and [were ourselves] besieging the aforesaid few in the castle of the city, and we were thus driven to eat the flesh of horses and asses. Moreover, on the second day after their arrival they killed Roger of Barneville. On the third day, they attacked the fortress which we had erected against the Antiochenes, but accomplished nothing. However, they did inflict a wound upon Roger, chatelain of Lille, from which he died. Seeing that they were accomplishing nothing on that side, they ascended the hills. However, when we went out against them, we were beaten and put to flight. Then they entered inside the wall, and that day and the following night we were only a stone's throw from each other. On the following day at daybreak they called upon Baphometh at the top of their voices, but we, calling upon our God in our hearts, made a charge upon them and drove them all outside the walls of the city. There Roger of Betheniville died. But they moved their camp and set siege to all the gates of the city, seeking to compel our surrender through lack of food.

Thereupon, when his servants had been placed in such tribulation, God stretched forth his right hand in aid and mercifully revealed the lance with which the body of Christ was pierced. It lay buried, moreover, to a depth of two men's stature beneath the floor in the church of St. Peter. So, when this precious gem was found, all our spirits were revived.

On [June 28,] the vigil of the apostles Peter and Paul, [our princes,] after taking counsel among themselves, sent envoys to Corbara to say: "The army of the Lord sends this message: 'Leave us and the inheritance of St. Peter, or otherwise thou shalt be put to flight by arms!'" When he heard this, Corbara unsheathed his sword and swore by his kingdom and throne that he would defend himself from all the Franks; and he further said that he himself owned the land and would possess it, justly or unjustly. For, he answered, they would hear no word from him until, abandoning Antioch, they denied Christ and professed the law of the Persians. When this message was heard, the Christians, cleansed by confession, and stoutly armed by partaking of the body and blood of Christ, went out from the gate ready for battle. The first to go forth was Hugh the Great, with his Franks; next the count of the Normans and the count of Flanders; after them, the venerable bishop of Puy and the battle line of the count of St. Gilles; after him, Tancred; and last of all, unconquered Bohemond. When, accordingly, the lines had been formed, with the lance of the Lord and the cross before them, they began battle with the greatest confidence. God helping, they turned in flight the Turkish princes, who were confused and utterly beaten, and killed countless numbers of them. Returning, therefore, with victory, we gave thanks to the Lord and celebrated the festival of the apostles with the greatest rejoicing. On that day the citadel was surrendered to us, the son of the king of Antioch having fled with Corbara. The king himself had been killed by peasants while fleeing in the mountains on the day that the city was surrendered.

We have sent this news to you, father, that you may take pleasure in the rescue of the Christians and the liberation of Antioch, and that you may pray God with greater devotion for all of us. For we place great faith in your prayers, and all that we accomplish we ascribe, not to our merit, but to your prayers. Now we pray you to keep our land in peace, and to defend the churches and the poor from the hands of tyrants. We pray, likewise, that you take counsel about the false pilgrims [that is, people who have taken the crusading vow but have not fulfilled it], either that they again take up the sign of the saving cross with penance, and resume the journey of the Lord, or that they undergo the peril of excommunication. Know for certain that the door of the land has been opened to us, and that, among our other good fortunes, the king of Babylon, by envoys sent to us, has said that he will obey our will. Farewell. We beseech in the name of the Lord Jesus that all whom this letter reaches pray God for us and our dead.

Questions: What was the significance of the discovery of the holy lance, according to Anselm? What role did relics and religious ritual play in the directing of crusading campaigns such as the siege of Antioch?

19. RALPH OF CAEN ON DIVISIONS AMONG THE CRUSADERS

Ralph of Caen arrived in the Holy Land in 1108 and became part of the crusading entourage of Tancred, nephew of Bohemond of Taranto. Around 1113, Ralph wrote The Deeds of Tancred. *This history, while clearly favoring his patron's family, demonstrates the growing divisions among the crusade leaders at the time of the siege of Antioch.*

Source: trans. A.C. Krey, *The First Crusade: The Accounts of Eye-witnesses and Participants* (Princeton: Princeton University Press, 1921), pp. 237-41; revised.

While Antioch was still resisting the princes of Gaul [that is, France], by whom it was encircled, a quarrel arose between the adherents of Bohemond and Raymond. Men of both parties were sent to gather grain. They found food and a fight [with each other] at the same time, and the grain was divided by the sword. Both parties were wounded, as well as frightened, and both sides returned home wounded. The princes were wrought up at the sight of the blood of their vassal host [that is, their soldiers and retainers], and they inflamed the minds of the wounded men to revenge whenever a similar affair should occur [but only outside the camp].... The soldiers' ready ears received this command willingly—a command difficult to revoke. Accordingly, when thereafter a greater band of one party met a smaller one of the other laden with provisions, the burdens of food were put down there, and their necks were loaded with a shower of blows; and thus the one that was stronger enjoyed the spoils. Then, the weaker party, thus despoiled, grieved that they had exerted themselves for others, and not for themselves. He who understood the tongue of either now lashed with it; meanwhile, the innocent were lashed for it. All from Narbonne, Auvergne, Gascony, and all this kind of people were for the Provençals; the remainder of Gaul, especially the Normans, conspired with the Apulians. The Bretons, Swabians, Huns, Ruthenians, and people of this kind were protected by the barbarity of their tongues. All this was going on outside the wall.

[Once the crusaders were inside] the city, also, the quarrel did not decrease, but rather increased, for when the besieged people were in the throes of famine, as mentioned above, there arose from the army of Raymond a versatile fabricator of lies, Peter, who preached that the salvation of the people had been revealed to him in this way: "St. Andrew, the apostle," he said, "appeared to me, when I was half asleep, and spoke this command in my ear. 'Arise and announce to the people who are laboring that consolation has come from heaven, which the lance that opened the side of the Lord will confer when it is found. It lies hidden beneath the soil within the church of St. Peter. Break the pavement at such a place (and he pointed out the place), and by digging there you will find the iron mentioned. When the horror of battle threatens, turn that against the enemy, and you will conquer through it.' Terrified, I thought that I had been deceived by a dream; and that I would not disclose it, but would remain silent forever, unless I was warned the second and the third time. The quiet of the next night was again enfolding me when the same apostle again returned, uttering the very statement which he had made before, but like one scolding and in wrath. 'Wherefore,' he said, 'didst thou shun me and remain silent? Thou alone art delaying the safety of many. The people have cried out to the Lord and have been heard; and still thy negligence leaves them as if neglected. Hasten, therefore, as quickly as possible to correct this, that thou mayest continue to live.' Frightened at these words, when I had emerged from the sleep, I was at the same time more certain and more troubled; yet, still I hesitated whether to keep the secret or disclose it. In this worry I passed a whole day, and half the night, with prayer and fasting, begging the Lord for the third visit, if the first two had really been from him. The cock had twice acclaimed the morning, when, at length, just before the third crow, sleep bound my tired limbs; then without delay he who had come a first time, who had come a second time, appeared there again, ever more terrible, ever more commanding. 'Rise up, go, lazy brute, mute dog, delayer of safety and victory, menace to your fellows, solace of your enemies. Thou hast trembled with fear where there was no fear; where it is thou hast no fear.' Threats and curses still continued, when my spirit, terrified with fear at the threats, carried me away from sleep; perspiration and trembling coursed over my body at the same time, and if fire was burning one side, the other was stiff with ice. By these steps I came to teach what I had learned; you, however, fathers and brothers, do not stop to test the truth of the matter; it remains for me to point out the place for you to dig."

When this rumor was brought to the ears of Raymond, he called a council and had Peter summoned to the church of St. Peter. When asked about the place, he pointed behind the altar, true to his story, and advised them to dig; and that his words might have weight, he likewise composed his expression. They dug, but without avail; the upturned earth could not return what had not been committed to it, and what it had not received. However, the man had secreted about him an Arabic spear point, from the chance finding of which he had contrived material for his deception. Therefore, seizing the hardened, worn, and aged point, which was in form and size unlike those which we used, he was encouraged thereby to believe that people would put faith in his new creations. Accordingly, when the time for the deception came, he took a spade, jumped into the pit and, turning to a corner, said, "Here we must dig. Here lies hidden what we seek. Here it will come forth." Then, multiplying blow on blow, often and more often, he pulled forth from the dug up ground the spear which had been fraudulently dropped by him. The darkness conspired in the deception; likewise, the throng of people with the darkness, and the narrowness of the pit with the throng. But when the sound of metal striking upon metal was heard, this same fabricator of lies held out the iron and filled the excited ears of the simple with these words: "Lo, behold! Heaven promised what the earth preserved; the apostle revealed what the prayer of the people obtained!" Scarcely had he said this when they went outside and, following the trophy with hymns and chants, showered it with gifts and wrapped it up in cloth of gold. This Raymond and those who supported him had fittingly arranged, but the men of other parties, too, in their rude simplicity, paid devotion to it with gifts. Before victory earnestly, after it much more earnestly, the Provençals said that the glory of the triumph should be ascribed to the lance, which was borne ahead in battle, as if it were a trophy. And so, the treasury of Raymond was enlarged, his spirit exalted, and his army became insolent. Some of the princes whom he had joined to himself, partly by flattery and partly by deference, sided with him.

But Bohemond, since he was no fool, scrutinized the matter in detail. For who was that dreamer? In what vagaries had he involved the people? What place had he pointed out to the diggers? In the fact that he himself had leaped into it, had dug and found it, Bohemond immediately detected a trick. He decided that the finding was invalid and proved the inventor false by keen conjectures: "Beautifully," said he, "was it contrived that St. Andrew should appear to a man who, I hear, frequents taverns, roams the streets, is a friend to vanities and ingrained with folly! The holy apostle chose a fine person to whom to disclose the secret of heaven! For to whom would that trick not be evident? If a Christian had hidden it, why did he pass over the nearest altar for a hiding place, or if a gentile, or a Jew, why was it hidden within the walls of a church? Why near an altar? If it is ascribed to neither, but to chance, in what historical account is Pilate found to have come to Antioch? Surely we knew that it was the lance of a soldier, and a soldier of Pilate. But what follows is delightful! I hear that the finder leaped in, after the diggers had been laboring in vain, and that was granted to one man in the darkness which had been denied many in the open. Oh, boorish foolishness! Oh, boorish credulity! Oh, credulity, easily won! So be it! His integrity corroborates the man, and nearness to the crucifixion the place. Is this most recent fraud of that man not evident enough? If he had walked purely, simply, in the way of God; if he had trusted in the apostle who appeared to him, he himself would not [alone] bear witness to this discovery but would obtain another's testimony. But why do I devote so much scorn to that person? Because the Provençals ascribe our victory, which is from above, like light from the Father, to their piece of iron. Let that grasping count and stupid rabble regard it as their own! We, however, have won and shall win in the name of our Lord Jesus Christ!" This said Bohemond, and with him those who looked more deeply below the surface, the counts of Normandy and Flanders, and the vice-prelate, Arnulf, and Tancred.

Accordingly, Raymond, wounded by the sharp points of Bohemond's arguments, sought vengeance by a thousand arts, or a thousand ways. Then, withdrawing, without a mediator, he said, "Either I will die soon, or I will avenge the insults of the son of Guiscard. If the meeting does not occur openly, let it come secretly. Let the dagger prevail, where the lance will not!... Since the custody of the city is mine, then the citadel on the hill, the chief palace, the market place, the bridge, and the gates belong to me; also the lance and most of the people are subject to me. What remains, except that, with Bohemond out of the way, I shall gain the principality?"

While he was turning this and much more over in his mind, he decided first of all that an uprising should be stirred up among the people, so that Bohemond would be overwhelmed from head to foot. In the beginning, oaths would be hurled back and forth in the market place; the clamor would rise to disturb the people; the leaders from both sides would bring aid to their men; and every arrow, every javelin, would be aimed at Bohemond. While Raymond was digesting this plot in his heart, like a lion, God willed that this injustice should not be concealed, and it was disclosed to Arnulf, and through him to Bohemond. Thus the plot was thwarted and the soul of a man, whose life had already been of the greatest advantage to those seeking Jerusalem, and was yet to be of great advantage, was saved from death.

Thus their anger had its beginning; thus began the kindling of their hate.... While their arms were idle and ease shut out war-like cares, the question of the finding of the above-mentioned spear point was to be put to test, for division was disturbing the people. These favored the lance, those condemned it, neither party at all reasonable. As a result, the chief leaders agreed that he who had been the beginning of the difficulty should himself end it, and should prove the matter in question by the ordeal of fire. Accordingly, when Peter had been brought in to the council, they decided that he should take nine steps hither and thither through the midst of burning, flaming branches, that by this test the finding would be proved true, if he were unhurt, or false, if he were burnt. A period of three days was set aside for a fast, and proper provision was made for prayer and vigil. So they separated. But soon, on the third day, they met again. Branches were set afire in a double row. Peter, dressed in a shirt and breeches, otherwise naked, proceeded through the midst of it, fell burned at the other end, and died on the following day. The people, upon seeing what was done, confessed that they had been deceived by his wordy guile, were sorry that they had erred, and testified that Peter was a disciple of Simon, the magician. But Raymond and his Provençal accomplices defended the accused with obstinate minds, proclaimed him a saint, threatened Arnulf, as the chief discoverer of the fraud which had been revealed and, finally, sent an armed band against him to overwhelm him unexpectedly at his house. Had he not previously warned the count of Normandy, in whose service he was, he would have come to an early death. The count was eating, with him the count of Flanders, and both were reclining. When they heard the cause of the commotion, their session was broken off. The counts separated, each to his own forces, and both sent arms to oppose the armed men. But frightened by the commotion of the Normans which they heard, they tried to cover up the matter, making believe that they were looking for something else and had some other intent. By this artifice they saved themselves; otherwise those whom flight spared would have grieved, not that they had taken up arms in vain, but that they had done so unfortunately.

Questions: By this account, what led to the hostilities between the crusade leaders at Antioch? Compare Ralph's account of the finding of the holy lance with that by Anselm of Ribemont. What arguments does Bohemond (Tancred's uncle) give against the relic's authenticity? What did Raymond and his supporters have to gain by the possession and promotion of the holy lance?

20. RAYMOND OF AGUILERS ON THE FALL OF JERUSALEM

By June of 1099 the crusaders were besieging Jerusalem. Raymond of Aguilers was a chaplain in the service of the crusading count of Toulouse, Raymond of St. Gilles. His history of the crusade provides an eyewitness account of the siege and fall of Jerusalem. The siege began on June 7 and concluded on July 15 with the breaching of the city walls and the massacre of many of the inhabitants by the crusading forces.

Source: trans. A.C. Krey, *The First Crusade: The Accounts of Eye-witnesses and Participants* (Princeton: Princeton University Press, 1921), pp. 257-62.

The duke [Godfrey of Bouillon] and the counts of Normandy and Flanders placed Gaston of Beert in charge of the workmen who constructed machines. They built mantlets and towers with which to attack the wall. The direction of this work was assigned to Gaston by the princes because he was a most noble lord, respected by all for his skill and reputation. He very cleverly hastened matters by dividing the work. The princes busied themselves with obtaining and bringing the material, while Gaston supervised the work of construction. Likewise, Count Raymond made William Ricau superintendent of the work on Mount Zion and placed the bishop of Albara in charge of the

Fig. 6: Siege machine. A European army uses a wooden siege tower on wheels to attack a city, as the crusaders did at Jerusalem. This nineteenth-century engraving is a copy of a fourteenth-century manuscript illumination. From P. Lacroix, *Military and Religious Life in the Middle Ages* (London, Chapman and Hall, 1874).

Saracens and others who brought in the timber. The count's men had taken many Saracen castles and villages and forced the Saracens to work, as though they were their serfs. Thus for the construction of machines at Jerusalem fifty or sixty men carried on their shoulders a great beam that could not have been dragged by four pair of oxen. What more shall I say? All worked with a singleness of purpose, no one was slothful, and no hands were idle. All worked without wages, except the artisans, who were paid from a collection taken from the people. However, Count Raymond paid his workmen from his own treasury. Surely the hand of the Lord was with us and aided those who were working!

When our efforts were ended and the machines completed, the princes held a council and announced: "Let all prepare themselves for a battle on Thursday; in the meantime, let us pray, fast, and give alms. Hand over your animals and your boys to the artisans and carpenters, that they may bring in beams, poles, stakes, and branches to make mantlets. Two knights should make one mantlet and one scaling ladder. Do not hesitate to work for the Lord, for your labors will soon be ended." This was willingly done by all. Then it was decided what part of the city each leader should attack and where his machines should be located.

Meanwhile, the Saracens in the city, noting the great number of machines that we had constructed, strengthened the weaker parts of the wall, so that it seemed that they could be taken only by the most desperate efforts. Because the Saracens had made so many and such strong fortifications to oppose our machines, the duke, the count of Flanders, and the count of Normandy spent the night before the day set for the attack moving their machines, mantlets, and platforms to that side of the city which is between the church of St. Stephen and the valley of Josaphat. You who read this must not think that this was a light undertaking, for the machines were carried in parts almost a mile to the place where they were to be set up. When morning came and the Saracens saw that all the machinery and tents had been moved during the night, they were amazed. Not only the Saracens were astonished, but our people as well, for they recognized that the hand of the Lord was with us. The change was made because the new point chosen for attack was more level, and thus suitable for moving the machines up to the walls, which cannot be done unless the ground is level; and also because that part of the city seemed to be weaker, having remained unfortified, as it was some distance from our camp. This part of the city is on the north.

Count Raymond and his men worked equally hard on Mount Zion, but they had much assistance from William Embriaco and the Genoese sailors, who, although they had lost their ships at Joppa, as we have already related, had been able, nevertheless, to save ropes, mallets, spikes, axes, and hatchets, which were very necessary to us. But why delay the story? The appointed day arrived and the attack began. However, I want to say this first, that, according to our estimate and that of many others, there were 60,000 fighting men within the city, not counting the women and those unable to bear arms, and there were not many of these. At the most we did not have more than twelve thousand able to bear arms, for there were many poor people and many sick. There were twelve or thirteen hundred knights in our army, as I reckon it, not more. I say this that you may realize that nothing, whether great or small, which is undertaken in the name of the Lord can fail, as the following pages show.

Our men began to undermine the towers and walls. From every side stones were hurled from the *tormenti* and the *petrariae* [that is, catapults], and so many arrows that they fell like hail. The servants of God bore this patiently, sustained by the premises of their faith, whether they should be killed or should presently prevail over their enemies. The battle showed no indication of victory, but when the machines were drawn nearer to the walls, they hurled not only stones and arrows, but also burning wood and straw. The wood was dipped in pitch, wax, and sulfur; then straw [was] fastened on by an iron band, and, when lighted, these firebrands were shot from the machines. [They were] all bound together by an iron band, I say, so that wherever they fell, the whole mass held together and continued to burn. Such missiles, burning as they shot upward, could not be resisted by swords or by high walls; it was not even possible for the defenders to find safety down behind the walls. Thus the fight continued from the rising to the setting sun in such splendid fashion that it is difficult to believe anything more glorious was ever done. Then we called on almighty God, our leader and guide, confident in his mercy. Night brought fear to both sides. The Saracens feared that we would take the city during the night or on the next day, for the outer works were broken through and the ditch was filled, so that it was possible to make an entrance through the wall very quickly. On our part, we feared only that the Saracens would set fire to the machines that were moved close to the walls, and thus improve their situation. So on both sides it was a night of watchfulness, labor, and sleepless caution: on one side, most certain hope, on the other doubtful fear. We gladly labored to capture the city for the glory of God; they less willingly strove to resist our efforts for the sake of the laws of Mohammed. It is hard to believe how great were the efforts made on both sides during the night.

When the morning came, our men eagerly rushed to the walls and dragged the machines forward, but the Saracens had constructed so many machines that for each one of ours they now had nine or ten. Thus they greatly interfered with our efforts. This was the ninth day, on which the priest had said that we would capture the city. But why do I delay so long? Our machines were now shaken apart by the blows of many stones, and our men lagged because they were very weary. However, there remained the mercy of the Lord which is never overcome nor conquered, but is always a source of support in times of adversity. One incident must not be omitted. Two women tried to bewitch one of the hurling machines, but a stone struck and crushed them, as well as three slaves, so that their lives were extinguished and the evil incantations averted.

By noon our men were greatly discouraged. They were weary and at the end of their resources. There were still many of the enemy opposing each one of our men; the walls were very high and strong, and the great resources and skill that the enemy exhibited in repairing their defenses seemed too great for us to overcome. But, while we hesitated, irresolute, and the enemy exulted in our discomfiture, the healing mercy of God inspired us and turned our sorrow into joy, for the Lord did not forsake us. While a council was being held to decide whether or not our machines should be withdrawn, for some were burned and the rest badly shaken to pieces, a knight on the Mount of Olives began to wave his shield to those who were with the count and others, signaling them to advance. Who this knight was we have been unable to find out. At this signal our men began to take heart, and some began to batter down the wall, while others began to ascend by means of scaling ladders and ropes. Our archers shot burning firebrands, and in this way checked the attack that the

Saracens were making upon the wooden towers of the duke and the two counts. These firebrands, moreover, were wrapped in cotton. This shower of fire drove the defenders from the walls. Then the count quickly released the long drawbridge which had protected the side of the wooden tower next to the wall, and it swung down from the top, being fastened to the middle of the tower, making a bridge over which the men began to enter Jerusalem bravely and fearlessly. Among those who entered first were Tancred and the duke of Lorraine, and the amount of blood that they shed on that day is incredible. All ascended after them, and the Saracens now began to suffer.

Strange to relate, however, at this very time when the city was practically captured by the Franks, the Saracens were still fighting on the other side, where the count was attacking the wall as though the city should never be captured. But now that our men had possession of the walls and towers, wonderful sights were to be seen. Some of our men (and this was more merciful) cut off the heads of their enemies; others shot them with arrows, so that they fell from the towers; others tortured them longer by casting them into the flames. Piles of heads, hands, and feet were to be seen in the streets of the city. It was necessary to pick one's way over the bodies of men and horses. But these were small matters compared to what happened at the Temple of Solomon, a place where religious services are ordinarily chanted. What happened there? If I tell the truth, it will exceed your powers of belief. So let it suffice to say this much, at least, that in the Temple and porch of Solomon, men rode in blood up to their knees and bridle reins. Indeed, it was a just and splendid judgment of God that this place should be filled with the blood of the unbelievers, since it had suffered so long from their blasphemies. The city was filled with corpses and blood. Some of the enemy took refuge in the Tower of David, and, petitioning Count Raymond for protection, surrendered the Tower into his hands.

Now that the city was taken, it was well worth all our previous labors and hardships to see the devotion of the pilgrims at the Holy Sepulcher. How they rejoiced and exulted and sang a new song to the Lord! For their hearts offered prayers of praise to God, victorious and triumphant, which cannot be told in words. A new day, new joy, new and perpetual gladness, the consummation of our labor and devotion, drew forth from all new words and new songs. This day, I say, will be famous in all future ages, for it turned our labors and sorrows into joy and exultation; this day, I say, marks the justification of all Christianity, the humiliation of paganism, and the renewal of our faith. "This is the day which the Lord hath made, let us rejoice and be glad in it," for on this day the Lord revealed himself to his people and blessed them.

On this day, the Ides of July, Lord Adhemar, bishop of Puy, [who had died at Antioch,] was seen in the city by many people. Many also testified that he was the first to scale the wall, and that he summoned the knights and people to follow him. On this day, moreover, the apostles were cast forth from Jerusalem and scattered over the whole world. On this same day, the children of the apostles regained the city and fatherland for God and the fathers. This day, the Ides of July, shall be celebrated to the praise and glory of the name of God, who, answering the prayers of his church, gave in trust and benediction to his children the city and fatherland which he had promised to the fathers. On this day we chanted the office of the resurrection, since on that day he, who by his virtue arose from the dead, revived us through his grace. So much is to be said of this.

Questions: What tactics were employed by the crusaders in the siege of Jerusalem? How did the city's people defend themselves? How does Raymond justify the massacre of so many inhabitants? How believable is his account?

21. LETTER OF POPE PASCHAL ON THE CAPTURE OF JERUSALEM

Paschal II (1099-1118) was the successor of Urban II as pope and a firm supporter of the crusades. This support is clearly demonstrated in this letter written to the clergy of France on the capture of Jerusalem.

Source: trans. A.C. Krey, *The First Crusade: The Accounts of Eye-witnesses and Participants* (Princeton: Princeton University Press, 1921), p. 279.

Paschal, bishop, servant of the servants of God, to all archbishops, bishops, and abbots throughout Gaul [that is, France]; greeting and apostolic blessing.

We owe boundless gratitude to the compassion of almighty God, since in our time he has deigned to wrest the church in Asia from the hands of the Turks and to open to Christian soldiers the very city of the Lord's suffering and burial. However, we ought to follow divine grace with what means he has given us, and effectively aid our brethren who have remained in those districts which were once the lands of the people of Palestine or Canaan. Urge, therefore, all the soldiers of your region to strive for remission and forgiveness of their sins by hastening to our mother church of the East; especially compel those who have assumed the sign of the cross in pledge of this journey to hasten thither, unless they are prevented by the hindrance of poverty. Moreover, we decree that those be held in disgrace who left the siege of Antioch through weak or questionable faith; let them remain in excommunication, unless they affirm with certain pledges that they will return. We furthermore command that all their possessions be restored to those brethren who are returning after the victory of the Lord, just as your recall was ordained in a synodal decree by Urban, our predecessor of blessed memory. Do thus in all matters, being so zealous in your duty that by common zeal our mother church of the East may be restored to her due state, the Lord granting it.

Questions: What does this letter tell us about the pope's long-term plans for crusading? What are his concerns for this venture? How does he strive to ensure its success?

22. ABU L-MUZAFFAR AL-ABIWARDI ON THE FALL OF JERUSALEM

While Europe rejoiced at the news of the fall of Jerusalem, this was not a sentiment shared by the majority in the East, especially those in the Holy Land. Muslims, Jews and eastern Christians had all been horrified by the brutality of the campaign and the indiscriminate slaughter of men, women and children by the triumphant crusaders. Although much was written about and against this atrocity, there was, initially, no active response. The Iraqi poet Abu l-Muzaffar al-Abiwardi was living in Baghdad at this time and may well have been aware of the pleas for aid made by those Muslims living in the Holy Land to the caliphs of Baghdad.

Source: trans. E.J. Costello and F. Gabrieli, *Arab Historians of the Crusades*, ed. F. Gabrieli (Berkeley: University of California Press, 1969), p. 12.

We have mingled blood with flowing tears, and there is no room left in us for
    pity(?).
To shed tears is a man's worst weapon when the swords stir up the embers of
    war.
Sons of Islam, behind you are battles in which heads rolled at your feet.
Dare you slumber in the blessed shade of safety, where life is as soft as an
    orchard flower?
How can the eye sleep between the lids at a time of disasters that would
    waken any sleeper?
While our Syrian brothers can only sleep on the backs of their chargers, or in
    vultures' bellies!
Must the foreigners feed on our ignominy, while you trail behind you the
    train of a pleasant life, like men whose world is at peace?
When blood has been spilt, when sweet girls must for shame hide their lovely
    faces in their hands!
When the white swords' points are red with blood, and the iron of the brown
    lances is stained with gore!
At the sound of sword hammering on lance young children's hair turns white.
This is war, and the man who shuns the whirlpool to save his life shall grind
    his teeth in penitence.

This is war, and the infidel's word is naked in his hand, ready to be sheathed
again in men's necks and skulls.
This is war, and he who lies in the tomb at Medina seems to raise his voice
and cry: "O sons of Hashim!
I see my people slow to raise the lance against the enemy: I see the Faith
resting on feeble pillars.
For fear of death the Muslims are evading the fire of battle, refusing to believe
that death will surely strike them."
Must the Arab champions then suffer with resignation, while the gallant
Persians shut their eyes to their dishonor?

*Questions: What is the poet calling for in this poem? What arguments does he use to
goad his fellow Muslims into action? What is the poet's view of warfare with the Christian forces?*

CHAPTER THREE:

THE CRUSADER STATES

Fig. 7: A fifteenth-century German woodcut of Jerusalem, with the Temple of Solomon (the Al-Aqsa Mosque) in the center. From P. Lacroix, *Manners, Customs, and Dress during the Middle Ages* (London: Chapman and Hall, 1874).

23. WILLIAM OF TYRE'S *HISTORY*

William, Catholic archbishop of Tyre in the kingdom of Jerusalem, was a Frank who had been born in the Holy Land and educated in France. He wrote his History of Deeds Done Beyond the Sea *in the 1160s and 1170s. For source material he relied not only on other histories and his own experience, but also on the documents and records of the crusader states. In the extracts below, he describes the establishment of the Latin (that is, European) kingdom of Jerusalem and the principality of Antioch, the third and fourth of the four crusader states to be founded during and after the First Crusade, as well as some of the problems facing the Franks in their new colonies and some of the strategies by which they addressed those problems.*

Source: trans. E.A. Babcock and A.C. Krey, *A History of Deeds Done beyond the Sea, by William Archbishop of Tyre* (New York: Columbia University Press, 1943), vol. I, pp. 379, 381-82, 391-92, 507-08, 524-26.

Thus [after the fall of Jerusalem to the crusaders,] through the superabundant grace of God the holy city had been restored to the Christian people and matters had been reduced to some degree of order. Seven days glided by in much rejoicing, tempered, indeed, by the fear of the Lord and spiritual gladness. On the eighth day the leaders assembled for consultation. It was their purpose, after invoking the grace of the Holy Spirit, to choose someone from among their own number to rule over the region and to bear the royal responsibility for that province.

But while they were deliberating over the matter, some of the clergy, puffed up with the spirit of pride and intent on their own interests rather than on those of Jesus Christ, also gathered. They sent a message to the chiefs saying that they had certain private matters which they wished to bring before those who were now sitting in council. On being admitted, they said, "It has been reported to the clergy that you have met for the purpose of choosing one of your number as king. This purpose of yours seems to us holy and well advised and, if it were reached in its proper order, worthy of being carried out with all care. It is undoubtedly true that spiritual matters are of higher importance than temporal and ought therefore to be considered first. In our opinion, the order should be reversed, and, before election to a secular office is thought of, some person of religious life, pleasing to God, ought to be chosen who will be capable of presiding over the church of God for its advancement and benefit. If it pleases you to proceed in this order, it will be most agreeable to us, and we are with you in body and spirit. But if not, we shall pronounce whatever you decree without our approval invalid and without force."...

The princes regarded the objections of the clergy ... as frivolous and of no importance. Though intent on carrying out their plan, yet they took the proposal under consideration…. [Eventually they proceeded to choose a king.]

After carefully considering all aspects of the matter, the [secular] electors unanimously agreed upon the duke [of Bouillon] as their choice. Godfrey was elected and escorted with great devotion to the Sepulcher of the Lord, attended by the singing of chants and hymns….

Godfrey was a devout man, whose heart was filled with pious care for all that pertained to the honor of the house of God. A few days after he was elected head of the kingdom, he began to offer the first fruits of his responsibility to the Lord. He established canons in the church of the Lord's Sepulcher and in the Temple of the Lord; and upon them he bestowed ample benefices known as prebends. At the same time also he gave them noble houses in the vicinity of these same churches beloved of God. He preserved the rule and regulations observed by the great and wealthy churches founded by pious princes beyond the mountains, and he would have conferred still greater gifts, had not death prevented…. Nevertheless, after his elevation to power, because of his humility of spirit, he refused to be invested with a crown of gold in the holy city, as is the fashion of kings. For he was content with, and showed reverence toward, that crown of thorns which, in that same city, the Savior of the human race, for our salvation, wore even to the passion of the cross. Hence, some people, not appreciating Godfrey's services, hesitate to place his name in the catalogue of the kings; such regard those outward acts which are done in the body as of greater value than those of a faithful spirit pleasing to God. To us he seems not merely a king, but the best of kings, a light and a mirror to others….

[In about 1116], the king [that is, Godfrey's successor Baldwin] realized with great concern that the holy city, beloved of God, was almost destitute of inhabitants. There were not enough people to carry on the necessary undertakings of the realm. Indeed there were scarcely enough to protect the entrances to the city and to defend the walls and towers against sudden hostile attacks. Accordingly, he gave much anxious thought to the problem, turning the question over in his own mind and talking with others concerning plans for filling it with faithful people, worshippers of the true God. The Gentiles [that is, the non-Christians] who were living there at the time the city was taken by force had perished by the sword, almost to a man; and if any had by chance escaped they were not permitted to remain in the city. For to allow anyone not belonging to the Christian faith to live in so venerated a place seemed like sacrilege to the chiefs in their devotion to God. The people of our country were so few in number and so needy that they scarcely filled one street, while the Syrians who had originally been citizens of the city had been so reduced through the many tribulations and trials endured in the time of hostilities that their number was as nothing….

Fig. 8: The twelfth-century tomb of Godfrey of Bouillon, first ruler of the kingdom of Jerusalem, in the Church of the Holy Sepulcher, as it appeared in 1828. From P. Lacroix, *Military and Religious Life in the Middle Ages* (London, Chapman and Hall, 1874).

The king felt that the responsibility for relieving the desolation of the city rested upon him. Accordingly, he made careful investigations in regard to some source whence he might obtain citizens. Finally he learned that beyond the Jordan in Arabia there were many Christians living in villages under hard conditions of servitude and forced tribute. He sent for these people and promised them improved conditions. Within a short time, he had the satisfaction of receiving them with their wives and children, flocks and herds, and all their households. They were attracted thither not only by reverence for the place but also by affection for our people and the love of liberty. Many, even without being invited, cast off the harsh yoke of servitude and came that they might dwell in the city worthy of God. To these the king granted those sections of the city which seemed to need this assistance most and filled the houses with them....

In [1118], certain pious and God-fearing nobles of knightly rank, devoted to the Lord, professed the wish to live perpetually in poverty, chastity, and obedience [that is, as monks]. In the hands of the patriarch they vowed themselves to the service of God as regular canons. Foremost and most distinguished among these men were the venerable Hugh de Payens and Godfrey of St. Omer. Since they had neither a church nor a fixed place of abode, the king granted them a temporary dwelling place in his own palace, on the north side by the Temple of the Lord.... The main duty of this order—that was enjoined upon them by the patriarch and the other bishops for the remission of sins—was, "that, as far as their strength permitted, they should keep the roads and highways safe from the menace of robbers and highwaymen, with especial regard for the protection of pilgrims."

Nine years after the founding of this order ... [the Templars] were as yet only nine in number. After this period, however, they began to increase, and their possessions multiplied. It was in the time of Pope Eugenius [III, 1145-53], it is said, that they began to sew on their mantles crosses of red cloth, that they might be distinguished from others. Not only the knights, but also the inferior brothers called sergeants, wore this sign. The Templars prospered so greatly that today [that is, around 1170] there are in the order about three hundred knights who wear the white mantle and, in addition, an almost countless number of lesser brothers.

They are said to have vast possessions, both on this side of the sea and beyond. There is not a province in the Christian world today which does not bestow some part of its possessions upon these brethren, and their property is reported to be equal to the riches of kings....

Questions: What were the immediate concerns of the crusaders after taking Jerusalem? What models did they follow in administering their new Middle Eastern territories? What problems arose, and how were they addressed? Why did the crusader states fail to attract Christian residents? What tensions are revealed in the text?

24. FULCHER OF CHARTRES'S *HISTORY*

Fulcher of Chartres went on the First Crusade with Stephen of Blois and later served as a chaplain in the service of Baldwin of Boulogne, who would become the second king of Jerusalem. Fulcher's history of the crusade and its aftermath, written between 1101 and 1127, is one of the better informed such works.

Source: trans. F.R. Ryan, in Fulcher of Chartres, *A History of the Expedition to Jerusalem, 1095-1127* (Knoxville: University of Tennessee Press, 1969), pp. 149-52, 238-39, 243, 267-68, 270-72.

Book II

... In the beginning of his reign Baldwin [I, the king of Jerusalem] as yet possessed few cities [that is, only Jerusalem, Bethlehem, and Joppa] and people. Through that same winter he stoutly protected his kingdom from enemies on all sides. And because they found out that he was a very skillful fighter, although he had few men, they did not dare to attack him. If he had had a greater force he would have met the enemy gladly.

Up to that time the land route was completely blocked to our pilgrims. Meanwhile they, French as well as English, or Italians and Venetians, came by sea as far as Joppa. At first we had no other port. These pilgrims came very timidly in single ships, or in squadrons of three or four, through the midst of hostile pirates and past the ports of the Saracens, with the Lord showing the way. When we saw that they had come from our own countries in the West, we promptly and joyfully met them as if they were saints. From them each of us anxiously inquired concerning his homeland and his loved ones. The new arrivals told us all that they knew. When we heard good news we rejoiced; when they told of misfortune we were saddened. They came on to Jerusalem; they visited the Holy of Holies, for which purpose they had come. Following that, some remained in the Holy Land, and others went back to their native countries. For this reason the land of Jerusalem remained depopulated. There were not enough people to defend it from the Saracens if only the latter dared attack us.

But why did they not dare? Why did so many people and so many kingdoms fear to attack our little kingdom and our humble people? Why did they not gather from Egypt, from Persia, from Mesopotamia, and from Syria at least a hundred times a hundred thousand fighters to advance courageously against us, their enemies? Why did they not, as innumerable locusts in a little field, so completely devour and destroy us that no further mention could be made of us in a land that had been ours from time immemorial? For we did not at that time have more than three hundred knights and as many footmen to defend Jerusalem, Joppa, Ramla, and also the stronghold of Haifa. We scarcely dared to assemble our knights when we wished to plan some feat against our enemies. We feared that in the meantime they would do some damage against our deserted fortifications.

Truly it is manifest to all that it was a wonderful miracle that we lived among so many thousands and as their conquerors made some of them our tributaries and ruined others by plundering them and making them captives. But whence came this virtue? Whence this power? Truly from him whose name is the Almighty, who, not unmindful of his people laboring in his name, in his mercy aids in their tribulations those who trust in him alone. Moreover God promises to reward with everlasting glory in the life to come those whom he sometimes makes happy with very little temporal reward.

Oh time so worthy to be remembered! Often indeed we were sad when we could get no aid from our friends across the sea. We feared lest our enemies, learning how few we were, would sometime rush down upon us from all sides in a sudden attack when none but God could help us. We were in need of nothing if only men and horses did not fail us. The men who came by sea to Jerusalem could not bring horses with them, and no one came to us by land. The people of Antioch were not able to help us, nor we them....

During that same winter season [of 1100-1101] a fleet of beaked Genoese and Italian ships [that is, warships] had stayed at the port of Laodicea. In the spring when the men saw that the weather was calm and suitable for navigation they sailed as far as Joppa with a favoring wind. When they reached port they were gladly received by the king. Because it was near Easter and since it was customary for all who could to celebrate this solemn occasion, they beached their ships and went up to Jerusalem with the king. On Easter Sabbath everyone was much disturbed because the holy fire failed to appear at the Sepulcher of the Lord. When the Easter solemnity was over, the king went back to Joppa and made a convention with the consuls of the above-mentioned fleet. It was agreed that as long as the Genoese cared to stay in the Holy Land for the love of God, if with his consent and assistance they and the king could take any of the cities of the Saracens, they should have in common a third part of the money taken from the enemy with no injury done to the Genoese, and the king should have the first and second parts. Moreover [the Genoese] should possess by perpetual and hereditary right a section in such a city captured in this way....

Book III

... In [1123] the Venetians were inspired to sail with a great fleet to Syria in order with the help of God to extend Jerusalem and the area adjacent, all for the advantage and glory of Christendom. They had left their own land the year before and had wintered on the island called Corfu, awaiting a favorable season for sailing further. Their fleet was of one hundred and twenty ships, excepting small boats and skiffs. Some vessels were beaked, some were merchant ships, and some triremes. They were built of these three types. In them were loaded very long timbers which when skillfully made into siege machinery by the carpenters could be used for scaling and seizing the high walls of cities.

In the spring when the sea routes were open to their ships the Venetians delayed no longer in fulfilling their long-standing vows to God. After they had made ample provision for the voyage and had set fire to the huts in which they had wintered and had invoked the help of God, they joyfully sounded their trumpets and hoisted their sails. The ships, painted in various colors, delighted with their brightness those who beheld them from afar. In them were fifteen thousand armed men, Venetians as well as pilgrims whom they had associated with themselves. In addition they took three hundred horses. And so when the wind blew gently from the north they expertly cut away from their gangplanks and set course for Methone [on the coast of Messinia] and then to Rhodes....

[Around the beginning of June the Venetian fleet] entered many of the ports of Palestine. Indeed rumor had for a long time foretold its arrival. As soon as the doge [that is, the leader] of the Venetians, who commanded this fleet, had landed at Acre, he was informed at once of what had happened in Joppa by land and sea, and how the Babylonians [that is, the Egyptians] had done as much damage as they could, and having accomplished their purpose, had departed. But if the doge wished to pursue them energetically he could certainly overtake them, with God's help. [The Frankish military operations continued, with Venetian help.]

... While we were waiting [during the summer of 1124] with ears open to learn any bit of news, behold! three messengers arrived in great haste bearing letters from our patriarch announcing the capture of Tyre. When this was heard a most joyful clamor arose. The "Te Deum Laudamus" was forthwith sung with exultant voice. Bells were rung, a procession marched to the Temple of God, and flags were raised on the walls and towers. Through all the streets many-colored ornaments were displayed, thankful gestures made, the messengers suitably rewarded according to their deserts, the humble and the great mutually congratulated themselves, and the girls were delightful as they sang in chorus.

Justly Jerusalem like a mother rejoices over her daughter Tyre at whose right hand she sits crowned as befits her rank. And Babylon mourns the loss of her prestige, which sustained her until recently, and the loss of her hostile fleet, which she used to send out against us each year. Indeed although Tyre is lessened in worldly pomp she is augmented in divine grace. For whereas among the heathen the city had a high priest or arch-priest in authority, according to the institutions of the fathers she shall have a primate or patriarch in Christian law. For where there were high priests, Christian archbishops shall be instituted to rule over provinces.... Praise be to God on high because he has returned Tyre to us, not by the might of men but by his own good pleasure and without the effusion of blood [that is, by surrender rather than by assault]. Tyre is a noble city, very strong and very difficult to take unless God lays upon it his own right hand. The people of Antioch failed us in this affair, for they furnished us no aid nor wished to be present at the task. But blessed be Pons of Tripoli since he was our most faithful ally....

The affairs of Tyre were settled as was proper. A tripartite division was made in which two equal parts were turned over to the authority of the city. The third part, lying within the city as well as around the harbor, was as a result of reciprocal concessions made one by one turned over to the Venetians to hold by hereditary right. Then all returned home....

At that time the sun appeared to us in dazzling color for almost one hour. It was changed by a new and hyacinthine beauty and transformed into the shape of the moon as in a two-pronged eclipse. This happened on [August 11, 1124,] when the ninth hour of the day was waning. Therefore do not marvel when you see signs in the heavens because God works miracles there as he does on earth. For just as in the heavens so also on earth he transforms and arranges all things as he wills. For if those things which he made are wonderful, more wonderful is he who made them. Consider, I pray, and reflect how in our time God has transformed the Occident [that is, the West] into the Orient [that is, the East].

For we who were occidentals have now become orientals. He who was a Roman or a Frank has in this land been made into a Galilean or a Palestinian. He who was of Rheims or Chartres has now become a citizen of Tyre or Antioch. We have already forgotten the places of our birth; already these are unknown to many of us or not mentioned any more. Some already possess homes or households by inheritance. Some have taken wives not only of their own people but Syrians or Armenians or even Saracens who have obtained the grace of baptism. One has his father-in-law as well as his daughter-in-law living with him, or his own child if not his stepson or stepfather. Out here there are grandchildren and great-grandchildren. Some tend vineyards; others till fields. People use the eloquence and idioms of diverse languages in conversing back and forth. Words of different languages have become common property known to each nationality, and mutual faith unites those who are ignorant of their descent. Indeed it is written, "The lion and the ox shall eat straw together" [Isaiah 62:25]. He who was born a stranger is now as one born here; he who was born an alien has become as a native.

Our relatives and parents join us from time to time, sacrificing, even though reluctantly, all that they formerly possessed. Those who were poor in the

Occident, God makes rich in this land. Those who had little money there have countless bezants here, and those who did not have a villa possess here by the gift of God a city. Therefore why should one return to the Occident who has found the Orient like this? God does not wish those to suffer want who with their crosses dedicated themselves to follow him, nay even to the end. You see therefore that this is a great miracle and one which the whole world ought to admire. Who has heard anything like it? God wishes to enrich us all and to draw us to himself as his dearest friends. And because he wishes it we also freely desire it, and what is pleasing to him we do with a loving and submissive heart in order that we may reign with him throughout eternity.

Questions: What does Fulcher see as the greatest problem facing the kingdom of Jerusalem? What additional ways were found to address it? Why did Christian-Muslim warfare continue after the First Crusade was over? According to Fulcher, how did the European settlers adapt to life in Palestine? What was his attitude toward this change? How thoroughly do you think the settlers were assimilated?

25. VENETIAN TREATY

In the preceding document, Fulcher of Chartres described the involvement of a Venetian fleet in the military affairs of the kingdom of Jerusalem, including the siege of Tyre in 1124. Just before the siege began, the following treaty of alliance was drawn up between the kingdom and the Venetians; it is preserved in the work of William of Tyre.

Source: trans. E.A. Babcock and A.C. Krey, *A History of Deed Done beyond the Sea, by William Archbishop of Tyre*, (New York: Columbia University Press, 1943), vol. I, pp. 553-55.

In every city of the above-mentioned king [of Jerusalem], under the rule of his successors also, and in the cities of all his barons, the Venetians shall have a church and one entire street of their own; also a square and a bath and an oven to be held forever by hereditary right, free from all taxation as is the king's own property.

In the square at Jerusalem, however, they shall have for their own only as much as the king is wont to have. But if the Venetians desire to set up at Acre, in their own quarter, an oven, a mill, a bath, scales, measures and bottles for measuring wine, oil, and honey, it shall be permitted freely to each person dwelling there without contradiction to cook, mill, or bathe just as it is freely permitted on the king's property. They may use the measures, the scales, and the measuring bottles as follows: when the Venetians trade with each other, they must use their own measures, that is the measures of Venice; and when the Venetians sell their wares to other races, they must sell with their own measures, that is, with the measures of Venice; but when the Venetians purchase and receive anything in trade from any foreign nation other than the Venetians, it is permitted them to take it by the royal measure and at a given price. For these privileges the Venetians need pay no tax whatever, whether according to custom or for any reason whatsoever, either on entering, staying, buying, selling, either while remaining there or on departing. For no reason whatever need they pay any tax excepting only when they come or go, carrying pilgrims with their own vessels. Then indeed, according to the king's custom, they must give a third part to the king himself.

Wherefore, the king of Jerusalem and all of us on behalf of the king agree to pay the doge of Venice, from the revenues of Tyre, on the feast day of the apostles Peter and Paul, three hundred Saracen bezants yearly, as agreed upon.

Moreover, we promise you, doge of Venice, and your people that we will take nothing more from those nations who trade with you beyond what they are accustomed to give and as much as we receive from those who trade with other nations.

In addition, that part of the same place and street of Acre which has at one end the house of Peter Zanni and at the other the monastery of St. Dimitrius, and also another part of the same street having one wooden house and two of stone, which were formerly reed huts, the same which King Baldwin of Jerusalem originally gave to the blessed Mark and to Doge Ordolafo and his successors in consideration of the acquisition of Sidon; these places, I say, we confirm to St. Mark and to you, Domenigo Michieli, doge of Venice, and to your successors by this same document. To you we give the power in perpetuity of holding and possessing it, and of doing with it whatever you please. Over the other part of the same street extending in a straight line from the house of Bernard of Neufchatel, which formerly belonged to John Julian, as far as the house of Gilbert of Jaffa, of the family of St. Lo, we give you exactly the same power which the king had. In addition, no Venetian in the whole domain of the king, or in the domains of his barons, need give any tribute whether in entering, or staying there, or going out for any pretext; but may be as free as in Venice itself.

But if a Venetian shall have a lawsuit or any litigation over any business against a Venetian, it shall be decided in the court of the Venetians. Again, if anyone feels that he has a quarrel or lawsuit against a Venetian, it shall be determined in the same court of the Venetians. But if a Venetian makes complaint against any other than a Venetian, the case shall be decided in the court of the king. Also when a Venetian dies, whether testate [that is, having written a will] or intestate (which we call without a tongue), his property shall accrue to the control of the Venetians. If any Venetian shall be shipwrecked, he shall not suffer loss of any of his property. If he dies in the shipwreck, the property which he leaves shall be sent back to his heirs or to other Venetians. Moreover, the Venetians shall have the same powers of justice and the same rights over the burghers of any people dwelling in the street and houses of the Venetians as the king has over his own people.

Finally the Venetians shall have a third part of the two cities of Tyre and Ascalon, with their appurtenances, and a third part of all the lands belonging to them from the feast day of St. Peter. This applies only to lands which are now subject to the Saracens and are not as yet in the hands of the Franks. If, through the aid of the Venetians or by any other means, the Holy Spirit shall give either of these cities or, God willing, both of them into the power of the Christians, a third part of such city or cities, as has been said, freely and with regal powers the Venetians shall hold with hereditary right forever, without let or hindrance, just as the king holds two parts.

Questions: Which conditions here are benefits to the Venetians, and why? Why are such rich benefits being granted? Which conditions here are not advantageous for the Venetians? What does the document tell us about conditions in the kingdom of Jerusalem at this time? How would this treaty change the crusader states?

26. LAWS OF THE KINGDOM OF JERUSALEM

The Christian government of Jerusalem set up two courts of law, the High Court and the Court of the Bourgeois (town-dwellers or commoners). The laws of both courts, covering many civil and some criminal matters, developed over the course of the twelfth and thirteenth centuries; they survive in a thirteenth-century Old French manuscript. Excerpted here, first, are some provisions from the Court of the Bourgeois dealing with commercial lawsuits between members of the different ethnic groups dwelling in the kingdom. The second section outlines tolls and customs, which were the major source of revenue for the kingdom of Jerusalem. The bezant was a Greek gold coin used as a standard monetary unit throughout the Mediterranean world; the karouble was probably worth one twenty-fourth of a bezant. The drachma was a Greek silver coin, worth less than the bezant; the raboin was worth one quarter of a bezant.

Sources: first section: trans. E. Amt from *Recueil des historiens des croisades: Lois*, Vol. II, *Assises de la cour des bourgeois*, ed. A.A. Beugnot (Paris: Imprimerie Royale, 1843), pp. 53-56; second section: trans. R.P. Falkner, *Translations and Reprints from the Original Sources of European History*, series I, vol. III (Philadelphia: University of Pennsylvania Department of History, n.d.), no. 2, pp. 19-23, revised.

Debt Collection Procedures

59. If it happens that a Frank makes a claim against a Syrian in court to have what the Syrian owes him, and the Syrian denies owing it, and the Frank has no guarantor for it, the law decrees that the Syrian must swear on the holy

cross that he owes him nothing; and by way of this ceremony the Syrian must be acquitted by the court. Likewise, if a Syrian makes a claim against a Frank in the court to have what the Frank owes him, and the Frank denies owing what he claims from him, and the Syrian has no guarantor for it, the Frank shall not make any oath to the Syrian, if he does not acknowledge the debt at all, according to the law and the court.

60. If a Frank makes a claim in court against a Saracen to have what the latter owes him, and the Saracen denies owing it, and the Frank has no guarantor for it, it is right that the Saracen must swear on the law that he owes the Frank nothing, and thereupon he must be acquitted. Likewise, if a Saracen makes a claim against a Frank in court to have what the Frank owes him, and the Frank does not have it for him, and the Saracen has no guarantor for it, the law decrees that the Frank should not make an oath to the Saracen, if he does not acknowledge the debt at all.

61. If it happens that a Frank makes a claim in court against a Griffon [that is, a Greek], concerning something that he claims is owed, and the Frank who claims this has no Griffon for a guarantor, who acknowledges the debt, other [that is, non-Griffon] guarantors are not sufficient for this, according to the law and to the court; because a Frank cannot be a guarantor against a Griffon, nor a Griffon against a Frank, according to the law of the kingdom of Jerusalem....

63. If it happens that a Syrian makes a claim in the court against a Nestorian [that is, a native Christian belonging to an eastern sect], concerning something that he claims is owed, and the Syrian has no Nestorian as a guarantor, other guarantors will not be sufficient for the Syrian, if the business was not conducted in the court, because a Syrian cannot be a guarantor against a Nestorian, according to the court of the kingdom of Jerusalem. Likewise, if a Nestorian makes a claim in court against a Syrian, concerning a debt which he owes him, and he denies the debt, and the Nestorian has no Syrian as a guarantor, other guarantors will not be valid, if the business was not conducted in the court, because a Nestorian cannot be a guarantor against a Syrian, according to the court of the kingdom of Jerusalem.

64. If it happens that a Nestorian makes a claim in court against a Jacobite [that is, a native Christian belonging to a certain Syrian sect], concerning something that he claims is owed him, and the Nestorian who claims it has no Jacobite for a guarantor, other guarantors will not be sufficient, if the loan was not made in court, because a Nestorian cannot be a guarantor against a Jacobite, according to the law and the court of Jerusalem. Likewise, if a Jacobite makes a claim in court against a Samaritan, concerning a debt which he owes him, and the Samaritan denies the debt, it is rightly his business to have two Samaritans as guarantors, because other guarantors are not valid for this, according to the law and the court of Jerusalem, because a Jacobite cannot be a guarantor against a Samaritan.

65. If it happens that a Samaritan makes a claim in court against a Saracen, concerning a debt that he owes him, and the Saracen denies that it is owed, it is the business of the Samaritan to have two Saracen guarantors, because other guarantors are not sufficient for the Samaritan, if the business was not done in court, for a Samaritan cannot be a guarantor against a Saracen, according to the court of the kingdom of Jerusalem. Likewise, if a Saracen makes a claim in court against a Jew, concerning a debt which is owed him, and the Jew denies it, it is rightly the Saracen's business to have two Jewish guarantors, and if he does not, other guarantors are not valid, if the loan was not made in court, because a Saracen cannot be a guarantor against a Jew, nor a Jew against a Saracen, nor a Saracen against a Jacobite, nor a Jacobite against a Syrian, for a debt, or for an inheritance, or for any other business, if it is not conducted in court, for the law decrees that concerning this rule, the guarantor must be of the same nationality as the one who makes the claim, as the law decrees: "That no member of any of the aforesaid nationalities is permitted, according to the custom of Jerusalem, to testify against someone of another nationality, in a civil case which is conducted in court."

Tax Rates

1. The old duties command that one should take at the custom house, for the sale of silk, for every 100 bezants, 8 bezants and 19 karoubles, as duty.
2. For the duty on cotton, the rule commands that one should take, per 100 b., 10 b. and 18 k. as duty.
3. For the duty of pepper, the rule commands that one should take, per 100 b., 11 b. and 5 k. as duty.
4. For cinnamon, the rule commands that one should take, per 100 b., 10 b. and 18 k. as duty.
5. For wool, the rule commands that one should take, per 100 b., 11 b. and 10 k. as taxes.
6. For the duty of alum, the rule commands that one should take, per 100 b., 11 b. and 5 k. as duty.
7. For the duty on varnish, the rule commands that one should take, per 100 b., 10 b. and 18 k. as duty.
8. For the duty on nutmegs or on nutmeg leaves, the rule commands that one should take as duty, per 100 b., 8 b. and ⅓ by law.
9. Of flax, the rule commands that one should take, per 100 b., 8 b. and 8 k. as duty.
10. For the duty upon cloves and the leaves of cloves, the rule commands that one should take, per 100 b., 9 b. and ⅓ by law.
11. For the duty on Indian hens, one should take the tenth.
12. For the wares which are brought by sea from the coast of Syria and

which cannot be sold, the rule is that they can be withdrawn and taken out of the country, but if the merchandise which cannot be sold be taken out beyond the chain [at the mouth of the harbor] they must be paid, per 100, for as much as may then be in the country, 8 b. per 100 b., and for that which may have been sold duty must be paid to the custom house according to that which is established for each kind and which one would have to pay. And be it understood that these duties shall be paid by the Saracens and by all the Syrians who may come with wares into this kingdom.

13. For the duty on musk, the rule commands that one should take, per 100 b., 8 b. and ⅓ as duty.

14. For the duty upon aloe wood, the rule commands that one should take 9 b. and ⅓ per 100 b. as duty.

15. For the duty on sugar, for that which is imported and exported by land and by sea, the rule commands that one should take, per 100 b., 5 b. as duty.

16. For the duty per camel's load of sugar, the rule commands that one should take 4 b. as duty.

17. For the duty on sugar which is brought by beasts of burden [other than camels], the rule commands that one should take 1 raboin per load as duty.

18. For all things which are exported by land to be taken to the pagans, the rule commands that one should take as duty per bezant 1k.

19. For the duty for the salt fish which is imported from Babylon, one should take the quarter, that is, of every 4 b., one of the four, as duty.

20. For the duty on flax which is imported from Babylon to Damascus, the rule commands that one should take in transit, for each camel, 1 b. and 2 k. as duty.

21. For the duty on alcana [that is, henna], the rule commands that one should take, for each sack, a duty of 18 ½ k.

22. For the duty on all the spices of retail shopkeepers, the rule commands that one should take as duty, per bezant, 1 k.

23. For the duty on sesame, the rule commands that one should take on importation, per 100 b., 10 b. as duty.

24. For the duty on sesame oil, the rule commands that one should take, per 100 b., 11 b. as duty.

25. For the duty on incense, the rule commands that one should take, per 100 b., 11 b. and 5 k. as duty.

26. The rule for [the spice] cardamom is that the law commands that one should take, per 100 b., 11 b. and 5 k. as duty.

27. For the duty on ivory, the law commands that one should take, per bezant, 2 k. as duty.

28. For the duty on sarcocoll [that is, Persian gum], the rule commands that one should take, per 100 b., 11 b. and 5 k.

29. For the duty on galega [that is, Indian ginger], the rule commands that one should take, per 100 b., 4 b. and 4 k.

30. For the duty upon the twigs and the leaves of lavender, the rule commands that one should take, per 100 b., 4 b. and 4 k.

31. For the duty on myrobalan [that is, a fruit used for dyeing and tanning], the rule commands that one should take, per 100 b., 4 b. and 4 k.

32. For the duty on cinnamon, the rule commands that one should take, per 100 b., 4 b. and 4 k.

33. For the duty on rhubarb, the rule commands that one should take, per 100 b., 4 b. and 3 k. as duty.

34. For the duty on ginger, the rule commands that one should take, per 100, 4 b. and 4 k. as duty.

35. For the duty on camphor, the rule commands that one should take, per 100 b., 11 b. and 8 k. as duty.

36. It is understood that the rule commands that one should take on borage, per 100 b., 11 b. and 5 k. as duty.

37. It is understood that the rule commands that one should take on aspic, per 100 b., 4 b. and 4 k. as duty.

38. It is understood that the rule commands that one should take on gariophylus [that is, a type of clove], per 100 b., 4 b. and 4 k. as duty.

39. It is understood that the rule commands that one should take an internal tax on ammonia, that is, per 100 b., 11 b. and 5 k.

40. It is understood that the rule commands that one should take an internal tax on Nabeth sugar.

41. It is understood that the rule commands that one should take an internal tax on dates.

42. It is understood that the rule commands that one should take on emery, per 100 b., 10 b. as duty.

43. It is understood that the rule commands that one should take on licorice, Saracen and Syrian, 1 and ½ tenths [per 100 b.], but on French [licorice] one should take only 13 b. per 100 b. as duty.

44. It is understood that the rule commands that one should take on sulfur of arsenic, per 100 b., 11 b. and 5 k. as duty.

45. It is understood that the rule commands that one should take on camphor root ... per 100 b., 11 b. and 5 k. as duty.

46. It is understood that the rule commands that one should take, on straps and saddles which are exported from the city, per bezant, 1 k. as duty.

47. It is understood that the rule commands that one should take an internal tax on yellow sulfur of arsenic.

48. It is understood that the rule commands that one should take on frank-incense, per 100 b., 10 b. and 8 k. as duty.

49. It is understood that the rule commands that one should take as duty, on all planks and beams which are exported by land, one quarter of what they cost.

50. It is understood that the rule commands that one should take as duty, on planks used to construct threshing floors, one tenth of what they cost.

51. It is understood that the rule commands that one should take as duty, on salt fish exported from the city, one quarter of what it cost.

52. It is understood that the rule commands that one should take, on fruit, per 100 b., 14 b. as duty....

54. It is understood that the rule commands that one should take as duty, on rafters, per b., 2 k.

55. It is understood that the rule commands that one should take, on olives, 20 b. [per 100 b.]

56. It is understood that the rule commands that one should take, on wine which is brought from Nazareth and from Saphourie and from Safran, per camel load, 12 drachmas as duty.

57. It is understood that the rule commands that one should take an internal tax on thread of Damascus.

58. It is understood that the rule commands that one should take as duty, on senna, per 100 b., 20 b.

59. It is understood that the rule commands that one should take, on red currants, per 100 b., 8 b. and ⅓, which is the amount of the duty.

60. It is understood that the rule commands that one should take, on wine which is imported from Antioch or from Lische or this side, per bezant, 1 k. as duty.

61. It is understood that the rule commands that one should take, on the shoes which the Saracens purchase, as tax on the sale, one tenth [of the value].

62. It is understood that the rule commands that one should take as duty, on wheat, one tenth.

63. It is understood that the rule commands that one should take, on eggs, the tenth as duty.

64. It is understood that the rule commands that one should take as duty, on hens and pullets, one tenth, that is, per 100 b., 10 b.

65. On the goats which are imported from the pagans, the rule commands that one should take one tenth as duty.

66. On geese which are brought into the city, the rule commands that one should take one tenth as duty.

67. On the oil which comes to the custom-house, the rule commands that one should take, per 100 b., 8 b. and 4 k. as duty.

68. On nut gall, the rule commands that one should take as duty 5 b. and 18 k. per 100 b.

69. On the wool which is imported from various parts, the rule commands that one should legally take, per 100 b., 10 b. and 18 k.

70. On wax, the rule commands that one should take, per 100 b., 2 b. and 5 k.

71. On pens, the rule commands that one should take an internal tax, that is, 11 b. and 5 k. per 100 b.

Questions: What do the laws reveal about commercial life in this society? How do they address the ethnic diversity of the kingdom? How are some ethnic groups advantaged over others? What kinds of goods were brought into the kingdom of Jerusalem? How were goods transported, and from where? Which items commanded the highest and lowest duties, in terms of percentage of value? Why? What situations are anticipated in these tax laws?

27. THE TRAVELS OF SAEWULF

As soon as the crusaders took Jerusalem, the volume of Christian pilgrimage from Europe increased. The author of the following narrative was an Englishman who went on pilgrimage to the Holy Land in 1102-03, just a few years after the end of the First Crusade. Among the places he describes are two of the most important Christian sites in crusader Jerusalem, the Church of the Holy Sepulcher and, on the Temple Mount, the so-called Temple of the Lord; the latter was actually the seventh-century mosque known as the Dome of the Rock, but it was believed by medieval Christians to be an ancient Jewish temple.

Source: trans. T. Wright, *Early Travels in Palestine* (London: Henry G. Bohn, 1848), pp. 31, 34, 36-40, 44, 46-48; revised.

I, Saewulf, though conscious of my own unworthiness, went to offer up my prayers at the Holy Sepulcher....

After leaving the isle of Cyprus, we were tossed about by tempestuous weather for seven days and seven nights, being forced back one night almost to the spot from which we sailed; but after much suffering, by divine mercy, at sunrise on the eighth day, we saw before us the coast of the port of Joppa, which filled us with an unexpected and extraordinary joy. Thus, after a course of thirteen weeks ... we put into the port of Joppa, with great rejoicings and thanksgivings, on a Sunday.... I was suddenly seized with a great desire of landing, and, having hired a boat, went into it, with all my companions; but, before I had reached the shore, the sea was troubled, and became continually more tempestuous. We landed, however, with God's grace, without hurt, and

Fig. 9: Twelfth-century map of Jerusalem. North is to the left. Bethlehem is shown in the lower right corner, while Nazareth is indicated by the small domed building near the top, just outside Jerusalem. Inside the city walls, the Temple of the Lord (the Dome of the Rock) is shown as a round shape at the top of the circle, the Temple of Solomon (the Al-Aqsa Mosque) is the complex building in the upper right quarter, and the Church of the Holy Sepulcher is the round shape near the bottom. Pilgrims and other travelers are also depicted. From J.R. MacPherson, ed., *Fetellus* (London, Palestine Pilgrims' Text Society, 1896).

entering the city weary and hungry, we secured a lodging, and reposed ourselves that night....

We went up from Joppa to the city of Jerusalem, a journey of two days, by a
mountainous road, very rough, and dangerous on account of the Saracens, who
lie in wait in the caves of the mountains to surprise those less capable of resisting by the smallness of their company, or the weary, who may chance to lag
behind their companions. At one moment, you see them on every side; at
another, they are altogether invisible, as may be witnessed by anybody traveling
there. Numbers of human bodies lie scattered in the way, and by the wayside,
torn to pieces by wild beasts. Some may, perhaps, wonder that the bodies of
Christians are allowed to remain unburied, but it is not surprising when we
consider that there is not much earth on the hard rock to dig a grave; and if
earth were not wanting, who would be so simple as to leave his company, and
go alone to dig a grave for a companion? Indeed, if he did so, he would be
digging a grave for himself rather than for the dead man. For on that road, not
only the poor and weak, but the rich and strong, are surrounded with perils....
We, however, with all our company, reached the end of our journey in safety.
Blessed be the Lord, who did not turn away my prayer, and has not turned his
mercy from me....

The entrance to the city of Jerusalem is from the west, under the citadel of
King David, by the gate which is called the gate of David. The first place to be
visited is the church of the Holy Sepulcher, ... not only because the streets
lead most directly to it, but because it is more celebrated than all the other
churches; and that rightly and justly, for all the things which were foretold and
forewritten by the holy prophets of our Savior Jesus Christ were there actually
fulfilled. The church itself was royally and magnificently built, after the discovery of our Lord's cross, by the archbishop Maximus, with the patronage of the
emperor Constantine, and his mother Helena. In the middle of this church is
our Lord's Sepulcher, surrounded by a very strong wall and roof, lest the rain
should fall upon the holy sepulcher, for the church above is open to the sky....

In the court of the church of our Lord's Sepulcher are seen some very holy
places, namely, the prison in which our Lord Jesus Christ was confined after he
was betrayed...; then, a little above, appears the place where the holy cross and
the other crosses were found, where afterwards a large church was built in
honor of Queen Helena, but which has since been utterly destroyed by the
pagans; and below, not far from the prison, stands the marble column to which
our Lord Jesus Christ was bound in the common hall, and scourged with most
cruel stripes. Near this is the place where our Lord was stripped of his garments by the soldiers; and next, the place where he was clad in a purple vest by
the soldiers, and crowned with the crown of thorns, and they cast lots for his
garments. Next we ascend Mount Calvary, where the patriarch Abraham

raised an altar, and prepared, by God's command, to sacrifice his own son; there afterwards the Son of God, whom he prefigured, was offered up as a sacrifice to God the Father for the redemption of the world. The rock of that mountain remains a witness of our Lord's passion, being much cracked near the foss [that is, the crevice] in which our Lord's cross was fixed....

We descend from our Lord's sepulcher, about the distance of two arbalest-shots, to the Temple of the Lord, which is to the east of the Holy Sepulcher, the court of which is of great length and breadth, having many gates; but the principal gate, which is in front of the Temple, is called "the beautiful," on account of its elaborate workmanship and variety of colors.... In the middle of [the] Temple is seen a high and large rock, hollowed beneath, in which was the Holy of Holies. In this place Solomon placed the Ark of the Covenant, having the manna and the rod of Aaron, ... and the two tablets of the Testament [that is, the Ten Commandments]; ... here the child Jesus was circumcised on the eighth day, and named Jesus, which is interpreted [as meaning] Savior; here the Lord Jesus was offered by his parents, with the Virgin Mary, on the day of her purification, and received by the aged Simeon; here, also, when Jesus was twelve years of age, he was found sitting in the midst of the doctors, hearing and interrogating them, as we read in the Gospel; here afterwards he cast out the oxen, and sheep, and pigeons, saying, "My house shall be a house of prayer;" and here he said to the Jews, "Destroy this temple, and in three days I will raise it up."...

The city of Bethlehem in Judea is six miles to the north of Jerusalem. The Saracens have left nothing there habitable, but everything is destroyed (as in the other holy places outside the walls of the city of Jerusalem) except the monastery of the blessed Virgin Mary, which is a large and noble building....

The city of Nazareth of Galilee, where the blessed Virgin Mary received the salutation of our Lord's nativity from the angel, is about four days' journey from Jerusalem.... The city of Nazareth is entirely laid waste and overthrown by the Saracens; but the place of the annunciation of our Lord is indicated by a very noble monastery....

Having, to the best of our power, visited and paid our devotion at all the holy places in the city of Jerusalem and the surrounding country, we took ship at Joppa on the day of Pentecost, on our return; but, fearing to meet the fleet of the Saracens, we did not venture out into the open sea by the same course we came, but sailed along the coast by several cities, some of which have fallen into the hands of the Franks, while others still remain in the power of the Saracens....

Questions: What perils did European pilgrims face in going to Jerusalem? What signs are there in the text of the short time that had elapsed since the First Crusade? How does Saewulf describe the condition of the Holy Land? How does the biblical past live for him in the places he has visited? How does his pilgrimage experience compare with that of Etheria (doc. 1)?

28. JOHN OF WURZBURG'S PILGRIM GUIDE

John of Wurzburg, a German priest, visited Palestine during the 1160s and wrote a typical pilgrim guidebook describing the holy sites, borrowing in places from other similar texts. His description of the major churches of Jerusalem is considered especially valuable by historians.

Source: trans. A. Stewart, *Description of the Holy Land by John of Wurzburg* (London: Palestine Pilgrims' Text Society, 1896), pp. 15-21, 35-41, 69; revised.

Now this same Temple of the Lord, which has been adorned by someone both within and without with a wondrous casing of marble, has the form of a beautiful rotunda, or rather of a circular octagon—that is, having eight angles disposed in a circle, with a wall decorated on the outside from the middle upwards with the finest mosaic work, for the remainder is of marble. This same lower wall is continuous, save that it is pierced by four doors, having one door towards the east, which adjoins a chapel dedicated to St. James.... On the north side it has a door leading to the canons' cloisters, upon the lintel whereof many Saracen letters are inscribed.... At the entrance to the Temple towards the west, above the vestibule, is an image of Christ, with this inscription around it: "My house shall be called the house of prayer." It also has a door on the south, looking toward the building of Solomon. On the west also it has a door looking towards the Sepulcher of our Lord, where also is the beautiful gate.... Each of the doorways has a handsome porch.

So much for the lower part of the wall; now in the upper part of the said wall, I mean where the admirable mosaic work is, there are windows inserted in such a manner that there are five on each of the eight sides, except the sides on which the doors of the Temple are, which contain only four windows; and the whole number of the windows is thirty-six. Between this external circumscribing wall and the inner great marble columns—which are twelve in number, and support the inner, narrower, higher, and altogether round wall, which is pierced by twelve windows, and has beneath it four piers of squared stones—between the former, I say, and the latter are sixteen columns and eight piers of squared marble, with a space of eight paces between them, which piers sustain on either side a roof, between the outer wider wall and the inner and narrower one, with most beautifully adorned beams above them support-

Fig. 10: The Temple Mount, in a late fifteenth-century woodcut. Published in the *Nuremberg Chronicle*, 1493.

ing the roof itself, affording an uninterrupted space for walking in any direction, and having leaden pipes to carry off the rain water. Above this narrower wall is raised on high a round vault, painted within, and covered without with lead, on the summit of which the figure of the holy cross has been placed by the Christians, which is very offensive to the Saracens, and many of them would be willing to expend much gold to have it taken away; for although they do not believe in Christ's passion, nevertheless they respect this Temple, because they adore their creator therein, which nevertheless must be regarded as idolatry on the authority of St. Augustine, who declares that everything is idolatry which is done without faith in Christ....

This Temple, so beautifully built and adorned, has on all sides of it a wide and level platform, paved with stones fitted together, which platform is of a square shape, and is ascended on three sides by many steps. Indeed, this platform is very ingeniously built up, in consequence of the nature of the ground. It has in its east wall a wide entrance through five arches, which are connected by four great columns, and this wall opens thus towards the Golden gate, through which our Lord on the fifth day before his Passion rode in triumph, sitting upon an ass, and was greeted by Jewish boys with palm branches, who sang praises and said, "Hosanna to the Son of David," etc. This gate by the divine protection has always remained unharmed, although since that time Jerusalem has often been captured and destroyed by hostile armies. This gate, moreover, in pious remembrance of our Lord's divine and mystic entrance when he came up from Bethany over the Mount of Olives to Jerusalem, is closed within, and blocked up with stones outside, and is never opened to anyone except on Palm Sunday, on which day every year, in memory of what there took place, it is solemnly opened to a procession and to the whole people, whether they be citizens or strangers. After the patriarch [of Jerusalem] has preached a sermon to the people at the foot of the Mount of Olives, when the service for that day is over, it is closed again for a whole year as before, except on the day of the Exaltation of the Holy Cross, upon which also it is opened....

As you descend the chief street there is a great gate, by which entrance is obtained into the wide courtyard of the Temple. On the right hand towards the south is the palace which Solomon is said to have built, wherein is a wondrous stable of such size that it is able to contain more than 2,000 horses or 1,500 camels. Close to this palace the Knights Templars have many spacious and connected buildings, and also the foundations of a new and large church which is not yet finished. For that house possesses much property and countless revenues both in that country and elsewhere. It gives a considerable amount of alms to the poor in Christ, but not a tenth part of that which is done by the Hospitallers. The house also has very many knights for the defense of the land of the Christians; but they have the misfortune, I know not whether truly or falsely, to have their fair fame aspersed with the reproach of treachery, which indeed was clearly proved in the well known affair of Damascus under King Conrad [that is, when the Templars allegedly accepted bribes from the enemy to persuade the king to lift the siege]....

The monument which contains the Holy Sepulcher of our Lord is almost round in form, and is decorated inside with mosaic work. It is entered from the east through a little door, in front of which is an antechamber of almost square shape, with two doors. Through one of these, persons entering the monument are admitted to the sepulcher, and through the other those who are leaving it pass out. In that antechamber also the guardians of the sepulcher dwell. It has also a third little door, which opens towards the choir. Outside this same monument, that is to say at the head of the sepulcher, there is an altar with a kind of square canopy built over it, whose three walls are beautifully formed of iron lattice work, and this altar is called the altar of the Holy Sepulcher. The monument has above it a cup-like dome, the upper surface of which is covered with silver, and which rises high in the air towards the wide space open to the sky, which is made in the larger building above it, which building being of a round form, on a circular ground plan, with a wide space all round the monument, has at its end a continuous wall adorned with painted figures of various saints on a large scale and lighted by numerous lamps. In the narrower circuit of this larger building eight round columns of marble, and the

Fig. 11: Façade and dome of the Church of the Holy Sepulcher, as it appeared in 1874, showing twelfth-century decoration. From P. Lacroix, *Military and Religious Life in the Middle Ages* (London, Chapman and Hall, 1874).

same number of square bases, adorned outside with the same number of marble slabs, and placed all round [the central point], sustain an entablature under the roof, which we have said is open in the middle....

We have said that the aforesaid number of columns are arranged in a circle; but now on the eastern side their number and arrangement are altered, because of the new church which has been built onto them, the entrance into which is at that point. This new and newly-added building contains a spacious choir of the canons, and a spacious sanctuary, which contains a high altar dedicated in honor of the ... Holy Resurrection, as is shown by a picture in mosaic work placed above it. For this picture contains the figure of Christ rising, having burst the gates of hell, and bringing up our ancient father Adam from thence. Outside the sanctuary of this altar and within the circuit of the cloister is contained a space sufficiently wide in all directions, both through this new church and also through the old building round about the aforementioned monument, to be suitable for a procession, which takes place every Sunday night from Easter to Advent at vespers, to the Holy Sepulcher.... In the like fashion the mass of the resurrection is celebrated on every Sunday throughout this time....

On [July 16], both in the giving of alms and in the prayers, they make solemn mention of all the faithful dead, more especially of those who fell on the occasion of the storming of Jerusalem, whose burying-place near the Golden Gate is most famous. Three days afterwards is the anniversary of [the death of] noble Duke Godfrey of happy memory, the chief and leader of that holy expedition, who was born of a German family. His anniversary is solemnly observed by the city with plenteous giving of alms in the great church, according as he himself arranged while yet alive.

But although he is there honored in this way for himself, yet the taking of the city is not credited to him with his Germans, who bore no small share in the toils of that expedition, but is attributed to the French alone.... Although, however, Duke Godfrey and his brother Baldwin, who was made king in Jerusalem after him, which the duke had through humility refused to be before him, were men of our country, yet since only a few of our people remained there with them, and very many of the others with great haste and homesickness returned to their native land, the entire city has fallen into the hands of other nations — Frenchmen, Lorrainers, Normans, Provençals, Auvergnats, Italians, Spaniards, and Burgundians, who took part in the crusade; and also no part of the city, not even in the smallest street, was set apart for the Germans. As they themselves took no care about the matter, and had no intention of remaining there, their names were never mentioned, and the glory of delivering the holy City was ascribed to the Franks alone; and they at this day, together with the aforesaid nations, bear rule in the aforesaid city and the neighboring country. Indeed, this province of Christendom would long ago have extended its boundaries beyond the Nile to the southward, and beyond Damascus to the northward, if there were therein as great a number of Germans as there are of the others....

Thus, as well as I am able, I have described the holy places in the sacred city, starting from the Church of the Holy Sepulcher, and going round about, through the gate of David, till I returned to the same place. I have omitted many of the chapels and smaller churches which are maintained there by men of various nations and languages. For there are Greeks, Bulgarians, Latins, Germans, Hungarians, Scots, Navarrese, Bretons, English, Franks, Ruthenians, Bohemians, Georgians, Armenians, Jacobites, Syrians, Nestorians, Indians, Egyptians, Copts, Capheturici, Maronites, and very many others, whom it would take long to tell: so with these let us make an end of this little work. Amen.

Questions: How are the major churches of Jerusalem decorated? What signs are there of their history? How does John's description of the Temple and the Holy Sepulcher compare with Saewulf's, written some sixty years earlier? What do we learn about crusader society? How does John's nationality enter into his description?

29. THE TRAVELS OF IBN JUBAYR

Abu 'l-Husayn Mohammed Ibn Ahmad Ibn Jubayr, a well-educated professional from the Muslim state of Granada in Spain, made a pilgrimage to Mecca in the early 1180s. His journey home took him north to Damascus and then through Frankish territory in order to catch a ship from Acre to Spain. In his account he mentions Saladin, a great Muslim leader whose achievements are described in Chapter IV (docs. 39, 40). (The dinar was a gold coin minted by many Mediterranean states, equivalent to the Greek bezant. The parasang is a Persian measure equal to about three miles.)

Source: trans. R.J.C. Broadhurst, *The Travels of Ibn Jubayr* (London: Jonathan Cape, 1952), pp. 313-22.

We left Damascus on the evening of Thursday the ... 13th of September [1184], in a large caravan of [Christian] merchants traveling with their merchandise to Acre. One of the strangest things in the world is that Muslim caravans go forth to Frankish lands, while Frankish captives enter Muslim lands. In this regard, as we were leaving, we observed a singular event. When Saladin was laying siege to the fortress of Kerak, ... taking advantage of the opening that fell to him, Saladin schemed an incursion on [Frankish] country. Unexpectedly he arrived at the city of Nablus and attacked it with his soldiers and took it. He took prisoner all within it and seized with it fortified places and villages.... The sultan [that is, Saladin] reached Damascus the first Saturday after our departure, and we learnt that he will rest his soldiers a little and then return to the fortress of Kerak. May God assist him, and in his power and glory cause it to fall to him. We ourselves went forth to Frankish lands at a time when Frankish prisoners were entering Muslim lands. Let this be evidence enough to you of the temperateness of the policy of Saladin.

We passed the night of Friday in Darayah, a village belonging to Damascus, and one and a half parasangs from it. We removed from there at daybreak on Friday to a village called Bait Jann, which lies among the hills. Thence we left, on the morning of Saturday, for the city of Banyas. Halfway on the road, we came upon an oak-tree of great proportions and with wide-spreading branches. We learnt that it is called "The Tree Measure," and when we enquired concerning it, we were told that it was the boundary on this road between security and danger, by reason of some Frankish brigands who prowl and rob thereon. He whom they seize on the Muslim side, be it by the length of the arms or a span, they capture; but he whom they seize on the Frankish side at a like distance, they release. This is a pact they faithfully observe and is one of the most pleasing and singular conventions of the Franks....

We moved from Tibnin — may God destroy it — at daybreak on Monday. Our way lay through continuous farms and ordered settlements, whose inhabitants were all Muslims, living comfortably with the Franks. God protect us from such temptation. They surrender half their crops to the Franks at harvest time, and pay as well a poll-tax of one dinar and five qirat for each person. Other than that, they are not interfered with, save for a light tax on the fruits of trees. Their houses and all their effects are left to their full possession. All the coastal cities occupied by the Franks are managed in this fashion, their rural districts, the villages and farms, belonging to the Muslims. But their hearts have been seduced, for they observe how unlike them in ease and comfort are their brethren in the Muslim regions under their [Muslim] governors. This is one of the misfortunes afflicting the Muslims. The Muslim community bewails the injustice of a landlord of its own faith, and applauds the conduct of its opponent and enemy, the Frankish landlord, and is accustomed to justice from him....

On the same Monday, we alighted at a farmstead a parasang distant from Acre. Its headman is a Muslim, appointed by the Franks to oversee the Muslim workers in it. He gave generous hospitality to all members of the caravan, assembling them, great and small, in a large room in his house, and giving them a variety of foods and treating all with liberality. We were amongst those who attended this party, and passed the night there. On the morning of Tuesday the ... 18th of September, we came to the city of Acre — may God destroy it. We were taken to the custom-house, which is a khan [that is, a building] prepared to accommodate the caravan. Before the door are stone benches, spread with carpets, where are the Christian clerks of the customs with their ebony ink-stands ornamented with gold. They write Arabic, which they also speak…. The merchants deposited their baggage there and lodged in the upper story. The baggage of any who had no merchandise was also examined in case it contained concealed [and dutiable] merchandise, after which the owner was permitted to go his way and seek lodging where he would. All this was done with civility and respect, and without harshness and unfairness. We lodged beside the sea in a house which we rented from a Christian woman and prayed God most high to save us from all dangers and help us to security….

Acre is the capital of the Frankish cities in Syria, the unloading place of [ships]… and a port of call for all ships. In its greatness it resembles Constantinople. It is the focus of ships and caravans, and the meeting-place of Muslim and Christian merchants from all regions. Its roads and streets are choked by the press of men, so that it is hard to put foot to ground. Unbelief and unpiousness there burn fiercely, and pigs and crosses abound. It stinks and is filthy, being full of refuse and excrement. The Franks ravished it from Muslim hands…, and the eyes of Islam were swollen with weeping for it; it was one of its griefs. Mosques became churches and minarets bell-towers, but God kept undefiled one part of the principal mosque, which remained in the hands of the Muslims as a small mosque where strangers could congregate to offer the obligatory prayers. Near its mihrab [that is, a niche showing the direction of Mecca] is the tomb of the prophet Salih — God bless and preserve him and all the prophets. God protected this part [of the mosque] from desecration by the unbelievers for the benign influence of this holy tomb….

[Tyre] has become proverbial for its impregnability, and he who seeks to conquer it will meet with no surrender or humility. The Franks prepared it as a refuge in case of unforeseen emergency, making it a strong point for their safety. Its roads and streets are cleaner than those of Acre. Its people are by disposition less stubborn in their unbelief, and by nature and habit they are kinder to the Muslim stranger. Their manners, in other words, are gentler. Their dwellings are larger and more spacious. The state of the Muslims in this city is easier and more peaceful….

An alluring worldly spectacle deserving of record was a nuptial procession which we witnessed one day near the port in Tyre. All the Christians, men and women, had assembled, and were formed in two lines at the bride's door. Trumpets, flutes, and all the musical instruments were played until she proudly emerged between two men who held her right and left [hands] as though they were her kindred. She was most elegantly garbed in a beautiful dress from which trailed, according to their traditional style, a long train of golden silk. On her head she wore a golden diadem covered by a net of woven gold, and on her breast was a like arrangement. Proud she was in her ornaments and dress, walking with little steps of half a span, like a dove, or in the manner of a wisp of cloud. God protect us from the seduction of the sight. Before her went Christian notables in their finest and most splendid clothing, their trains falling behind them. Behind her were her peers and equals of the Christian women, parading in their richest apparel and proud of bearing in their superb ornaments. Leading them all were the musical instruments. The Muslims and other Christian onlookers formed two ranks along the route, and gazed on them without reproof. So they passed along until they brought her to the house of the groom; and all that day they feasted. We thus were given the chance of seeing this alluring sight, from the seducement of which God preserve us....

There can be no excuse in the eyes of God for a Muslim to stay in any infidel country, save when passing through it, while the way lies clear in Muslim lands. They will face pains and terrors such as the abasement and destitution of the capitation [that is, a tax on non-Christians] and more especially, amongst their base and lower orders, the hearing of what will distress the heart in the reviling of him [that is, Mohammed] whose memory God has sanctified, and whose rank he has exalted; there is also the absence of cleanliness, the mixing with the pigs, and all the other prohibited matters too numerous to be related or enumerated. Beware, beware of entering their lands....

Questions: Compare this account with the Christian travelers' accounts above. What are the concerns of this traveler? How does he describe the crusader states? What are the relations between Franks and Muslims? What does the author mean by "seduction" in his description of the Frankish wedding procession?

30. MEMOIRS OF USAMAH IBN MUNQIDH

Usamah Ibn Munqidh, a Syrian prince and diplomat whose life spanned most of the twelfth century, wrote his memoirs as a collection of anecdotes drawn from his own experiences for the purposes of moral and practical instruction. He spent most of his later life in Damascus but had traveled extensively in Syria, Palestine, and Egypt, and he had a wide circle of acquaintances.

Source: trans. G.R. Potter, *The Autobiography of Ousâma*, by Ousâma Ibn Mounkidh (London: George Routledge & Sons, Ltd., 1929), pp. 86-87, 164-65, 172-73, 176-77, 184-85.

Relations with the Franks

The Franks (may Allah turn from them!) have none of the virtues of men except bravery. It is only the knights who are given prominence and superiority among them. The knights are really the only men who count among them. They are also considered as the arbiters of councils, judgments, and decisions. One day I demanded justice of them for some flocks of sheep which the [Frankish] lord of [Banyas] had taken in the forest. Just then there was peace between us, and I was living at Damascus. I said to King Fulk [of Jerusalem], son of King Fulk: "This lord has committed an act of hostility against us and has carried off our flocks. It was at the time when the sheep were lambing; their lambs died at birth. He has given them back to us after he has caused the death of their offspring."

The king at once said to six or seven knights: "Hold a session and do him justice." They left the room, went apart, and discussed the matter until they had come to an agreement. They then returned to the room where the king held audience and said, "We have decided that the lord of [Banyas] is bound to compensate them for the loss that he has caused them by the death of their lambs." The king ordered him to pay this debt. He entreated, importuned, and implored me; finally I accepted 400 dinars as payment from him. Now, once a decision has been pronounced by the knights, neither the king nor any other chief of the Franks can alter it or diminish it, such is the importance of the knight in their eyes!

The king said to me: "O Usamah, by the truth of my religion, yesterday I experienced an exceeding great joy." I answered, "May Allah make the king joyful! What have you had to be joyful about?" The king answered, "I have been told that you are a noble knight. I hadn't the least idea that you were a knight." "My master," [I] answered, "I am a knight after the manner of my race and my family." What they specially admire about a knight is his thinness and tallness....

Among the Franks who had been taken to my father's house [as captives] was an old woman with one of her daughters, young and well formed, and a stalwart son. The son became a [Muslim] and his [belief] was of a high standard as far as one could judge from his prayers and fasting. He learnt the art of working in marble in the school of an artist who paved my father's house in marble. Then, his stay there being prolonged, my father married him to a woman of a religious family and gave him everything that was necessary for his marriage and to set him up. His wife bore him two sons who grew up in the midst of us. They were five or six years old when their father, the workman Raoul, whose joy they were, set off with them and their mother, taking all he had in his house, to rejoin the Franks at Apamea. He became Christian again, together with his children, after years of [Islam], prayer, and faith. May Allah the most high cleanse the world of this race!

...I will report some Frankish characteristics and my surprise as to their intelligence.

In the army of King Fulk, son of King Fulk, there was a respectable Frankish knight who had come from their country to make a pilgrimage and then return. He made my acquaintance and became so intimate with me that he called me "my brother." We liked one another and were often together. When he got ready to go back over the sea and return to his own country, he said to me, "My brother, I am returning home and I should like, with your permission, to take your son with me to bring him to our countries." (I had with me my son, aged fourteen.) "He will see our knights, and he will learn wisdom and knowledge of chivalry there. When he returns, he will have taken on the bearing of an intelligent man." My ear was hurt by his words, which did not come from a wise head. If my son had been taken prisoner, captivity could have brought him no worse fate than to be taken to the Frankish countries. I answered, "By your life, that was my intention, but I have been prevented by the affection that his grandmother, my mother, has towards my son. She let him leave with me only after making me swear to bring him back to her." "Is your mother still living then?" he asked. "Yes," I replied. He said to me, "Don't disappoint her."...

It is always those who have recently come to live in Frankish territory who show themselves more inhuman than their predecessors who have been established amongst us and become familiarized with the [Muslims].

A proof of the harshness of the Franks (the scourge of Allah upon them!) is to be seen in what happened to me when I visited Jerusalem. I went into the mosque al-Aqsa. By the side of this was a little mosque which the Franks had converted into a church. When I went into the mosque al-Aqsa, which was occupied by the Templars, who were my friends, they assigned me this little mosque in which to say my prayers. One day I went into it and glorified Allah. I was engrossed in my praying when one of the Franks rushed at me, seized me, and turned my face to the east, saying, "That is how to pray!" A party of Templars made for him, seized his person, and ejected him. I returned

THE CRUSADES: A READER

to my prayers. The same man, escaping attention, made for me again and turned my face round to the east, repeating, "That is how to pray!" The Templars again made for him and ejected him; then they apologized to me and said to me, "He is a stranger who has only recently arrived from Frankish lands. He has never seen anyone praying without turning to the east." I answered, "I have prayed sufficiently for today." I went out and was astonished to see how put out this demon was, how he trembled and how deeply he had been affected by seeing anyone pray in the direction of the *qiblah* [that is, the niche pointing toward Mecca]....

The Franks understand neither the feeling of honor nor the nature of jealousy. If one of them is walking with his wife and he meets another man, the latter takes the woman's hand and goes and talks to her while the husband stands aside waiting for the end of the interview. If the woman prolongs it unreasonably, the husband leaves her alone with her companion and goes [on his way]....

Among the Franks, we notice those who have come to dwell in our midst and who have become accustomed to the society of [Muslims]. They are greatly superior to those who have more recently joined them in the country which they occupy. They form, in fact, an exception which must not be made into a rule.

Thus, I sent one of my friends to Antioch to settle some business. At this time the chief of the city was Theodoros Sophianos. There were bonds of friendship between us. His authority prevailed in Antioch. One day he said to my friend: "I have received an invitation from one of my Frankish friends; come with me and see their customs."

This is what my friend told me: "I went with him and we entered the house of one of the old knights who had come on the first Frankish expedition. He had been struck off the subsidy rolls and exempted from all military service, and in addition had been endowed with a fief at Antioch, from which he obtained his livelihood. At his order, they brought in a magnificent table furnished with the purest and most perfect food. However, my host noticed that I abstained from eating. 'Eat,' he said to me, 'you will find it good. For I do not eat Frankish food, but I have Egyptian cooks and eat only what they cook. Further, no pork ever comes into my house.' I decided to eat, but with care. Then we took our leave of our host. Some days later, I was going through the marketplace when a Frankish woman attached herself to me, uttering barbarous cries in their language, and I did not understand a word that she was saying. A crowd gathered round me. They were Franks, and I began to feel that my death was near. Just then, this same knight appeared. He saw me, came up, and said to the woman, 'What have you to do with this [Muslim]?' 'He is,' she said, 'the murderer of my brother Hurso.' Now Hurso was a knight of Apamea who had been killed by a soldier from Hama. The Christian knight reproached the woman, saying, 'You have before you a bourgeois, that is to say, a merchant, who does not fight, and is not even present at battles.' He then reprimanded the assembled crowd, which dispersed. Then he took my hand and went with me. It was thanks to that meal that I escaped certain death."

Muslim Women

On [a day when fighting was going badly for our people], my mother (may Allah have mercy upon her!) distributed my swords and my padded tunics. She went to one of my elder sisters and said to her, "Put on your shoes and your coat." She obeyed and my mother took her to a balcony of the house which dominated the valley to the east. She made her sit down there and sat down herself on the threshold of the door to the balcony. Allah (glory be to him!) gave us the victory over the [enemy]. I came to my house to get one of my weapons and found nothing but scabbards of swords and leather bags for tunics. I asked my mother, "Where are my weapons?" She answered, "Dear

Fig. 12: Muslim woman in a burka, with mesh face panel, from a late medieval wood-cut.

son, I have given the arms to those who were fighting for us, and I did not suppose that you were alive." I then said, "And what is my sister doing here?" She replied, "My dear son, I made her sit on the balcony and I sat behind her. As soon as I should have seen the [enemy] come to us, I would have pushed her and hurled her into the valley, to see her dead rather than taken into captivity among peasants and ravishers." I thanked my mother, and my sister thanked her also, showing her gratitude. In truth this point of honor is stricter than points of honor among men.

An old woman named Fanoun, who had served my grandfather, the emir Abou 'l-Hasan 'Ali (may Allah have mercy upon him!), on this day covered her face with a veil, seized a sword, and rushed into the fight. She did not stop until she saw us get the upper hand and triumph over our enemies.

Questions: What is Usamah's attitude toward the Franks? What do we learn about life in the crusader states and Muslim territories from this text? Compare his account of the Franks with that of Ibn Jubayr, above. Which one is better informed? What does Usamah reveal about Muslim values?

31. THE ITINERARY OF BENJAMIN OF TUDELA

Benjamin of Tudela, a rabbi in the Spanish kingdom of Navarre, traveled throughout the Mediterranean region in the late 1160s. His report on his travels is the only significant Jewish account of the crusader states in the twelfth century.

Source: trans. M.N. Adler, *The Itinerary of Benjamin of Tudela: Critical Text, Translation and Commentary* (New York: Philipp Feldheim, Inc., 1907), pp. 14–27; revised.

[From Tarsus] it is two days' journey to Antioch the great, situated on the river Orontes…. This is the great city which Antiochus the king built. The city lies by a lofty mountain, which is surrounded by the city wall. At the top of the mountain is a well, from which a man appointed for that purpose directs the water by means of twenty subterranean passages to the houses of the great men of the city. The other part of the city is surrounded by the river. It is a strongly fortified city, and is under the sway of Prince Bohemond the Poitevin, surnamed le Baube [that is, the Stammerer]. Ten Jews dwell here, engaged in glass-making, and at their head are Rabbi Mordecai, Rabbi Chayim, and Rabbi Samuel. From here it is two days' journey to Leda, or Ladikiya, where there are about 100 Jews, at their head being Rabbi Chayim and Rabbi Joseph.

Thence it is two days' journey to Gebela, which is Baal-Gad, at the foot of Lebanon. In the neighborhood dwells a people called Al-Hashishim [that is, the Assassins]. They do not believe in the religion of Islam, but follow one of their own folk, whom they regard as their prophet, and all that he tells them to do they carry out, whether for death or life. They call him the sheik Al-Hashishim, and he is known as their elder. At his word these mountaineers go out and come in. Their principal seat is Kadmus, which is Kedemoth in the land of Sihon. They are faithful to each other, but a source of terror to their neighbors, killing even kings at the cost of their own lives. The extent of their land is eight days' journey. And they are at war with the sons of Edom who are called the Franks, and with the ruler of Tripoli…. At Tripoli in years gone by there was an earthquake, when many gentiles [that is, non-Jews] and Jews perished, for houses and walls fell upon them. There was great destruction at that time throughout the land of Israel, and more than 20,000 souls perished.

Thence it is a day's journey to Jubail, which borders on the land of the children of Ammon, and here there are about 150 Jews. The place is under the rule of the Genoese, the name of the governor being William Embriacus…. There are about 200 Jews there, at their head being Rabbi Meir, Rabbi Jacob, and Rabbi Simchah. The place is situated on the sea-border of the land of Israel. From there it is two days' journey to Beirut, or Beeroth, where there are about fifty Jews, at their head being Rabbi Solomon, Rabbi Obadiah, and Rabbi Joseph. Thence it is one day's journey to Sidon, a large city, with about twenty Jews. Ten miles from there a people dwell who are at war with the men of Sidon; they are called Druses, and are pagans of a lawless character. They inhabit the mountains and the clefts of the rocks; they have no king or ruler, but dwell independent in these high places, and their border extends to Mount Hermon, which is a three days' journey. They are steeped in vice…. There are no resident Jews among them, but a certain number of Jewish handicraftsmen and dyers come among them for the sake of trade, and then return, the people being favorable to the Jews. They roam over the mountains and hills, and no man can do battle with them.

From Sidon it is half a day's journey to Sarfend, which belongs to Sidon. Thence it is a half-day to New Tyre, which is a very fine city, with a harbor in its midst. At night-time those that levy dues throw iron chains from tower to tower, so that no man can go forth by boat or in any other way to rob the ships by night. There is no harbor like this in the whole world. Tyre is a beautiful city. It contains about 500 Jews, some of them scholars of the Talmud, at their head being Rabbi Ephraim of Tyre, the Dayan, Rabbi Meir from Carcassonne, and Rabbi Abraham, head of the congregation. The Jews own seagoing vessels, and there are glass-makers amongst them who make that fine Tyrian glassware which is prized in all countries. In the vicinity is found sugar of a high class, for men plant it here, and people come from all lands to buy it. A man can ascend the walls of New Tyre and see ancient Tyre, which the sea has

THE CRUSADES: A READER

now covered, lying at a stone's throw from the new city. And should one care to go forth by boat, one can see the castles, market-places, streets, and palaces in the bed of the sea. New Tyre is a busy place of commerce, to which merchants flock from all quarters.

One day's journey brings one to Acre, the Acco of old, which is on the borders of Asher; it is the commencement of the land of Israel. Situated by the Great [that is, Mediterranean] Sea, it possesses a large harbor for all the pilgrims who come to Jerusalem by ship. A stream runs in front of it, called the brook of Kedumim. About 200 Jews live there, at their head being Rabbi Zadok, Rabbi Japheth, and Rabbi Jonah. From there it is three parasangs to Haifa ... on the seaboard, and on the other side is Mount Carmel, at the foot of which there are many Jewish graves. On the mountain is the cave of Elijah, where the Christians have erected a structure called St. Elias. On the top of the mountain can be recognized the overthrown altar which Elijah repaired in the days of Ahab. The site of the altar is circular, about four cubits remain thereof, and at the foot of the mountain the brook Kishon flows. From here it is four parasangs to Capernaum, which is the village of Nahum....

Six parasangs from here is Caesarea, ... and here there are about 200 Jews and 200 Cuthim. These are the Jews of Shomron, who are called Samaritans. The city is fair and beautiful, and lies by the sea. It was built by Caesar, and called after him Caesarea. Thence it is half a day's journey to Kako.... There are no Jews here. Thence it is half a day's journey to Sebastiya, which is the city of Samaria, and here the ruins of the palace of Ahab the son of Omri may be seen. It was formerly a well-fortified city by the mountainside, with streams of water. It is still a land of brooks of water, gardens, orchards, vineyards, and olive groves, but no Jews dwell here. Thence it is two parasangs to Nablus, ... where there are no Jews; the place is situated in the valley between Mount Gerizim and Mount Ebal, and contains about 1,000 Cuthim, who observe the written law of Moses alone, and are called Samaritans. They have priests of the seed [of Aaron], and they call them Aaronim, who do not intermarry with Cuthim, but wed only amongst themselves. These priests offer sacrifices, and bring burnt-offerings in their place of assembly on Mount Gerizim, as it is written in their law — "And thou shalt set the blessing on Mount Gerizim." They say that this is the proper site of the Temple. On Passover and the other festivals they offer up burnt-offerings on the altar which they have built on Mount Gerizim, as it is written in their law — "Ye shall set up the stones upon Mount Gerizim, of the stones which Joshua and the children of Israel set up at the Jordan." They say that they are descended from the tribe of Ephraim. And in the midst of them is the grave of Joseph, the son of Jacob our father, as it is written — "and the bones of Joseph buried they in Shechem." ...

From [Gibeon the Great] it is three parasangs to Jerusalem, which is a small city, fortified by three walls. It is full of people whom the [Muslims] call Jacobites, Syrians, Greeks, Georgians, and Franks, and of people of all tongues. It contains a dyeing-house, for which the Jews pay a small rent annually to the king, on condition that besides the Jews no other dyers be allowed in Jerusalem. There are about 200 Jews [or, alternatively, about four Jews] who dwell under the Tower of David in one corner of the city. The lower portion of the wall of the Tower of David, to the extent of about ten cubits, is part of the ancient foundation set up by our ancestors, the remaining portion having been built by the Muslims. There is no structure in the whole city stronger than the Tower of David. The city also contains two buildings, from one of which—the hospital—there issue forth 400 knights; and therein all the sick who come thither are lodged and cared for in life and in death. The other building is called the Temple of Solomon; it is the palace built by Solomon the king of Israel. Three hundred knights are quartered there, and issue therefrom every day for military exercise, besides those who come from the land of the Franks and the other parts of Christendom, having taken upon themselves to serve there a year or two until their vow is fulfilled. In Jerusalem is the great church called the Sepulcher, and here is the burial-place of Jesus, unto which the Christians make pilgrimages.

Jerusalem has four gates—the gate of Abraham, the gate of David, the gate of Zion, and the gate of Gushpat, which is the gate of Jehoshaphat, facing our ancient Temple, now called the Temple of the Lord. Upon the site of the sanctuary Omar ben al Khataab erected an edifice with a very large and magnificent cupola, into which the gentiles do not bring any image or effigy, but they merely come there to pray. In front of this place is the western wall, which is one of the walls of the Holy of Holies. This is called the Gate of Mercy, and thither come all the Jews to pray before the wall of the court of the Temple. In Jerusalem, attached to the palace which belonged to Solomon, are the stables built by him, forming a very substantial structure, composed of large stones, and the like of it is not to be seen anywhere in the world. There is also visible up to this day the pool used by the [ancient Jewish] priests before offering their sacrifices, and the Jews coming thither write their names upon the wall. The gate of Jehoshaphat leads to the valley of Jehoshaphat, which is the gathering-place of nations. Here is the pillar called Absalom's Hand, and the sepulcher of King Uzziah.

In the neighborhood is also a great spring, called the Waters of Siloam, connected with the brook of Kidron. Over the spring is a large structure dating from the time of our ancestors, but little water is found, and the people of Jerusalem for the most part drink the rainwater, which they collect in cisterns in their houses....

In front of Jerusalem is Mount Zion, on which there is no building, except a place of worship belonging to the Christians. Facing Jerusalem for a distance of three miles are the cemeteries belonging to the Israelites, who in the days of old buried their dead in caves, and upon each sepulcher is a dated inscription, but the Christians destroy the sepulchers, employing the stones thereof in building their houses. These sepulchers reach as far as Zelzah in the territory of Benjamin. Around Jerusalem are high mountains....

From Jerusalem it is two parasangs to Bethlehem, which is called by the Christians Beth-Leon, and close thereto, at a distance of about half a mile, at the parting of the way, is the pillar of Rachel's grave, which is made up of eleven stones, corresponding with the number of the sons of Jacob. Upon it is a cupola resting on four columns, and all the Jews that pass by carve their names upon the stones of the pillar. At Bethlehem there are two Jewish dyers. It is a land of brooks of water, and contains wells and fountains.

At a distance of six parasangs is St. Abram de Bron, which is Hebron; the old city stood on the mountain, but is now in ruins; and in the valley by the field of Machpelah lies the present city. Here there is the great church called St. Abram, and this was a Jewish place of worship at the time of the Muslim rule, but the gentiles have erected there six tombs, respectively called those of Abraham and Sarah, Isaac and Rebekah, Jacob and Leah. The custodians tell the [Christian] pilgrims that these are the tombs of the patriarchs, for which information the pilgrims give them money. If a Jew comes, however, and gives a special reward, the custodian of the cave opens unto him a gate of iron, which was constructed by our forefathers, and then he is able to descend below by means of steps, holding a lighted candle in his hand. He then reaches a cave, in which nothing is to be found, and a cave beyond, which is likewise empty, but when he reaches the third cave behold there are six sepulchers, those of Abraham, Isaac, and Jacob, respectively facing those of Sarah, Rebekah, and Leah. And upon the graves are inscriptions cut in stone; upon the grave of Abraham is engraved "This is the grave of Abraham"; upon that of Isaac, "This is the grave of Isaac, the son of Abraham our father"; upon that of Jacob, "This is the grave of Jacob, the son of Isaac, the son of Abraham our father"; and upon the others, "This is the grave of Sarah," "This is the grave of Rebekah," and "This is the grave of Leah." A lamp burns day and night upon the graves in the cave. One finds there many casks filled with the bones of Israelites, as the members of the house of Israel were wont to bring the bones of their fathers thither and to deposit them there to this day....

Questions: Compare this traveler's account with those of the Christian and Muslim authors above. What makes a site holy for Benjamin? What does he tell us of Jewish economic life in medieval Palestine? Why does he inventory the Jewish presence in the Holy Land? What are the relations between Jews, Muslims, and Christians in this text?

32. BURCHARD OF MOUNT SION ON THE PEOPLE OF PALESTINE

Burchard of Mt. Sion was a German Dominican friar who lived in Palestine from the mid-1270s to the mid-1280s. His description of the Holy Land is considered one of the most reliable and discriminating of the many pilgrim guides written by European visitors. Nevertheless, the following discussion of religions and ethnic groups contains much that is inaccurate.

Source: trans. A. Stewart, *Burchard of Mount Sion* (London: Palestine Pilgrims' Text Society, 1896), pp. 102–08, 111; revised.

There are dwelling therein men of every nation under heaven, and each man follows his own rite, and, to tell the truth, our own people, the Latins, are worse than all the other people of the land. The reason for this, I think, is that when any man [in Europe] has been a malefactor, as, for example, a homicide, a robber, a thief, or an adulterer, he crosses the sea as a penitent, or else because he fears for his skin, and therefore dares not stay at home. Wherefore men come thither from all parts—from Germany, Italy, France, England, Spain, Hungary, and all other parts of the world; yet they do but change their climate, not their mind: for when they are there, after they have spent what they brought with them, they have to earn some more, and therefore return again [like dogs] to their own vomit, and do worse than they did before. They lodge pilgrims of their own nation in their houses, and these men, if they know not how to take care of themselves, trust them, and lose both their property and their honor. They also breed children, who imitate the crimes of their fathers, and thus bad fathers beget sons worse than themselves, from whom descend most vile grandchildren, who tread upon the holy places with polluted feet. Hence it comes to pass that, because of the sins of the dwellers in the land against God, the land itself, and the place of our redemption, is brought into contempt.

Besides the Latins there are many other races there; for example, the Saracens, who preach Mohammed and keep his law. They call our Lord Jesus Christ the greatest of the prophets, and confess that he was conceived of the Holy Ghost and born of the Virgin Mary. But they deny that he suffered and was buried, but choose to say that he ascended into heaven, and sits at the right hand of the Father, because they admit him to be the Son of God. But they declare that Mohammed sits on God's left hand. They are very unclean, and have as many wives as they can feed; yet, nevertheless, they practice unnatural sins, and have *ephebiae* [that is, brothels of young men] in every city. Yet they are very hospitable, courteous, and kindly.

Besides these there are the Syrians. The whole land is full of these. They are Christians, but keep no faith with the Latins. They are clothed most wretchedly, and are stingy, giving no alms. They dwell among the Saracens, and for the most part are their servants. In dress they are like the Saracens, except that they are distinguished from them by a woolen belt.

The Greeks in like manner are Christians, but schismatics, save that a great part of them returned to obedience to the [Roman] church at a General Council held by our lord [Pope] Gregory X [in 1274, in France]. In the Greek church all the prelates are monks, and are men of exceeding austerity of life and wondrous virtue.

The Greeks are exceedingly devout, and for the most part greatly honor and revere their prelates. I have heard one of their patriarchs say in my presence, "We would willingly live in obedience to the church of Rome, and venerate it; but I am much surprised at my being ranked below the inferior clergy, such as archbishops and bishops. Some archbishops and bishops wish to make me, a patriarch, kiss their feet, and do them service, which I do not hold myself bound to do, albeit I would willingly do so for the pope, but for no one else."

There are also Armenians, Georgians, Nestorians, Nubians, Jacobites, Chaldeans, Medes, Persians, Ethiopians, Egyptians, and many other peoples who are Christians. Of those there is an infinite number. Each group of them has its own patriarch and obeys him. Their prelates declare that they would most willingly belong to the church of Rome. Of these the Nestorians, Jacobites, and the like are so named after certain heretics who once were their chiefs.

Moreover, there are in the Holy Land Midianites, who now are called Bedouins and Turcomans, who apply themselves solely to feeding flocks and camels, of which they have exceedingly great numbers. These people have no fixed dwellings, but wherever they learn that there is pasture, thither they go and pitch their tents. They are exceedingly warlike, yet only use swords and lances in battle. They do not use arrows, saying that it is base beyond measure to steal away a man's life with an arrow. They are brave in war, but wear only a red shirt, and over it a large flowing mantle, covering their heads only with a cloth. All Syria is full of them, but for the most part they dwell round about the River Jordan, from Lebanon even to the wilderness of Paran, because there are mountains for sheep and goats, and plains for cattle and camels. The sheep in those parts, and especially the rams, are very big, and have tails of such a size that one tail is as much as three or four men can eat.

Round about the castle of Arachas, beyond Tripoli, up to the castle of Krak des Chevaliers, dwell Saracens called Vannini. Adjoining them are the Saracens called Assassins, who dwell in the mountains beyond Antaradus near the castle of Margat. They have many castles and cities and a fertile land, and are said to have forty thousand fighting men. They have one chief, not by hereditary succession, but by personal merit, who is called the Old Man of the Mountains—not because of his age, but of his wisdom. These people are said to be of Persian origin. I have passed through a part of their country. They are obedient even to death, and at their superior's bidding slay anyone at all, and say that thereby they gain paradise, even if they themselves are slain before they have fulfilled their orders.... The boundary between these people's land and that of the Christians is marked by some stones, on which on the side of the Christians are carved crosses, and on that of the Assassins knives. None of the sultans have hitherto been able to subdue them, but they make their own laws and customs and follow them as they choose. They are a terror to all the nations round about because of their exceeding fierceness.

Now, it must be noted as a matter of fact (although some, who like to talk about what they have never seen, declare the contrary) that the whole East beyond the Mediterranean Sea, even unto India and Ethiopia, acknowledges and preaches the name of Christ, save only the Saracens and some Turcomans who dwell in Cappadocia, so that I declare for certain, as I have myself seen and have heard from others who know, that always in every place and kingdom (besides Egypt and Arabia, where Saracens and other followers of Mohammed chiefly dwell), you will find thirty Christians and more for one Saracen. But the truth is that all the Christians beyond the sea are easterners by nation, and although they are Christians, yet, as they are not much practiced in the use of arms, when they are assailed by the Saracens, Turks, or any other people whatsoever, they yield to them and buy peace and quiet by paying tribute, and the Saracens, or other lords of the land, place their bailiffs and tax-gatherers therein. Hence it arises that their kingdom is said to belong to the Saracens, whereas, as a matter of fact, all the people are Christians save those bailiffs and tax-gatherers and their families, as I have seen with my own eyes in Cilicia and Lesser Armenia, which is subject to the rule of the Tartars [that is, Mongols].... Many, too, are frightened when they are told that in parts beyond seas there dwell Nestorians, Jacobites, Maronites, Georgians, and other sects named after heretics whom the [Roman] church has condemned, where these men are thought to be heretics, and to follow the errors of those after whom they are called. This is by no means true. God forbid! But they are men of simple and devout life; yet I do not deny that there may be fools among them, seeing that even the church of Rome itself is not free from fools....

The chief prelate of the Armenians and Georgians is called the catholicus. I stayed with him for 14 days, and he had with him many archbishops and bishops, abbots, and other prelates. In his diet, his clothes, and his way of life, he was so exemplary, that I have never seen anyone, religious or secular, like him.... He and all his prelates used to fast all Lent on bread and water, and so did the king [of Armenia] and all his nobles, save on the feast of the Annunciation, when in my presence the catholicus allowed himself to eat some fish and drink wine.... I have seen many other very commendable practices in that land, among laymen, clerks, and monks, which in our land would scarce be believed to be done.

Questions: When summarizing Muslim beliefs and characteristics, on what does Burchard focus? How do his knowledge of and attitude toward Islam compare with those of Christian writers encountered in previous chapters? What is his attitude toward the native Christians of the Middle East? Toward his fellow Europeans? What does he tell us about life in Palestine?

CHAPTER FOUR:

THE SECOND AND THIRD CRUSADES

Fig. 13: The great seal of Third Crusade leader Richard I of England, "the Lionheart," reproduced in a nineteenth-century engraving. From C. Knight, *Old England: A Pictorial Museum* (London: James Sangster & Co., 1845).

33. IBN AL-QALANISI ON ZENGI AND NUR AD-DIN

For nearly 44 years after the fall of Jerusalem, the crusaders ruled their new territories with little interference from the surrounding Islamic emirs. Warring among themselves, these emirs lacked the unity necessary to expel the crusaders from the Holy Land. This began to change, however, with the rise of Imad ad-Din Zengi, emir of Mosul and Aleppo, who called a jihad, a holy war, against the crusaders. Zengi was succeeded by his son Nur ad-Din, who worked to expand and consolidate the Islamic forces under the banner of jihad. In the two passages below, Ibn al-Qalanisi, a contemporary of these events, highlights the divisions among the Muslim rulers at the time of Zengi (referred to here by the title "atabeg") and the efforts of his son Nur ad-Din to unite these factions.

Source: trans. H.A.R. Gibb, *The Damascus Chronicle of the Crusades* (London: Luzac & Co., 1932), pp. 256–62, 333–37.

In [August, 1139,] news was received that 'Imad al-Din Atabeg [that is, Zengi], having completed his reorganization of the defense of Ba'albek and its tower, and repaired the breaches in its fortifications, was engaged in making ready for his descent upon the city of Damascus. Subsequently news arrived of his departure thence with the 'askar [that is, armed forces] and of his arrival in the Biqa' in [the autumn].

He dispatched an envoy to the emir Jamal al-Din Mohammed, son of Taj al-Muluk Buri b. Atabeg, lord of Damascus, demanding that he should surrender the city to him and receive in compensation for it whatsoever might be dictated by his choice and suggestion. On the rejection of his demand, he moved from the Biqa' and encamped at Darayya, in the outskirts of Damascus, on Wednesday, 13th Second Rabi' [that is, Dec. 6]. As he was encamping at Darayya the advance guards had become engaged with one another; he captured a number of them, and the remainder fled to the town. Thereafter on Friday, 28th Second Rabi', he advanced to the town with his 'askar in fighting formation.... He defeated a considerable number of the armed bands of the town and the Ghuta, and put them to the sword; some of them suffered death or captivity, others returned to the town either wounded or unharmed. On this day the town was on the verge of destruction, had it not been for the mercy of God. The atabeg returned to his camp with those who had been captured over and above those who had been killed, and refrained from fighting for some days.

[Zengi] continued to send messages and to try to wheedle [the prince] into surrendering the city [of Damascus] and accepting instead Hims, Ba'albek, and what other places he might suggest. Jamal al-Din Mohammed b. Taj al-Muluk inclined to give his consent to this proposal, on account of the guarantee which it offered for the establishment of peace, the sparing of bloodshed, the prosperity of the provinces, and the restoration of calm, but when he asked advice on the matter from others they refused to entertain it. The atabeg continued to deploy his 'askar for attack on occasional days, but without putting vigor into the fighting or rigorously enforcing the blockade, in the desire to spare bloodshed, with the restraint of one who was desirous of peace and loath to engage in combats and despoiling. In First Jumada [which began December 24] Jamal al-Din fell a victim to a lingering disease, which was now more, now less, oppressive, coming and going, diminishing and increasing, until it became so aggravated that all hope of his recovery was lost. Neither medical skill nor the charms of sorcerers availed him against it, and he remained in this condition until he came to his predestined end and passed to the mercy of God on the eve of Friday, 8th Sha'ban [that is, March 29], at the same hour in which his brother Shihab al-Din Mahmud b. Taj al-Muluk (God's mercy upon them both) was assassinated. The people marveled at this coincidence of time and hour, and magnified God and hallowed his name. Jamal al-Din was prepared for burial and buried in the mausoleum of his grandmother in al-Faradis.

The leaders and holders of authority [in Damascus] after his death took counsel together and agreed to fill the gap caused by his loss by setting up his son, the emir 'Adb al-Dawla Abu Sa'id Abaq b. Jamal al-Din Mohammed, in his place. Pledges of loyal obedience and faithful service, confirmed by the most solemn oaths, were duly taken to him in this capacity. Order and administration was established on a sound footing, dissension was brought to an end, disturbance was succeeded by tranquillity, and distress of mind by calmness. 'Imad al-Din [Zengi] Atabeg, on learning of this turn of affairs, advanced with his 'askar towards the city, eager to take advantage of any dissension which might be caused between the leaders by his death, so that he might attain thereby the fulfillment of some of his demands. The case turned out to be contrary to his hopes and the reverse of his imaginings. From none of the troops or armed bands of Damascus did he meet with anything but determination to pursue the struggle and steadfastness in the charge and the combat. He withdrew therefore to his camp weakened in spirit, and downcast at this failure.

Meanwhile an agreement had been [made between the Muslim rulers of Damascus and] the Franks to take common action and support one another, and to unite and join forces in driving off the atabeg and preventing the achievement of his aims. A formal treaty to this effect was signed with solemn oaths and a guarantee of loyal execution of their promise. In consideration of this the Franks asked for a stipulated sum of money to be paid to them forthwith, that it might assist them and strengthen them in their undertaking, and for a number of hostages to ensure their ease of mind. Their requests were granted; the money was paid to them and hostages sent from among the relatives of the commanders. Thereupon they began to make preparations to send reinforcement and to give support, and they wrote letters to one another urging them to assemble from all the castles and cities in order to drive off the atabeg and prevent him from attaining his ambition at Damascus, before he should become too firmly settled to be dislodged and his might should become invincible, and he should be victorious over the Frankish bands and attack their cities.

The atabeg, on his part, on learning the truth of the position in regard to this decision and to their assembling together to attack him in conjunction with the army of Damascus, retired from his camp at Darayya on Sunday, 15th Ramadan [that is, May 4], and made for Hawran, in order to oppose the Franks if they should approach him, and to pursue them if they should keep at a distance from him. He pursued this policy for some time, and then returned to the Ghuta of Damascus and encamped at 'Adhra' on Wednesday, 24th Shawwal [that is, June 12]. Having burned a number of farms in the Marj and the Ghuta as far as Harasta al-Tin, he withdrew northwards on the following Saturday, on learning that the Franks had encamped with all their forces at al-Madan.

The terms of the treaty with the Franks provided, amongst the promises made to them, for the recapture of the frontier fort of Banyas from Ibrahim b. Turghut and its surrender to them. Now it happened that Ibrahim b. Turghut, its governor, had gone out with his party towards [Frankish-held] Tyre, in order to raid it, and there encountered Raymond, lord of Antioch, on his way to support the Franks in giving assistance to the men of Damascus. They engaged in battle, and Raymond routed Turghut, who was himself killed in the encounter together with a few of his party. The remainder of them returned to Banyas, fortified themselves in it, and mustered for its defense the men of Wadi'l-Taim and elsewhere, and all whom they could collect. The emir Mu'in al-Din marched thither with the 'askar of Damascus, encamped before it, and remained during the whole of Shawwal [which began May 20], engaging it with catapults and besieging it with military operations of various kinds, accompanied by a considerable detachment of the army of the Franks. News was received that the emir 'Imad al-Din Atabeg had alighted before Ba'albek and had sent during Shawwal to summon the Turkmens from their abodes in order to proceed to Banyas and to drive off the besiegers from it. The troops continued operations in this wise until the end of this year.... The siege of Banyas was prosecuted without intermission until the supplies in it were exhausted and the garrison were short of food. It was then surrendered to Mu'in al-Din, and the commander who was in it was compensated with a fief and a benefaction which satisfied him. Mu'in al-Din, having surrendered it to the Franks and carried out the terms of his agreement with them, set out thence to return to Damascus at the end of Shawwal [that is, the middle of June], having achieved his hopes and stultified his labors.

On the morning of Saturday, 7th Dhu'l-Qa'da [that is, June 22], 'Imad al-Din Atabeg appeared outside Damascus with his 'askar on a flying raid. He ... approached the city wall unperceived, as the people were still in the last moments of their sleep. When dawn broke and the news of his arrival became known, shouts and cries were raised and the people rushed to arms and assembled on the walls. The gate was opened and the cavalry and footsoldiers made a sortie. 'Imad al-Din had in the meantime dispersed his 'askar in detachments to Hawran, the Ghuta, the Marj, and all the outlying districts for the purpose of raiding, while he himself remained with his personal guard facing the 'askar of Damascus, in order to prevent any of them from pursuing any of his raiding horsemen. Battle was joined between him and the 'askar of Damascus, and a considerable number of both sides were wounded. He then withdrew from the engagement, owing to his preoccupation with the squadrons whom he had dispersed to carry out the raids. An innumerable quantity of horses at pasture, sheep and goats, cattle, and furnishings fell into their hands, as their raid was so unexpected and took everyone by surprise. The atabeg halted at Marj Rahit on the same day, until his men assembled with their spoils, and set off to return by the northern road carrying a prodigious quantity of booty....

[After Zengi's death in 1146, his son Nur ad-Din took up the jihad against the Franks.]

On Thursday, 27th First Rabi' [that is, May 2], Nur ad-Din arrived in his capital [that is, Aleppo] in order to arrange for the issue of weapons and the dispatch of them to the 'askar. After a stay of a few days he set out at once to join the assembled squadrons of the Turkmens and Arabs, to engage in the holy war with the infidel antagonists. Immediately on his arrival he proceeded to carry out the business on which he had come. He gave orders to dispatch what mangonels [that is, catapults] and weapons were required to the victorious 'askar and to make proclamation in the city calling upon those who had undertaken to engage in the holy war and upon the volunteer bands from both the men of the city and strangers to equip themselves and prepare to wage a struggle with the Franks, the upholders of polytheism and heresy. He himself made haste to set out at once to the victorious 'askar, pressing on his journey without hesitation or delay, on Saturday, the last day of First Rabi', and he was followed up by a vast multitude, imposing in its numbers, of armed bands, volunteers, religious teachers, Sufis, and pious devotees.

On the following Saturday, 7th Second Rabi' [that is, May 18], and after the descent of al-Malik al-'Adil Nur ad-Din upon Banyas with his 'askar and his siege of it with catapults, a carrier-pigeon arrived from the victorious 'askar in the outskirts of Banyas with a letter publishing news of the arrival of a courier from Asad al-Din's camp with the Turkmens and Arabs at Hunin, bringing a report to the following effect. The Franks (God forsake them) dispatched a troop of their principal leaders and warriors, numbering more than a hundred horse exclusive of followers, in order to fall upon this party, imagining that they were only a handful of men and not knowing that they were some thousands strong. When the Franks approached them, the Muslims leapt towards them as lions to their prey and overwhelmed them with slaughter, capture, and spoliation, and none but a few of them escaped. The prisoners, the heads of the slain, and their equipment of ... horses, bucklers, and lances arrived at the city on the Monday following the date mentioned, and were paraded through it, whereupon all hearts were rejoiced and multiplied thanks to God for this further bounty granted in succession to the previous one — may he hasten their destruction and overthrow. This mark of divine favor was followed by the arrival of a carrier-pigeon from the camp at Banyas on Tuesday, the morrow of that day, announcing the capture of the city of Banyas by the sword after four hours had passed of this same Tuesday, when, the sap [that is, tunnel under the walls] having been finished and fire thrown into it, the tower which had been undermined fell down, the troops forced their way in through the gap, plied the sword in slaying its inhabitants and plundered its contents. Those who escaped fled to the citadel, but the siege of them was still proceeding and their capture would not long be delayed by the favor of God most high — may God further it and bring it speedily to pass.

It befell thereafter, in accordance with the foreordained decrees, that the Franks assembled together from their fortresses, with the determination to rescue Humphrey, lord of Banyas, and his Frankish companions who were besieged along with him in the citadel of Banyas. These for their part had come to the verge of destruction and had exerted themselves to obtain terms of capitulation from the lord Nur ad-Din, offering to surrender what they still held of the citadel and all its contents, if they might be released in safety, but he would not consent to their request and desire. When the king of the Franks arrived from the direction of the mountain with his host of horse and foot, taking by surprise the two armies, that which was encamped before Banyas to besiege it, and that which was holding the road in order to prevent access to it, policy necessitated their withdrawal from thence, and the Franks reached the fortress and relieved those who were holding it. When, however, they saw that the wall of Banyas and the dwelling of its inhabitants were entirely in ruins they despaired of rebuilding it after such destruction. This was in the last ten days of Latter Rabi' [that is, June 12-20].

On Wednesday, 9th First Jumada [that is, June 19], the pigeons arrived with letters from the camp of Nur ad-Din conveying information that al-Malik al-'Adil Nur ad-Din, learning that the camp of the Frankish infidels was at al-Mallaha, between Tiberias and Banyas, set out with his victorious 'askar of Turks and Arabs and marched with all speed. When he was almost upon them and they, taken by surprise, saw his standards overshadowing them, they made speed to don their armor and to mount, and dividing into four detachments they charged upon the Muslims. Thereupon the king Nur ad-Din dismounted and his stout warriors dismounted with him, and they smote them with arrows and spears, so that in less time than it takes to tell it, their feet slipped with them and death and destruction overwhelmed them. God, the mighty, the omnipotent, sent down his aid upon his faithful followers and his abandonment upon the stiff-necked infidels; we overpowered their horsemen with slaughter and captivity, and the swords extirpated their footsoldiers. They were a great number and a vast assembly, but none of them escaped, according to the report of a reliable informant, save ten men whom destiny had respited and to whose hearts fear had lent wings. It was said that their king (God curse them) was amongst them, and it was said that he was one of the slain, but no information was obtained concerning him, though a vigorous search was made for him. Of the 'askar of Islam there were lost none but two men, one of whom was a noted warrior, who had slain four of the infidel braves, and was himself slain at the arrival of his destined hour, the other an unknown stranger. Each of them passed away a martyr, rewarded and recompensed (God's mercy upon them). The hands of the 'askeris were filled with an innumerable quantity of the horses, equipment, beasts, and baggage furniture of the Franks, and their church with its famous apparatus came into the hands of the king Nur ad-Din. This was a mighty conquest and manifest aid from God, the powerful, the giver of victory—may God increase thereby the might of Islam and abase polytheism and its faction.

The prisoners and the heads of the slain reached Damascus on the Monday following the date of the victory. They had set the Frankish horsemen in pairs upon camels, each pair being accompanied by one of their standards unfurled, to which were attached a number of skins of their heads with their hair. Their leaders and the commanders of their fortresses and provinces were set each one upon a horse, each wearing his coat of mail and helmet and with a standard in his hand, while the footsoldiers—serjeants and Turcopoles—were roped together in threes or fours or fewer or more. An uncountable number of the townsfolk—old men, young men, women, and children—came out to see what God (exalted is his name) had granted to the whole body of Muslims in this brilliant victory, and they multiplied their praises and glorification to God, and their fervent prayers for al-Malik al-'Adil Nur ad-Din, their defender and protector.

Questions: What accounts for the divisions among the Muslim emirs? Where did they turn for help against each other? Did the Franks work to maintain this unstable situation? What was jihad, *as defined by Nur ad-Din? How did he go about promoting this idea to his potential followers?*

34. IBN AL-ATHIR ON THE FALL OF EDESSA

The fall of Edessa to Zengi's Muslim army in 1144, described in the following selection, was a major turning point in the fortunes of the crusader states. Moreover, the loss of this city was felt deeply throughout Europe and prompted the calling of the Second Crusade. Ibn al-Athir (1160-1223), although writing some time after this event, is nevertheless considered to be one of the most reliable Islamic historians for the crusader period.

Source: trans. E.J. Costello and F. Gabrieli, *Arab Historians of the Crusades*, ed. F. Gabrieli (Berkeley: University of California Press, 1969), pp. 50-52.

On [Dec. 23, 1144] the atabeg 'Imad ad-Din Zengi Ibn Aq Sunqur seized from the Franks the city of Edessa and other forts in the Jazira. The Franks had penetrated far into this area, as far as Amid and Nusaibin, Ras al-'Ain and ar-Raqqa. Their influence extended from near Mardin to the Euphrates, and covered Edessa, Saruj, al-Bira, Sinn Ibn 'Utair, Jamlin, al-Mu'azzar, Quradi and other cities as well. All these and other regions west of the Euphrates belonged to Joscelin, the most famous of the Franks and the leader of their army by virtue of his valor and command of strategy. Zengi knew that if he made a direct attack on Edessa the Franks would concentrate there to defend it, and it was too well fortified to be an easy conquest. He moved to Diyar Bakr, to give the Franks the impression that his interests lay elsewhere and that he was in no position to attack their kingdom. When the Franks felt sure that he could not extract himself from the war he was fighting with the Artuqids and other princes at Diyar Bakr, and so felt safe from him, Joscelin left Edessa and crossed the Euphrates to move westwards. As soon as Zengi's spies informed him of this, he issued orders to his army to set out the next day for Edessa. His emirs were summoned to his presence, and he ordered food to be served. "No one," he said, "shall eat with me at this table unless he is prepared to hurl his lance with me tomorrow at the gates of Edessa." The only ones who dared to come forward were a solitary emir and a youth of humble birth whose bravery and prowess were known to all, for he had no equal in battle. The emir said to [the young man]: "What are you doing here?" but the atabeg intervened: "Leave him, for his, I can see, is not a face that will be lagging behind me in battle."

The army set out and reached the walls of Edessa. Zengi was the first to charge the Franks, but the young man was at his side. A Frankish knight lunged at Zengi from the side, but the emir faced him and transfixed him with his lance, and Zengi was saved.

They besieged the city and attacked it for three weeks. Zengi made several assaults on it, and used sappers to mine the walls. He was straining every nerve in the struggle, for fear that the Franks should marshal their forces and march on him to relieve the fortress. Then the sappers undermined the wall and it collapsed, and Zengi took the city and besieged the citadel. The citizens and their goods were seized, the young taken captive, the men killed. But when Zengi inspected the city he liked it and realized that it would not be sound policy to reduce such a place to ruins. He therefore gave the order that his men should return every man, woman and child to his home together with the goods and chattels looted from them. This was done in all but a very few cases, in which the captor had already left the camp. The city was restored to its former state, and Zengi installed a garrison to defend it. Then he received the surrender of Saruj and other cities west of the Euphrates.

Questions: What kind of a military leader was Zengi? In this and the previous document, what was his attitude toward his conquered enemies? How do the writers of this and the previous document understand historical causation? Given the context of both this and the previous documents, why was Zengi's capture of Edessa a momentous event for the Islamic world?

35. LETTER OF BERNARD OF CLAIRVAUX

The loss of Edessa shocked Europe and prompted a new crusade, of which the Cistercian abbot Bernard of Clairvaux (1090-1153) was, without doubt, the spiritual heart and soul. Called by Pope Eugenius III on December 1, 1145 (see his proclamation of privileges in doc. 46), the Second Crusade was promoted by Bernard and his fellow Cistercian monks throughout Europe through letters, preaching, and overseeing the taking of crusader vows. The letter below is typical of addresses made by Bernard and his followers.

Source: trans. J.H. Robinson, *Readings in European History, Vol.1: From the Breaking up of the Roman Empire to the Protestant Revolution* (Boston: Ginn & Company, 1904), pp. 330-33; revised.

To the lords and very dear fathers, the archbishops and bishops, with the whole clergy and the faithful people of eastern France and Bavaria: Bernard, called abbot of Clairvaux, desires that they may abound in the spirit of strength.

I write to you with respect to a matter which concerns the service of Christ, in whom is our salvation. This I say in order that the Lord's authority may excuse the unworthiness of the person who speaks; let the consideration of its usefulness to yourselves also excuse the faults of my address. I, indeed, am of small account; but I have no small love for you all, in the bowels of Jesus Christ. This, now, is my reason for writing to you, that I may thus approach you as a whole. I would rather do so by word of mouth, if the opportunity, as well as the will, were afforded me.

Fig. 14: The abbey church at Vézelay in France, where Bernard of Clairvaux preached the Second Crusade in 1146. The engraving shows it as it appeared in the nineteenth century. From P. Lacroix, *Military and Religious Life in the Middle Ages* (London, Chapman and Hall, 1874).

Behold, brethren, now is the accepted time, now is the day of salvation. The earth also is moved and has trembled, because the God of heaven has begun to destroy the land which is his: his, I say, in which the word of the Father was taught, and where he dwelt for more than thirty years, a man among men; his, for he enlightened it with miracles, he consecrated it with his own blood; in it appeared the first fruits of his resurrection. And now, for our sins, the enemies of the cross have raised blaspheming heads, ravaging with the edge of the sword the land of promise. For they are almost on the point, if there be not one to withstand them, of bursting into the very city of the living God, of overturning the sanctuaries of our redemption, of polluting the holy places of the spotless Lamb with purple blood. Alas! they rage against the very shrine of the Christian faith with blasphemous mouths, and would enter and trample down the very couch on which, for us, our life lay down to sleep in death.

What are you going to do then, O brave men? What are you doing, O servants of the cross? Will you give what is holy to the dogs, and cast your pearls before swine? How many sinners there, confessing their sins with tears, have obtained pardon, after the defilement of the heathen had been purged by the swords of your fathers! The wicked man sees and is grieved; he gnashes with his teeth, and consumes away. He prepares the instruments of sin, and will leave no sign or trace of so great piety, if ever (which God forbid!) he gain possession of this holiest of holy places. Verily that would be an irremediable grief to all time, an irrecoverable loss, a vast disgrace to this most graceless generation, and an everlasting shame.

What are we then to think, brethren? Is the Lord's arm shortened so that it cannot save, because he calls his weak creatures to guard and restore his heritage? Can he not send more than twelve legions of angels, or merely speak the word and the land shall be set free? It is altogether in his power to effect what he wishes; but I tell you, the Lord, your God, is trying you. He looks upon the sons of men to see if there be any to understand, and seek, and bewail his error. For the Lord has pity upon his people, and provides a sure remedy for those that are afflicted.

Think what care he uses for your salvation, and wonder. Behold the abyss of his love, and trust him, O you sinners. He wills not your death, but that you may turn and live; for now he seeks occasion, not against you, but for your benefit. What opportunity of salvation has God not tried and sought out, when the almighty deigns to summon to his service murderers, robbers, adulterers, perjurers, and those guilty of other crimes, as if they were a people that dealt righteously? Doubt him not, O sinners; God is kind. If he willed to punish you, he not only would not seek your service, but would not accept it when offered.

Again I say, weigh the riches of the goodness of the highest God; hear his plan of mercy. He makes or feigns a need for himself, while he desires to help you in your necessity. He wills to be held a debtor, that he may give pay to those that fight for him, pardon of sins, and everlasting glory. Therefore I may call it a highly favored generation which has happened upon a time so full of indigence; upon which has come that acceptable year of the Lord, a very jubilee; for this blessing is spread over the whole world, and all fly eagerly to the sign of life.

Since, therefore, your land is fruitful in brave men, and is known to be full of robust youth, since your praise is in the whole world, and the fame of your valor has filled the entire earth, gird up your loins manfully, and take up arms in zeal for the Christian name. Let not your former warlike skill cease, but only that spirit of hatred in which you are accustomed to strike down and kill one another and in turn be overcome yourselves. How dire a madness goads those wretched men, when kinsmen strike each other's bodies with the sword, perchance causing the soul also to perish! But he does not escape who triumphs; the sword shall go through his own soul also, when he thinks to have slain his enemy only. To enter such a combat is madness, not valor: it is not to be ascribed to bravery, but rather to foolishness.

But now, O brave knight, now, O warlike hero, here is a battle you may fight without danger, where it is glory to conquer and gain to die. If you are a prudent merchant, if you are a desirer of this world, behold I show you some great bargains; see that you lose them not. Take the sign of the cross, and you shall gain pardon for every sin that you confess with a contrite heart. The material itself, being bought, is worth little; but if it be placed on a devout shoulder it is, without doubt, worth no less than the kingdom of God. Therefore they have done well who have already taken the heavenly sign: well and wisely also will the rest do, if they hasten to lay upon their shoulders, like the first, the sign of salvation.

Besides, brethren, I warn you, and not only I, but God's apostle, "Believe not every spirit." We have heard and rejoice that the zeal of God abounds in you, but it behooves no mind to be wanting in wisdom. The Jews must not be persecuted, slaughtered, nor even driven out. Inquire of the pages of holy writ. I know what is written in the psalms as prophecy about the Jews. "God hath commanded me," says the church, "Slay them not, lest my people forget."

[The Jews] are living signs to us, representing the Lord's passion. For this reason they are dispersed into all regions, that now they may pay the just penalty of so great a crime, and that they may be witnesses of our redemption. Wherefore the church, speaking in the same psalm, says, "Scatter them by thy power; and bring them down, O Lord, our shield." So has it been. They have been dispersed, cast down. They undergo a hard captivity under Christian princes. Yet they shall be converted at evening, and remembrance of them shall be made in due season. Finally, when the multitude of the gentiles shall have entered in, then "all Israel shall be saved," says the apostle. Meanwhile he

THE CRUSADES: A READER

who dies remains in death.

I do not enlarge on the lamentable fact that where there are no Jews, there Christian men *judaize* even worse than they in extorting usury — if, indeed, we may call them Christians and not rather baptized Jews. Moreover, if the Jews be utterly trampled down, how shall the promised salvation or conversion profit them in the end?...

This also we must warn you, dearest brethren, that if any love to bear rule among you, and wish, by hastening, to anticipate the army of his country, he shall by no means attempt to do it. If he pretend to have been sent by us, it is not true; or if he show letters as if given by us, I warn you that they are altogether false or obtained by fraud. It is necessary to choose warlike and skillful leaders, and for the army of the Lord to set out together, that it may have strength everywhere, and not be liable to sustain injury from any.

There was in the former expedition, before Jerusalem was taken, a certain man, Peter by name, of whom (if I am not mistaken) you have often heard mention. He went alone, at the head of a mass of people who had entrusted themselves to his care, and led them into so great dangers that none, or at least very few, escaped death, either by hunger or the sword. So there is danger lest, if you do likewise, the same fate should overtake you also, which may God, who is forever blessed, avert from you. Amen.

Questions: What effect did the loss of Edessa have upon the Christian communities both in the Holy Land and in the West? Given that the Holy Land was still, for the most part, in Christian hands, how did Bernard stir up enthusiasm for the Second Crusade? According to Bernard, what was the main reason for going to the aid of the crusader states? What concerns did he have for this crusade? How did he hope to avoid the excesses of the earlier Peasants' Crusade?

36. ODO OF DEUIL: *THE JOURNEY OF LOUIS VII TO THE EAST*

The preaching of the Second Crusade by Bernard of Clairvaux and others resulted in the organization of two major crusading factions: the French, led by King Louis VII, and the Germans, under the German (or Holy Roman) emperor, Conrad III. Leaving Europe in May and June of 1147, both armies fared badly in their efforts to reach the Holy Land, especially the Germans, who lost almost the whole of their fighting force in a battle with the Turks in Anatolia. The French found themselves fighting both the Muslims and the Byzantines (the latter having been ordered by the eastern emperor to defend Byzantine territory from the crusaders). So depleted were both armies that when the combined force finally arrived in Antioch, there were not enough soldiers to launch a successful campaign to retake Edessa, the primary goal of the crusade.

Odo of Deuil (d. 1162) was the chaplain of King Louis VII of France and an eye-witness to the events of the Second Crusade. A monk of the Abbey of St. Denis, he was instructed by the head of that institution, Abbot Suger, to take notes while on crusade. Odo later used these notes to write his Journey of Louis VII to the East.

Source: trans. V.G. Berry, *Odo of Deuil: The Journey of Louis VII to the East* (New York: W.W. Norton & Company Inc., 1948), pp. 7-9, 41-45, 63-67, 87-91.

In the year ... 1146, the illustrious king of the Franks and duke of the Aquitanians, Louis [VII], son of King Louis, in order to be worthy of Christ, undertook to follow him by bearing his cross on Easter in Vézelay, at the age of twenty-five. On the preceding Christmas, when the same devout king had held court at Bourges, he had revealed for the first time to the bishops and magnates of the realm, whom he had purposely summoned in greater numbers than usual for his coronation, the secret in his heart. On that occasion the pious bishop of Langres spoke in his episcopal capacity concerning the devastation of Rohes, whose ancient name is Edessa, and the oppression of the Christians and the arrogance of the heathen; and by this doleful theme he aroused great lamentation, while at the same time he admonished all that, together with their king, they should fight for the King of all in order to succor the Christians. There burned and shone in the king the zeal of faith, the scorn of pleasure and of earthly glory — an example finer than any discourse; but what the bishop sowed by word the king did not harvest immediately through his example. Therefore another time was appointed, Eastertide at Vézelay, where all were to assemble on the Sunday before Palm Sunday, and where those who should be divinely inspired were to take up the glorious cross on Easter Sunday.

Meanwhile the king, who was ever active in the undertaking, sent messengers concerning it to Pope Eugenius at Rome. They were received gladly and sent home glad, bearing letters sweeter than any honeycomb, which enjoined obedience to the king and moderation in arms and clothing, which promised those taking the easy yoke of Christ the remission of all sins and the protection of their wives and children, and which contained certain other provisions that seemed advisable to the pope's holy wisdom and solicitude. He wished personally to give the initial blessing to such a holy undertaking, but, since he could not, hindered as he was by the tyranny of the Romans, he delegated that charge to Bernard, the holy abbot of Clairvaux....

Thus far we were engaged in play, because we neither suffered injuries from men's ill will nor feared dangers arising from the cunning of crafty men. However, from the time when we entered Bulgaria, a land belonging to the Greeks, our valor was put to the test and our emotions were aroused. When about to enter the uninhabited portion, we stocked ourselves in the poor town of Brandiz with provisions, most of which Hungary supplied via the Danube. There the fleet which the Germans had brought and abandoned was so huge that for a long time it furnished the citizens with building material and firewood. Our men took the smaller types of these boats and, after crossing the stream, brought supplies from a certain Hungarian castle which was not far away. Here we first encountered the copper money "staminae," and for one of these we unhappily gave five [pennies], or rather we lost a mark on twelve [shillings]. Thus, at the entrance to their own land the Greeks stained themselves with perjury, for you should remember what has already been said, namely, that the messengers had sworn on behalf of their emperor to furnish us a suitable market and exchange. But we crossed the wasteland and entered the exceedingly beautiful and rich territory which stretches without interruption all the way to Constantinople. Here for the first time wrongs began to arise and to be noticed; for the other countries, which sold us supplies properly, found us entirely peaceful. The Greeks, however, closed their cities and fortresses and offered their wares by letting them down from the walls on ropes. But food furnished in such measure did not suffice our throng. Therefore, the pilgrims, unwilling to endure want in the midst of plenty, procured supplies for themselves by plunder and pillage.

Some thought, however, that this state of affairs was the fault of the Germans who preceded us, since they had been plundering everything....

The Germans were unbearable even to us. One time, for instance, some of our men who wished to escape the press of the crowd around the king, and therefore went ahead, lodged near them. Both groups went to market; but the Germans did not allow the Franks to buy anything until after they themselves had had all they wanted. From this situation arose a dispute, or rather a brawl; for, when one person accuses another in a very loud voice without understanding him, there is a brawl. Thereupon the Franks, after this exchange of blows, returned from market with their supplies; that is, the Germans, scorning the pride of the few Franks, because they themselves were many, took arms against them and fell upon them furiously, and the Franks, likewise armed, resisted spiritedly. But God put an end to the wicked encounter, for night fell rapidly. Their anger could neither be quenched nor lulled by that night, for in the morning they arose, raging more bitterly; but wise men among them, falling at the knees of the fools, calmed this rage by humility and reason.

Thus, the Germans disturbed everything as they proceeded, and the Greeks therefore fled our peaceful king, who followed after. Nonetheless, the congregations of the churches and the entire clergy always received him with due reverence and honor, issuing forth from their cities with icons and other Greek paraphernalia. Also, the duke of Sofia, a kinsman of the emperor's who always kept close to the king during the journey, both established peace for the inhabitants and saw to procuring part of the market for the pilgrims. He served the king honorably in regard to provisions, but Louis, keeping little or nothing of this for himself, divided the entire amount, some with the poor, and some with the rich. And so peace was maintained more strictly with Louis, because he was less needy and commanded more respect than the others. But there preceded and followed him many divisions who gained plenty for themselves, either from the market, whenever that was possible, or from plunder, because they had the power to do that....

Constantinople, the glory of the Greeks, rich in renown and richer still in possessions, is laid out in a triangle shaped like a ship's sail. In its inner angle stand [the church of] Santa Sophia and Constantine's palace, in which there is a chapel that is revered for its exceedingly holy relics. Moreover, Constantinople is girt on two sides by the sea; when approaching the city we had the Arm of St. George on the right and on the left a certain estuary, which, after branching from the Arm, flows on for about four miles. In that place the Palace of Blachernae, although having foundations laid on low ground, achieves eminence through excellent construction and elegance and, because of its surroundings on three sides, affords its inhabitants the triple pleasure of looking out upon sea, fields, and city. Its exterior is of almost matchless beauty, but its interior surpasses anything that I can say about it. Throughout it is decorated elaborately with gold and a great variety of colors, and the floor is marble, paved with cunning workmanship; and I do not know whether the exquisite art or the exceedingly valuable stuffs endow it with the more beauty or value. The third side of the city's triangle includes fields, but it is fortified by towers and a double wall which extends for about two miles from the sea to the palace. This wall is not very strong, and it possesses no lofty towers; but the city puts its trust, I think, in the size of its population and the long period of peace which it has enjoyed. Below the walls lies open land, cultivated by plow and hoe, which contains gardens that furnish the citizens all kinds of vegetables. From the outside underground conduits flow in, bringing the city an abundance of sweet water.

The city itself is squalid and fetid and in many places harmed by permanent darkness, for the wealthy overshadow the streets with buildings and leave these dirty, dark places to the poor and to travelers; there murders and robberies and other crimes which love the darkness are committed. Moreover, since people live lawlessly in this city, which has as many lords as rich men and almost as many thieves as poor men, a criminal knows neither fear nor shame, because crime is not punished by law and never entirely comes to light. In every respect she exceeds moderation; for, just as she surpasses other cities in wealth, so, too, does she surpass them in vice. Also, she possesses many churches unequal to Santa Sophia in size but equal to it in beauty, which are to be marveled at for their beauty and their many saintly relics. Those who had the opportunity entered these places, some to see the sights and others to worship faithfully.

Conducted by the emperor, the king also visited the shrines and, after returning, when won over by the urgency of his host's requests, dined with him. That banquet afforded pleasure to ear, mouth, and eye with pomp as marvelous, viands as delicate, and pastimes as pleasant as the guests were illustrious. There many of the king's men feared for him; but he, who had entrusted the care of himself to God, feared nothing at all, since he had faith and courage; for one who is not inclined to do harm does not easily believe that anyone will harm him.

Although the Greeks furnished us no proof that they were treacherous, I believe that they would not have exhibited such unremitting servitude if they had had good intentions. Actually, they were concealing the wrongs which were to be avenged after we crossed the Arm. However, it was not held against the Greeks that they closed the city gates to the [crusading] throng, since it had burned many of their houses and olive trees, either for want of wood or by reason of arrogance and the drunkenness of fools. The [French] king frequently punished offenders [in his own army] by cutting off their ears, hands, and feet, yet he could not thus check the folly of the whole group. Indeed, one of two things was necessary, either to kill many thousands at one time or to put up with their numerous evil deeds....

Romania [in Asia Minor], a land which is very broad and exceedingly rugged with stony mountains, lies beyond, extending to Antioch on the south and bordering Turkey on the east. Although all Romania was formerly under Greek jurisdiction, the Turks now possess a great part and, after expelling the Greeks, have devastated another part; but where the Greeks still hold castles the two peoples divide the revenues. In such subjection the Greeks retain the territory the Franks procured [during the First Crusade] because they went in quest of Jerusalem; and the lazy people would have lost all if they had not defended themselves by importing knights from various nations, thus compelling gold to redeem gold. Nevertheless, they always lose (but since they possess much they cannot lose all at once), for mercenaries do not suffice a people without forces of its own. Nicomedia first showed us this; set among thorns and brambles, her lofty ruins testify to her former glory and her present masters' inactivity. In vain does a certain estuary of the sea, which terminates in the city three days after rising in the Arm, offer her the advantage of good transportation.

From this city three routes, unequal in length and unlike in character, lead to Antioch. The one bearing to the left is the shorter. Had it no drawbacks, it could be traveled in three weeks; but after twelve days it arrives at Iconium, the [Turkish] sultan's very fine capital, and then, five days after passing the Turks, at the land of the Franks. Now a strong army, secure in its faith and numbers, would discount all that if it were not alarmed in winter by the snow-clad mountains. The road bearing right is richer and more peaceful; but, in following the broken coastline, it delays travelers thrice over, since it crosses rivers and rushing streams which are as much to be feared in the winter as are the snow and the Turks on the first road. The middle route, however, is tempered by the advantages and disadvantages of the other two, since it is longer, but safer, than the shorter route, and shorter and safer, but poorer, than the longer route. Therefore the Germans who had preceded us had separated. Led by the emperor, the majority took the left-hand route through Iconium, by ill luck; with the emperor's brother, however, the rest turned to the right, pursuing a course which was unfortunate in every respect. Now the middle lot, which mitigates the disadvantages of the other two, fell to us. Thus, when, goaded on by Greek rumors to overtake and to take over in the Germans' footsteps, we had left Nicaea behind on the left and were camping beside the Nicene lake, suddenly there arrived German nobles who had been sent after the king by their emperor and dolefully reported that, contrary to our desire and belief, the Germans had fled back to Nicaea.

On hearing this our men were grieved with stupefaction and stupefied with grief that such a strong army had failed so suddenly and that our enemies and God's had triumphed so easily over our allies.

Questions: How did the crusaders conduct themselves on the way to the Holy Land? What reasons are given for their difficulties and divisions? What do we learn from Odo's narrative about Constantinople and Byzantine relations with the West? How does the crusade compare with Bernard's original vision of this venture? Why did the Second Crusade fall short of his ideal?

37. JOHN KINNAMOS: *THE DEEDS OF JOHN AND MANUEL COMNENUS*

As mentioned by Odo of Deuil in the previous document, the German contingent of the Second Crusade had arrived in the East before the French army. The Deeds of John and Manuel Comnenus, by the Greek historian John Kinnamos, gives a Byzantine view of the Second Crusade. In the passage below, Kinnamos, who had served as secretary to the Byzantine emperor Manuel and was writing in the early 1180s, describes the German campaign and relations between Manuel and the German emperor Conrad, the leader of the German force.

Source: trans. C.M. Brand, *The Deeds of John and Manuel Comnenus*, by John Kinnamos (New York: Columbia University Press, 1976), pp. 70-72.

As stated, the Germans had been frequently defeated by the Turks and lost many of their men; once they abandoned passage through Philomilion, they hastened back. Coming to [Nicaea] they met there the French who were marching on the road, and the other kings who were bringing with them large forces: one of these ruled the Czechs' nation, and had seemingly been appointed king by Conrad; the other, that of the Poles, who are a Scythic people and dwell beside the western Hungarians....

Therefore, and because the risk of taking second place to the French on the roads threatened them, they marched as far as Philadelphia together; from there Conrad, unable to endure being slighted by the French, determined to return: he wrote to the [Byzantine] emperor and revealed his plan. As he [that is, Manuel] desired to separate the kings from each other, and sympathized with the man, he replied thus: "Men who claim to grow a little wise customarily observe matters not according to turns of fortune, but individually, apart from any sudden alteration. So when you were prospering we decided not to treat you beyond your worth, and now that you are in a moderately bad situation, we do not hesitate to welcome you back with those same things which we were eager to do in honor of a relative, the ruler of such nations, and to take counsel together regarding the present circumstances, on account of the said [reasons] as well as of being of the same religion...."

The letter concluded in such terms. Conrad had previously perceived his own folly, but not knowing what he should do, he had unwillingly followed the French. When the emperor's letter reached him, believing the thing a piece of luck, he received the advice with pleasure and speedily returned; reaching the Hellespont, he crossed to Thrace by the ferry there. He encountered the emperor who was making a stay there and returned to Byzantium with him [in the winter of 1147-48]. There amusements succeeded one another: imperial residences, varied spectacles, horse races, and splendid receptions, whereby his exhausted body recuperated.

Furnished with sufficient funds, he set out for Palestine with [ships]; Nicephorus Dasiotes commanded his ship and provided other service. There he met the other kings and performed appropriate rites at the life-giving tomb of Christ; while the others set out for their individual homelands as best they might, he left there with the said ships and landed at Thessalonica. He saw the emperor there for a second time and again joined in discussions and conversations with him. The emperor reminded him of what had been previously agreed; this was, that Italy [that is, Apulia and Calabria] should be restored to the empress [Bertha-]Irene for her marriage-gift, as she was his [that is, Conrad's] relative and he had betrothed her to the emperor. After he and [his nephew and heir] Frederick had pledged their agreements with additional oaths, they departed from the Romans' land. So Conrad's affairs had their conclusion there [in the winter of 1148-49]....

Having returned to his native land, Conrad soon ended his life [in 1152], without having completed anything which he had promised the emperor.

Questions: What reasons are given for the failure of the German campaign? What part did the Byzantine emperor play in this crusade? What, perhaps, motivated his actions?

38. ANALYSES OF THE SECOND CRUSADE

The Second Crusade was a dismal failure. Edessa remained in Muslim hands. Louis VII's four-day siege of Damascus (begun July 24, 1148) served only to strengthen the position of Nur ad-Din, as the people of this city, previously allied with the kingdom of Jerusalem, turned to the Muslim leader for help. Moreover, the crusade further strained relations between Byzantium and the West—so much so that many in Europe now viewed Byzantium, not Islam, as the real enemy of the crusader states. The failure of the crusade was met with disbelief and anger in the West, and blame was freely distributed. Below are two reactions to the debacle, the first by an anonymous writer from Germany who offers a very hostile view of the crusade; the second is Bernard of Clairvaux's own analysis of the failings of the crusade in a letter sent to Pope Eugenius III.

Source: trans. J.A. Brundage, *The Crusades: A Documentary Survey* (Milwaukee: The Marquette University Press, 1962), pp. 121-24.

Anonymous Annals of Würzburg

God allowed the western Church, on account of its sins, to be cast down. There arose, indeed, certain pseudo prophets, sons of Belial, and witnesses of anti-Christ, who seduced the Christians with empty words. They constrained all sorts of men, by vain preaching, to set out against the Saracens in order to liberate Jerusalem. The preaching of these men was so enormously influential that the inhabitants of nearly every region, by common vows, offered themselves freely for common destruction. Not only the ordinary people, but kings, dukes, marquises, and other powerful men of the world as well, believed that they thus showed their allegiance to God. The bishops, archbishops, abbots, and other ministers and prelates of the church joined in this error, throwing themselves headlong into it to the great peril of bodies and souls.... The intentions of the various men were different. Some, indeed, lusted after novelties and went in order to learn about new lands. Others there were who were driven by poverty, who were in hard straits at home; these men went to fight, not only against the enemies of Christ's cross, but even against the friends of the Christian name, wherever opportunity appeared, in order to relieve their poverty. There were others who were oppressed by debts to other men or who sought to escape the service due to their lords, or who were even awaiting punishment merited by their shameful deeds. Such men simulated a zeal for God and hastened chiefly in order to escape from such troubles and anxieties. A few could, with difficulty, be found who had not bowed their knees to Baal, who were directed by a holy and wholesome purpose, and who were kindled by love of the divine majesty to fight earnestly and even to shed their blood for the holy of holies.

Bernard of Clairvaux

...As you know we have fallen upon grave times, which seemed about to bring to an end to not only my studies but my very life, for the Lord, provoked by our sins, gave the appearance of having judged the world prematurely, with justice, indeed, but forgetful of his mercy. He spared neither his people nor his name. Did not the heathen say: "Where is their God?" [Ps. 113b:2.]. Nor do I wonder, for the sons of the church, those who bear the label "Christians," have been laid low in the desert and have either been slain by the sword or consumed by famine....

We said "Peace, and there is no peace" [Jer.6:14]; we promised good things, "and behold trouble" [Jer.14:19]. It might seem, in fact, that we acted rashly in this affair, or had "used lightness" [II Cor. 1:17]. But "I did not run my course like a man in doubt of my goal" [I Cor. 9:26], for I acted on your orders, or rather on God's orders given through you...The judgments of the Lord are true indeed. Who does not know that? This judgment, however, "is a great deep" [Ps. 32:7], so much so, that it seems to me not unwarranted to call him blessed who is not scandalized thereat.

How, then, does human rashness dare reprove what it can scarcely understand? Let us put down some judgments from on high, which are "from everlasting" [Ps. 24:6], for there may, perhaps, be consolation in them.... I speak of a matter which is unknown to no one, but of which no one now seems to be aware. Such is the human heart, indeed, that what we know when we need it not, is lost to us when it is required.

When Moses was going to lead the people out of the land of Egypt, he promised them a better land. Otherwise would that people, who knew only earthy things, ever have followed him? He led them away—but he did not lead them into the land which he had promised them. The sad and unexpected outcome, however, cannot be laid to the rashness of the leader, for he did everything at the Lord's command, with "the Lord aiding them and attesting his word by the miracles that went with them" [Mark 16:20]. But, you may say, they were a stiff-necked race, forever contending against the Lord and Moses his servant. Very well, they were rebellious and unbelieving; but what about these other people? Ask them. Why should it be my task to speak of what they have done? One thing I shall say: how could they make progress when they were always looking backwards as they walked? Was there a time in the whole journey when they were not in their hearts returning to Egypt? But if the Jews were vanquished and "perished because of their iniquity" [Ps. 72:19], is it any wonder that those who did likewise suffered a similar fate? Would anyone say that the fate of the former was contrary to God's promise? Neither, therefore, was the fate of the latter....

These few things have been said by way of an apology, so that your conscience may have something from me, whereby you can hold yourself and me excused, if not in the eyes of those who judge causes from their results, then at least in your own eyes. The perfect and final apology for any man is the testimony of his own conscience. As for myself, I take it to be a small matter to be judged by those "who call evil good, and good evil, whose darkness is light, whose light darkness" [Isa. 5:20].

If one or the other must be done, I would rather that men murmur against us than against God. It would be well for me, if he deigns to use me for his shield.... I shall not refuse to be made ignominious, so long as God's glory is not attacked.

Questions: What motivations for crusading does the Würzburg chronicler identify? What, according to the Würzburg author, was the primary reason for the failure of the Second Crusade? How does this view compare with that of Bernard of Clairvaux?

39. BAHA AD-DIN'S *LIFE OF SALADIN*

Salah al-Din Yusuf, or Saladin, as he is known in the West, served in both an adminis-
trative and military capacity under Zengi and Nur ad-Din. He conquered Egypt in
1171 and, upon the death of Nur ad-Din (in 1174), was able to take control of Syria as
well. Saladin then turned his attention to the crusader states. This long, drawn-out cam-
paign culminated in the Battle of Hattin in 1187, where the crusader army suffered a
crushing defeat. Saladin has come down to us as a legendary figure—the epitome of
medieval chivalry. He was praised in the Islamic sources for his goodness and piety as
well as for his military success. The historian Baha ad-Din become one of Saladin's
retainers in 1188. His Life of Saladin *offers many personal details about the Muslim*
leader and the way in which he ruled.

Source: trans. C.R. Conder, *The Life of Saladin by Beha ed-Din* (London: Palestine Pilgrims' Text
Society, 1897), pp. 20-24, 38-45; revised.

1. What I have observed of Saladin's attachment to the principles of religion, and his respect for every part of the holy law

In our collection of authentic traditions stands the following saying of the holy
Prophet [that is, Mohammed]: "Islam is built upon five columns: confession of
the unity of God, the regular performance of prayer, payment of the tenth in
charity, the fast of the month Ramadan, and pilgrimage to the holy house of
God [in Mecca]." Saladin—may God be merciful to him!—truly believed in
the doctrines of the faith, and often recited prayers in praise of God. He had
accepted the dogmas of religion upon demonstrable proofs, the result of his
conversations with the most learned doctors and the most eminent juriscon-
sults. In these arguments he acquired knowledge that enabled him to speak to
the purpose when a discussion took place in his presence, although he did not
employ the technical language of the lawyers. These conversations confirmed
him in a true faith, which remained undisturbed by any doubt, and, in his case,
prevented the arrow of speculation from overshooting the mark, and striking
at last on doubt and infidelity.

The learned doctor Kotb ed-Uin en-Nisaburi had composed an exposition
of Islam for the benefit of this prince, containing all that was necessary for him
to know. As [Saladin] was much pleased with this treatise, he made his younger
sons learn it by heart, so that good doctrine might be established in their souls
from their tenderest years. I have myself seen him take this book and read it
aloud to his children, after they had committed its contents to memory.

As to prayer, he was always regular in his attendance at the public service
[on Fridays], and he said one day that for several years he had never failed in

this duty. When he was ill, he used to send for the imam [that is, teacher] alone, and forcing himself to keep on his feet, would recite the Friday prayers. He recited the usual prayers regularly, and, if he woke during the night, said a prayer. If he did not wake, he used to pray before the morning prayer. As long as consciousness lasted, he never failed to say his prayers. I saw him perform this duty regularly during his last illness, and he discontinued it only during the three days in which his mind was wandering. When he was traveling, he used to get down from his horse at the appointed hours to pray.

Let us speak of his tenth in charity. The sum of money he left at his death was not large enough to be submitted to this tax; his private charities had absorbed everything. He who had possessed such abundant wealth left in his treasury, when he died, only forty-seven Nasri dirhems [equivalent to Greek drachmas], and a single Tyrian gold piece [that is, a gold coin minted at Tyre]. He left neither goods, nor house, nor real estate, neither garden, nor village, nor cultivated land, nor any other species of property.

Let us pass to the fast of the month Ramadan. Several of these fasts remained to be fulfilled, as he had not observed them in consequence of his frequent illnesses. It was the duty of the kadi [that is, judge] el-Fadel to keep an account of the number of these days. The prince—may God have mercy on him!—was in the last year of his life, and was dwelling at Jerusalem, when he began to make reparation for the fasts he had omitted. He then fasted for a period exceeding the ordinary month, for he had still a fast of two Ramadans to keep, which he had been prevented from observing by constant disorders of the body, and the continual cares of the holy war. Fasting did not suit his health; but thus, by the inspiration of God, he undertook to repair his omissions during that year. It fell to me to keep account of the days, for the kadi was absent. It was useless for his physician to disapprove of what he was doing. The prince would not listen to him, and said, "I do not know what may happen." It seems as though God had inspired Saladin to save his responsibility by paying his debt, and so he continued to fast until the days were wholly accomplished.

Let us now speak of the pilgrimage. He always intended to perform it, and, above all, in the last year of his life. He had made up his mind, and given orders for the necessary preparations to be made. We had collected provisions for the journey, and all was ready for the start, when he decided to postpone the pilgrimage till the following year on account of want of time and lack of money sufficient for one of his high rank. But God decreed as he did decree. What I have related on that subject is a thing known to all the world.

Saladin was very fond of hearing the Quran read, and he used to argue with the imam. This man had to be master of all knowledge connected with the text of the Quran and to know the book by heart. When the prince passed the night in the alcove [of his tent], he used to charge the man on guard to read him two, three, or four sections. When he gave public audiences, he would have from one to twenty verses, and sometimes more, read by men accustomed to do so. One day he passed a little boy who was reading the Quran very well at his father's side, and was so pleased that he had the boy called, and gave him some of the food set aside for his own special use. Also he granted to him and his father part of the produce of a certain field. His heart was humble, and full of compassion; tears came readily into his eyes. When he was listening to the reading of the Quran, his heart melted, and tears generally flowed down his cheeks. He was very fond of listening to the recital of traditions [that is, the sayings of Mohammed] when the narrator could trace each tradition that he related to its source, and when he was learned in such lore. If one of the doctors visited the court, he received him personally, and made those of his sons who happened to be present, as well as the mamluks [that is, military slaves] on duty, listen to the traditions recited. He would order all those who were present to be seated during the narration, as a sign of respect. If any of the doctors of traditional lore were such characters as do not frequent the gates of sultans, and are unwilling to present themselves in such places, Saladin would go himself to seek them out and listen to them. When he was at Alexandria, he often visited Hafiz el-Isfahani, and learnt from him a great number of traditions. He himself was fond of reading traditions, so he used to make me come into his private chamber, and there, surrounded by books of traditions which he had had collected, he would begin to read; and whenever he came to a tradition containing an instructive passage, he was so touched that the tears came into his eyes....

5. Of his zeal in fighting in God's cause

God almighty said (Quran 29:69): "Those who fight strenuously for us we will surely guide in our way, for, verily, God is with those who do well." There are numerous texts in the Quran exhorting us to fight for the faith. And, of a truth, the sultan entertained an ardent passion for the holy war; his mind was always filled with it. Therefore one might swear, in absolute security and without risk of perjury, that from the time when he first issued forth to fight the infidel, he spent not a single piece of gold or silver except for the carrying on of the holy war or for distribution among his troops. With him to wage war in God's name was a veritable passion; his whole heart was filled with it, and he gave body and soul to the cause. He spoke of nothing else; all his thoughts were of instruments of war; his soldiers monopolized every idea. He showed all deference to those who talked of the holy war and who encouraged the people to take part in it. His desire to fight in God's cause forced him to leave his family, his children, his native land, the place of his abode, and all else in his land. Leaving all these earthly enjoyments, he contented himself with dwelling beneath the shadow of a tent, shaken to the right hand and to the left by the breath of every wind....

8. His care to be polite:

The holy Prophet said: "I have been sent to make manifest in all their beauty the noble qualities of the soul." When any man gave his hand to the Prophet he clasped it until the other withdrew it. And so, too, our sultan was very noble of heart; his face expressed kindliness, his modesty was great, and his politeness perfect. No visitor ever came to him without being given to eat, and receiving what he desired. He greeted everyone, even infidels, politely. For instance, after the conclusion of peace in the month of Shawâl, in the year 588 [that is, Oct. to Nov. 1192], he left Jerusalem to journey to Damascus, and whilst he was on his way he saw the [Frankish] prince of Antioch, who had come up unexpectedly, and was standing at the entrance of his tent. This prince had come to ask something from him, and the sultan gave him back el-'Amk, which territory he had acquired in the year 584 [that is, 1188–1189], at the time of the conquest of the coastal lands. So, too, I was present at Nazareth when the sultan received the visit of the [Frankish] lord of Sidon; he showed him every mark of respect, treated him with honor, and admitted him to his own table. He even proposed to him that he should embrace Islam, set before him some of the beauties of our religion, and urged him to adopt it.

He always gave a kind reception to sheiks, to all learned and gifted men, and to the various influential persons who came to see him. He enjoined us to present to him every notable sheik passing through the camp, so that he might exercise his generosity....

I was present one day when a Frankish prisoner was brought before him. This man was in such a state of excitement that his terror was visible in every feature. The interpreter asked him the cause of his fear, and God put the following answer in the mouth of the unfortunate fellow: "Before I saw his face I was greatly afraid, but now that I am in the presence [of Saladin] and can see him, I am certain that he will do me no harm." The sultan, moved by these words, gave him his life, and sent him away free.

I was attending the prince on one of the expeditions he used to make on the flanks of the enemy, when one of the scouts brought up a woman, rending her garments, weeping and beating her breast without ceasing. "This woman," the soldier said, "came out from among the Franks, and asked to be taken to the sultan; so I brought her here." The sultan asked her, through his interpreter, what was the matter, and she replied: "Some Muslim thieves got into my tent last night and carried off my child, a little girl. All night long I have never ceased begging for help, and our princes advised me to appeal to the king of the Muslims. 'He is very merciful,' they said. 'We will allow you to go out to seek him and ask for your daughter.' Therefore they permitted me to pass through the lines, and in you lies my only hope of finding my child." The sultan was moved by her distress; tears came into his eyes, and, acting from the generosity of his heart, he sent a messenger to the market-place of the camp, to seek her little one and bring her away, after repaying her purchaser the price he had given. It was early morning when her case was heard, and in less than an hour the horseman returned, bearing the little girl on his shoulder. As soon as the mother caught sight of her, she threw herself on the ground, rolling her face in the dust, and weeping so violently that it drew tears from all who saw her. She raised her eyes to heaven, and uttered words which we did not understand. We gave her back her daughter, and she was mounted to return to the enemy's army.

The sultan was very averse to the infliction of corporal punishment on his servants, even when they cheated him beyond endurance. On one occasion two purses filled with Egyptian gold pieces had been lodged in the treasury; these were stolen, and two purses full of copper coins left in their place. All he did was to dismiss the people employed in that department from his service.

In the year 583 [that is, 1187], at the battle of Hattin—a famous day's fight of which, please God, we shall speak in its proper place—Prince Arnat [that is, Reynald of Châtillon], lord of el-Kerak, and the king of the Franks of the seacoast [that is, Guy of Lusignan], were both taken prisoner, and the sultan commanded them to be brought before him. This accursed Arnat was a great infidel, and a very strong man. On one occasion, when there was a truce between the Muslims and the Franks, he had treacherously attacked and carried off a caravan that passed through his territory, coming from Egypt. He seized these people, put them to torture, and put some of them in grain-pits, and imprisoned some in narrow cells. When they objected that there was a truce between the two peoples, he replied: "Ask your Mohammed to deliver you." The sultan, to whom these words were reported, took an oath to slay the infidel with his own hand, if God should ever place him in his power. The day of the battle of Hattin God delivered this man into the hands of the sultan, and he resolved at once to slay him, that he might fulfill his oath. He commanded him to be brought before him, together with the king. The latter complained of thirst, and the sultan ordered a cup of sherbet to be given him. The king, having drunk some of it, handed the cup to Arnat, whereupon the sultan said to the interpreter: "Say to the king, 'It is you who give him drink, but I give him neither to drink nor to eat.'" By these words he wished it to be understood that honor forbade him to harm any man who had tasted his hospitality.

He then struck him on the neck with his own hand, to fulfill the vow he had made. After this, when he had taken Acre, he delivered all the prisoners, to the number of about four thousand, from their wretched durance, and sent them back to their own country and their homes, giving each of them a sum of money for the expenses of his journey. This is what I have been told by many persons, for I was not present myself when it took place.

The sultan was of a sociable disposition, of a sweet temper, and delightful to talk with. He was well acquainted with the pedigrees of the old Arabs, and with the details of their battles; he knew all their adventures; he had the pedigrees of their horses at his fingers' ends, and was master of all curious and strange lore. Thus in conversation with him people always heard things which they could never have learned from others. In company, he put everyone at their ease. He comforted those who were in trouble, questioned those who were ill on the nature of their malady, on the treatment they had adopted, on their diet, and on the changes they experienced in their system. He insisted strictly upon due seemliness in conversation, never suffering anyone to be spoken of except with respect; he would talk with none but persons of good conversation, lest his ears should be offended; having his tongue under perfect control, he never gave way to abusive language; he could also control his pen, and never made use of cutting words in writing to a Muslim. He was most strict in the fulfillment of his promises....

This is but a meager sketch of his lofty disposition and of his noble character. My aim has been to be concise, and to avoid prolixity lest I should weary my readers. I have mentioned nothing that I have not witnessed, adding thereto information obtained from credible authorities which I have myself tested. What I have here told is but a part of that which I was able to observe while in the sultan's service, and it is little indeed in comparison with all that could be told by his life-long friends, and those who have grown old in his service. But what I have given will convince an intelligent reader of the grandeur and purity of the prince's character and feelings.... May God hallow his soul and shed the light of his mercy upon his tomb!

Questions: According to Baha ad-Din, why is Saladin a worthy leader of the Islamic forces? What was Saladin's view of holy war? What were the aims of his campaign? Can one use this text to compare Saladin's conduct in warfare with that of the crusade leaders?

40. IMAD AD-DIN ON THE BATTLE OF HATTIN

As the Islamic forces continued to gather under Saladin, the unity of the crusader states was beginning to show the strain of the varying ambitions of its leaders. One noble in particular, Reynald of Châtillon, has been blamed by many historians for these divisions and the subsequent loss of Christian territory. Reynald had acted independently from other crusade leaders, ignoring treaties with the Muslims and attacking their trade caravans, as described in the previous document. Refusing the orders of the king of Jerusalem to halt these attacks, Reynald's actions split the crusaders into two camps: moderates and hawks. While Saladin prepared his ever-growing Islamic army for war, the moderates argued for delay, believing that time would diminish Saladin's forces. The more zealous of the Franks, however, pressed to march out to meet him in battle, and it was this rash plan which was ultimately adopted. The armies met on July 3, 1187, in a dry, desolate place called Hattin, near the Sea of Galilee. The battle was a crushing defeat for the crusader state forces. Imad ad-Din (1125-1201), who gives an account of the battle below, was Saladin's secretary. Although rather florid in its style, his narrative of the battle includes many important details not found in the Christian sources.

Source: trans. E.J. Costello and F. Gabrieli, *Arab Historians of the Crusades*, ed. F. Gabrieli (Berkeley: University of California Press, 1969), pp. 129-37.

Saladin surrounded [the town of] Tiberias with his personal guard and his most faithful troops. He advanced the infantry and sappers ... and the artillery, surrounded the walls and began to demolish the houses, giving battle fiercely and not sparing the city in the attack. This was Thursday, and he was at the head of his troops. The sappers began to mine one of the towers. They demolished it, knocked it down, leapt onto it and took possession of it. Night fell, and while the dawn of victory was breaking for them, the night of woe was darkening for enemy. The citadel put up resistance and the [Frankish] countess [Eschiva] shut herself up there with her sons. When the count [that is, Raymond of Tripoli] heard that Tiberias had fallen and his princedom been taken he was seized with consternation and lost all his strength of purpose, putting himself completely in the hands of the [other] Franks. "From today onwards," he said, "not to act is no longer possible. We must at all costs drive the enemy back. Now that Tiberias is taken and the whole princedom with all my possessions, acquired or inherited, is lost, I cannot resign myself or recover from this reverse." The king [of Jerusalem] was his ally and offered no opposition, but consented to this without hypocrisy, with sincere and unmixed affection, in a friendly manner completely lacking in coldness. He gave him precise promises without having to be asked twice, and set out on the march with his army, his sight and his hearing, his dragons and demons, beasts and wolves, the followers of his error and the faction of his evil deeds. The earth trembled beneath their feet, the heavens were clouded with the dust thrown up by them. News came [to the Muslims] that the Franks had mounted and were on the move with the ranks of their steadfast faith, who leapt into the attack, drawn up for battle and flooding over the ground, creeping forward on the defensive, kindling the fire of war, responding to the cry of vengeance, running to reach their dwellings. This was Friday 24 Rabi' II [that is, July 3]. As soon as the news was verified the sultan confirmed that his decision, based on his earlier judgment, was accurate, and rejoiced to hear that they were on the march; "If our objective is gained," he said, "our request will have been heard in full and our ambition will have been achieved. Thanks be to God, our good fortune will now be renewed, our swords sharp, our courage valiant, our victory swift. If they are really defeated, killed and captured, Tiberias and all Palestine will have no one left to defend them or to impede our conquest."

Thus he sought God's best [fortune] and set off, casting all delay aside. On Friday 24 Rabi' II the Franks were on the march toward Tiberias with all their forces, moving as fast as if they were always going downhill. Their hordes rolled on, their lions roared, their vultures flew above them, their cries rose up, the horizon was hidden by the clouds of them, their heads sought eagerly for those who were to strike them off. They looked like mountains on the march, like seas boiling over, wave upon wave, with their crowding ranks, their seething approach-roads and mutilated barbarian warriors. The air stank, the light was dimmed, the desert was stunned, the plain dissolved, destiny hung over them, the Pleiades sent dust down upon them, the chargers' saddle-cloths brushed the ground and swept it, their hurrying hooves scored the earth. The knights clad in mail went with raised visors amid the swords, the hardened warriors and heroes of battle were loaded down with the apparel of war, and their number was complete. Ahead of them the sultan had drawn up his battalions and strengthened all his resolve for the fight. He set his army to face them and kept a watch on their vanguard in case they should charge; he cut off their access to water and filled in the wells, which caused them great hardship. He prevented their getting down to the water and set himself between them and their objective, keeping them at a distance. This was on a burningly hot day, while they themselves were burning with wrath. The Dog Star was blazing with merciless heat that consumed their water supplies and offered no support against thirst.

Night separated the two sides and the cavalry barred both the roads. Islam passed the night face to face with unbelief, monotheism at war with trinitarianism, the way of righteousness looking down upon error, faith opposing polytheism. Meanwhile the several circles of hell prepared themselves and the several ranks of heaven congratulated themselves; Malik (the guardian of hell) waited and Ridwan (the guardian of paradise) rejoiced. Finally, when day dawned and the morning gleamed out, when dawn sent waves of light across the sky and the clangor of the trumpets startled the crow from the dust, when the swords awoke in their sheaths and the lances flamed with eagerness, when the bows stirred and the fire glowed, when blades were unsheathed and pre-varication ripped away, then the archers began to scorch with their burning shafts men destined for hell fire; the bows hummed and the bowstrings sang, the warriors' pliant lances danced, unveiling the brides of battle, the white blades appeared naked out of the sheath amid the throng, and the brown lances were pastured on entrails. The Franks hoped for a respite and their army in desperation sought for a way of escape. But at every way out they were barred, and tormented by the heat of war without being able to rest. Tortured by the thirst they charged, with no other water than the "water" of the blades they gripped. The fire of arrows burned and wounded them, the fierce grip of the bows seized tenaciously upon them and struck them dead. They were impo-tent, driven off, pushed to extremes and driven back, every charge thrown off and destroyed, every action or attack captured and put in chains. Not even an ant could have escaped, and they could not defend themselves by charging. They burned and glowed in a frenzied ferment. As the arrows struck them down those who had seemed like lions now seemed like hedgehogs. The arrows beat them down and opened great gaps in their ranks. They sought refuge on the hill of Hattin to protect them from the flood of defeat, and Hat-tin was surrounded by the flags of destruction. The sword-blades sucked away their lives and scattered them on the hillsides; the bows found their targets, the wild fates stripped them, disasters crushed them, destruction picked them out, they became death's target and fate's prey. When the count [Raymond of Tripoli] realized that they were defeated his anguish was clear to see. He gave up all effort and planned a way of escape. This was even before the main body of the army was roused and the embers were fanned, before the war was set alight and the flame burned. His band went off to find a way of escape and took the road across the wadi [that is, streambed], refusing to stop. He went off like a flash of lightning in his folly, before the leak became too big; he fled with a few followers and did not return to the attack. Thus he absented him-self from the fight, seized by an unconquerable terror that forced him to flee. The fighting grew more violent as lance crossed lance and sword struck sword. The Franks were surrounded whichever way they turned and completely encircled. They began to pitch their tents and to rally their troops, setting up their pavilions on Hattin, while the gallant archers hammered away at their swords. But they were prevented from planting and raising their tents, and plucked from the roots and branches of life. They hoped to improve their position by dismounting from their horses, and they fought tenaciously, but the swords went through them as a torrent flows and our army surrounded them as hellfire surrounds the damned. Finally they resorted to saddling the ground, and their girth clasped the nipples of the plain.

The devil and his crew were taken, the king and his counts were captured, and the sultan sat to review his chief prisoners, who came forward stumbling in their fetters like drunken men. The grand master of the Templars was brought in his sins, and many of the Templars and Hospitallers with him. The king Guy and his brother Geoffrey were escorted in, with Hugh of Jubail, Humphrey, and Prince Arnat of al-Karak.... [Arnat, Reynald of Châtillon, was executed as described by Baha ad-Din, above.]

This defeat of the enemy, this our victory occurred on a Saturday, and the humiliation proper to the men of Saturday [that is, the Jews] was inflicted on the men of Sunday [that is, the Christians], who had been lions and now were reduced to the level of miserable sheep. Of these thousands only a few individuals escaped, and of all those enemies only a few were saved. The plain was covered with prisoners and corpses, disclosed by the dust as it settled and victory became clear. The prisoners, with beating hearts, were bound in chains. The dead were scattered over the mountains and valleys, lying immobile on their sides. Hattin shrugged off their carcasses, and the perfume of victory was thick with the stench of them. I passed by them and saw the limbs of the fallen cast naked on the field of battle, scattered in pieces over the site of the encounter, lacerated and disjointed, with heads cracked open, throats split, spines broken, necks shattered, feet in pieces, noses mutilated, extremities torn off, members dismembered, parts shredded, eyes gouged out, stomachs disemboweled, hair colored with blood, the praecordium slashed, fingers sliced off, the thorax shattered, the ribs broken, the joints dislocated, the chests smashed, throats slit, bodies cut in half, arms pulverized, lips shriveled, foreheads pierced, forelocks dyed scarlet, breasts covered with blood, ribs pierced, elbows disjointed, bones broken, tunics torn off, faces lifeless, wounds gaping, skin flayed, fragments chopped off, hair lopped, backs skinless, bodies dismembered, teeth knocked out, blood spilt, life's last breath exhaled, necks lolling, joints slackened, pupils liquefied, heads hanging, livers crushed, ribs staved in, heads shattered, breasts flayed, spirits flown, their very ghosts crushed; like stones among stones, a lesson to the wise....

At the same time as the king was taken, the "true cross" was also captured, and the idolaters who were trying to defend it were routed. It was this cross, brought into position and raised on high, to which all Christians prostrated themselves and bowed their heads. Indeed, they maintain that it is made of the wood of the cross on which, they say, he whom they adore was hung, and so they venerate it and prostrate themselves before it. They had housed it in a casing of gold, adorned with pearls and gems, and kept it ready for the festival of the Passion, for the observance of their yearly ceremony. When the priests exposed it to view and the heads (of the bearers) bore it along all would run and cast themselves down around it, and no one was allowed to lag behind or hang back without forfeiting his liberty. Its capture was for them more important than the loss of the king and was the gravest blow that they sustained in that battle. The cross was a prize without equal, for it was the supreme object of their faith. To venerate it was their prescribed duty, for it was their God, before whom they would bow their foreheads to the ground, and to which their mouths sang hymns. They fainted at its appearance, they raised their eyes to contemplate it, they were consumed with passion when it was exhibited and boasted of nothing else when they had seen it. They went into ecstasies at its reappearance, they offered up their lives for it and sought comfort from it, so much so that they had copies made of it which they worshipped, before which they prostrated themselves in their houses and on which they called when they gave evidence. So when the great cross was taken great was the calamity that befell them, and the strength drained from their loins. Great was the number of the defeated, exalted the feelings of the victorious army. It seemed as if, once they knew of the capture of the cross, none of them would survive that day of ill-omen. They perished in death or imprisonment, and were overcome by force and violence. The sultan encamped on the plain of Tiberias like a lion in the desert or the moon in its full splendor.

Questions: What tactics were employed by Saladin to ensure victory at Hattin? What was the fate of Reynald of Châtillon? What does Imad ad-Din's account of the capture of the cross reveal about the Muslim view of Christian practices?

41. ROGER OF WENDOVER ON THE FALL OF JERUSALEM

Saladin's victory at Hattin paved the way for his conquest of Jerusalem on October 2, 1187. Saladin accepted the city's surrender but, unlike the armies of the First Crusade, did not permit the massacre of its inhabitants. The Christians were granted their freedom, at a price, and those who could pay left the city and made for the coast. Those who could not afford the ransom were sold into slavery. Roger of Wendover was a thirteenth-century English historian whose work incorporates material from a number of other writers. The passage below records the last days of Frankish rule at Jerusalem and the fall of the city to Saladin's forces.

Source: trans. J.A. Giles, *Roger of Wendover's Flowers of History* (London: H.G. Bohn, 1849), Vol. II, pp. 58-63; revised.

Sibylla is Crowned Queen of Jerusalem

About this time, Baldwin the young king of Jerusalem died, and there was no one to succeed him on the throne, except Sibylla, wife of Guy count of Joppa, sister of the leprous king, and mother of the boy-king, just deceased; but as the truce between Saladin and the Christians was just on the point of expiring, the protection of the kingdom was in a critical state, which would brook no longer a delay. A council of the nobles was therefore held, and it was agreed that Sibylla, wife of Guy, as heiress of the kingdom, should be crowned queen, and repudiate Guy, as unequal to the government. Sibylla rejected the sovereignty on these terms, until the nobles, in granting it to her, bound themselves by oath to obey as king the man whom she should choose as her husband. Guy also himself entreated her not to neglect the care of the kingdom on his account. Thus, after some delay, Sibylla acquiesced in tears, and being solemnly crowned queen, received the homage of all the people, whilst Guy her husband, deprived at the same moment of his bride and his crown, returned to his own people. Meanwhile, a report was spread, and soon confirmed by facts, of the hostile approach of Saladin; upon which the queen, convoking her ecclesiastic and temporal nobles, deliberated with them about choosing a king; and, whereas they had all previously allowed her to choose whomsoever she pleased, and now anxiously looked to the choice which she should make, she said to Guy, who was standing by among the others, "My lord Guy, I choose you for my husband, and give up myself and my kingdom to you as the future king." All were astonished at her words, and wondered that so simple a woman had baffled so many wise councilors. Her conduct was in fact worthy of great praise, both in point of modesty and discretion; for she saved the crown for her husband, and her husband for herself.

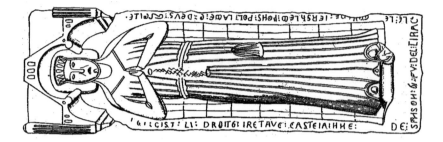

Fig. 15: A drawing of the tomb effigy of Queen Sybilla of Jerusalem, who shortly before her death in 1187 maneuvered to keep her husband Guy de Lusignan on the throne as king (see doc. 41). Sybilla had inherited the throne in her own right. From P. Lacroix, *Military and Religious Life in the Middle Ages* (London, Chapman and Hall, 1874).

About this time, ... the mother of Saladin, on her way from Egypt to Damascus with a large and splendid retinue, passed through the Christian territories which lie on the other side of Jordan, trusting to the truce; but Reynald of Châtillon, assaulting the company, carried off all their valuables, but Saladin's mother saved herself by flight. Saladin, aroused by this injury, demanded restitution and satisfaction, according to the terms of the treaty, and Reynald, when called upon to give it, returned a harsh and insulting reply. Upon this, Saladin rejoiced beyond measure that the Christians had first infringed the treaty, and prepared himself for war and for revenge.... [The battle of Hattin was fought.]

How the Holy City and Almost All the Kingdom was Subdued by Saladin

Saladin, having obtained this victory [at Hattin], returned to Tiberias, and when he had reduced the only fortress which remained, he sent the king and his prisoners to Damascus. Then entering Galilee he found no one to oppose him, and coming to Ptolemais took it without bloodshed. From there he proceeded to Jerusalem, and planted his machines on all sides round the walls: the citizens erected such defenses as they were able, but their bows, cross-bows, and stone-engines were plied in vain. The people, in terror, flocked round the patriarch and the queen, who at that time governed the city, and entreated that terms might be entered into with Saladin for surrender. A capitulation was in consequence effected, more worthy to be lamented than to be described; that every man should pay a ransom of ten bezants, a woman five, and a child one; but in the whole city there were fourteen thousand of both sexes, who, being unable to pay this ransom, were reduced to perpetual slavery. Thus the holy city was surrendered to the enemies of Christ: the sepulcher fell into the hands of those who persecuted him who was buried therein, and those who blaspheme the crucified are in possession of his cross! Saladin entered the city with the sound of timbrels and trumpets, and hastening to the Temple removed the cross erected there, and all the other objects which Christians held in veneration. He then caused the Temple to be sprinkled within and without with rose-water, and the superstitions which belong to his religion to be proclaimed in all its four corners; the church of the resurrection and the tomb of our Lord was let to certain Syrians at a stipulated tribute; after which Saladin sallied forth and reduced all the other cities and towns except Ascalon, Tyre, and Krak beyond Jordan, otherwise called Mount Royal....

How at the Preaching of the Crusade Many Took the Cross

In 1188, Frederick [Barbarossa] the [Holy] Roman emperor took the cross on the preaching of Henry bishop of Alba, a legate of the apostolic see, who had been sent by Pope Clement, and at the same time Philip king of the French and Henry king of the English came to a conference in Normandy, between Trie and Gisors, for the purpose of rendering assistance to the Holy Land, where, after long deliberations, they in the presence of Philip count of Flanders mutually agreed to take the sign of the cross, and to hasten their journey together to Jerusalem. Thereupon the king of the English first took the sign of the cross at the hands of the archbishop of Rheims and William of Tyre, the latter of whom had been entrusted by our lord the pope with the office of legate in the affairs of the crusade in the western part of Europe. After this the king of the French and Philip count of Flanders also took the cross, and the example thus shown was so powerful, that throughout the kingdoms and dominions of the two above named kings, the cross was eagerly assumed by archbishops, bishops, dukes, marquises, counts, barons, and soldiers, as well as by the middle and lower classes of the people promiscuously. It was agreed between the princes that the French should all wear red, the English white, and the followers of the count of Flanders green, crosses. Concerning dominions, fortresses, and all their possessions, it was agreed that, until their pilgrimage was accomplished, and each of them had passed forty days in his own country, all things should remain as they were before their taking the cross.

Questions: What was the political situation in Jerusalem prior to Saladin's capture of the city? What role did the hereditary queen, Sybilla, play? From the descriptions of the battle of Hattin in this and the previous document, why did the Franks lose so badly? What is this author's view of Saladin and his actions?

42. LETTERS ON THE FALL OF JERUSALEM

The recapture of Jerusalem was seen as a significant event by the Muslims of this peri-od; more than sixty Islamic letters (along with numerous poems and sermons) on the subject survive. Jerusalem, whose religious importance had waxed and waned throughout the course of Islamic history, was now viewed as a symbol of the unity and strength of Islam. The significance of Jerusalem was not lost on Saladin. From the timing of his entry into Jerusalem (on the exact date of Mohammed's legendary Night Journey to the city) to his ordering of a commemorative sermon by the well-known preacher Ibn al-Zaki, Saladin orchestrated the event with an eye toward posterity. For the Christian West, the loss of Jerusalem was devastating and prompted the immediate call for another crusade.

Source: trans. W. Robson, *The History of the Crusades*, by J.F. Michaud (New York: A.C. Armstrong & Son, 1881), vol. III, pp. 372-76, 380-84; revised.

Saladin to the Imam Nassir Del-din-illah Aboul Abbas Ahmed

The servant [that is, Saladin] has written this letter, which contains the account of the auspicious events of which he is the author....

The land of Jerusalem is become pure.... God is become one God, and he was three. The houses of the infidel are destroyed, the dwellings of polytheism are cast down. The Muslims have taken possession of the fortified castles. Our enemies will not return to them again, for they are branded with the seal of weakness and degradation. God has placed beauty where deformity was....

This province [of Palestine] is full of wells, lakes, islands, mosques, minarets, population, armies. The servant will change the tares of error for the good seed of the true faith; he will cast down the crosses of the churches, and will cause the izan [that is, the summons to prayers] to be heard. He will change into pulpits the places [that is, altars] on which the infidels immolated, and of churches he will make mosques.

There remained nothing but Jerusalem; every banished man, every fugitive had here taken refuge; those from afar as well as those near had here shut themselves up; they considered themselves as there protected by the favor of God; they believed that their church would intercede for them. Then the ser-vant arrived before the city; he beheld a city well peopled; he beheld troops who had agreed to die; for whom death would be sweet if their city was doomed to fall. He came to one side of the city, but he found that the valleys were deep; that bad passages were numerous; that the walls, like a necklace, sur-rounded it, and that towers, like large beads, were placed along the middle of the walls. Then he directed his course to another side, where there was such an ascent as he desired, a place and an asylum for the cavalry; he surrounded this side and made his approaches to it; he caused his tent to be pitched in a spot exposed to the attempts of the enemy; he attacked the walls vigorously, and at length got possession of them. The besieged sent to him, offering to pay him a tribute for a certain time; they wished to obtain a cessation of their distress, and wait for reinforcements. The servant deferred his answer, and drew his machines nearer — the machines that are the sticks and cords that punish castles for their resistance. Their strokes prepared the victory. Possession was taken of the towers; the walls were void of combatants; stone crumbled away into dust again, as it had been at first. The gates fell into the hands of the army of the servant. Then the infidels despaired; the leader of the impiety came out then...; he requested that the city should be taken by capitulation and not by storm; the abjection of ruin and distress was imprinted upon his countenance, which before had shone with the glory of royalty; he prostrated himself in the dust, he before whom nobody had dared to raise their eyes, and said: "There [pointing to the city] are thousands of captive Muslims; this is the determination of the Franks: if you take the city by force, if you place the burden of war heavily on their backs, they will immediately kill their captives; they will afterwards kill their wives and children; then they will have nothing to wish for but death; but not one of them will die without having sacrificed many of your people." The officers were of opinion that the city should be taken by capitulation; for, they said, if it is taken by storm, there is no doubt but that the besieged will rush headlong into danger and will sacrifice their lives for a thing they have so well defended. In the sorties they had previously made they had displayed incredible courage, and their attacks had been terrible....

But God has driven them out of this territory, and has cast them down; he has favored the partisans of the truth, and has shown his anger against the infidels. These had protected this city by the sword; they had raised buildings at the point of the sword and with columns of soldiers. These have placed churches there, and houses ... of the Hospitallers [and others]. In these houses are precious things in marble.

The servant has restored the Al-Aqsa mosque to its ancient destination. He has placed imams in it who will there celebrate the true worship. The khothbeh [that is, sermon] was made there on Friday, the 14th of Chaaban. Little was wanting to make the heavens open with joy, and the stars dance. The word of God has been exalted; the tombs of the prophets which the infidels had stained, have been purified....

Papal Bull of Gregory VIII, 1187

Gregory, bishop, servant of the servants of God; to all those of the worshippers of our Lord Jesus Christ to whom these letters shall come, health and the apostolic benediction.

Having learnt the terrible severity of the judgments which the divine hand has exercised over Jerusalem and the Holy Land, we have been, we and our brethren, penetrated with such horror, afflicted with such lively grief, that, in the painful uncertainty of what it would be best for us to do on this occasion, we have only been able to partake of the sorrows of the psalmist, and to claim with him, "Lord, the nations have invaded thy heritage, they have profaned thy holy temple; Jerusalem is no more than a desert, and the bodies of the saints have served as pasture to the beasts of the earth, and to the birds of the heavens." For in consequence of the internal dissensions which the wickedness of men, by the suggestion of the demon, had given birth to in the Holy Land, behold Saladin, without any warning, at the head of a formidable army, comes pouring down upon the city. The king and the bishops, the Templars and the Hospitallers, the barons and the people, hasten to the rescue, bearing with them the cross of the Lord, that cross which, in memory of the passion of Christ, who was nailed to it, and which thus purchased the redemption of the human race, was regarded as the most secure rampart to be opposed to the attacks of the infidels. The conflict begins; our brethren are conquered; the holy cross falls into the hands of the enemies; the king is made prisoner, the bishops are massacred, and such of the Christians as escape death cannot avoid slavery. Flight saves a few, and very few; and these tell us that they saw the whole of the Templars and Hospitallers perish before their eyes. We think it useless, beloved brethren, to inform you how, after the destruction of the army, the enemies spread themselves over the whole kingdom, and rendered themselves masters of most of the cities, with the exception of a small number, which still resist. It is here we are compelled to say with the prophet, "Who will change my eyes into a fountain of tears, that I may weep night and day the massacre of my people?" Nevertheless, far from allowing ourselves to be cast down, or to be divided, we ought to be persuaded that these reverses are only to be attributed to the anger of God, against the multitude of our sins; that the most efficacious manner of obtaining the remission of them is by tears and groans, and that at last, appeased by our repentance, the mercy of the Lord will raise us up again, more glorious for the abasement into which he has plunged us.... We ought not then to attribute our disasters to the injustice of the judge who chastises, but rather to the iniquity of the people who have sinned....

The people of these countries had beforehand reason to fear that which has now happened to them, when the infidels got possession of a part of the frontier cities. Would to God that they had then had recourse to penitence, and that they had appeased, by a sincere repentance, the God they had offended! For the vengeance of that God is always only delayed. He does not surprise the sinner; he gives him time for repentance, until at length his exhausted mercy gives place to his justice. But we who, amidst the dissolution spread over this country ought to give our attention, not only to the iniquities of its inhabitants, but to our own, and to those of all Christian people, and who ought, still further, to dread the loss of those of the faithful that still remain in Judea, and the ravages with which the neighboring countries are threatened, amidst dissensions which prevail between Christian kings and princes, and between villages and cities; we who see nothing on all sides but scandals and disorders, we ought to weep with the prophet, and repeat with him, "Truth and the knowledge of God are not upon earth; I see nothing reign in their place but falsehood, homicide, adultery, and thirst for blood."

It is everywhere urgent to act, to efface our sins by voluntary penance, and, by the help of true piety, to return to the Lord our God, in order that, corrected of our vices, and seeing the malice and ferocity of the enemy, we may do for the support of the cause of the Lord, as much as the infidel does not fear to attempt to do every day against him. Think, my beloved brethren, for what purpose you came into this world, and how you ought to leave it; reflect that you will thus pass through all that concerns you. Employ, then, the time you have to dispose of in good actions, and in performing penance; give that which belongs to you, because you did not make yourself, because you have nothing which is yours alone....

We will labor to reconquer that land upon which the truth descended from heaven, and where it did not refuse to endure the opprobrium of the cross for our salvation. We will not hold in view either a love of riches or a perishable glory, but your holy will, O my God! you who have taught us to love our brothers as ourselves, and to consecrate to you those riches, the disposal of which, with us, is so often independent of your will.... "Let us prepare ourselves, let us show ourselves courageous, because it is better to perish in fight than to behold the evils of our nation, and the profanation of holy things."

We promise, then, to all those who, with a contrite heart and an humble mind, will not fear to undertake this painful voyage, and who will be determined to do so by motives of a sincere faith, and with the view of obtaining the remission of their sins, a plenary indulgence for their faults, and the life everlasting which will follow.

Whether they perish there, or whether they return, let them know that, by the mercy of the all powerful God, and by the authority of the holy apostles Peter and Paul, and by our own, they are liberated from all other penance that may have been imposed upon them, provided always that they may have made an entire confession of their sins.

The property of the crusaders and their families will remain under the special protection of the archbishops, bishops, and other prelates of the church of God.

No examination shall be made as to the validity of the rights of possession of a crusader, with regard to any property whatever, until his return or his decease be certain; and till that time his property shall be protected and respected.

He cannot be compelled to pay interest, if he owe any to anybody.

The crusaders are not to march clothed in sumptuous habits, with dogs, birds, or other such objects, which only display luxury and ostentation; but they are to have what is necessary, are to be clothed simply, and are rather to resemble men who are performing a penance, than such as are in search of a vain glory...

The anger of the supreme judge being never so effectively appeased as when we seek to subdue our carnal desires, [and] as we have no doubt that the misfortunes which have recently fallen upon Jerusalem and the Holy Land from the invasion of the Saracens have been produced by the crimes of the inhabitants and those of the Christian people, we, with the unanimous advice of our brethren, and the approbation of a great number of bishops, order that, from this day, for five years, the fast of Lent shall be observed every Friday, during the whole day.

We further order, that in all places where divine service is celebrated, it shall be at nine o'clock, and that from the Advent of the Lord to his nativity.

Every one, without distinction, abstaining from eating flesh on the Friday and Saturday of each week, we and our brethren further interdict the use of it on Tuesdays among ourselves, unless personal infirmities, a festival, or some other good cause excuse us; hoping by this means that the Lord will be appeased, and will leave us his benediction.

Such are our regulations on this subject, and whoever shall infringe them shall be considered as a transgressor of the fast of Lent.

Questions: Why was the taking of Jerusalem so important to Saladin? What did he consider to be the most significant result of this event? Compare his account with the narrative by the Christian writer Roger of Wendover in the previous document. According-ing to Gregory VIII, what were the reasons for the loss of Jerusalem? How did he pro-pose to counter this disaster?

43. TAXATION AND REGULATIONS FOR THE THIRD CRUSADE

Gregory VIII, in his call for a crusade, had insisted on the establishment of a truce between the warring factions of Europe so that its participants could leave their lands without fear and concentrate on the matter at hand. This was especially important in the case of the French and English kings, who had, up to this time, been engaged in skirmishes and schemes to take one another's territory. Papal legates hammered out a truce between Henry II of England and Philip Augustus of France. The next step was to finance this venture, and to this end the so-called Saladin Tithe was announced by both kings. Highly unpopular, the Saladin Tithe was collected in England but eventually repealed in France. Both Henry and Philip vowed to take the cross, but Henry died in 1189 and was succeeded by his son, Richard I (the Lionheart). Under pressure from the church and public opinion, both Richard and Philip agreed that they would depart for the Holy Land as a united force in July of 1190. Preachers were sent out across Europe to recruit crusading soldiers, and codes of conduct stipulating how crusaders were to behave were formulated. Such regulations are known from the First Crusade onward.

Source: trans. J.A. Giles, *The Annals of Roger de Hoveden* (London: H.G. Bohn, 1853), Vol. II, pp. 79-81, 140-41, 160-63; revised.

Ordinances of 1188

...Henry [II], king of England, after he had thus taken the cross, came to LeMans, where on his arrival, he gave orders that everyone [in his kingdom] should give one-tenth of his revenues in the present year, and one-tenth of his chattels, as alms in a subsidy to the land of Jerusalem. The following articles were excepted from the levy: the arms, horses, and garments of men-at-arms, and the horses, books, clothes, vestments, and all kinds of sacred vessels belonging to the clergy, and also all kinds of precious stones belonging to either the clergy or the laity. Excommunication was pronounced beforehand by the archbishops, bishops, and rural deans, in each parish, against anyone who would not lawfully pay his aforementioned tithe in the presence and at the assessment of those whose duty it was to be present there.

Furthermore, the said money was to be collected in each parish in the presence of the priest of the parish, the rural dean, one Templar, one Hospitaller, one member of the household of our lord the king, one yeoman of the baron's household, his clerk, and the clerk of the bishop. And if anyone should give less, according to their conscientious assessment, than he ought to give, four or six lawful men of the parish were to be chosen, who, on oath, were to state the amount that he ought to have stated, on which he would be bound to add the amount by which it was deficient. Clerks, however, and knights who would take the cross, were not to pay any such tithes; but the revenues from their demesnes, and whatever their vassals should owe as their due, were to be collected by the abovenamed persons, and to be remitted to them untouched.

... It was also enacted by the kings [of France and England], and the archbishops, bishops, and other princes of the land ... that no one [among the crusaders] should swear profanely, and that no one should play at games of chance or at dice; and no one was after the ensuing Easter to wear beaver, or grey fur, or sable, or scarlet; and all were to be content with two dishes [at a meal]. No one was to take any woman with him on the pilgrimage, unless, perhaps, some laundress accompany him on foot, about whom no suspicion could be entertained; and no person was to have his clothes in rags or torn....

Ordinances of 1190

"Richard, by the grace of God king of England, duke of Normandy and Aquitaine, and count of Anjou, to all his subjects about to proceed by sea to Jerusalem, greeting. Know ye that we, by the common counsel of fit and proper men, have made the enactments written below [for the crusade].

"Whoever shall slay a man on shipboard shall be bound to the dead man and thrown into the sea. If he shall slay him on land, he shall be bound to the dead man and buried in the earth. If anyone shall be convicted, by means of lawful witnesses, of having drawn a knife with which to strike another, or shall strike another so as to draw blood, he shall lose his hand. And if he shall strike a blow with his hand, without shedding blood, he shall be plunged in the sea three times. If anyone shall utter disgraceful language or abuse, or shall curse his companion, he shall pay an ounce of silver for every time he has so abused him. A robber who is convicted of theft shall have his head cropped like that of a hired fighter, and boiling pitch shall be poured over it, and then the feathers of a cushion shall be shaken out upon him, so that he may be known, and as soon as the ships touch land he shall be put ashore...."

On October 8, the king of France and the king of England, ... by the advice and consent of the whole army of the pilgrims, ... enacted that ... no man in the army was to play at any kind of game for money, with the exception of knights and the clergy, who, in one day and night, were not to lose more than twenty shillings; and if any knight or clerk should lose more than twenty shillings in any natural day, as often as such persons should exceed twenty shillings they were to pay one hundred shillings [toward the relief of the Holy Land].... The kings, however, were to play at their good pleasure; and in the lodgings of the two kings their men-at-arms might play as far as the sum of twenty shillings, with the permission of the kings. Also, in the presence of archbishops, bishops, earls, and barons, with their sanction, men-at-arms might play as far as the sum of twenty shillings. But if any men-at-arms or mariners, or others of the lower orders, should be found playing without permission, men-at-arms were to be whipped naked for three days in front of the army, unless they were able to ransom themselves at the arbitration of the persons before named; and the same was to apply to other servants of similar rank. But if mariners should so play, they were to be plunged into the sea, first thing in the morning, on three successive days, after the tradition of sailors, once each day, unless they were able to ransom themselves at the arbitration of the persons before mentioned.

Furthermore, if any pilgrim, while on his journey, should borrow anything from another person, he was to pay back what he had borrowed; but as to what he had borrowed before setting out, he was not to be bound to make repayment during the pilgrimage.

Furthermore, if any mariner hired for wages, or any men-at-arms or any other person whatever, clerks and knights excepted, should leave his master while on the said pilgrimage, no one else was to receive [that is, hire] him, except by permission of his master....

As for ... merchants, in whatever commodity they should deal, they were bound to make no more than one penny profit in every ten pence....

No person was to buy any dead flesh to sell the same again, nor yet any living beast, unless he should kill it within the camp.

No person was to sell his wine at too high a price....

Questions: What did the Saladin Tithe require of every person? How was its collection ensured? Who and what were exempt from this tax? What do the laws concerning conduct en route to the Holy Land tell us about life and discipline within the crusader armies? About social rank?

44. ACCOUNTS OF THE THIRD CRUSADE

Once the Third Crusade got under way, the tensions between its leaders only worsened. The first and third excerpts below are from The Itinerary of the Pilgrims and Deeds of Richard, *one of the best sources for the Third Crusade. Compiled by one Richard, an English Augustinian canon, in the early thirteenth century, it is believed to be based on sources that include accounts by a Templar eyewitness and by Ambroise, a French cleric writing in the mid-1190s. The second account below is by the well-informed English historian Richard of Devizes.*

Source: trans. J.A. Giles, *Chronicles of the Crusades, Being Contemporary Narratives...*, ed. H.G. Bohn (London: Henry G. Bohn, 1848), pp. 55-56, 60-64, 99-101, 151, 200, 206, 209-10, 217-21; revised.

Itinerary of the Pilgrims and Deeds of Richard

The [German] army now entered the Armenian territories: all rejoiced at having left a hostile kingdom, and at their arrival in the country of the faithful. But, alas! a more fatal land awaited them, which was to extinguish the light and joy of all.... On the borders of Armenia there was a place, surrounded on one side by steep mountains, on the other side by the river Selesius. While the packhorses and baggage were passing this river, the victorious emperor [Frederick Barbarossa] halted... [and] in consequence of the packhorses crossing the river, became at last impatient of the delay; and wishing to accelerate the march, he prepared to cross the nearest part of the stream, so as to get in front of the packhorses and be at liberty to proceed. O sea! O earth! O heaven! the ruler of the [Holy] Roman Empire, ever august, in whom the glory of ancient Rome again flourished, ... was overwhelmed in the waters and perished! And though those who were near him hastened to his assistance, yet his aged spark of life was extinguished by a sudden though not premature death....

When his funeral rites had been performed, they left the fatal spot as soon as possible, bearing with them the body of the emperor adorned with royal magnificence, that it might be carried to Antioch. There the flesh, being boiled from the bones, reposes in the church of the apostolic see, and the bones were conveyed by sea to Tyre, to be transported from there to Jerusalem.... The [emperor's army], arriving at Antioch after many and long fastings, gave way too plentifully to their appetites, and [many] died of sudden repletion, and so ... the greater part of the great army perished, and most of the survivors returned to their own countries. A small body of them, ashamed to return, served under the emperor's son....

After Easter [1191] there arrived [at Acre] Philip, king of France, and not long after him, Richard, king of England.... Around [Acre] the besiegers lay in countless multitudes, chosen from every nation throughout Christendom and under the face of heaven, and well fitted for the labors and fatigues of war; for the city had now been besieged a long time, and had been afflicted by constant toil and tribulation, by the pressure of famine, and every kind of adversity, as we have before described. Moreover, beyond the besiegers was seen the Turkish army, not in a compact body, but covering the mountains and valleys, hills and plains, with tents, the colors of whose various forms were reflected by the sun.... King Richard beheld and counted all their army, and when he arrived in port, the king of France and a whole army of natives, and the princes, chiefs, and nobles, came forth to meet him and welcome him, with joy and exultation, for they had eagerly longed for his arrival....

The city of Acre, from its strong position, and its being defended by the choicest men of the Turks, appeared difficult to take by assault. The French had hitherto spent their labor in vain in constructing machines and engines for breaking down the walls, with the greatest care; for whatever they erected, at a great expense, the Turks destroyed with Greek fire or some devouring conflagration....

King Richard was not yet fully recovered from [a] sickness; nevertheless, anxious for action, and strenuously intent upon taking the city, he made arrangements that his men should assault the city, in the hope that under divine providence he should succeed. For this purpose, he caused a hurdle to be made ... with the most subtle workmanship. This the king intended to be used for crossing over the trench outside the city. Under it he placed his most experienced crossbowmen, and he caused himself to be carried thither on a silken bed, to honor the Saracens with his presence, and animate his men to fight; and from it, by using his crossbow, in which he was skilled, he slew many with darts and arrows. His sappers also dug a mine under the tower, at which a petrary was directed; and having made a breach, they filled it with logs of wood, and set them on fire; when, by the addition of frequent blows from the petrary, the tower fell suddenly to the ground with a crash.... [The assault continued, and the city's inhabitants eventually agreed to surrender it.]

After this a great discord arose between the two kings.... Affairs being in this position, at the end of the month of July, within which the Turks had promised to restore the holy cross and receive back their hostages, a rumor spread among the army that the king of France, on whom the hope of the people rested, intended to return home, and was making active preparations for his journey. Oh how wicked and how insulting a proceeding, while as yet so much work remained on hand, to wish to go away, when his duty was to rule so large a multitude of people, and when his presence was so necessary to encourage the Christians to so pious a work.... The king of France alleged sickness as the cause of his return, and said that he had performed his vow as far as he was able.... It must not be denied, at the same time, that the king of France expended much labor and money in the Holy Land for the assaults on the city, and that he gave aid and assistance to very many, and that by the influence of his presence, he procured the more speedy execution and consummation of ... the capture of the city.... But when the inflexible determination of the king of France to return [home] became known to all, and his refusal to yield to the murmurs of his men, or their supplications to remain, the French would have renounced their subjection to him, if it could have been done.... But for all that, the king of France hastened his voyage as much as possible, and left in his stead the duke of Burgundy, with a large number of men. Moreover, he begged King Richard to supply him with two galleys, and the king readily gave him two of his best; how ungrateful [Philip] was for this service was afterward seen.

King Richard was of the opinion that the king of France should enter into a covenant for the preservation of their mutual security; for they, like their fathers, regarded each other with mistrusts, under the veil of friendship, which even in the following generation never expelled fear. King Richard was therefore anxious with this uneasy feeling, and required an oath from the king of France to keep his faith not to do injury to his men or territory knowingly or purposely, while he, King Richard, remained in a foreign land; but if on any occasion any action [by Richard's vassals] that should appear reprehensible went unpunished, King Richard on his return should have forty days' notice before the king of France should proceed to obtain redress. The king of France took the oath which was required faithfully to observe all these conditions, and gave the duke of Burgundy and Count Henry as hostages, and five or more others, whose names are lost. How faithfully [Philip] kept his covenant and oath is very well known to all the world; for he had no sooner reached his own country, than he set it in commotion and threw Normandy into confusion [by attacking Richard's lands there]....

King Richard ... turned his attention to packing up the petraries and mangonels for transportation. For when the time had expired which had been fixed by the Turks for the restoration of the cross and the ransom of the hostages, after waiting three weeks, according to the conditions, to see if Saladin would keep his word and covenant, the king regarded him as a transgressor, as Saladin appeared not to care about it at all; and perhaps this happened by the dispensation of God, so that something more advantageous might be obtained. But the Saracens asked further time to fulfill their promise and make search for the cross....

When it became clearly evident to King Richard that a longer period had elapsed than had been agreed, and that Saladin was obdurate and would not bother to ransom the hostages, he called together a council of the chiefs of the people, by whom it was resolved that the hostages should all be hanged, except a few nobles of the higher class, who might ransom themselves or be exchanged for some Christian captives. King Richard, aspiring to destroy the Turks root and branch, and to punish their wanton arrogance, as well as to abolish the law of Mohammed, and to vindicate the Christian religion, on the Friday before the Assumption of the blessed virgin Mary, ordered 2,700 of the Turkish hostages to be led forth from the city and hanged; his soldiers marched forward with delight to fulfill his commands and to retaliate, with the assent of divine grace, by taking revenge upon those who had destroyed so many of the Christians with missiles from bows and crossbows.... [The crusaders then moved toward Jerusalem, arriving in its vicinity in mid-1192, after much fighting and many delays.]

Richard of Devizes

Richard, the king of the English, had already spent two years in conquering the region around Jerusalem, and during all that time no aid had been sent to him from any of his realms. Nor yet were his only and uterine brother, John, count of Mortain, nor his justiciars, nor his other nobles, observed to take any care to send him any part of his revenues, and they did not even think of his return. However, the church prayed to God for him without ceasing. The king's army shrank daily in the promised land, and besides those who were slain by the sword, many thousands of people perished every month by the too sudden extremities of the nightly cold and the daily heat. When it appeared that they would all have to die there, everyone had to choose whether he would die as a coward or in battle.

On the other side, the strength of the infidels greatly increased, and their confidence was strengthened by the misfortunes of the Christians; their army was relieved at certain times by fresh troops; the weather was natural to them; the place was their native country; their labor, health; their frugality, medicine. Amongst us, on the contrary, that which brought gain to our adversaries became a disadvantage. For if our people had too little to eat even once in a week, they were rendered less effective for seven weeks after. The mingled nation of French and English fared sumptuously every day, at whatever cost, while their treasure lasted; and (no offense to the French) they ate until they were sick. The well-known custom of the English was continually kept up even under the clarions and the clangor of the trumpet or horn: with due devotion they drained their wine-cups to the dregs. The merchants of the country, who brought the victuals to the camp, were astonished at their wonderful and extraordinary habits, and could scarcely believe even what they saw to be true, that one people, and that small in number, consumed three times more bread and a hundred times more wine than that on which many nations of the infidels had been sustained, and some of those nations innumerable. And the hand of the Lord was deservedly laid upon them according to their merits. Such great lack of food followed their great gluttony, that their teeth scarcely spared their fingers, as their hands presented to their mouths less than their usual allowance. To these and other calamities, which were severe and many, a much greater one was added by the sickness of the king.

The king was extremely sick, and confined to his bed; his fever continued without intermission; the physicians whispered that it was an acute semitertian fever. And as they despaired of his recovery even from the beginning, terrible dismay was spread from the king's abode through the camp. There were few among the many thousands who did not consider fleeing, and the utmost confusion of dispersion or surrender would have followed, had not Hubert Walter, bishop of Salisbury, immediately assembled the council. By strenuous argument he won this concession: that the army should not break up until a truce was requested from Saladin. All the armed men stood in array more steadily than usual, and with a threatening look concealing the reluctance of their mind, they feigned a desire for battle. No one spoke of the king's illness, lest the secret of their intense sorrow should be disclosed to the enemy; for it was well known that Saladin feared the charge of the whole army less than that of the king alone; and if he should know that he was sick in bed, he would instantly pelt the French with cow-dung, and intoxicate the best of the English drunkards with a dose which should make them tremble....

[The Muslims eventually proposed a truce in these terms:] If it pleased King Richard, for the space of three years, three months, three weeks, three days and three hours, such a truce would be observed between the Christians and the infidels, that whatever either one party or the other in any way possessed he would possess without molestation to the end. During the interval the Christians would be permitted at their pleasure to fortify Acre only, and the infidels Jerusalem. All contracts, all commerce, every act and every thing would be mutually carried on by all in peace. [Saladin's brother] Saffadin himself was dispatched to the English as the bearer of this offer....

While King Richard was sick at Jaffa, word was brought to him that the duke of Burgundy was taken dangerously ill at Acre. It was the day for the king's fever to take its turn, and through his delight at this report, it left him. The king immediately with uplifted hands imprecated a curse upon the duke, saying, "May God destroy him, for he would not destroy the enemies of our faith with me, although he had long served in my pay." ... [Eventually,] having resumed his strength of body more by the greatness of his mind than by repose or nourishment, he issued a command for the whole coast from Tyre to Ascalon, that all who were able to serve in the wars should come to fight at the king's expense. A countless multitude assembled before him, the greater part of whom were on foot. Having rejected them as useless, he mustered the cavalry and found scarcely 500 knights and 2,000 shield-bearers whose lords had perished. And not discouraged by their small number, he, being a most excellent orator, strengthened the minds of the fearful with a timely speech. He commanded that it be proclaimed through the companies that on the third day they must follow the king to battle, either to die as martyrs or to take Jerusalem by storm. This was the sum of his project, because as yet he knew nothing of the truce. For there was no one who dared even hint to him, when he had so unexpectedly recovered, that which they had undertaken without his knowledge, through fear of his death. However, Hubert Walter, bishop of Salisbury, took counsel with Count Henry concerning the truce and obtained his ready concurrence in his wishes. So having deliberated together how they might safely hinder such a hazardous engagement, they conceived of the one stratagem out of a thousand, namely, to try to dissuade the people from the enterprise. And the matter turned out most favorably; the spirit of those who were going to fight had so greatly failed even without dissuasion, that on the appointed day, when the king, according to his custom leading the van, mar-shaled his army, of all the knights and shield-bearers no more than 900 were found. On account of which defection, the king, greatly enraged, even raving, and gnawing the pine rod which he held in his hand, at length opened his indignant lips as follows: "O God!" said he, "O God, my God, why hast thou forsaken me? For whom have we foolish Christians, for whom have we Eng-lish come hither from the furthest parts of the earth to bear our arms? Is it not for the God of the Christians? O fie! How good art thou to us thy people, who now are for thy name given up to the sword; we shall become a portion for foxes. O how unwilling should I be to forsake thee in so forlorn and dreadful a position, were I thy lord and advocate as thou art mine! In sooth, my standards will in future be despised, not through my fault but through thine; in sooth, not through any cowardice of my warfare, art thou thyself, my King and my God, conquered this day, and not Richard thy vassal."

He spoke, and returned to the camp extremely dejected; and as a fit occa-sion now offered, Bishop Hubert and Henry, count of Champagne, approach-ing him with unwonted familiarity, as if nothing had yet been arranged, begged under diverse pretexts the king's consent for making such overtures to the infidels as were necessary. And thus the king answered them: "Since a trou-bled mind is usually more likely to thwart than to afford sound judgment — I, who am greatly troubled in mind, authorize you, whom I see to be calm of mind, to arrange what you shall think most proper for the good of peace." Having gained their desires, they chose messengers to send to Saffadin upon these matters; Saffadin, who had returned from Jerusalem, was suddenly announced to be at hand. The count and the bishop went to meet him, and being assured by him of the truce, they instructed him how he must speak with the lord their king. Being admitted to an interview with the king as one who previously had been his friend, Saffadin could scarcely prevail upon the king not to destroy himself but to consent to the truce. For so great were the man's strength of body, mental courage, and entire trust in Christ, that he could hardly be prevailed upon not to undertake in his own person a single combat with a thousand of the choicest infidels, as he was destitute of soldiers. And as he was not permitted to attack, he chose this evasion, that, after a truce of seven weeks, the stipulations of the compact being preserved, it should remain for him to choose whether it were better to fight or to forbear. The two parties put their right hands to the final agreement, that they would faithfully observe it; and Saffadin, more honored than burdened with the king's present, went back again to his brother, to return at the expiration of the term for the final conclusion or breaking of the above truce.

Richard, king of England, held a council at Acre, and there prudently regulating the government of that state, he appointed his nephew, Henry, count of Champagne, on whom he had formerly conferred Tyre, to be captain and lord of the whole promised land. But he thought it proper to defer his consecration as king till he might perhaps be crowned at Jerusalem. King Richard, now thinking to return home, with the assistance of Count Henry appointed men for all the strongholds in his territories and found Ascalon alone without garrison or inhabitants, for lack of people. Wherefore, taking precaution that it might not become a receptacle of the infidels, he caused the ramparts and fortifications of the castle to be cast down.

The seventh day of the seventh week appeared, and behold Saffadin, with many emirs who desired to see the face of the king, drew near. The truce was confirmed on both sides by oath, with this provision being added to what had been previously agreed, that during the continuance of the truce no one, whether Christian or infidel, should inhabit Ascalon, and that all the fields pertaining to the town should still belong to the Christians. Hubert, bishop of Salisbury, and Henry, captain of Judea, together with a numerous band, went up to Jerusalem to worship in the place where the feet of Christ had stood. And there was woeful misery to be seen—captive confessors of the Christian name, wearing out a hard and constant martyrdom; chained together in gangs, their feet blistered, their shoulders raw, their backsides goaded, their backs wealed, they carried materials to the hands of the masons and stone-layers to make Jerusalem impregnable against the Christians. When the captain and bishop had returned from the sacred places, they endeavored to persuade the king to go up; but the worthy indignation of his great heart could not consent to receive by the courtesy of the infidels that which he could not obtain by the gift of God.

Itinerary of the Pilgrims and Deeds of Richard

[King Richard] urged the sailors to spread their canvas to the winds, so that they might the sooner cross over the expanse of sea that lay before them, ignorant indeed of the tribulations and sorrows that awaited him, and the calamities that he was to suffer from the treachery that had long before been transmitted to France, by which it was contrived that he should be wickedly thrown into prison [by a German prince], though he justly suspected no such evil in the service of God, and in so laborious a pilgrimage. O how unequally was he recompensed for his exertions in the common cause! His inheritance was seized by another [that is, his brother John], his castles in Normandy were unjustly taken [by Philip of France], his rivals made cruel assaults upon his rights without provocation, and he only escaped from captivity by paying a ransom to the emperor of Germany. To gather the money for his ransom, the taxes were raised to the uttermost; a large collection was levied upon all his land...; for the chalices and hallowed vessels of gold and silver were gathered from the churches, and the monasteries were obliged to do without their utensils; neither was this unlawful according to the decrees of the holy fathers, nay, it was even a matter of necessity, inasmuch as no saint, many though there be, ever during life suffered so much for the Lord as King Richard in his captivity in Austria and in Germany. He who had gained so many triumphs over the Turks was nefariously circumvented by the brethren of his own faith, and seized by those who agreed with him in name only as members of the creed of Christ.... But out of that captivity, by God's usual mercy, his own activity, and the care of his faithful servants, he was at length set at liberty for a large sum of money, because he was known to be a man of great power. At last restored to his native soil and the kingdom of his ancestors, in a short time he restored all to tranquillity....

Questions: What considerations might influence a crusade leader to return home before completing his mission? What role did morale play in this campaign? What factors influenced morale? How did each side try to gain advantages during negotiations? What kind of military leader was Richard? Why did he refuse to visit Jerusalem? What does the aftermath of the crusade reveal about crusading ideals?

CHAPTER FIVE:

THE CULTURE AND LOGISTICS OF CRUSADING

Fig. 16: A thirteenth-century ship, as represented on the wax seal of the English port of Dover. From P. Lacroix, *Military and Religious Life in the Middle Ages* (London, Chapman and Hall, 1874).

45. GERALD OF WALES ON PREACHING A CRUSADE

The crusading experience often began when the potential crusader heard a sermon calling on Christians to "take the cross"—and a vow to go on crusade. The prolific twelfth-century writer Gerald of Wales here recounts taking part in a preaching tour made to recruit holy warriors for the Third Crusade.

Source: trans. J.A. Giles, *The Historical Works of Giraldus Cambrensis* (London: H.G. Bohn, 1863), pp. 331-33, 337-38, 367-68, 371, 396-99, 425-26, 443, 467-68; revised.

In the year 1188 A.D., ... when Saladin, prince of the Egyptians and Damascenes, by a signal victory gained possession of the kingdom of Jerusalem, Baldwin, archbishop of Canterbury, a venerable man, distinguished for his learning and sanctity, journeyed from England for the service of the holy cross and entered Wales near the borders of Herefordshire.

The archbishop proceeded to Radnor on Ash Wednesday, ... where, a sermon being preached by the archbishop on the subject of the Crusades and explained to the Welsh by an interpreter, the author of this book was the first to arise, impelled by the urgent pleading and promises of the king and the persuasions of the archbishop and the justiciar, and, falling down at the feet of the holy man, devoutly took the sign of the cross. His example was instantly followed by Peter, bishop of St. David's, a monk of the abbey of Cluny, and then by Eineon, son of Eineon Clyd, prince of Elfael, and many other persons. Eineon, rising up, said to Rhys, whose daughter he had married, "My father and lord! With your permission I hasten to avenge the injury offered to the greatest Father of all." Rhys himself was so fully determined to set out on the holy pilgrimage, as soon as the archbishop should enter his territories on his return, that for nearly fifteen days he was employed in making the necessary preparations for so distant a journey with great solicitude. But then his wife ... by female artifices diverted him wholly from his noble purpose....

Having crossed the river Wye, we proceeded into Brecknockshire, and on preaching a sermon at Hay, we observed some amongst the multitude, who were to be signed with the cross, fly for refuge to the archbishop in the castle, leaving their garments in the hands of their friends or wives, who endeavored to hold them back. Early in the morning we began our journey to Aberhodni, and the word of the Lord being preached at Llanddew, we spent the night there....

A sermon having been delivered at Abergavenny, and many persons converted to the cross, a certain nobleman of those parts, named Arthenus, came to the archbishop, who was proceeding towards the castle of Usk, and humbly begged pardon for having neglected to meet him sooner. Being questioned whether he would take the cross, he replied, "That ought not be done without the advice of my friends." The archbishop then asked him, "Are you not going to consult your wife?" To which he modestly answered, with a downcast look, "When the work of a man is to be undertaken, the counsel of a woman ought not to be asked." And instantly he received the cross from the archbishop....

At the castle of Usk, a multitude of persons influenced by the archbishop's sermon, and by the exhortations of the good and worthy William, bishop of Llandaff, who faithfully accompanied us through his diocese, were signed with the cross; Alexander, archdeacon of Bangor, acted as interpreter to the Welsh. It is remarkable that many of the most notorious murderers, thieves, and robbers of the neighborhood were converted here, to the astonishment of the spectators....

On our journey from Carmarthen to the Cistercian monastery called Whitland, the archbishop was informed of the murder of a young Welshman, who had been devoutly hastening to meet us; when turning out of the road, the archbishop ordered the corpse to be covered with the cloak of his almoner [that is, his official in charge of charity], and with a pious supplication he commended the soul of the murdered youth to heaven. Twelve archers of the adjacent castle of St. Clears, who had assassinated the young man, were on the following day signed with the cross at Whitland, as a punishment for their crime....

A sermon having been delivered at Haverfordwest by the archbishop, and the word of God preached to the people by the archdeacon, whose name appears on the title-page of this work [that is, Gerald], many soldiers and commoners were induced to take the cross. It appeared wonderful and miraculous, that, although the archdeacon addressed them both in the Latin and French tongues, those persons who understood neither of those languages were equally affected, and flocked in great numbers to the cross....

We slept [one] night in the monastery of St. Dogmael, where, as well as on the next day at Aberteivi, we were handsomely entertained by the prince Rhys. On the Cemmeis side of the river, not far from the bridge, the people of the neighborhood being assembled together, and Rhys and his two sons, Malgon and Gruffydd, being present, the word of the Lord was persuasively preached by both the archbishop and the archdeacon, and many were induced to take the cross. One of them was an only son and the sole comfort of his mother, far advanced in years, who, steadfastly gazing on him, as if inspired by the Deity, uttered these words: "O most beloved Lord Jesus Christ, I give you hearty thanks for having conferred on me the blessing of bringing forth a son, whom you may think worthy of your service." Another woman at Aberteivi, of a very different way of thinking, held her husband fast by his cloak and belt, and publicly and audaciously prevented him from going to the archbishop to take the cross. But three nights afterward, she heard a terrible voice saying, "You have taken away my servant from me; therefore what you most love shall be taken away from you." On her relating this vision to her husband, they were struck with mutual terror and amazement; and on falling asleep again, she accidentally smothered her little boy, whom, with more affection than prudence, she had taken to bed with her. The husband, relating to the bishop of the diocese both the vision and its fatal prediction, took the cross, which his wife spontaneously sewed on her husband's arm....

We remained [a] night at Bangor, the metropolitan see of North Wales, and were well entertained by the bishop of the diocese. On the next day, mass being celebrated by the archbishop before the high altar, the bishop of that see, at the urging of the archbishop and other persons, more persistent than persuasive, was compelled to take the cross, to the general concern of all his people of both sexes, who expressed their grief on this occasion by a loud and lamentable outcry....

From Wenlock, we passed by the little cell of Brumfeld, the notable castle of Ludlow, through Leominster to Hereford; ... thus describing, as it were, a circle, we came to the same point from which we had commenced this laborious journey through Wales.

During this long and laudable legation, about three thousand men were signed with the cross, well skilled in the use of arrows and lances, and versed in military matters, impatient to attack the enemies of the faith, profitably and happily engaged for the service of Christ, if only the expedition of the holy cross had been forwarded with an alacrity equal to the diligence and devotion with which the forces were collected....

Questions: Why did Gerald himself take the cross? What kinds of people did the preachers try to recruit for the crusade? What reactions did they encounter? What does this text reveal about the opinions of ordinary people about crusading?

46. PRIVILEGES AND INDULGENCES

An "indulgence" was a church-granted remission of penalties (especially of time to be in purgatory) for sin; such spiritual benefits had been promised to Christian holy warriors against Islam since the time of the Muslim invasion of Spain in the eighth century (see doc. 6). The term "privilege" in the crusading context refers to the practical protections and advantages promised to crusaders, their families, and their lands, either by the church or by secular authorities, to facilitate their long-term absence from home. For additional privileges and indulgences, see Gregory VIII's proclamation of the Third Crusade (doc. 42) and the decrees of the Fourth Lateran Council (doc. 62).

Sources: Eugenius III: trans. W. Robson, *The History of the Crusades*, by J.F. Michaud (New York: A.C. Armstrong & Son, 1881), Vol. III, pp. 370-72, revised; *Cor nostrum*: trans. E. Amt from Latin text in *Alexandri III Romani Pontificis Opera Omnia*, from. J.-P. Migne (Paris: *Patrologiae Cursus Completus, Series Latina*, vol. 200, 1855), cols. 1294-1296; Innocent III: trans. O. J. Thatcher and E.H. McNeal, *A Sourcebook for Medieval History: Selected Documents Illustrating the History of Europe in the Middle Age* (New York: Charles Scribner's Sons, 1905), pp. 537; others: trans. D.C. Munro, *Translations and Reprints from the Original Sources of European History*, series I, vol. I (Philadelphia: University of Pennsylvania Department of History, 1902), no. 2, pp. 12-15, 18-19, revised.

Urban II, 1095 (from William of Malmesbury, *Chronica Majora*)

If anyone through devotion alone, and not for the sake of honor or gain, goes to Jerusalem to free the church of God, the journey itself shall take the place of all penance.

Eugenius III, 1146

The servant of the servants of God, to his dear son Louis, illustrious and glorious king of the French, to his dear sons, the princes, and to all the faithful of the kingdom of France, health and apostolic benediction.

We know by the history of times past, and by the traditions of our fathers, how many efforts our predecessors made for the deliverance of the church of the East. Our predecessor, Urban, of happy memory, sounded the evangelic trumpet, and employed himself with unexampled zeal, in summoning the Christian nations from all parts of the world to the defense of the Holy Land. At his voice the brave and intrepid warriors of the kingdom of the Franks, and the Italians, inflamed with a holy ardor, took arms, and delivered, at the cost of their blood, the city in which our Savior deigned to suffer for us, and which contains the tomb, the monument of his passion. By the grace of God, and by the zeal of our fathers, who defended Jerusalem, and endeavored to spread the Christian name in those distant countries, the conquered cities of Asia have been preserved up to our days, and many cities of the infidels have been attacked and their inhabitants have become Christians. Now, for our sins, and those of the Christian people (which we cannot repeat without grief and lamentation), the city of Edessa—which in our own language is called Rohas, and which, if we can believe the history of it, when the East was subjected to the pagan nations, alone remained faithful to Christianity—the city of Edessa is fallen into the hands of the enemies of the cross.

Several other Christian cities have shared the same fate; the archbishop of that city with his clergy, and many other Christians have been killed; relics of the saints have been given up to the insults of the infidels and dispersed. The greatest danger threatens the church of God and all Christendom. We are persuaded that your prudence and your zeal will be conspicuous on this occasion;

you will show the nobleness of your sentiments and the purity of your faith. If the conquests made by the valor of the fathers are preserved by the valor of the sons, I hope you will not allow it to be believed that the heroism of the French has degenerated. We warn you, we pray you, we command you, to take up the cross and arms. I warn you for the remission of your sins — you who are men of God — to clothe yourselves with power and courage, and stop the invasion of the infidels, who are rejoicing at the victory gained over you; to defend the church of the East, delivered by our ancestors; to wrest from the hands of the Muslims many thousands of Christian prisoners who are now in chains. By the present generation, and your valor, the reputation of which is spread throughout the universe, will not only preserve itself without stain, but will acquire a new splendor.... We, who watch over the church and over you, with a parental solicitude, we grant to those who will devote themselves to this glorious enterprise the privileges which our predecessor Urban granted to the soldiers of the cross. We have likewise ordered that their wives and their children, their worldly goods, and their possessions, should be placed under the safeguard of the church, of the archbishops, the bishops, and the other prelates. We order, by our apostolic authority, that those who shall have taken the cross shall be exempt from all kinds of pursuit on account of their property, until their return, or until certain news be received of their death. We order, besides, that the soldiers of Jesus Christ should abstain from wearing rich habits, from having great care in adorning their persons, and from taking with them dogs for the chase, falcons, or anything that may corrupt the manners of the warriors. We warn them, in the name of the most high, that they should only concern themselves with their warhorses, their arms, and everything that may assist them in contending with the infidels. The holy war calls for all their efforts, and for all the faculties they have in them; they who undertake the holy voyage with a right and pure heart, and who shall have contracted debts, shall pay no interest. If they themselves, or others for them, are under obligations to pay usurious interest, we release them from them by our apostolic authority. If the lords from whom they hold will not, or cannot, lend them the money necessary, they shall be allowed to engage their lands or possessions to ecclesiastics, or any other persons. As our predecessor has done, by the authority of the all-powerful God, and by that of the blessed St. Peter, prince of the apostles, we grant absolution and remission of sins, and we promise life eternal to all those who shall undertake and complete the said pilgrimage, or who shall die in the service of Jesus Christ, after having confessed their sins with a contrite and humble heart.

Alexander III, papal bull *Cor nostrum*, 1181

Bishop Alexander, servant of the servants of God, to his dear sons, the noble men, the dukes and princes, counts, barons, and all God's faithful, to whom these letters shall come, greeting and apostolic blessing.

Evil rumors, which have come to us from those returning from the Holy Land, have disturbed our heart and those of all our brothers with great sorrow, and scarcely anyone who is counted as a Christian is able to hear, without tears and sighs, the things that are miserably recounted concerning the state of that land....

Strive to the utmost, therefore, not to let Christianity succumb to paganism; for it is better to counteract evil before it arrives than to seek a remedy after being injured. We therefore, by apostolic authority, do concede and confirm, to those who take up this work on behalf of Christ, the same indulgence of sins which our fathers and predecessors the Roman pontiffs Urban and Eugenius established. And we decree that their wives, too, and their children, and their goods and possessions, shall remain under our protection, and under that of the blessed Peter, and of archbishops, bishops, and other prelates of the church: and we very strictly prohibit any adversary of those who peacefully possess these things from lodging any suit against them after they have taken the cross, until they return, or until their death is established for certain. And let it be lawful for them, freely and without any disapproval, to mortgage their lands or their other possessions to churches, or to churchmen, or to other faithful persons, as sureties for the expenses of this journey, if their neighbors or even their lords (to whose fiefs their lands belong) do not want to or cannot lend them the money. Moreover, to any fighting men, well suited to the defense of that land, who go to those holy places with the fervor of devotion, and fight there for two years against the Saracens for the defense of the Christian name, we, trusting in the love of Jesus Christ and in the authority of the blessed apostles Peter and Paul, grant absolution for all their sins which they have confessed with contrite and humble hearts: unless perchance they have stolen others' goods, or have extorted interest, or have committed thefts, for all of which they must make full restitution. But if is not possible for them to make the amends they owe, nonetheless they will receive pardon for their sins, as we have said. And those men who stay there for a year, as we have said, shall obtain indulgence of half the penance laid on them and remission of their sins. And to all who wish to visit the sepulcher of the Lord on account of the present need, whether they die on the journey or reach that place, we permit the labor of the journey to serve as penance, and obedience and remission of all sins, so that from the prison of this present life they may come, God permitting, to that blessing which "eye has not seen, nor ear heard; nor has it entered into the human heart" [I Cor. 11] what God has promised to those who love him.

King Philip II of France, 1188

In the name of the holy and indivisible Trinity, Amen. It has been decided by the lord Philip, king of the Franks, by the advice of the archbishops, bishops, and barons of his land:

1. That bishops, prelates, and clerks of the conventual churches, and knights who have taken the cross, shall have a respite of two years — dating from the first feast of All Saints [that is, Nov. 1] after the departure of the king — in paying the debts which they owed to Jews or Christians before the king took the cross; that is, on the first feast of All Saints the creditors shall have a third of the debt, and on the following feast of All Saints a second third of the debt, and on the third feast of All Saints the last third of the debt. Also, for each one, from the day on which he takes the cross, interest on debts previously contracted shall cease.

2. If a knight who is the legitimate heir, son, or son-in-law of a knight not taking the cross, or of a widow, and who is under the jurisdiction of his father or mother, takes the cross, his father and mother shall have a respite from their debts, in accordance with the above ordinance.

3. If, however, their son or son-in-law, who has taken the cross, is no longer under their jurisdiction, or if he is not a knight, or if he has not taken the cross, they shall not enjoy a respite through this decree.

4. Also, within a fortnight after the next feast of St. John the Baptist [that is, June 24], those debtors who have lands and revenues shall, through the lords in whose territory the lands are, assign the lands and revenues to their creditors, in order that from these the creditors may collect their debts at the aforesaid times and according to the aforesaid form. The lords shall not be able to prevent those assignments, unless they themselves settle with the creditor for the debt.

5. Those who do not have sufficient lands or revenues to make an assignment for their debts shall give their creditors sureties or bail that they will pay their debts at the dates fixed. And unless they give security, as has been arranged, through assignment of lands, or sureties, or bail if they have no lands, within a fortnight after the next feast of St. John the Baptist, they shall not have the respite which is granted to others.

6. If any crusader who is a clerk or knight is in debt to a crusader who is a clerk or knight, he shall have a respite from his debt until the next feast of All Saints — provided, however, that he furnishes good security for paying his debt at the time indicated.

7. If any one of those who have taken the cross shall have assigned to anyone gold, silver, grain, or any other personal property a week before the [feast of the] Purification of the Blessed Mary [that is, Feb. 2] or after that time, the creditor shall not be compelled to give him a respite on that account.

8. If anyone buys from another, who has not taken the cross, the usufruct [that is, the use and profits] of his lands for one year at a fixed price, the bargain shall stand.

9. If any knight or clerk shall have mortgaged his lands or revenues to a citizen who is also a crusader, or shall have assigned them for a period of years, the debtor this year shall receive the produce of the lands or the revenues; and the creditors, as a recompense for this year, shall hold the property for one year after the completion of the years for which the mortgage or assignment ought to continue. However, if the creditor shall have cultivated the mortgaged lands or vineyards, he shall have one-half the grain this year for his labor.

10. All bargains made a week before the Purification of the Blessed Virgin, or after that date, shall hold good.

11. For all debts on which he obtains a respite, the debtor must give as good security as, or better than, he had previously given. If a dispute arises about the security, the council of the lord of the creditor shall demand as good security as, or better than, before. And if the security is not fixed by that lord, it shall be fixed by the council of the prince of the land.

12. If any lord or prince under whose jurisdiction the said creditors or debtors shall be shall not wish to observe, or shall not cause to be observed, this decree concerning the respite for debts or the assignments, he shall be warned by his archbishop or bishop; if he shall not make amends within forty days, he may be placed by the same under a sentence of excommunication. Nevertheless, as long as the lord or prince shall be willing to prove, in the presence of his archbishop or bishop, that in this respect he has not failed in his duty to either the creditor or debtor, and that he is prepared to comply with the decree, the archbishop or bishop shall not have the power to excommunicate him.

13. No crusader, whether clerk, knight, or anyone else, shall be obliged to defend himself in a lawsuit concerning the land of which he was tenant, from the day on which he takes the cross until he returns from his undertaking, unless the suit had been brought against him before he had taken the cross.

Letter of Innocent III to King of Denmark, 1210

We commend you because, fired with zeal for the orthodox faith and for the praise of God and for the honor of the Christian religion, you have taken the cross and have drawn your royal sword to repress the cruelty of an infidel people [that is, the Turks]. And we also give you our apostolic favor, and take under the protection of St. Peter, as well as under our own, your person and your kingdom with all your possessions, decreeing that so long as you are engaged in this work all your possessions shall remain intact and free from all molestation. Nevertheless we urge upon you to take all possible precautions to protect you and yours, in order that you may not suffer any loss.

Edict of King Louis IX of France, 1270

If the king, or a count, or a baron, or any lord who had the right of jurisdiction in his land, arrests a clergyman, or crusader, or any man of religion, even if he is a layman, the lord ought to deliver him to the holy church, whatever may be his crime. And if the clerk has committed a crime for which the penalty is death by hanging, and is not tonsured, the secular justice ought to try him. But if he is tonsured and wears the habit of a clerk, even if he is a thief, no confession, no answer that he may make, can injure him, for he is not before his regular judges; and any confession made by one who is not before his regular judges has no value, according to the law written in the Decretals [that is, canon law]....

Questions: Compare these indulgences with early medieval indulgences (doc. 6) and the provisions of the Fourth Lateran Council (doc. 62). How did the spiritual benefits of crusading develop over time? What practical protections were extended to crusaders? How reliable was papal protection of crusaders' lands and possessions? How did crusading affect those who stayed at home in Europe? How might crusaders use the crusading privileges to their own benefit? What concerns had to be balanced against the privileges of crusaders?

47. PERSONAL ARRANGEMENTS

Below are documents in which individuals who have taken the cross make various property arrangements and other provisions for their absence or death on crusade.

Sources: Provision for sons: trans. E. Amt from *The Thame Cartulary*, ed. H.E. Salter (Oxford: Oxfordshire Record Society, 1947), p. 53; contract: trans. H.G. Richardson and G.O. Sayles, *The Governance of Mediaeval England from the Conquest to Magna Carta* (Edinburgh: Edinburgh University Press, 1963), p. 465; waiver: trans. E. Amt from *The Cartulary of the Knights of St. John of Jerusalem in England: Secunda Camera, Essex*, ed. M. Gervers (Oxford: Oxford University Press for the British Academy, 1982), pp. 113-14; disposition: trans. H.T. Riley, *Memorials of London and London Life in the XIIIth, XIVth, and XVth Centuries* (London: Longmans, Green, and Co., 1868), pp. 68-69, revised.

Provision for Sons, c. 1170

Let everyone know, now and in the future, that I, Hugh de Braimuster, being about to set out for Jerusalem, have given to my son Hugh half my land in England wherever it is, and the fief of Robert de St. Clare which is in Braimuster.... And if my son Hugh, after my death, will not agree to this pact, let my son Odo permit him to have the proper portion of my land according to the judgment of the court, ... and Hugh will be in possession according to the first agreement until the court has considered what part of the land Hugh ought to have. Each of them has confirmed this agreement by oath, and for my part I confirm this with my seal.

Waiver of Crusader Privilege, c. 1260

To all people to whom this present writing shall come, William, son of Henry of Halstead, sends greeting in the Lord. Know that I owe to the house of the Hospital of St. John of Jerusalem at Little Maplestead and to the brothers of that house 40s. in legal money, payable to the said brothers within eight days upon their demand or that of their representative. If it should happen (as it should not) that I make any transgression against the said brothers or their tenants (saving my own prosecution or defense or that of my right), and if I am delinquent in any payment, I wish and concede that both the archdeacon of Middlesex, with his official and his dean, and the guardians of the privileges of the prior and brothers of the hospital of St. John of Jerusalem in England may, jointly or separately, at the sole accusation of the said brothers or their representative (who will show this charter), publicly and solemnly excommunicate and denounce me. And I agree that I will remain excommunicated thereafter, until I make full satisfaction to the same brothers, both in the aforesaid sum of money and in their expenses, if they have to send anyone after me. And I

Fig. 17: The seal of a French nobleman. Personal documents such as those in this chapter would be authenticated with such a seal in wax. From P. Lacroix, *Military and Religious Life in the Middle Ages* (London, Chapman and Hall, 1874).

renounce royal protection, the legal rights bestowed by ordination, the privilege granted to those who take the cross, and every customary and legal exemption, all indulgences and privileges acquired from the apostolic seat, every special or general objection, and every remedy of civil or canon law, and for the greater security of this charter I have affixed my seal to it. These are the witnesses: Brother Thomas of Derminton, Master Robert of Twinstead, Brother Ralph of Godesfelt, Robert the chaplain, Hugh Joy, and others.

Contract of Service, 1270

To all those who shall see or hear this writing, Adam of Jesmond wishes salvation in our Lord. Know that I have agreed with my lord Edward, the eldest son of the king of England, to go with him to the Holy Land, accompanied by four knights, and to remain in his service for a whole year to commence at the coming voyage of September. And in return he has given me, to cover all expenses, 600 marks in money and transport, that is to say the hire of a ship and water for as many persons and horses as are appropriate for knights. And should it happen that I am detained by sickness or any other accident, which God forbid, a knight in my place and my knights aforesaid will undertake his service fully for the year or else I will return to him so much money as shall be necessary to complete the period which is lacking from the year, and this shall be at my option. And if it should by chance happen that God's will shall be that my aforesaid lord, Sir Edward, shall die, I shall be bound to him whom my lord shall leave or send in his place, [just the same] as to himself, according to the form above written. And in witness hereof I have caused my seal to be set to this writing. Given at Westminster the twentieth day of July in the fifty-fourth year from the coronation of our lord King Henry, son of King John.

Crusader's Disposition of Property, 1309

To all persons who shall see or hear these present letters, I, John de Lue, knight, send greetings in God. Whereas Sir Richard de Lue, my brother, made me joint tenant, with Anneis, my sister, of his houses and all his tenement that he had in the lane called Seething Lane in London, the which tenement the heirs of Messire Henry de Grey — to whom may God grant mercy — hold by enfeoffment and gift, which the said Sir Richard afterwards made to the afore-said Sir Henry, such houses and tenement being held, bound, and obligated to me for a yearly rent of 40 shillings, as is contained in an obligatory writing of his, under the hand of the said Sir Richard, and sealed with his seal, and of which rent I have been seised under his hand, part of the same being still in arrears; and whereas I am not able now to wait and raise and get in the same, by reason of my journey, which I have undertaken to make to the Holy Land, in devoutness, and for the salvation of my soul: know ye that I do assign and attorn in my stead Elizabeth, my dear partner, to demand and receive the same rent of 40 shillings, with the arrears, and by distraint to levy the same in my name from the tenement aforesaid, and to do all things in the same matter, for her own profit, as well as I myself ever could have done in my own proper person. For I have left and given, for always, unto the same Elizabeth, my part-ner, to help with her living and her sustenance, this same yearly rent of 40 shillings each year, and the arrears which are due unto me, with all my right and claim which I have or may have, at any time, in the houses and tenement aforesaid. In witness of which matter, unto this writing I have set my seal. Given at London, on Wednesday, the feast of St. Barnabas the Apostle [that is, 11 June], in the second year of the reign of King Edward, son of King Edward.

Questions: What concerns did crusaders have as they set out? How might these be diff-erent from their concerns at other times, or before other journeys? What necessary arrangements are not included in these documents?

48. LITURGY FOR PILGRIMS AND CRUSADERS

When an individual "took the cross," he or she usually did so in a spontaneous or ad hoc ceremony, rather than in a formal ritual administered by the church. But the church did develop procedures for the blessing of pilgrims, including the armed pilgrim or crusader, before their journeys. The ceremony printed here is from a liturgical tradition that was common to many parts of England. The scrip (or small bag) and staff that are mentioned were the traditional equipment of the pilgrim.

Source: trans. F.E. Warren, *The Sarum Missal in English* (London: De La More Press, 1911), pp. 166-73; revised and extended.

First, the following Psalms are said over them prostrate in front of the altar, after they have made their confessions, beginning thus:

Psalm: Unto thee, O Lord, will I lift up my soul. My God, I have put my trust in thee. O let me not be confounded, neither let mine enemies triumph over me.... [Ps. 25]

Psalm: Have mercy upon me, O God, according to thy loving kindness: according unto the multitude of thy tender mercies blot out my transgressions. Wash me thoroughly from mine iniquity, and cleanse me from my sin.... [Ps. 51]

Psalm: Whoso dwelleth under the defense of the most high, shall abide under the shadow of the Almighty. I will say unto the Lord, thou art my hope, and my stronghold; my God, in him will I trust.... [Psalm 91]

After each Psalm: Glory be to the Father, and to the Son, and to the Holy Ghost. As it was in the beginning, is now, and ever shall be, world without end. Amen.

Lord, have mercy upon us.
Christ, have mercy upon us.
Lord, have mercy upon us.

Our Father, which art in heaven, hallowed be thy name. Thy kingdom come. They will be done, in earth as it is in heaven. Give us this day our daily bread. And forgive us our trespasses, as we forgive them that trespass against us.

   V. And lead us not into temptation,
   R. But deliver us from evil.
   V. I said, Lord, be merciful unto me;

R. Heal my soul, for I have sinned against thee.
V. The Lord show thee his ways;
R. And teach thee his paths.
V. The Lord direct thy steps according to his word;
R. That no unrighteousness get the dominion over thee.
V. O that thy ways were made so direct;
R. That thou mightest keep the statutes of the Lord.
V. The Lord uphold thy goings in his paths;
R. That thy footsteps slip not.
V. Blessed be the Lord God daily;
R. The God of our salvation prosper thy way before thee.
V. The good angel of the Lord accompany thee;
R. And dispose thy way and thine actions aright, that thou mayest return again to thine own place with joy.
V. Blessed are those that are undefiled in the way;
R. And walk in the law of the Lord.
V. Let the enemy have no advantage against thee;
R. And let not the son of wickedness approach to hurt thee.
V. O Lord, arise, help us,
R. And deliver us for thy name's sake.
V. Turn us again, O Lord God of hosts;
R. And show the light of thy countenance upon us, and we shall be whole.
V. Lord, hear my prayer;
R. And let my crying come unto thee.
V. The Lord be with you.
R. And with thy spirit.

Let us pray.

Assist us, O Lord, in these our supplications, and dispose the way of thy servant N. towards the attainment of thy salvation, that among all the changes and chances of the journey through life, he may ever be defended by thy help....

Let us pray.

O God, who leadest unto life, and guardest with thy fatherly protection them that trust in thee, we beseech thee that thou wouldest grant unto these thy servants N. here present, going forth from amongst us, an escort of angels; that they, being protected by thy aid, may be shaken by no fear of evil, nor be depressed by any lingering adversity, nor be troubled by any enemy lying in wait to assail them; but that having prosperously accomplished the course of their appointed journey, they may return unto their homes; and having been received back in safety, may pay due thanks unto thy name....

Here shall the pilgrims rise from their prostration, and the blessing of the scrip and staff shall follow, thus:

    V. The Lord be with you.
    R. And with thy spirit.

Let us pray.

O Lord Jesus Christ, who of thy unspeakable mercy, and at the bidding of the Father, and with the cooperation of the Holy Ghost, didst will to come down from heaven, and to seek the sheep that was lost through the wiles of the devil, and to bear it back on thine own shoulders to the flock of the heavenly country, and didst command the sons of mother church by prayer to ask, by holy living to seek, and by knocking to persevere, that they may be able to find more quickly the rewards of saving life: we humbly beseech thee that thou wouldest vouchsafe to sanctify and bless (+) these scrips (*or* this scrip), and these staves (*or* this staff), that whosoever, for the love of thy name, shall desire to wear the same, like the armor of humility, at his side, or to hang it from his neck, or to carry it in his hands, and so on his pilgrimage to seek the prayers of the saints, with the accompaniment of humble devotion, may be found worthy, through the protecting defense of thy right hand, to attain unto the joys of the everlasting vision, through thee, O Savior of the world....

    Here the priest shall sprinkle the scrip with holy water, and place it on the neck of the pilgrim, saying:

In the name of our Lord Jesus Christ receive this scrip, the habit of thy pilgrimage; that after being well chastened thou mayest be found worthy both to reach in safety the thresholds of the saints, whither thou desirest to go; and that when thy journey is finished thou mayest return to us in safety....

Let it be done to each person, if there be more than one.
Then shall the priest deliver the staff to each one, saying:

Receive this staff for the support of thy journey, and for the labor of thy pilgrimage; that thou mayest be able to overcome all the hosts of the enemy, and to arrive in safety at the thresholds of the saints, whither thou desirest to go; and that when thy journey hath been obediently accomplished, thou mayest again return to us with joy....

And thus let him say to others, if there be more than one.
Blessing of a cross for one on a pilgrimage to Jerusalem.

V. The Lord be with you.
R. And with thy spirit.

Let us pray.

O God of unconquered power, and boundless pity, the entire aid and consolation of pilgrims, who givest to thy servants most invincible armor: we pray thee that thou wouldest vouchsafe to bless (+) this cross, which is humbly dedicated to thee; that the banner of the venerated cross, the figure whereof hath been depicted upon it, may be a most invincible strength to thy servant against the wickedest temptation of the ancient enemy; that it may be a defense by the way, a guard in thy house, and a protection to us everywhere....

Here shall holy water by sprinkled upon the dress [that is, the clothing bearing the cross]. *Then if any of those present be about to journey to Jerusalem, a vestment shall be given to him marked with the cross, the priest saying thus:*

Receive this vestment, marked with the cross of our Lord and Savior, that through it there may accompany thee safety, blessing, and strength for a prosperous journey to the sepulcher of [Christ]....

And thus shall it be done to the rest, if there be more than one present.
(The branding of a cross upon the flesh of pilgrims going to Jerusalem has been forbidden by canon law under pain of the greater excommunication.)

This done, there shall be said a mass for travelers, after the manner of a simple feast of nine lessons.

Questions: Which aspects of the journey to the Holy Land are emphasized here? What messages is the church communicating to the pilgrims and crusaders? What effect was this ceremony intended to have? What effects was it likely to have on the individual being blessed and on observers?

49. BERNARD OF CLAIRVAUX: *IN PRAISE OF THE NEW KNIGHTHOOD*

Bernard of Clairvaux, the Cistercian abbot who had preached the Second Crusade (see doc. 35), also actively promoted the new military order of the Knights Templar. Sometime before 1136, at the request of Hugues de Payens, founder of the Templars, he wrote a treatise extolling their way of life, which is excerpted below. In other parts of the treatise he paints a very negative picture of secular knights and their activities. Bernard's view of the Templars is highly idealized, even in comparison with the Templars' own rules and regulations.

Source: trans. C. Greenia, *In Praise of the New Knighthood* (Kalamazoo: Cistercian Publications, Inc., 2000), pp. 38-41, 45-48.

Chapter 3. On the New Knighthood

But the knights of Christ may safely do battle in the battles of their Lord, fearing neither the sin of smiting the enemy nor danger of their own downfall, inasmuch as death for Christ, inflicted or endured, bears no taint of sin, but deserves abundant glory. In the first case one gains for Christ, and in the second one gains Christ himself, who freely accepts the death of the foe in vengeance, and yet more freely gives himself in consolation to his fallen knight.

The knight of Christ, I say, may strike with confidence and succumb more confidently. When he strikes, he does service to Christ, and to himself when he succumbs. Nor does he bear the sword in vain. He is God's minister in the punishment of evil doers and the praise of well doers. Surely, if he kills an evil doer, he is not a man-killer, but, if I may so put it, an evil-killer. Clearly he is reckoned the avenger of Christ against evildoers, and the defender of Christians. Should he be killed himself, we know he has not perished, but has come safely home. The death which he inflicts is Christ's gain, and that which he suffers, his own. At the death of the pagan, the Christian exults because Christ is exalted; in the death of the Christian the King's liberality is conspicuous when the knight is ushered home to be rewarded. In the one case a just person shall rejoice at regarding vindication; in the other man shall say, "Truly there is a reward for the just; truly it is God who judges the earth" [Ps. 57:12].

Yet this is not to say that the pagans are to be slaughtered when there is any other way of preventing them from harassing and persecuting the faithful; but only that it now seems better to destroy them than to allow the rod of sinners to continue to be raised over the lot of the righteous, lest perchance the righteous set their hand to iniquity.

What then? If it is never permissible for a Christian to strike with the sword, why then did the Savior's precursor bid soldiers be content with their pay, and not rather ban military service to them? But if, as is the case, it is legitimate for all those ordained to it by the Almighty—provided they have not embraced a higher calling—then to whom, I ask, may it more rightly be allowed than to those into whose hands and hearts is committed on behalf of all of us Sion, the city of our strength? So that once the transgressors of divine law have been expelled, the righteous nation that preserves the truth may enter in security.

Surely then the nations who choose warfare should be scattered [Ps. 67:31], those that molest us should be cut away [Gal. 5:12], and all the workers of iniquity should be dispersed from the city of the Lord [Ps. 100:8]—those who busy themselves carrying off the incalculable riches placed in Jerusalem by Christian people, profaning holy things [Lev. 19:8] and possessing the sanctuary of God as their heritage [Ps. 82:13]. Let both swords [Luke 22:38] of the faithful fall upon the necks of the foe to the destruction of every lofty thing lifting itself up against the knowledge of God [2 Cor. 10:4-5], which is the Christian faith, lest the Gentiles [that is, non-Christians] should then say, "Where is their God?" [Ps. 113:2]... Do you not see how often these ancient witnesses authorize the new knighthood?...

Chapter 4. On the Lifestyle of the Knights of the Temple

And now as an exemplar, or at least an embarrassment, for those of our knights who are apparently fighting not for God, but for the devil, we will briefly set forth the life and virtues of these knights of Christ: how they conduct themselves at home as well as in battle, how they appear in public, and how the knighthood of God and of the world differ from one another.

First, discipline is in no way lacking, and obedience is never despised. As Scripture testifies, the undisciplined son shall perish, and rebellion is as much a sin as witchcraft; to refuse obedience is like the crime of idolatry. They come and they go at the bidding of their superior. They wear what he gives them and do not presume to wear or to eat anything from another source. Both in raiment and in rations they shun every excess and have regard only for what is necessary. They live in cheerful community and sober company, without wives and without children. So that their evangelical perfection will lack nothing, they dwell united in one family with no personal property whatever, careful to keep the unity of the Spirit in the bond of peace. You may say that the whole multitude has but one heart and one soul, to the point that no one follows his own will, but seeks instead to follow the commander.

They never sit in idleness or wander about aimlessly, but on the rare occasions when they are not on duty, they are always careful to earn their bread by repairing their worn armor and torn clothing, or simply by setting things to order. For the rest, they are guided by the common needs and by the will of their master.

There is little distinction of persons among them, and deference is shown to ability, not to nobility. They rival one another in mutual consideration, and they carry one another's burdens, thus fulfilling the law of Christ. No arrogant word, no idle deed, no unrestrained laugh, not even the slightest whisper or murmur, is left uncorrected once it has been detected. They forswear dice and chess, they abhor the hunt; they take no delight, as is customary, in the ridiculous cruelty of falconry. Jesters, wizards, bards, bawdy minstrels and jousters, they despise and reject as so many vanities and deceitful follies. They cut their hair short, cognizant that, according to the apostle, it is shameful for a man to cultivate flowing locks. They never dress, and seldom wash, their hair—content to let it appear tousled and dusty, darkened by chain mail and heat.

When a battle is at hand, they arm themselves [on the inside] with faith and [on the outside] with steel rather than with gold. Thus armed and not embellished, they strike fear rather than incite greed in the enemy. They seek out strong, swift horses, rather than those which are dappled and well-plumed. They set their minds on fighting to win rather than on parading for show. They take no thought for glory but seek to be formidable rather than flamboyant. Then too, they are not quarrelsome, reckless, or impulsively foolhardy, but they draw up their ranks deliberately, prudently, and providently, arraying themselves in the line of battle as we read about in the fathers [of the church]. Indeed, the true Israelites march into battle as men of peace.

Yet once in the thick of battle, they set aside this earlier gentleness, as if to say, "Do I not hate those who hate you, O Lord; am I not disgusted with your enemies?" [Ps. 138:21]. These men charge the enemy, regarding the foe as sheep, never—no matter how outnumbered they are—as ruthless barbarians or as awesome hordes. Nor do they presume on their own strength, but trust for victory in the Lord of Sabaoth. They are mindful of the words of the Maccabees, "It is simple enough for a multitude to be vanquished by a handful. It makes no difference in the God of heaven whether he grants deliverance by the hands of few or of many; for victory in war does not depend on a big army, but bravery is the gift from heaven." As they have on numerous occasions experienced, one man may pursue a thousand, and two put ten thousand to flight.

Thus in an astounding and unique manner they appear gentler than lambs, yet fiercer than lions. Consequently I do not know if it would be more appropriate to refer to them as monks or as soldiers, or whether it would perhaps be better to recognize them as being both, for they lack neither monastic meekness nor military might. What can we say about this, except that this is the Lord's doing, and it is marvelous in our eyes. God has hand-picked such troops, and from among the most valiant men of Israel he has recruited from the ends of the earth servants to guard vigilantly and faithfully that sepulcher which is the bed of the true Solomon; all bearing sword in hand, and superbly trained to war.

Questions: How did Bernard reconcile the monastic and warrior ideals? How might similar themes have inspired lay knights going on crusade? Compare Bernard's picture of the Templars with those sketched by William of Tyre, John of Würzburg, and Usamah ibn Munqidh (docs. 23, 28, 30).

50. THE RULE OF THE TEMPLARS

The military order of the Knights Templar, praised by Bernard of Clairvaux in the previous selection, was founded around 1119 (see William of Tyre, doc. 23) and achieved papal recognition in 1128. The earliest version of its Primitive Rule (its first official regulations), in Latin, dates to about 1129; a French version, excerpted below, was written between 1135 and 1147. The Hierarchical Statutes of the order, also excerpted below, were composed around 1165.

Source: trans. J.M. Upton-Ward, *The Rule of the Templars: The French Text of the Rule of the Order of the Knights Templar* (Woodbridge, Suffolk: The Boydell Press, 1992), pp. 21-22, 35, 58-60.

The Primitive Rule

9. You who renounce your own wills, and you others serving the sovereign king with horses and arms, for the salvation of your souls, for a fixed term, strive everywhere with pure desire to hear matins [that is, the morning service] and the entire service according to canonical law and the customs of the regular masters of the holy city of Jerusalem. O you venerable brothers, similarly God is with you, if you promise to despise the deceitful world in perpetual love of God, and scorn the temptations of your body: sustained by the food of God and watered and instructed in the commandments of our Lord, at the end of the divine office, none should fear to go into battle if he henceforth wears the tonsure.

10. But if any brother is sent through the work of the house and of Christianity in the East—something we believe will happen often—and cannot hear the divine office, he should say instead of matins thirteen paternosters; seven for each hour and nine for vespers. And together we all order him to do so. But those who are sent for such a reason and cannot come at the hours set

to hear the divine office, if possible the set hours should not be omitted, in order to render to God his due.

The Manner in Which Brothers Should be Received

11. If any secular knight, or any other man, wishes to leave the mass of perdition and abandon that secular life and choose your communal life, do not consent to receive him immediately, for thus said my lord St. Paul: ... "Test the soul to see if it comes from God." Rather, if the company of the brothers is to be granted to him, let the Rule be read to him, and if he wishes to studiously obey the commandments of the Rule, and if it pleases the master and the brothers to receive him, let him reveal his wish and desire before all the brothers assembled in chapter and let him make his request with a pure heart.

On Excommunicated Knights

12. Where you know excommunicated knights to be gathered, there we command you to go; and if anyone there wishes to join the order of knighthood from regions overseas, you should not consider worldly gain so much as the eternal salvation of his soul. We order him to be received on condition that he come before the bishop of that province and make his intention known to him. And when the bishop has heard and absolved him, he should send him to the master and brothers of the Temple, and if his life is honest and worthy of their company, if he seems good to the master and brothers, let him be mercifully received....

On Secular Knights

65. Those who serve out of pity and remain with you for a fixed term are knights of the house of God and of the Temple of Solomon; therefore out of pity we pray and finally command that if during his stay the power of God takes any one of them, for love of God and out of brotherly mercy, one pauper be fed for seven days for the sake of his soul, and each brother in that house should say thirty paternosters....

66. We command all secular knights who desire with a pure heart to serve Jesus Christ and the house of the Temple of Solomon for a fixed term to faithfully buy a suitable horse and arms, and everything that will be necessary for such work....

Fig. 18: Krak de Chevaliers, one of the Templar castles in Palestine, reconstructed in a nineteenth-century engraving. The garrisoning of massive desert castles that controlled strategic areas was an important function of the military orders in holding the crusader states. From P. Lacroix, *Military and Religious Life in the Middle Ages* (London, Chapman and Hall, 1874).

On the Commitment of Sergeants

67. As the squires and sergeants who wish to serve charity in the house of the Temple for the salvation of their souls and for a fixed term come from diverse regions, it seems to us beneficial that their promises be received, so that the envious enemy does not put it in their hearts to repent of or renounce their good intentions.

Hierarchical Statutes

How the Brothers Form the Line of March

156. When the convent wishes to ride, the brothers should not saddle up, nor load the baggage, nor mount, nor move from their places unless the marshal has the order called or commands it; but tent pegs, empty flasks, the camping axe, the camping rope and fishing net may be put on the horses before the

order to load the baggage is given. And if any brother wishes to speak to the marshal he should go to him on foot, and when he has spoken to him he should return to his place; and he should not leave his place before the order to mount is given, for as long as his companions are in camp.

157. When the marshal has the order to mount called, the brothers should look over their campsite so that nothing of their equipment is left behind, and then they should mount and go quietly with their troop, at a walk or amble, their squires behind them, and position themselves in the line of march if they find an empty place for themselves and their equipment; and if he does not find it empty, he may ask the brother who had taken it, who may give it to him if he wishes, but need not if he does not wish to. And when they have joined the line of march, each brother should give his squire and his equipment a place in front of him....

159. No brother should leave his troop to water his horses or for anything else, without permission; and if they pass by running water in peaceful territory, they may water their horses if they wish; but they may not endanger the line of march. And if they pass by water whilst on reconnaissance, and the standard bearer passes by without watering the horses, they should not do so without permission; and if the standard bearer stops to water his horses, they may do likewise without permission. And if the alarm is raised in the line of march, the brothers who are near the shout may mount their horses and take up their shields and lances, and keep calm and await the marshal's order; and the others should go towards the marshal to hear his command.

160. When there is a war and the brothers are lodged in an inn or established in camp, and the alarm is raised, they should not leave without permission, until the banner is taken out; and when it is taken out they should all follow it as soon as possible, and they should not arm or disarm without permission; and if they are lying in ambush or guarding pasture, or somewhere they are reconnoitering, or they are going from one place to another, they should not remove bridle or saddle or feed their horses without permission.

How Brothers Should Go in a Squadron

161. When they are established in squadrons, no brother should go from one squadron to another, nor mount his horse nor take up his shield or lance without permission; and when they are armed and they go in a squadron they should place their squires with lances in front of them, and those with horses behind them, in such a way that the marshal or the one who is in his place commands; no brother should turn his horse's head towards the back to fight or shout, or for anything else, while they are in a squadron.

163. And if it happens by chance that any Christian acts foolishly [in battle], and any Turk attacks him in order to kill him, and he is in peril of death,

and anyone who is in that area wishes to leave his squadron to help him, and his conscience tells him that he can assist him, he may do so without permission, and then return to his squadron quietly and in silence....

When the Marshal Takes up the Banner to Charge

164. When the marshal wishes to take the banner on God's behalf ... the marshal should order up five or six or up to ten knight brothers to guard him and the banner; and these brothers should overwhelm their enemies all round the banner, to the best of their ability, and they should not leave or go away; rather they should stay as near to the banner as they can, so that, if necessary, they may assist it. And the other brothers may attack in front and behind, to the left and the right, and wherever they think they can torment their enemies in such a way that, if the banner needs them they may help it, and the banner help them, if necessary.

168. And if it happens that the Christians are defeated, from which God save them, no brother should leave the field to return to the garrison, while there is a piebald banner [that is, a Templar banner] raised aloft; for if he leaves he will be expelled from the house forever. And if he sees that there is no longer any recourse, he should go to the nearest Hospital or Christian banner if there is one, and when this or the other banners are defeated, henceforth the brother may go to the garrison, to which God will direct him.

Questions: How are the monastic and knightly aspects of Templar life balanced in the Rule? How are they in conflict, and how are they compatible? What kinds of people, in the view of the Rule's authors, might want to join the Templars temporarily? Why would they want to do this? What do we learn about warfare from this text? What principles governed Templar practices on the march and in battle?

51. FINANCIAL ACCOUNTS

The following document records some of the French king Louis IX's spending on his crusade to the Middle East. In the accounts, twelve pence (d.) equal one shilling (s.), and twenty shillings equal one pound or livre (£). For Louis's crusade, see Chapter IX (doc. 84).

Source: trans. E. Amt; French text in *Recueil des historiens des Gaules et de la France*, vol. 21, ed. J.-D. Guigniaut and N. de Wailly (Paris: Académie des Inscriptions et Belles-Lettres, 1855), pp. 513-15.

These are the expenses of the king St. Louis and of the queen when they were overseas, and for war and ships, the king's ransom, building operations, and ransoming captives, and other items appearing below, for 2,120 days, which is three years and 25 days; that is, from the octave of Ascension 1250 to the octave of Ascension 1253.

Expenditures of the household of the king St. Louis and the queen when they were overseas, and for war and ships, from the octave of Ascension 1250 to the octave of Ascension 1251, for 384 days, which is one year and 19 days:

	£	s.	d.
Cost of food, with provisions and wages for the members of the household	28,990	15	8
Cloaks for knights and clerks	331	5	0
Robes and furs for the king	228	15	2
Harness and robes for [knights and clerks]	9,367	4	2
Gifts of robes and of money	1,410	15	8
Alms	1,689	16	8
Household crossbowmen and sergeants-at-arms	3,507	12	6
For 136 war-horses, riding-horses, and mules, and 15 camels purchased for the household	3,032	10	3
Total household expenses for the time aforesaid:	48,558	15	I

Expenditures for war and ships for the time aforesaid:	£	s.	d.
Pay of knights on wages	50,195	5	9
Gifts and promises to knights serving for a year without wages	23,213	14	8
Mounted crossbowmen and sergeants	17,170	0	6
Replacements and [new] horses	22,383	5	10
Crossbowmen and sergeants on foot	30,164	12	4
Carpenters, miners, and other workers	2,010 15	9	
Customary expenditure, including £3,914 5s. 2d. to ransom captives	72,907	3	6
Loans made against wages	2,096	6	4
[Other] money paid out	400	59	6
Payments for ships	20,258	16	6
Total for war and ships for the time aforesaid:	240,800	60	8
Total of the household expenditures, war, and ships, for the time aforesaid:	289,361	15	9
Item, paid in this period to ransom the king	167,100	58	8

Similar expenditures for the household, war, and ships from the octave of Ascension 1251 to the octave of Ascension 1252, for 351 days, in the Holy Land:

Cost of food	31,595	11	10
Robes and furs for the king	104	12	9
Cloaks for knights and clerks	312	10	0
Harness and robes for the same [knights and clerks]	12,910	8	11
Gifts of robes and of money	771	10	0
Alms	1,515	3	9
Household crossbowmen and sergeants-at-arms	4,494	6	6
105 war-horses, riding-horses, and mules purchased for the household	1,916	18	11
Total expenditures of the household for the king and queen for the time aforesaid:	53,621	2	8

Expenses for war and for ships for the time aforesaid:			
Pay of knights on wages	57,093	17	10
Gifts and promises to knights serving without wages	23,253	18	4
Mounted crossbowmen and sergeants	22,242	13	6
Replacements for 264 horses	6,789	17	0
Crossbowmen and sergeants on foot	29,575	0	6
Carpenters, artillerymen, and other workers	689	12	3
Customary expenses, including £41,366 14s. 9d. for workers in various places overseas, and £967 13s. 9d. to ransom captives	66,793	19	6
Payments for ships	5,725	15	0
Total for war and ships for the time aforesaid:	212,164	13	11
Total expenses of the household of the king and queen, and of war and ships, for the time aforesaid:	265,758	16	7

Similar expenses for the household, for war and ships, from the octave of Ascension 1252 to the octave of Ascension 1253, which time was 385 days, that is, one year and 20 days:

Total expenditures for the king's household:	60,678	10	10
Total for war and ships:	270,547	15	5
Total of the last two sums:	331,226	6	3
Total of the above days: 2120 days, that is, three years and 25 days.			
Total wages of knights serving for the said 3 years and 25 days:	177,938	15	7

(It should be noted that, as appears from the above accounts, each of the said knights received daily wages of just 7s. 6d., and so the number of knights each day comes to 424, so that the wages came to £157 17s. 6d. per day)

Total of gifts and payments made to knights serving
 without wages for the entire time aforesaid: 65,189   8   6

(These gifts and payments, if apportioned as are the customary wages of the knights above, that is 7s. 6d. per day for each knight, would be enough for 155 knights each day, for the entire time aforesaid, costing, per day, £58 4s. 1d. or thereabouts.)

Total for the said knights, calculated at the customary   243,128   4   0
 wage as above:

(Thus the king could have in his company each day, for the entire time aforesaid, 529 knights, [costing] about £217 19d. per day.)

Total of the household expenses for all three years and
 25 days above, for both the king and the queen: 162,858   8   7
(That is, per day, about £145 8s. 2d.)

Total for the king's ransom: 167,102   18   8
Total for war for the aforesaid time: 594,600   4   10
(That is, per day, £530 17s. 10d.)

Total for ships for this entire time: 32,026   2   8
Total for building operations overseas for this entire time: 95,839   2   6
Total for ransoming captives.   1,050   0   0
Total of all these expenditures for the three years and 25 days
 aforesaid; that is, for the household expenses of the king
 and queen, for the king's ransom, for war, ships, building
 operations, and for the ransoming of captives: 1,053,476   17   3

Questions: What were the comparatively larger and smaller expenses of the crusade? How much did a horse cost? Which expenses reflect the specific circumstances of this crusade (see doc. 84)? What different arrangements were made to provide soldiers for the crusade? What different jobs and specialties existed in the army? What clues about life on crusade does the text offer?

52. TRAVEL INFORMATION

The book entitled Secrets for True Crusaders to Help Them Recover the Holy Land *was written in about 1321 by Marino Sanuto, a prominent citizen of Venice. At this point the Europeans had lost their territories in Palestine. Although Marino had visited only Acre in the Holy Land, he was able to assemble, in his own guidebook, facts and lore from a number of other travelers' works. The excerpt below indicates the sort of specific practical information that was available for those planning expeditions to the Middle East. A league was a variable length; here it measures between two and three miles.*

Source: trans. A. Stewart, *Part XIV of Book III of Marino Sanuto's Secrets for True Crusaders to Help Them to Recover the Holy Land* (London: Palestine Pilgrims' Text Society, 1896), pp. 61-63; revised.

The description of the road from the promised land to Cairo by land, across the wilderness, is as follows:

From Gaza it is three leagues to Darum; it is a good road, with water and plenty of grass. Thence to Raphat, two leagues; good road, plenty of water and all things. Thence to Zasque, four leagues; not much sand, good grassy road, plenty of good water. Thence to Heus, four leagues; road leads over sand, fairly good water. Thence to Laris, four leagues; road all over sand, good enough water, and a place for buying and selling. Thence to Burelaui, four leagues; road all over sand, good water and plenty of it. Thence to Bouser, four leagues; here the road divides into the upper and lower road; the lower is the most commonly used, and passes by the place called Sabaquet Baridoil, where King Baldwin died. From Bouser to Tarade is two leagues; plenty of grass, and good water; there is a market there. Thence to Asbede, four leagues; there likewise is much sand, plenty of grass land, good water, and a market. Thence to Viteleb, five leagues; much sand, poor grass, and very bad water, but plenty of it. Thence to Naherlersibia, four leagues; much sand, but good water. Thence to Catie ...; this is a good village, and fairly good water; here the road divides into upper and lower; both roads lead to Habesse, an excellent village; the lower road is the more commonly used of the two.

The upper road is as follows: From Chatie to Hahras, five leagues; plenty of sand and water, but bad water. Thence to Bonuruch, four leagues; much sand, and the water is exceeding bad, bitter, and salty. Thence to Hucar, four short leagues; much sand and bad water. Thence to Asebbi, four leagues; much sand, grass, and good water; there is a market there. Thence to Hesiuone, four leagues; much sand and good water from a river. Thence to Masinach, three leagues; much sand, and good water from a river. After Sbesbie tilled land begins, and from thence to Vacaria, a good village, is two long leagues. There is plenty of water from a river. Thence to Habesse, three leagues. The road is

good, the land fertile, and the village is full of all good things. Thence to Bel-
beis, three leagues; the land is arable, and the village large and fertile. Thence
to Abirelcara, three leagues; fruitful land, good water, and plenty of it. Thence
to Hus, four leagues; fruitful land, good water, and plenty of it. Thence to
Quiriaci, three leagues; fruitful land, and fertile. Thence to Cairo, three
leagues; good road.

The lower road: From Chatie to Aguorabi, four leagues; much sand, very
little water, and that is salty. Thence to Chauseyr, five leagues; much sand, and
plenty of water, but very bad water. Thence to Birchisce, four leagues; not
much sand, plenty of water, but salt water. Thence to Salchie, a good village,
four leagues; abundance of good water. Thence, to Habesse, six leagues; good
road, plenty of good water from a river. Thence to Cairo, as before. Thus the
wilderness reaches for about seventy leagues, and the tilled land for twenty and
more, between Gaza and Cairo.

*Questions: What kind of information does Sanuto assemble here? How would it be
helpful to travelers? Would this be sufficient information for people planning a crusade or
a pilgrimage? How reliable was this information likely to be? What other sources of
information would be available to a traveler?*

53. THE SAGA OF SIGURD THE CRUSADER

*Having taken the cross, received the church's blessing, and made the necessary practical
arrangements, the crusader was ready to depart. Not all crusaders participated in the large
expeditions to which historians have assigned numbers; many went east on their own or
in small groups to assist the crusader states. The action in the following excerpt from the*
Heimskringla, *or* Chronicle of the Kings of Norway, *took place in about 1110.*

Source: trans. T. Wright, *Early Travels in Palestine* (London: Henry G. Bohn, 1848), pp. 50-51, 57-58, 61-62; revised.

After King Magnus Barefoot's fall, his sons, Eystein, Sigurd, and Olaf, took the
kingdom of Norway. Eystein got the northern, and Sigurd the southern parts
of the country.... King Sigurd was chosen king when he was thirteen or fourteen years old, and Eystein was a year older. When King Magnus's sons were
chosen kings, the men who had followed Skopte Ogmundsson returned
home. Some had been to Jerusalem, some to Constantinople; and there they
had made themselves renowned, and they had many kinds of novelties to talk
about. By these extraordinary tidings many men in Norway were incited to
the same expedition; and it was also told that the northmen [that is, Scandina-
vians] who liked to go into the military service at Constantinople found many

opportunities of getting property. Then these northmen desired much that one of the two kings, either Eystein or Sigurd, should go as commander of the troop which was preparing for this expedition. The kings agreed to this, and provided the equipment at their common expense. Many great men, both of the lendermen and bonders [that is, high-ranking people], took part in this enterprise; and when all was ready for the journey, it was determined that Sigurd should go, and Eystein, in the meantime, should rule the kingdom upon their joint account....

Four years after the fall of King Magnus, King Sigurd sailed with his fleet of sixty ships from Norway.... [He stopped in Spain to fight, and then traveled on to the Holy Land.]

King Sigurd stayed a long time in the land of Jerusalem in autumn, and in the beginning of winter.

King Baldwin [of Jerusalem] made a magnificent feast for King Sigurd and many of his people, and gave him many holy relics. By the orders of King Baldwin and the patriarch, there was taken a splinter off the holy cross; and on this holy relic both made oath, that this wood was of the holy cross, upon which God himself had been tortured. Then this holy relic was given to King Sigurd; with the condition that he, and twelve other men with him, should swear to promote Christianity with all his power, and erect an archbishop's seat in Norway if he could; and also that the cross should be kept where the [late] holy King Olaf reposed, and that he should introduce tithes, and also pay them himself. After this King Sigurd returned to his ships at Acre; and then King Baldwin prepared to go to Syria, to a town called Saet, which some think had been Sidon. This castle, which belonged to the heathens, he wished to conquer and lay under the Christians. On this expedition King Sigurd [in 1110] accompanied him with all his men, and sixty ships; and after the kings had besieged the town some time it surrendered, and they took possession of it, and of a great treasure of money; and their men found other booty....

Thereafter King Sigurd returned to his ships, and made ready to leave Palestine. They sailed north to the island of Cyprus; ... [next they went to Greece and spent some time there as guests of the Byzantine emperor.] Then King Sigurd left Constantinople; but many northmen remained, and went into the emperor's pay. Then King Sigurd traveled from Bulgaria, and through Hungary, Pannonia, Swabia, and Bavaria.... When King Sigurd came to Sleswick in Denmark, Earl Eilif made a sumptuous feast for him; and it was then midsummer. In Heidaby he met the Danish king Nicolaus, who received him in the most friendly way, made a great entertainment for him, accompanied him north to Jutland, and gave him a ship provided with everything needful. From thence the king returned to Norway, and was joyfully welcomed on his return to his kingdom. It was the common talk among the people, that none had ever made so honorable a journey from Norway as this journey of King Sigurd. He was twenty years of age, and had been three years on these travels.

Questions: What motivations for crusading are apparent in this text? What kind of experience did these crusaders have? What were Baldwin's concerns in dealing with them? What light is shed on crusading by the statement of Sigurd's age?

54. STORIES OF WOMEN CRUSADERS

The extracts below show some of the ways in which women participated in crusading. The first, by the Greek historian Niketas Choniates, describes noblewomen who went on the Second Crusade; their leader is usually assumed to be the French queen, Eleanor of Aquitaine. The second, reporting an incident during the Third Crusade, comes from The Itinerary of the Pilgrims and Deeds of Richard. *The third, from the memoirs of a knight named Ramon Muntaner, concerns the French invasion of Spain in 1283 under the pretext of a holy war declared by the pope against the Christian king Peter of Aragon.*

Sources: Choniates: trans. H.J. Magoulias, *O City of Byzantium, Annals of Niketas Chonniates* (Detroit: Wayne State University Press, 1984), p. 35; Itinerary: trans. G.A. Giles, *Chronicles of the Crusades, Being Contemporary Narratives*, ed. H.G. Bohn (London: Henry G. Bohn, 1848), p. 128; Muntaner: trans. G.G. Coulton, *A Medieval Garner: Human Documents from the Four Centuries Preceding the Reformation* (London: Constable, 1910), pp. 438-39; revised.

Annals of Niketas Choniates

But while the [Greek] emperor governed the empire in this fashion, a cloud of enemies, a dreadful and death-dealing pestilence, fell upon the Roman borders: I speak of the campaign of the Germans, joined by other kindred nations [that is, the Second Crusade]. Females were numbered among them, riding horseback in the manner of men, not on coverlets sidesaddle but unashamedly astride, and bearing lances and weapons as men do; dressed in masculine garb, they conveyed a wholly martial appearance, more mannish than the Amazons. One stood out from the rest as another Penthesilea [that is, the mythical queen of the Amazons] and from the embroidered gold which ran around the hem and fringes of her garment was called Goldfoot.

The Itinerary of the Pilgrims and Deeds of Richard

On another occasion [during the siege of Acre in 1191], amongst those who were carrying earth to make a mound in the ditch for assaulting the town more easily, was a woman who labored with great diligence and earnestness, and went to and fro unceasingly, and encouraged others unremittingly, in order that the work might be accomplished; but her zeal put an end to her life and labors; for while a crowd of all sexes and ages were constantly coming and going to complete the work in question, and while the aforesaid woman was occupied in depositing what she had brought, a Turk, who had been lying wait for her, struck her a mortal blow with a dart. As she fell to the ground, writhing with the violence of her pain, she entreated her husband and many others who had come up to assist her, with tears in her eyes, and very urgently, saying, "By your love for me, my dearest lord, by your piety as my husband, and the faith of our marriage contracted of old, permit not my corpse to be removed from this place; but I pray and beseech you, that since I can do nothing more towards the fulfillment of the work, I may deem myself to have done some good, if you will allow my lifeless body to be laid in the trench instead of earth, for it will soon be earth." This she urged with supplications to all the multitude that stood around, and soon after gave up the ghost. Oh! wonderful faith of the weaker sex! Oh! zeal of woman, worthy of imitation, for she ceased not, even dead, to help those who labored, and in her death continued to show her zeal in the cause!

Memoirs of Ramon Muntaner

There was a lady at Perelada whom I knew and saw: men called her Marcadera because she sold merchandise [that is, in Spanish, *mercaderia*]; she was a very doughty woman, solid and big of bones. One day while the French army lay encamped before Perelada, she went forth to fetch herbs from the garden outside the walls: she put on a man's quilted doublet and armed herself with sword and shield and lance, and thus went forth into her garden. And as she stooped in the garden she heard a sound of bells, whereupon she marveled, and stopped picking her colewort, and went to see what this might be, when lo! in the way between her garden and her neighbor's, she saw a French knight fully harnessed on his horse, which was all hung about with little bells at his breastband; he rode hither and thither to find a way out of that path. When she was aware of him, she strode forward a step and dealt him so shrewd a thrust with her lance through the cuisses [that is, thigh armor] that she drove also through thigh and saddle, and even wounded the horse also. When the beast felt the hurt, he reared and kicked again, and would surely have thrown his rider, but that he was bound by a chain to the saddle. What more shall I say? She drew her sword and ran round by a little gate and smote the beast so sore on the head that he staggered. What more? She seized the rein and cried to the knight, "Yield, or you are a dead man!" and he, that thought himself but dead, cast away his sword and yielded himself prisoner. She therefore took up the sword, drew the lance from his side, and led him to Perelada. The king and the prince made merry over this story, and would often bid the lady tell them how she had taken him. In brief, the knight and his armor were hers; he ransomed himself for 200 gold pieces, which fell to her share. Thereby may you know God's anger against the French.

Questions: What roles were these women playing in the respective military campaigns? What were their motivations? How were their actions limited by their sex? How were they viewed by contemporaries? Compare them to the Muslim women described by Usamah Ibn Munqidh in document 30.

55. CRUSADING SONGS

Crusading was a pervasive theme in medieval song, both religious and secular, because it inspired kings and peasants alike, it separated lovers, and it brought exotic new locales to the attention of Europeans. The first song below, written in French, exhorts knights to accompany Louis VII on the Second Crusade. The second was written about the same time in Provençal, the language of southern France, by the noted musician Marcabrun. One of the best-known crusading songs, it tells of crusading opportunities in both the Middle East and Spain. The third song below, written by the Italian nobleman Rinaldo d'Aquino in the mid-thirteenth century, adopts the voice of a woman left behind by her crusader lover.

Sources: "Chevalier, Mult Es Guariz": trans. E. Amt from text ed. N. Clare, liner notes, *Music of the Crusades* (New York: London Records, 1971); other songs: trans. J.J. Wilhelm, *Medieval Song: An Anthology of Hymns and Lyrics* (New York: E.P. Dutton & Co., Inc., 1971), pp. 123-25, 205-07.

Chevalier, Mult Es Guariz
[Knights, Much is Promised]

Knights, your salvation is assured
Since God has made appeal to you
Against Almoravids and Turks,
Who to our Lord dishonor do.
Against all right, they've seized his fiefs.
At this we suffer in accord,
For it was there that God was first
Obeyed and recognized as Lord.

Refrain:
Who goes along with King Louis
Will never be afraid of hell,
His soul will go to paradise,
Where angels of the Lord do dwell.

Rohais [that is, Edessa] is taken, as you know,
And Christians troubled sore and long.
The churches there are empty now,
And masses are no longer sung.
O knights, you should consider this,
You who in arms are so renowned,
And then present your bodies to
One who for you with thorns was crowned.

Refrain
Let us go conquer Moses there
Who stands upon Mount Sinai's heights;
Let's take him from the Saracens,
And so the staff with which he strikes
The Red Sea waters and they part
When Israel's host did with him go;
And Pharaoh followed in their wake,
and drowned with all his men below.

Refrain

Pax in Nomine Domini
[Peace in the Name of the Lord]

Pax in Nomine Domini!
Marcabrun made the words and the song:
Hear what he says.
The most gracious Lord of Heaven
Out of his sweetness has fashioned
For our use here a washing tub,
Unlike any other (except the one
Overseas in the vale of Josephat).
But to this one I summon you.

For the Lord who knows all that is
And all that will be, and all that was

Has promised us
Honor in the name of the emperor.
And the beauty to come—do you know?—
For those who will go to the tub:
More than the star of morning joy,
If only they'll avenge the wrongs
To God, here and in Damascus.

In Spain, over here, Marquis Ramon
And those from the Temple of Solomon
Suffer the weight
And the pain of the [pagan] pride.
And so youth gets a vile report.
And the cry for this washing tub
Rolls over the richest overlords
Who're feeble, failing, bereft of nerve,
For they don't value joy nor fun.

The Franks are all degenerates
If they say no to the task of God
That I command.
Ah, Antioch! Virtue and valor
are mourned in Guyenne and Poitou!
God our Lord, to your washing tub
Bring the count's soul in peace;
And here guard Poitiers and Niort,
O Lord who issued from the tomb!

Giammi Non Mi Conforto
[Never Again that Comfort for Me]

Never again that comfort,
Never that joyous heart.
The ships down in the harbor
Are straining to depart.
Away all the people run
To lands across the sea.
But me—poor weeping thing—
What shall become of me?

Away, away he'll run,
Fade quietly out of sight,

Leaving me here alone.
All day, all the night
Many will be the sighs
That assail me constantly
Not in heaven, nor on earth
Will life exist for me.

O holy, holy Savior
Who from Mary came our way!
Watch, protect that lover,
Since you're taking him away.
O reverenced and feared
Power from above!
In your hands I place
My tender love.

O cross that saves mankind,
You plummet me to error,
Twisting my grievous mind
Beyond all hope of prayer.
Why, O pilgrim cross,
Why this bitter turn?
Bowed beneath my loss,
I kindle; O I burn.

The Emperor who rules the world
In his peaceful sway
Ravages poor little me
By taking my hope away.
O reverenced and feared
Power from above!
In your hands I place
My tender love.

When he took up the cross,
I didn't know the end was this:
Whatever love he gave me
I repaid him kiss for kiss.
Now I'm thrust aside —
Yes, condemned to prison —
Now I'm forced to hide

In lifelong derision.

The ships are in their moorings.
Soon they'll depart.
With them and that rabble
Sails my heart.
O Father, O Creator,
Guide them to holy haven,
By your sacred cross
They're all enslaven.
And O darling, I beg you:

Take pity on my hysteria.
Write me a little sonnet.
Send it to me from Syria!
Night and day I'll know
Only this bitter strife.
In lands beyond the ocean
Lies my whole life.

Questions: What do the songs reveal about the emotional world of the crusaders? What themes are common throughout? In each song, what is the attitude of the speaker toward God? Toward the holy war?

CHAPTER SIX:

THE AGE OF INNOCENT III

Fig. 19: A papal bull is read by an archbishop in a modern engraving of a late medieval manuscript illumination. From C. Knight, *Old England: A Pictorial Museum* (London: James Sangster & Co., 1845).

56. LETTERS OF INNOCENT III

Pope Innocent III (1198-1216) was second only to Urban II in his influence on the development and direction of the crusading movement. More than any other crusading pope, Innocent believed fervently in the crusading cause and, unlike his predecessors, felt it was his duty to take an active role in the planning and implementation of this enterprise. In addition to the promotion of crusades centering on the Holy Land, Innocent went further than any other pontiff in the calling of European crusades. He expanded the crusades in the Baltic region and Spain (see Chapters VIII and IX, below), he initiated a purely political crusade against an Italian noble in 1199, and he broadened and redefined crusading in ways this chapter will examine. One of the earliest examples of his far-reaching interest is the first letter below, establishing the first direct taxation of the church by the papacy (this version is addressed to one German city, but similar letters were sent throughout Europe). Although this policy met with resistance, taxation of the church gradually became a standard means of raising money for crusading. The second letter below was written in the context of the lucrative trade that many Italian cities had established with the Islamic world; the Italians were known to put their profits above the concerns of the western church and its crusading aims.

Sources: Magdeburg: trans. L. and J. Riley-Smith, *The Crusades: Ideal and Reality, 1095-1274* (London: Edward Arnold, 1981), pp. 145-48; Venice letter: trans. O.J. Thatcher and E.H. McNeal, *A Source Book for Medieval History: Selected Documents Illustrating the History of Europe in the Middle Ages* (New York: Charles Scribner's Sons, 1905), pp. 536-37.

To the Archbishop and Clergy of Magdeburg, 1199

... We have been discussing the subject of aid to the Holy Land with our brothers; and because we do not want to appear to lay heavy burdens on the shoulders of our subjects, which we are not willing to move even with a finger of our own, only talking but doing very little, we have, with the approval of the bishops and other religious men residing at the apostolic see, arranged that a tenth part of all our revenues in money and in kind is allotted for the aid of the eastern province [that is, the crusader states]. We have subtracted not a little from this tenth because of our needs, for which our means are not enough since the present circumstances are more serious than usual and, because of this, demand heavier expenditure; our intention is to give you, and through you the laity, an example of generosity, following the example of him who began to do and to teach, and, although we cannot give anything that is ours, at least to return a little of his own to him who in his mercy has given us everything. And so as to assign necessary aid to the Holy Land in men as well as in goods, we propose to send there our beloved sons the cardinals Soffred, priest of the title of St. Praxedis, and Peter, deacon of St. Maria in Via Lata, on whom we have already placed the sign of the cross. They will go before the army of the Lord, acting in our stead, so that everyone may have recourse to them as though to one head.

Because we feel very strongly that this is in no way enough, for it is little, really very little, to answer to the so very many needs of that province, we command you all by apostolic letters, and we order each of you strictly under the threat of divine judgment on behalf of God almighty in the strength of the Holy Spirit, to render at least a fortieth part of all his ecclesiastical revenues in money and in kind for the aid of the Holy Land, after deducting the usuries which he cannot avoid paying. We, trusting in the mercy of almighty God and the authority of the blessed apostles Peter and Paul, relax a quarter of the penance imposed on all clergy, both subordinates and prelates, who pay this fortieth willingly and faithfully, as long as they practice no deceit and support the payment with pious devotion. But you should also know that anyone who refuses in so great a need to give such trifling aid to his Creator and Redeemer, from whom he has received body and soul and every good thing he has, is blameworthily severe and severely to be blamed; and we who, although unworthy, act in God's stead on earth can in no way hide the seriousness of this fault. Nor must you in any way believe that we are intending to use this to impose a law on you to your cost, thinking that from now on a fortieth may be exacted from you as if it were a duty or a custom. We do not wish you, moreover, to be damaged in any way on account of this and, grieving that a crisis of such great need has come upon ourselves and you, we pray that a similar crisis will not occur again. Nevertheless, if it is not possible for this aid to be levied in Magdeburg on account of hostility to it or some other obvious impediment, we wish and command you, our brothers the archbishop and bishops in the metropolitan church, to arrange to meet without delay in two or three places in the province of Magdeburg and discuss amongst yourselves the terms of the apostolic mandate concerning the rendering of aid to the Holy Land. After his return each of you should call a council in his diocese immediately and order on our authority the abbots and priors, both of exempt houses and others, archdeacons and deans and the entire clergy living in the diocese to assess their revenues in money and in kind by just reckoning. They must send without delay, within three months of the announcement being made to them, a fortieth part of their value to a suitable place in the same diocese, with the bishop himself and several religious as witnesses; some faithful and discerning laymen must also be summoned as a safeguard. And we order you to do this, our brothers the archbishop and bishops, with the same strictness.

But we exempt from this general rule Cistercian monks, Premonstratensian canons, and Grandmontine and Carthusian hermits, to whom we are sending a special injunction on this matter. We do not wish those who take pains to assess their revenues in money and kind diligently to run the risk of transgressing the aforementioned order if perhaps they do not pay the full fortieth through ignorance rather than with full deliberation; but they must pay in full once they have realized that they have paid too little mistakenly. If, God forbid, anyone deliberately withholds any part of the fortieth he owes, he should be completely immune from the penalty for his fault once he has made due satisfaction. No one should be amazed or even disturbed that we have ordered this under such threats, since the greatest necessity demands it; for, although service to God ought to be offered voluntarily, we read in the Gospel about the guests at the wedding feast whom the Lord ordered to be forced to enter. We command you, moreover, our brothers the archbishop and bishops, to have the same fortieth urgently exacted and faithfully collected throughout your dioceses, according to the plan mentioned above, to have it deposited in a safe place and to send an account of it all to us as quickly as possible by means of your letters and special envoys.

In addition to all of this we order that an empty trunk be placed in each church, locked with three keys; the first is to be put in the charge of the bishop, the second in the charge of the priest of the church, and the third in the charge of some devout laymen. All the faithful should be advised to put their alms in it for the remission of their sins — the amount will depend on what the Lord inspires them to give — and this ought to be publicly and repeatedly announced once a week at mass in all churches, for the remission of sins and especially for the remission of the sins of those who make offerings. We allow you, our brothers the archbishop and bishops, to substitute the gift of alms for the performance of penance imposed on those who are willing to come to the assistance of the Holy Land with their goods, with the advice of men of good judgment who have considered the station in life of the persons involved and the value of the offerings and have also taken into consideration the warmth of their devotion.

In addition to this we want you to summon to your side two brothers, when you can find them, one of the Hospital of Jerusalem and the other of the Knighthood of the Temple, and two other devout laymen and knights of good judgment or other fighting men who have taken the sign of the Lord's cross. If crusaders cannot afford the journey you should make suitable grants to them from the same cash, after receiving a sufficient assurance from them that they will remain to defend the eastern land for a year or more, according to the amount of the grant, and that if, God forbid, they should die on the way, the aid they have received will not be converted to other uses but must rather be made over for the upkeep of fighting men. And when they return they must not be released from the assurance they made until they have shown you letters from the king or patriarch or masters of the Hospital of Jerusalem or the Knighthood of the Temple or our legate giving you evidence of their stay.

Because the critical situation demands and the common good requires the Christian people to hurry to the Holy Land without delay, bringing aid not only in material goods but also in person against the pagans, we order you our brothers, and we command you by means of this apostolic letter, to press on wisely and conscientiously, in person and with the help of other suitable men, with the task of encouraging and persuading the faithful, so that those who are in a position to fight the war of the Lord take the sign of the cross in the name of the Lord of Hosts, while the rest piously donate alms according to their means. For we, trusting in the mercy of God and the authority of the blessed apostles Peter and Paul, by that power of binding and loosing that God has conferred on us, although unworthy, grant all those submitting to the labor of this journey personally and at their own expense full forgiveness of their sins, for which they have repented in their hearts and by word of mouth, and as the reward of the just we promise them a greater share of eternal salvation. To those who do not personally campaign, but only send suitable men to stay there for at least a year at their own expense, according to their means and station in life, and to those similarly who personally fulfill another's vow to pilgrimage, although at another's expense, we concede full forgiveness of their sins. We also wish all to share in this remission of sins who, according to the amount of their aid and the depth of their devotion, donate a fitting proportion of their goods to the aid of that land....

To Venice, 1198

... In support of the eastern province, in addition to the forgiveness of sins which we promise those who, at their own expense, set out thither, and besides the papal protection which we give those who aid that land, we have renewed that decree of the Lateran council [held under Pope Alexander III in 1179], which excommunicated those Christians who shall furnish the Saracens with weapons, iron, or timbers for their galleys, and those who serve the Saracens as helmsmen or in any other way on their galleys and other piratical craft, and which furthermore ordered that their property be confiscated by the secular princes and the consuls of the cities, and that, if any such persons should be taken prisoner, they should be the slaves of those who captured them. We furthermore excommunicated all those Christians who shall hereafter have anything to do with the Saracens either directly or indirectly, or shall attempt to give them aid in any way so long as the war between them and us shall last. But recently our beloved sons, Andreas Donatus and Benedict Grilion, your messengers, came and explained to us that your city was suffering great loss by this our decree, because Venice does not engage in agriculture, but in shipping and commerce. Nevertheless, we are led by the paternal love which we have for you to forbid you to aid the Saracens by selling them, giving them, or exchanging with them, iron, flax (oakum), pitch, sharp instruments, rope, weapons, galleys, ships, and timbers, whether hewn or in the rough. But for the present and until we order to the contrary, we permit those who are going to Egypt to carry other kinds of merchandise whenever it shall be necessary. In return for this favor you should be willing to go to the aid of the province of Jerusalem and you should not attempt to evade our apostolic command. For there is no doubt that he who, against his own conscience, shall fraudulently try to evade this prohibition, shall be under divine condemnation....

Questions: How did Innocent endeavor to soften the blow of the new taxation? How did he try to ensure the payment of the tax? How was it to be collected? What does the letter to Venice tell us about commercial activity between East and West? To what extent was the pope willing to compromise, and why?

57. ACCOUNTS OF THE FOURTH CRUSADE

Innocent III called a crusade in the first year of his pontificate and soon afterwards began to raise money for this venture and send out crusade preachers. These efforts bore fruit in 1200 when a group of mainly French nobles began to plan what would be the Fourth Crusade. They decided to travel east by sea, and the city of Venice, a major trading power in the Mediterranean, was selected to supply the crusade with the necessary ships and provisions. As will be seen below, the crusade leaders soon ran into logistical difficulties and found themselves deeply in debt to the Venetians, who then pressured the crusaders into attacking the Christian city of Zara, a commercial rival of Venice on the eastern coast of the Adriatic Sea. Later, the crusade became fatally embroiled in Byzantine politics.

Source: D.C. Munro, *Translations and Reprints from the Original Sources of European History*, series 1, vol. III (Philadelphia: University of Pennsylvania Department of History, n.d.), no. 1, pp. 2-15; revised.

Villehardouin: *The Conquest of Constantinople*

[The crusaders' envoys addressed the doge of Venice:] "Sire, we have come to you on behalf of the noble barons of France who have taken the cross in order to avenge the shame of Jesus Christ and to reconquer Jerusalem, if God will permit. And because they know no people who are as able to assist them as you and your people, they pray you, for God's sake, to pity the land of Out-remer and the shame of Jesus Christ, and to endeavor to furnish them trans-ports and ships of war."

"Under what conditions?" asked the doge.

"Under any conditions that you may propose or advise, if they are able to fulfill them," replied the messengers.

"Certainly," replied the doge [to his associates], "it is a great undertaking that they have asked of us and they seem to be considering an important mat-ter;" [and to the messengers] "we will give you an answer in a week, and do not wonder if the time seems long, for such a great undertaking deserves much thought."

At the time fixed by the doge, they returned to the palace. I cannot tell you all that was said, but the conclusion of the conference was as follows:

"My lords," said the doge, "we will tell you what we have decided, if we can get the Grand Council and the people of the country to agree to it; and you shall decide whether you can fulfill your part.

"We will furnish [ships] for carrying 4,500 horses and 9,000 esquires, and vessels for 4,500 knights and 20,000 foot-soldiers. The agreement shall be to furnish food for nine months for all these horses and men. That is the least that we will do, on condition that we are paid four marks per horse and two marks per man.

"And we will observe all these conditions which we explain to you, for one year, beginning the day we leave the harbor of Venice to fight in the service of God and of Christianity, wherever we may go. The sum of these payments indicated above amounts to 85,000 marks.

"And we will do still more: we will add fifty armed galleys, for the love of God; on the condition that as long as our alliance shall last, of every conquest of land or money that we make, by sea or land, we shall have one-half and you the other. Now deliberate whether you can fulfill these conditions."

The messengers went away, saying that they would talk it over and reply the next day. They consulted and discussed that night and then resolved to agree to it. The next day they went to the doge and said: "Sire, we are ready to make this agreement." The doge said that he would speak to his people and tell them the result....

It was explained in council that they would go to Babylon [that is, Cairo], because at Babylon they could do more injury to the Turks than anywhere else. And in public it was announced that they would go across the sea. It was then Lent [March, 1201], and on St. John's day the following year, the 1202nd year after the incarnation of Jesus Christ, the barons and pilgrims were to be at Venice and the vessels were to be ready on their arrival.

Robert of Clari: The Conquest of Constantinople

While the pilgrims were staying on the island of St. Nicholas [in Venice], the doge of Venice and the Venetians went to speak to them and demanded the pay for the navy which had been prepared. And the doge said to them that they had acted wrongly in commanding through their messengers that vessels should be prepared for 4,000 knights and their equipment, and for 100,000 footsoldiers. Of these 4,000 knights, there were not more than 1,000 present, for the others had gone to other ports. And of these 100,000 footsoldiers there were not more than 50,000 or 60,000. "Nevertheless," said the doge, "we want you to pay us the sum which you promised." When the crusaders heard this, they debated and arranged that each knight should pay four marks and four marks for each horse, and each esquire two marks; and those who paid less, should pay one mark. When they collected this money, they paid it to the Venetians. But 50,000 marks still remained due.

When the doge and the Venetians saw that the pilgrims had not paid more, they were all so incensed that the doge said to the pilgrims, "My lords, you have imposed upon us shamefully. For, as soon as your messengers had made the agreement with me and my people, I issued orders throughout my whole land that no merchant should undertake a voyage, but all were to aid in preparing this fleet. They have been waiting ever since and have gained nothing for the last year and a half; and, accordingly, they have lost much. Therefore my men and I want you to pay us the money which you owe us. If you do not pay us, you shall not leave this island before we get our money; and no one shall bring you anything to eat or drink." The doge, however, was a very excellent man and did not prevent the people from bringing enough food and drink.

When the count and the crusaders heard what the doge said they were much troubled and grieved. They made another collection and borrowed all the money they could from those who were thought to have any. They paid it all to the Venetians, but after this payment 36,000 marks still remained due. They said to the Venetians that they had been imposed upon; that the army was greatly impoverished by this last collection; that they could not pay any more money at all, for they had hardly enough to support the army.

When the doge perceived that they could not pay all the money and that they were in sore straits, he said to his people: "Sirs, if we let these people go back to their own country, we shall always be considered base and tricky. Let us go to them and say that, if they are willing to pay us the 36,000 marks which they owe us out of their part of the first conquests which we make, we will carry them across the sea." The Venetians were well pleased with the doge's proposition.

Accordingly, they went to the camp of the pilgrims. When they came thither, the doge said to the crusaders: "Sires, we have agreed, I and my people, that if you are willing to guarantee faithfully to pay us the 36,000 marks, which you owe us, out of your share of the first conquests, we will carry you across the sea."

When the crusaders heard what the doge proposed they were very glad and fell at his feet for joy. They bound themselves very willingly to do faithfully what the doge had proposed. They were so joyous that night that there was no one so poor that he did not make a great illumination, and each one carried great torches made of candles on the end of his lance, both outside of the camp and inside, so that the whole army seemed intoxicated....

Afterwards the doge came to the army and said: "Sirs, it is now winter; we cannot cross the sea, nor does this depend upon me. For I would have had you cross already, if it had not depended upon you. But let us do the best we can. There is a city near here, named Zara. The people of this city have done us much evil, and I and my men want to punish them, if we can. If you will take my advice, we will go there this winter and stay until Easter. Then we will make ready our navy and go to Outremer at Lady Day [that is, March 25]. The city of Zara is very rich and well supplied with all kinds of provisions." The barons and the nobles among the crusaders agreed to what the doge proposed. But no one in the army knew this plan, except the leaders.... [The crusaders proceeded to Zara.]

Villehardouin

The day after the feast of St. Martin [that is, Nov. 11], some people from Zara came to speak to the doge of Venice, who was in his tent. They said to him that they would surrender the city and all their property to his mercy, if their lives were spared. The doge said that he would not accept these or any other conditions without the advice of the counts and barons, and that he would go and discuss the matter with them.

While he went to talk to the counts and barons, that party, of which I have already spoken, who wanted to break up the army, said to the messengers: "Why do you want to surrender your city? The pilgrims will not attack you and you have nothing to fear from them. If you can defend yourselves against the Venetians, you need have no anxiety." And they sent one of them, Robert de Boves, who went to the walls of the city and announced the same thing. So the messengers returned to the city and the plan of surrender was given up.

The doge of Venice, when he came to the counts and barons, said to them: "Sirs, the people yonder want to surrender the city to my mercy, on condition that their lives be spared. But I will not make this agreement or any other without your advice." The barons replied: "Sire, we advise you to make this agreement and we pray you to do so." He said he would, and they all went back together to the doge's tent to make this agreement. They found that the messengers had gone away, following the advice of those [crusaders] who wanted to break up the army.

Then the abbot of Vaux of the order of Cîteaux rose and said to them: "Sirs, I forbid you, in the name of the pope at Rome, to attack this city; for the inhabitants are Christians and you are pilgrims."

When the doge heard this he was much irritated and troubled. He said to the counts and barons: "Sirs, this city was practically in my power, and your people have taken it from me; you had promised that you would aid me in conquering it; now I require you to do so."

Then the counts and barons and those who belonged to their party held a conference and said: "Those who have prevented this agreement have committed a very great outrage, and it was not right for them to try to break up the army. Now we shall be disgraced, if we do not aid in capturing the city." They went to the doge and said to him: "Sire, we will aid you in capturing the city, in spite of those who wish to prevent it."…

[They attacked Zara for five days, after which the inhabitants again offered to surrender.]

Accordingly the city was surrendered to the mercy of the doge of Venice, on condition that the lives of the inhabitants should be spared. Then the doge went to the counts and barons and said to them: "Sirs, we have conquered this city, by the grace of God and through your aid. It is now winter and we can not leave here until Easter. For we should find no provisions elsewhere; and this city is very rich and very well supplied with everything needful. Let us divide it accordingly into two parts; we will take one-half of it and you the other half."

Robert of Clari

In the meantime the crusaders and the Venetians remained at Zara during the winter. They considered how great the expense had been and said to one another that they could not go to Babylon or Alexandria or Syria; for they had neither provisions nor money for the journey. They had already used up everything they had, either during the sojourn that they had made or in the great price that they had paid for the vessels. They said that they could not go and, even if they should go, they would accomplish nothing; they had neither provisions nor money sufficient to support them.

The doge of Venice saw clearly that the pilgrims were ill at ease. He addressed them, saying: "Sirs, Greece is a very rich land and bountifully supplied with everything. If we can find a sufficient excuse for going there and taking food and other things, so as to recuperate ourselves, it would seem to me advisable, and then we could easily go across the sea." Then the marquis [Boniface of Montferrat] rose and said: "Sir, I was in Germany at the emperor's court last Christmas. There I saw a young man who was the emperor's brother-in-law. This young man was the son of the emperor Kyrsac of Constantinople from whom his brother had taken the empire of Constantinople by treason. Whoever could get this young man," said the marquis, "could certainly go to the land of Constantinople and take provisions and other things; for this young man is the rightful heir." ... [After much discussion the crusaders decided to invite Alexis, the claimant of the Byzantine throne, and he soon arrived in the camp.]

Then all the barons of the army and the Venetians were summoned. When they had all assembled, the doge of Venice rose and said to them: "My lords, we have now a sufficient excuse for going to Constantinople, if you think it wise, for we have the lawful heir." Now some who did not want to go to Constantinople spoke thus: "Bah! What are we going to do at Constantinople? We have our pilgrimage to make and intend to go to Babylon or Alexandria. Our ships are rented for only one year and the year is already over."

The others said in reply: "What are we going to do at Babylon or Alexandria, since we have neither provisions nor money enough to go? It is better to go where we have a sufficient excuse for obtaining money and provisions by conquest, than to go where we shall die of hunger. Then we can do it, and he offers to go with us and to pay for our ships and our navy another year at his own expense." And the marquis of Montferrat did all in his power to urge our going to Constantinople, because he wished to take vengeance for a wrong which the emperor of Constantinople had done him....

[The crusaders proceeded to Constantinople, where Alexis and his father were restored to power.]

Afterwards all the barons assembled one day at the palace of the emperor and demanded of him their pay. He replied that he would pay them, but he wished first to be crowned. Accordingly they made preparations and set a day for the coronation. On that day [Alexis] was crowned emperor with due ceremony, with the consent of his father, who willingly granted it. After he had been crowned, the barons demanded their pay. He said he would very willingly pay what he could, and at that time he paid 100,000 marks. Of this sum the Venetians received one-half, for they were to receive one-half of the conquests. Of the 50,000 which remained, 36,000, which the Franks still owed for the vessels, were paid to the Venetians. And all those who had advanced money to pay for the passage were paid out of the 14,000 marks which the pilgrims had left. [But the promised resources for the crusade were not forthcoming.]

Villehardouin

[The crusaders' representatives] dismounted from their horses at the gate, entered the palace, and found the emperor Alexis and the emperor Isaac, his father, seated upon two thrones, side by side. Near them was seated the empress, who was the father's wife, the son's stepmother, and the sister of the king of Hungary, a good and beautiful lady. A great number of nobles were with them, and it certainly seemed the court of a rich prince.

According to the agreement with the other messengers, Conon of Bethune, who was very rich and very eloquent, spoke: "Sire, we have been sent to you by the barons of the army and by the doge of Venice. Know that they reproach you because of the great service which they have done you, which everybody knows and which is apparent to you. You have sworn to them, you and your father, to keep the agreement that you have made with them; and they have your written compact. You have not kept your agreement with them as you ought.

"They have summoned you many times, and we summon you in their name, before all your barons, to keep the agreement which you have made with them. If you do so, all will be well; if you do not keep it, know that in the future they will consider you neither as lord nor as friend; but they will try to get their rights in any way they can. They announce to you that they would injure neither you, nor any one else, before the defiance; for they have never acted treasonably, and in their country it is not the custom to do so. You have heard what we have said to you and you can do as you please."

The Greeks marveled much at this defiance and great insult. They said that no one had ever been so bold before as to defy the emperor of Constantinople in his own halls. The emperor Alexis looked savagely at the messengers, and so did all the Greeks, though they had on many occasions in the past looked very friendly.

Robert of Clari

At these words the barons left the palace and returned to their camp. After returning they deliberated upon the course to follow. Meanwhile they sent two knights to the emperor and demanded again that he should pay them. He replied to the messengers that he would pay nothing, he had already paid too much, and that he was not afraid of any one. He also commanded them to go away and leave his land; they were to understand that if they did not depart, he would injure them. Then the messengers went back and told the barons the emperor's reply. When the barons heard this, they deliberated as to what they should do. The doge said that he wanted to speak to the emperor.

He sent a messenger to demand that the emperor should come to the harbor to speak to him. The emperor went on horseback. The doge prepared four armed galleys; he went in one and took the other three for protection. When he was near the shore he saw the emperor who had come on horseback. He addressed the latter as follows: "Alexis, what do you think you are going to do? Remember we have raised you from a very humble estate. We have made you lord and crowned you emperor. Will you not keep your agreement with us and will you not do more?"

"No," replied the emperor, "I will not do anything more."

"No?" said the doge, "wretched boy, we have raised you from the mire, and we will throw you into the mire again; and be sure that I will do you all the injury that I can, from this time on."...

[The crusaders then decided to attack Constantinople, but their initial assaults were unsuccessful. During the siege Alexis and his father were deposed and both died; and a new emperor was crowned.]

When the pilgrims saw [that their attack had failed], they were very angry and grieved much; they went back from the other side of the harbor to their lodgings. When the barons had returned and had gotten ashore, they assembled and were much amazed, and said that it was on account of their sins that they did not succeed in anything and could not capture the city. Meanwhile the bishops and the clergy in the army debated and decided that the war was a righteous one, and that they certainly ought to attack the Greeks. For formerly the inhabitants of the city had been obedient to the law of Rome and now they were disobedient, since they said that the law of Rome was of no account, and called all who believed in it "dogs." And the bishops said that for this reason one ought certainly to attack them, and that it was not a sin, but an act of great charity.

Then it was announced to all the host that all the Venetians and every one else should go and hear the sermons on Sunday morning; and they did so. Then the bishops preached to the army ... and they showed to the pilgrims that the war was a righteous one; for the Greeks were traitors and murderers, and also disloyal, since they had murdered their rightful lord, and were worse than Jews. Moreover, the bishops said that, by the authority of God and in the name of the pope, they would absolve all who attacked the Greeks. Then the bishops commanded the pilgrims to confess their sins and receive the communion devoutly; and said that they ought not to hesitate to attack the Greeks, for the latter were enemies of God. They also commanded that all the evil women should be sought out and sent away from the army to a distant place. This was done; the evil women were all put on a vessel and were sent very far away from the army.

Villehardouin

Then the members of the host debated and consulted upon the best course to pursue. The discussion was long and stormy, but the following was the result of the deliberation: If God granted that they should capture the city, all the booty that was taken should be brought together and divided fairly, as was fitting. And, if they captured the city, six men should be chosen from the Franks and six from the Venetians; these were to take oath upon relics that they would elect as emperor him whom they should judge to be the most useful for the good of the land. And he whom they chose as emperor should have one-quarter of all the conquests both in the city and outside; and in addition he should have the palace of the Lion's Mouth and of Blachern. The other three-quarters should be divided into two parts, one-half for the Venetians and one-half for the crusaders. Then twelve of the wisest of the army of the pilgrims and twelve of the Venetians should be chosen to divide the fiefs and the offices among the men and to define the feudal service which each one owed to the emperor.

This compact was guaranteed and sworn to by both the Franks and the Venetians, with the condition that any one who wished could go away within one year from the end of March. Those who remained in the country must perform the feudal service to the emperor, as it might be arranged. Then the compact was made and sworn to and all who should not keep it were excommunicated by the clergy.

Questions: What went wrong in the negotiations with the Venetians? What were the consequences of this mistake? How did the Venetians turn the crusaders against Zara and Constantinople? How did the people of Constantinople view the crusader force? Was the original purpose of crusading enlarged or distorted by these events?

58. DOCUMENTS ON THE SACK OF CONSTANTINOPLE

The siege of Constantinople began on April 9, 1204, and the crusaders broke through the walls on the 12th. The new emperor abandoned his throne and the city was subjected to three horrific days of unchecked pillaging. In addition to the looting, rape and murder of the Greek inhabitants, the crusaders also took a great interest in Byzantium's holy sanctuaries. Churches were stripped of all their treasures, including holy relics. The first of the accounts below is by Niketas Choniates, an early thirteenth-century Greek historian. Next, Gunther of Paris, who wrote soon after the crusade, describes the plundering activities of one French abbot. In the final two documents Innocent III, who had excommunicated the crusaders after they took Zara, responds to the news of their conquest of Constantinople.

Sources: second papal letter: trans. J.A. Brundage, *The Crusades: A Documentary History* (Milwaukee, WI: Marquette University Press, 1962), pp. 208-09; others: trans. D.C. Munro, *Translations and Reprints from the Original Sources of European History*, series 1, vol. III (Philadelphia: University of Pennsylvania Department of History, n.d.), no. 1, pp. 15-20, revised.

Niketas Choniates

How shall I begin to tell of the deeds wrought by these nefarious men! Alas, the images, which ought to have been adored, were trodden under foot! Alas, the relics of the holy martyrs were thrown into unclean places! Then was seen what one shudders to hear, namely, the divine body and blood of Christ was spilled upon the ground or thrown about. They snatched the precious reliquaries, thrust into their bosoms the ornaments which these contained, and used the broken remnants for pans and drinking cups—precursors of Antichrist, authors and heralds of his nefarious deeds which we momentarily expect. Manifestly, indeed, by that race then, just as formerly, Christ was robbed and insulted and his garments were divided by lot; only one thing was lacking, that his side, pierced by a spear, should pour rivers of divine blood on the ground.

Nor can the violation of the great church [of St. Sofia] be listened to with equanimity. For the sacred altar, formed of all kinds of precious materials and admired by the whole world, was broken into bits and distributed among the soldiers, as was all the other sacred wealth of so great and infinite splendor.

When the sacred vases and utensils of unsurpassable art and grace and rare material, and the fine silver, wrought with gold, which encircled the screen of the tribunal and the ambo, of admirable workmanship, and the door and many other ornaments, were to be borne away as booty, mules and saddled horses were led to the very sanctuary of the temple. Some of these which were

Fig. 20: In a drawing based on a sixteenth-century fresco, the Fourth Crusaders storm Constantinople. From P. Lacroix, *Military and Religious Life in the Middle Ages* (London, Chapman and Hall, 1874).

unable to keep their footing on the splendid and slippery pavement, were stabbed when they fell, so that the sacred pavement was polluted with blood and filth.

Nay more, a certain harlot, a sharer in their guilt, a minister of the furies, a servant of the demons, a worker of incantations and poisonings, insulting Christ, sat in the patriarch's seat, singing an obscene song and dancing frequently. Nor, indeed, were these crimes committed and others left undone, on the ground that these were of lesser guilt, the others of greater. But with one consent all the most heinous sins and crimes were committed by all with equal zeal. Could those, who showed so great madness against God himself, have spared the honorable matrons and maidens or the virgins consecrated to God?

Nothing was more difficult and laborious than to soften by prayers, to render benevolent, these wrathful barbarians, vomiting forth bile at every unpleasing word, so that nothing failed to inflame their fury. Whoever attempted it was derided as insane and a man of intemperate language. Often they drew their daggers against any one who opposed them at all or hindered their demands.

No one was without a share in the grief. In the alleys, in the streets, in the temples, complaints, weeping, lamentations, grief, the groaning of men, the shrieks of women, wounds, rape, captivity, the separation of those most closely united. Nobles wandered about ignominiously, those of venerable age in tears, the rich in poverty. Thus it was in the streets, on the corners, in the temple, in the dens, for no place remained unassailed or defended the suppliants. All places everywhere were filled full of all kinds of crime. Oh, immortal God, how great the afflictions of the men, how great the distress!

Gunther of Paris

While the victors were rapidly plundering the conquered city, which was theirs by right of conquest, the abbot Martin began to cogitate about his own share of the booty, and lest he alone should remain empty-handed, while all the others became rich, he resolved to seize upon plunder with his own sacred hands. But, since he thought it not meet to handle any booty of worldly things with those sacred hands he began to plan how he might secure some portion of the relics of the saints, of which he knew there was a great quantity in the city.

Accordingly, having a presentiment of some great result, he took with him one of his two chaplains and went to a church which was held in great reverence because in it the mother of the most famous emperor Manuel had a noble grave, which seemed of importance to the Greeks, but which our people held for naught. There a very great amount of money brought in from all the surrounding country was stored, and also precious relics which the vain hope of security had caused the Greeks to bring in from the neighboring churches and monasteries. Those whom the Greeks had driven out had told us of this before the capture of the city. When many pilgrims broke into this church and some were eagerly engaged in stealing gold and silver, others precious stones, Martin, thinking it unbecoming to commit sacrilege except in a holy cause, sought a more retired spot where the very sanctity of the place seemed to promise that what he desired might be found.

There he found an aged man of agreeable countenance, having a long and hoary beard, a priest, but very unlike our priests in his dress. Thinking him a layman, the abbot, though inwardly calm, threatened him with a very ferocious voice, saying: "Come, perfidious old man, show me the most powerful relics you have, or you shall die immediately." The latter, terrified by the sound rather than the words, since he heard but did not understand what was said, and knowing that Martin could not speak Greek, began in the Romanian language, of which he knew a little, to entreat Martin and by soft words to turn away the latter's wrath, which in truth did not exist. In reply, the abbot succeeded in getting out a few words of the same language, sufficient to make the old man understand what he wanted. The latter, observing Martin's face and dress, and thinking it more tolerable that a religious man should handle the sacred relics with fear and reverence, than that worldly men should, perchance, pollute them with their worldly hands, opened a chest bound with iron and showed the desired treasure, which was more grateful and pleasing to Martin than all the royal wealth of Greece. The abbot hastily and eagerly thrust in both hands and, working quickly, filled with the fruits of the sacrilege both his own and his chaplain's bosom. He wisely concealed what seemed the most valuable and departed without opposition.

Moreover, what and how worthy of veneration those relics which the holy robber appropriated were, is told more fully at the end of this work. When he was hastening to his vessel, so stuffed full, if I may use the expression, those who knew and loved him, saw him from their ships as they were themselves hastening to the booty, and inquired joyfully whether he had stolen anything, or with what he was so loaded down as he walked. With a joyful countenance, as always, and with pleasant words he said: "We have done well." To which they replied: "Thanks be to God."...

Therefore "blessed be the Lord God, who only does wondrous things," who in his unspeakable kindness and mercy has looked upon and made glorious his church at Paris through certain gifts of his grace, which he deigned to transmit to us through the venerable man, already so frequently mentioned, Abbot Martin. In the presence of these the church exults and by their protection any soul faithful to God is aided and assisted. In order that the readers' trust in these may be strengthened, we have determined to give a partial list.

First, of the highest importance and worthy of all veneration: a trace of the blood of our Lord Jesus Christ, which was shed for the redemption of all mankind.

Second, a piece of the cross of our Lord on which the Son of the Father, the new Adam, sacrificed for us, paid the debt of the old Adam.

Third, a not inconsiderable piece of St. John [the Baptist], the forerunner of our Lord.

Fourth, the arm of St. James, the apostle, whose memory is venerated by the whole church.

There were also relics of the other saints, whose names are as follows:

Christopher, the martyr.

George, the martyr.

Theodore, the martyr.

The foot of St. Cosmas, the martyr.

Part of the head of Cyprian, the martyr.

Pantaleon, the martyr.

A tooth of St. Lawrence.

Demetrius, the martyr.

Stephen, the proto-martyr.

Vincentius, Adjutus, Mauritius and his companions.

Crisantius and Darius, the martyrs.

Gervasius and Protasius, the martyrs.

Primus, the martyr.

Sergius and Bacchus, the martyrs.

Protus, the martyr.

John and Paul, the martyrs.

Also relics from the following: the place of the nativity of our Lord; Calvary; our Lord's sepulcher; the stone rolled away; the place of our Lord's ascension; the stone on which John stood when he baptized the Lord; the spot where Christ raised Lazarus; the stone on which Christ was presented in the temple; the stone on which Jacob slept; the stone where Christ fasted; the stone where Christ prayed; the table on which Christ ate the supper; the place where he was captured; the place where the mother of our Lord died; his grave; the grave of St. Peter, the apostle; the relics of the holy apostles Andrew and Philip; the place where the Lord gave the law to Moses; the holy patriarchs Abraham, Isaac, and Jacob; St. Nicholas, the bishop; Adelasius, the bishop; Agricius, the bishop; John Chrysostom; John, the almsgiver; the milk of the mother of our Lord; Margaret, the virgin; Perpetua, the virgin; Agatha, the virgin; Agnes, the virgin; Lucia, the virgin; Cecilia, the virgin; Adelgundis and Euphemia, the virgins.

Letters of Innocent III

To all the clergy and people in the Christian army at Constantinople:

If the Lord had granted the desires of his humble servants sooner, and had transferred, as he has now done, the empire of Constantinople from the Greeks to the Latins before the fall of the Holy Land, perhaps Christianity would not be weeping today over the desolation of the land of Jerusalem. Since, therefore, through the wonderful transference of this empire God has deigned to open to you a way to recover that land, and the detention of this may lead to the restoration of that, we advise and exhort you all, and we enjoin upon you for the remission of your sins, to remain for a year in Romania [that is, the Byzantine Empire], in order to strengthen the empire in its devotion to the apostolic see and to us, and in order to retain it in the power of the Latins; and to give wise advice and efficient aid to Baldwin, our most beloved son in Christ, the illustrious emperor of Constantinople; unless, perchance, your presence in the Holy Land should be necessary before that time, in which case you ought to hasten to guard it before the year elapses.

To Peter, cardinal priest of the title of St. Marcellus, legate of the apostolic see:

We were not a little astonished and disturbed to hear that you and our beloved son the cardinal priest of the title of St. Praxida and legate of the apostolic see, in fear of the looming perils of the Holy Land, have left the province of Jerusalem (which, at this point is in such great need) and that you have gone by ship to Constantinople. And now we see that what we dreaded has occurred and what we feared has come to pass.... For you, who ought to have looked for help for the Holy Land, you who should have stirred up others, both by word and by example, to assist the Holy Land, on your own initiative ... sailed to Greece, bringing in your footsteps not only the pilgrims, but even the natives of the Holy Land who came to Constantinople, following our venerable brother, the archbishop of Tyre. When you had deserted it, the Holy Land remained destitute of men, void of strength. Because of you, its last state was worse than the first, for all its friends deserted with you; nor was there any admirer to console it.... We ourselves were not a little agitated and, with reason, we acted against you, since you had fallen in with this counsel and because you had deserted the land which the Lord consecrated by his presence, the land in which our King marvelously performed the mystery of our redemption....

It was your duty to attend to the business of your legation and to give careful consideration, not to the capture of the empire of Constantinople, but rather to the defense of what is left of the Holy Land and, with the Lord's leave, the restoration of what has been lost. We made you our representative and we sent you to gain, not temporal, but rather eternal riches. And for this purpose, our brethren provided adequately for your needs.

We have just heard and discovered from your letters that you have absolved from their pilgrimage vows and their crusading obligations all the crusaders who have remained to defend Constantinople from last March to the present. It is impossible not to be moved against you, for you neither should nor could give any such absolution.

Whoever suggested such a thing to you and how did they ever lead your mind astray?...

How, indeed, is the Greek church to be brought back into ecclesiastical union and to a devotion for the apostolic see when she has been beset with so many afflictions and persecutions that she sees in the Latins only an example of perdition and the works of darkness, so that she now, and with reason, detests the Latins more than dogs? As for those who were supposed to be seeking the ends of Jesus Christ, not their own ends, whose swords, which they were supposed to use against the pagans, are now dripping with Christian blood, they have spared neither age nor sex. They have committed incest, adultery, and fornication before the eyes of men. They have exposed both matrons and virgins, even those dedicated to God, to the sordid lusts of boys. Not satisfied with breaking open the imperial treasury and plundering the goods of princes and lesser men, they also laid their hands on the treasures of the churches and, what is more serious, on their very possessions. They have even ripped silver plates from the altars and have hacked them to pieces among themselves. They violated the holy places and have carried off crosses and relics.

Furthermore, under what guise can we call upon the other western peoples for aid to the Holy Land and assistance to the empire of Constantinople? When the crusaders, having given up the proposed pilgrimage, return absolved to their homes; when those who plundered the aforesaid empire turn back and come home with their spoils, free of guilt; will not people then suspect that these things have happened, not because of the crime involved, but because of your deed? Let the Lord's word not be stifled in your mouth. Be not like a dumb dog, unable to bark. Rather, let them speak these things publicly, let them protest before everyone, so that the more they rebuke you before God and on God's account, the more they will find you simply negligent. As for the absolution of the Venetian people being falsely accepted, against ecclesiastical rules, we will not at present argue with you....

Questions: According to Niketas, what was the worst crime committed by the crusaders in the taking of Constantinople? How does Gunther justify Abbot Martin's theft of relics? What sorts of relics were most admired by this light-fingered monk? What enabled Innocent finally to accept the fiasco of the Fourth Crusade? In Innocent's mind, what was the most lamentable consequence of the fall of the city?

59. BERNARD OF GUI'S MANUAL FOR INQUISITORS

As crusading under Innocent III came to be defined as the right response to any threat against Christianity, the mechanisms of this movement were also applied to what many believed to be the greatest danger to Christendom—the rise of Christian heretical movements within Europe. One of these, the Albigensian or Cathar heresy, had appeared in southern France during the twelfth century and had gained a considerable following there. Faced with this threat to Christianity and the authority of the church, Innocent initially sought to suppress the Albigensians by sending out preachers, including St. Dominic of Caleruega (1170-1221) and his followers, the friars of the new Dominican order, which Innocent officially recognized in 1216. The Dominicans soon came to play a major role in the Inquisition, the ecclesiastical judicial institution created to investigate and prosecute heresy. Bernard of Gui was a Dominican friar appointed to the Inquisition in 1307. He dealt primarily with Albigensian heretics and wrote The Manual for Inquisitors, *which is excerpted below, based on his own experiences and earlier sources.*

Sources: description of Cathars: trans. J.H. Robinson, *Readings in European History, Vol.1: From the Breaking Up of the Roman Empire to the Protestant Revolution* (Boston: Ginn & Company, 1904), pp. 381-83; instructions: trans. H.C. Lea, *A History of The Inquisition of the Middle Ages* (New York: The Macmillan Company, 1922), pp. 411-14; revised.

Description of the Cathars

It would take too long to describe in detail the manner in which these same Manichaean heretics preach and teach their followers, but it must be briefly considered here.

In the first place, they usually say of themselves that they are good Christians, who do not swear, or lie, or speak evil of others; that they do not kill any man or animal, nor anything having the breath of life, and that they hold the faith of the Lord Jesus Christ and his Gospel as Christ and his apostles taught. They assert that they occupy the place of the apostles, and that, on account of the above-mentioned things, they of the Roman church, namely the prelates, clerks, and monks, and especially the inquisitors of heresy, persecute them and call them heretics, although they are good men and good Christians, and that they are persecuted, just as Christ and his apostles were by the Pharisees.

Moreover they talk to the laity of the evil lives of the clerks and prelates of the Roman church, pointing out and setting forth their pride, cupidity, avarice, and uncleanness of life, and such other evils as they know. They invoke, with their own interpretation and according to their abilities, the authority of the Gospels and the Epistles against the condition of the prelates, churchmen, and monks, whom they call Pharisees and false prophets, who say, but do not.

Then they attack and vituperate, in turn, all the sacraments of the church, especially the sacrament of the eucharist, saying that it cannot contain the body of Christ, for had this been as great as the largest mountain Christians would have entirely consumed it before this. They assert that the host comes from straw, that it passes through the tails of horses, to wit, when the flour is cleaned by a sieve [of horse hair]; that, moreover, it passes through the body and comes to a vile end, which, they say, could not happen if God were in it.

Of baptism, they assert that water is material and corruptible, and is therefore the creation of the evil power and cannot sanctify the soul, but that the churchmen sell this water out of avarice, just as they sell earth for the burial of the dead, and oil to the sick when they anoint them, and as they sell the confession of sins as made to the priests.

Hence they claim that confession made to the priests of the Roman church is useless, and that, since the priests may be sinners, they cannot loose nor bind, and, being unclean themselves, cannot make others clean. They assert, moreover, that the cross of Christ should not be adored or venerated, because, as they urge, no one would venerate or adore the gallows upon which a father, relative, or friend had been hung. They urge, further, that they who adore the cross ought, for similar reasons, to worship all thorns and lances, because as Christ's body was on the cross during the passion, so was the crown of thorns on his head and the soldier's lance in his side. They proclaim many other scandalous things in regard to the sacraments.

Moreover they read from the Gospels and the Epistles in the vulgar tongue [that is, in vernacular translations], applying and expounding them in their favor and against the condition of the Roman church in a manner which it would take too long to describe in detail; but all that relates to this subject may be read more fully in the books they have written and infected, and may be learned from the confessions of such of their followers as have been converted.

Instructions for Interrogation

When a heretic is first brought up for examination he assumes a confident air, as though secure in his innocence. I ask him why he has been brought before me. He replies, smiling and courteous, "Sir, I would be glad to learn the cause from you."

> Inquisitor: "You are accused as a heretic and that you believe and teach otherwise than [the] holy church believes."
>
> Accused: (Raising his eyes to heaven, with an air of the greatest faith) "Lord, thou knowest that I am innocent of this, and that I never held any faith other than that of true Christianity."

Inquisitor: "You call your faith Christian, for you consider ours as false and heretical. But I ask whether you have ever believed as true another faith than that which the Roman church holds to be true?"

Accused: "I believe the true faith which the Roman church believes, and which you openly preach to us."

Inquisitor: "Perhaps you have some of your sect at Rome whom you call the Roman church. I, when I preach, say many things, some of which are common to us both, as that God lives, and you believe some of what I preach. Nevertheless you may be a heretic in not believing other matters which are to be believed."

Accused: "I believe all things that a Christian should believe."

Inquisitor: "I know your tricks. What the members of your sect believe you hold to be that which a Christian should believe. But we waste time in this fencing. Say simply, Do you believe in one God the Father, and the Son, and the Holy Ghost?"

Accused: "I believe."

Inquisitor: "Do you believe in Christ born of the Virgin, suffered, risen, and ascended to heaven?"

Accused: (Briskly) "I believe."

Inquisitor: "Do you believe the bread and wine in the mass performed by the priests to be changed into the body and blood of Christ by divine virtue?"

Accused: "Ought I not to believe this?"

Inquisitor: "I don't ask if you ought to believe, but if you do believe."

Accused: "I believe whatever you and other good doctors order me to believe."

Inquisitor: "Those good doctors are the masters of your sect; if I accord with them you believe with me; if not, not."

Accused: "I willingly believe with you if you teach what is good to me."

Inquisitor: "You consider it good to you if I teach what your other masters teach. Say, then, do you believe the body of our Lord Jesus Christ to be in the altar?"

Accused: (Promptly) "I believe."

Inquisitor: "You know that a body is there, and that all bodies are of our Lord. I ask whether the body there is of the Lord who was born of the Virgin, hung on the cross, arose from the dead, ascended, etc.?"

Accused: "And you, sir, do you not believe it?"

Inquisitor: "I believe it wholly."

Accused:	"I believe likewise."
Inquisitor:	"You believe that I believe it, which is not what I ask, but whether you believe it."
Accused:	"If you wish to interpret all that I say otherwise than simply and plainly, then I don't know what to say. I am a simple and ignorant man. Pray don't catch me in my words."
Inquisitor:	"If you are simple, answer simply, without evasions."
Accused:	"Willingly."
Inquisitor:	"Will you then swear that you have never learned anything contrary to the faith which we hold to be true?"
Accused:	(Growing pale) "If I ought to swear, I will willingly swear."
Inquisitor:	"I don't ask whether you ought, but whether you will swear."
Accused:	"If you order me to swear, I will swear."
Inquisitor:	"I don't force you to swear, because as you believe oaths to be unlawful, you will transfer the sin to me who forced you; but if you will swear, I will hear it."
Accused:	"Why should I swear if you do not order me to?"
Inquisitor:	"So that you may remove the suspicion of being a heretic."
Accused:	"Sir, I do not know how unless you teach me."
Inquisitor:	"If I had to swear, I would raise my hand and spread my fingers and say, 'So help me God, I have never learned heresy or believed what is contrary to the true faith.'"

Then trembling as if he cannot repeat the form, [the accused] will stumble along as though speaking for himself or for another, so that there is not an absolute form of oath and yet he may be thought to have sworn. If the words are there, they are so turned around that he does not swear and yet appears to have sworn. Or he converts the oath into a form of prayer, as God help me that I am not a heretic or the like; and when asked whether he had sworn, he will say: "Did you not hear me swear?" And when further hard pressed he will appeal, saying, "Sir, if I have done amiss in aught, I will willingly bear the penance, only help me to avoid the infamy of which I am accused through malice and without fault of mine."

But a vigorous inquisitor must not allow himself to be worked upon in this way, but proceed firmly till he makes these people confess their error, or at least publicly abjure heresy, so that if they are subsequently found to have sworn falsely, he can, without further hearing, abandon them to the secular arm [that is, turn them over to the government for punishment]. If one consents to swear that he is not a heretic, I say to him, "If you wish to swear so as to escape [being burned at] the stake, one oath will not suffice for me, nor ten, nor a hundred, nor a thousand, because you dispense each other for a certain number of oaths taken under necessity, but I will require a countless number. Moreover, if I have, as I presume, adverse witnesses against you, your oaths will not save you from being burned. You will only stain your conscience without escaping death. But if you will simply confess your error, you may find mercy." Under this anxiety, I have seen some confess.

Questions: From the description of the Albigensians, what can be learned about their beliefs? What is the purpose of the interrogation of heretics, according to Gui? By what means does the interrogator seek to gain a confession? How, in this account, does the heretic try to avoid betraying himself?

60. WILLIAM OF TUDELA'S *SONG OF THE CATHAR WARS*

Preaching proved unsuccessful against the Albigensians, and in 1207 Peter of Castelnau, the papal legate for this area, excommunicated Count Raymond VI of Toulouse, who had been linked to the Albigensians. Then Peter was murdered in early 1208 by one of Raymond's retainers, and soon afterwards Innocent III launched the Albigensian Crusade. This war, which raged from 1209 to 1229, was characterized by politics, bloody power struggles, and a land grab by the northern French nobles who made up the bulk of the crusading force. The main leaders were, on the Albigensian side, Count Raymond (d. 1222), and, on the papal side, the heir to the French throne, the future king Louis VIII (1223-26) and Simon de Montfort (d. 1218), the appointed leader of the crusade. Raymond VI's heir, Raymond VII, agreed to the Peace of Paris in 1229, which ended the Albigensian Crusade. The Albigensian heresy, however, persisted and was finally subdued by the Inquisition (see previous document).

The Song of the Cathar Wars covers the period between 1204 and 1218. It has two authors, William of Tudela and a later anonymous writer who finished the last two thirds of the poem. Although the poem was written as a performance piece, both texts are believed to be an accurate account of the events. The section printed here is from the beginning of the poem and is by William of Tudela.

Source: trans. J. Shirley, in William of Tudela and an anonymous successor, *The Song of the Cathar Wars: A History of the Albigensian Crusade* (Aldershot: Scolar Press, 1996), pp. 11-16.

Of course you all know how this heresy — God send his curse on it! — became so strong that it gained control of the whole of the Albigeois, of the Carcassès and most of Lauragais. All the way from Béziers to Bordeaux many or indeed most people believed in or supported it. When the lord pope and the other clergy saw this lunacy spreading so much faster than before and tightening its grip every day, each of them in his own jurisdiction sent out

Fig. 21: The siege of Toulouse and death of Simon de Montfort in 1218, as depicted in a nineteenth-century engraving of a thirteenth-century French stone sculpture. From P. Lacroix, *Military and Religious Life in the Middle Ages* (London, Chapman and Hall, 1874).

preachers. The Cistercian order led the campaign, and time and again it sent out its own men. Next, the bishop of Osma [in Spain] arranged a meeting between himself and the other legates with these Bulgars [that is, the heretics] at Carcassonne. This was very well attended, and the king of Aragon [that is, Peter II, 1174-1213] and his nobles were present. Once the king had heard the speakers and discovered how heretical they were, he withdrew, and sent a letter about this to Rome....

God grant me his blessing, what shall I say? They think more of a rotten apple than of sermons, and went on just the same for about five years. Those lost fools refused to repent, so that many were killed, many people perished, and still more will die before the fighting ends. It cannot be otherwise....

Led by Brother Arnold, abbot of Cîteaux, friend of God, the preachers traveled on foot and horseback among the wicked and misbelieving heretics, arguing with them and vigorously challenging their errors, but these fools paid no attention and despised everything they said.

At this time [the papal legate] Peter of Castelnau was traveling out of Provence on his pacing mule. He reached the Rhône at St. Gilles, and there he excommunicated the count of Toulouse for supporting the mercenaries who were ravaging the countryside. Thereupon an evil-hearted squire, hoping to win the count's approval, stepped like a traitor behind the legate, drove his sharp sword into his spine, and killed him. The man fled at once on his fast horse to his home town of Beaucaire, where he had kinsmen....

You can be sure the pope was not pleased when he heard of his legate's death. He grasped his chin in anger and called on St. James of Compostela and on St. Peter of Rome who lies in the chapel there. He spoke his anathema and then dashed out the candle. Brother Arnold of Cîteaux was present, and so too were Master Milo, that fine Latinist, and the twelve cardinals all in a circle. There it was they made the decision that led to so much sorrow, that left so many men dead with their guts spilled out and so many great ladies and pretty girls naked and cold, stripped of gown and cloak. From beyond Montpellier as far as Bordeaux, any that rebelled were to be utterly destroyed....

The abbot of Cîteaux, however, sat with his head bent. Then he rose and, standing by a marble column, said to the pope: "By St. Martin, my lord, this talking is a waste of time! Come, have your letters written in good Latin, and then I can set off. Send them to France, to the Limousin, to Poitou, the Auvergne, and Périgord; have the indulgence proclaimed here too and all over the world as far as Constantinople. Proclaim that any man who does not take the cross shall drink no wine, shall not eat off a cloth morning or night, shall wear neither linen nor hemp, and when he dies shall lie unburied like a dog." He fell silent, and his advice seemed right to all who were there.

Everyone greatly respected the abbot of Cîteaux (who later became archbishop of Narbonne, the best who ever wore the miter there), and when he had spoken, no one said a word. Then the pope, looking thoroughly unhappy, spoke as follows: "Go to Carcassonne, brother, and to great Toulouse on the Garonne and lead the armies against the ungodly. Cleanse the troops from their sins in the name of Christ, and in my name preach to them and exhort them to drive the heretics out from amongst the virtuous." ...

As soon as they had taken leave, the abbot mounted and rode to Cîteaux, where all the [Cistercian abbots] had gathered for the chapter-general on the feast of the Holy Cross in summer, as is their custom. In the presence of the whole assembly, he sang mass and explained that they were to go here and there about the world, over the whole length and breadth of holy Christendom. Then, once they knew their sins would be forgiven, men took the cross in France and all over the kingdom....

The count of Toulouse, lord of Beaucaire, saw that his nephew the viscount was against him, saw too all his enemies poised to attack, and knew that the crusaders would invade all and any part of his lands without hesitation. He sent into Gascony therefore, to his comrade the archbishop of Auch, being sure he would not refuse to travel on his behalf, and to the abbot of Condom, a man of noble birth, to Raymond of Rabastens, a generous giver, and to the prior of the Hospital [of Toulouse], a good physician. All these were to go to Rome and then to the [German] emperor. They would speak to the pope, for they were eloquent men, and would make some arrangement.

These envoys rode off to Rome as fast as they could. Why make a long story of it? They said enough and they made gifts enough to reconcile their lord pope and the count of Toulouse. This is how it was settled: Raymond was to make seven of his strongest castles over to the lord pope as a guarantee of future obedience. The pope sent a most worthy clerk called Milo, who was to give the count his orders (this Milo died at St. Gilles before the end of the year).

When the viscount of Béziers heard that Count Raymond had indeed made peace, he bitterly repented and would have been glad to make terms too if he could. But Milo despised him and refused his request. So the viscount summoned his forces from his whole fief, horse and foot, every able-bodied man, and waited inside Carcassonne for the crusading armies to arrive. How wretched were those who had stayed at Béziers! I doubt if as many as fifty or a hundred of them escaped death.

Questions: Where do the author's sympathies lie? In the poem, what is the pope's view of the crusade? Why did Raymond's negotiations with the pope succeed while those of the count of Béziers with the clerk Milo failed? What does this episode tell us about diplomacy between secular leaders and the papacy?

61. ACCOUNTS OF THE CHILDREN'S CRUSADE

The Children's Crusade of 1212 was not a movement planned or even encouraged by Innocent III. Rather, it grew out of people's dissatisfaction with traditional crusades to the Holy Land—crusades which had, of late, resulted in failure and humiliating loss. The belief that weakness and humility could succeed where strength and arrogance had failed was widespread, and this wave of popular piety sparked off numerous movements or pilgrimages including that known as the Children's Crusade and, later in the thirteenth century, the so-called Shepherds' Crusade (doc. 85). Records of the Children's Crusade are sketchy at best, and there are no first-hand narratives; some historians have even argued that it never occurred. Below are four accounts from France and Germany.

Sources: Cologne and Trier: trans. J. Shinners, *Medieval Popular Religion, 1000-1500: A Reader* (Peterborough: Broadview Press, 1997), pp. 398-99; Marbach and Laon: trans. R.H. Cooke in J.F.C. Hecker, *The Epidemics of the Middle Ages*, trans. B.G. Babington (London: Trübner & Co., 1895), pp. 354, 357, revised by J. Shinners.

Royal Chronicles of Cologne

An absolutely marvelous thing occurred that same year [1212], all the more marvelous since such a thing was unheard of in the world. For around Easter and Pentecost from all Germany and France with no encouragement or preaching but driven by unknown inspiration many thousands of children from six years old all the way to young manhood abandoned the plows and wagons they drove, or the cattle they herded, or whatever else they had at hand, and—though their unwilling parents, kinfolk, and friends tried to hold them back—suddenly ran one after the other and undertook a crusade. In groups of twenty, fifty, or a hundred, with their banners aloft they began heading for Jerusalem. Many people asked them by whose counsel or encouragement they had exposed themselves to this kind of life, especially since for quite some years before many kings, more dukes, and countless people going at it with their mighty hands had returned with the business unfinished; but they were still just youngsters with neither the power nor the strength to do anything, and so everyone judged them to be foolish and imprudent for attempting to do this. They answered briefly: they made themselves obedient to divine assent in this. Thus, whatever God wanted them to do they would endure gladly and with a compliant heart. And so making a little progress on the way, some turned back at Mainz, some at Piacenza, some at Rome. Others reached Marseilles, but whether they crossed the sea or what became of them is uncertain. But one thing is sure: of the many thousands who had set out, barely a few returned home.

Annals of Marbach

At this time [1212] a frivolous expedition occurred, as children and foolish men marked themselves as crusaders without any discretion, more out of curiosity than for their salvation. People of both sexes, boys and girls alike, not just minors but also grownups, married women with virgins, set out with empty purses, not only through all Germany, but also through parts of France and Burgundy. Their parents and friends could use no means to restrain them, for they used every effort to join that expedition, so that everywhere in the villages and the fields they left their tools and whatever they had in hand at the time and joined bands as they passed by. And just as we are often a crowd easily prone to belief when faced with such novelties, many thought that this happened not through some foolheadedness but through divine inspiration and a certain piety, and so they aided them with provisions, furnishing them food and other necessities. But when the clergy and some of the others of sounder mind spoke against it, and judged the expedition to be in vain and useless, the laity vehemently objected, saying that the clerics were unbelievers, and that they opposed this more out of their envy and greed than for its truth and righteousness. But since no affair that begins without the balance of reason and the strength of counsel has a good end, after this stupid multitude reached the regions of Italy, they were separated and scattered through the cities and towns; many were kept by the inhabitants of the land as servants and handmaids. Others are said to have reached the sea where they were carried off by the sailors and mariners and transported to other distant parts of the world. But the rest came to Rome where they ... realized that their effort was frivolous and empty. Still, they were by no means absolved from the vow to take the cross, except the boys under the age of discretion and those who were oppressed by old age. Thus deceived and perplexed, therefore, they began their return. Those who had once passed through the land in crowds and never without a song of encouragement among their troops, now returned singly and silently, barefoot and famished, held in scorn by everyone; and many virgins had been raped and had lost the flower of their chastity.

Anonymous Chronicle of Laon

In the month of June of the same year [1212] a certain boy, by occupation a shepherd, of a village named Cloyes near the town of Vendôme, said that the Lord had appeared to him in the form of a poor pilgrim, had received bread from him, and had delivered letters to him to be taken to the king of the French. When he came, together with his fellow shepherd-boys, nearly thirty thousand people assembled around him from all parts of France. While he stayed at St. Denis, the Lord worked many miracles through him, as many have witnessed. There were also many other boys who were held in great veneration by the common multitude in many places because they were also believed to work miracles, to whom a multitude of boys gathered wishing to proceed to the holy boy Stephen under their guidance. All acknowledged him as master and prince over them. At length the king [Philip II], having consulted the masters of Paris about this gathering of boys, commanded them to return to their homes; and so this childish enthusiasm was as easily ended as it had begun. But it seemed to many that, by means of such innocents gathered of their own accord, the Lord would do something great and new upon the earth, but it turned out much differently.

Deeds of Trier

For certain children gathered together from all the towns and villages of Germany, and, as if by divine inspiration, they met in each place, united into a troop, and headed for the road to Jerusalem as if they meant to recapture the Holy Land. The leader and head of this journey was Nicholas, a boy from Cologne, who bore over him a cross having the shape of the Greek letter *tau*, which was put forward as a mark of his holiness and miraculous qualities, though it was hard to tell what kind of material or metal it was made of. When the children arrived at Brindisi [in southern Italy], the local bishop, sensing something underhanded, did not permit them to cross the sea. For Nicholas's father sold them to the heathens, and this happened from the evil deed of demons. Because of this, the boy himself died, and his father met a bad death back in Cologne. Even more of the children died; for when they were on their way people generously aided them, but on their journey back home they gave them nothing.

Questions: How were the child crusaders viewed by ordinary people? By church and secular leaders? By the various authors of these accounts? What do we learn here about people's view of crusading? What inconsistencies are there in the texts? What does this indicate about the event?

62. DECREES OF THE FOURTH LATERAN COUNCIL

In 1215, Innocent III held a great council to discuss, among other issues, plans for a new crusade. The Fourth Lateran Council is notable for its crusading legislation, which creat-ed a model framework for future crusades. Innocent himself never saw the realization of the council's plans: he died on July 16, 1216, in the midst of a preaching campaign for what was to become the Fifth Crusade.

Source: O.J. Thatcher and E.H. McNeal, *A Sourcebook for Medieval History: Selected Documents Illus-trating the History of Europe in the Middle Ages* (New York: Charles Scribner's Sons, 1905), pp. 538-44.

Since we earnestly desire to liberate the Holy Land from the hands of the wicked, we have consulted wise men who fully understand the present situa-tion. And at the advice of the holy council we decree that all crusaders who shall determine to go by sea shall assemble in the kingdom of Sicily a year from the first of next June. They may gather at their convenience either at Brindisi, Messina, or in any other place on either side of the strait. If the Lord permits, we shall also be there in order that the Christian army may, with our advice and aid, be well organized, and set out with the divine benediction and papal blessing.

1. Those who determine to go by land shall be ready at the same date, and they shall keep us informed of their plans in order that we may send them a suitable legate to counsel and aid them.

2. All clergymen of whatever rank who go on the crusade shall diligently devote themselves to prayer and exhortation, by word and example teaching the crusaders always to have the fear and the love of God before their eyes and not to say or do anything to offend the divine majesty. Even if they sometimes fall into sin, they shall rise again by true penitence. They shall show humility of heart and of body, and observe moderation in their way of living and in their dress. They shall altogether avoid dissensions and rivalries, and shun hatred and envy. Thus, equipped with spiritual and material arms, they shall fight more securely against the enemies of the faith, not resting on their own power but hoping in the divine strength.

3. These clergymen shall receive all the income of their benefices for three years, just as if they were residing in them, and, if it is necessary, they may pawn their benefices for the same length of time.

4. In order that this holy undertaking may not be prevented or delayed, we earnestly command all prelates, each in his own locality, to urge and insist that all who have taken the cross fulfill their vows to the Lord. And, if necessary,

they may compel them to do so, in spite of all their subterfuges, by putting their persons under excommunication and their lands under the interdict. We except, however, those who may find some real hindrance in the way, on account of which we may decide that their vow may be commuted or put off.

5. In addition to these things, that nothing relating to Christ's business may be neglected, we command patriarchs, archbishops, bishops, abbots, and all others who have the care of souls, zealously to preach the crusade to those who are under their charge, by the Father, Son, and Holy Spirit, one only true eternal God, beseeching kings, dukes, princes, marquises, counts, barons, and other magnates, as well as the communes of cities, villages, and towns, that those who do not go in person to aid the Holy Land may, in proportion to their wealth, furnish a suitable number of fighting men and provide for their necessary expenses for three years. This they shall do for the remission of their sins according to the terms published in our general letter, and, for the sake of greater clearness, repeated below. Not only those who give their own ships, but also those who shall try to build ships for this purpose, shall have a share in this remission of sins.

6. If any shall be found so ungrateful to the Lord as to refuse, we warn them that they must answer for it to us before the terrible judge on the last day. Let all such consider with what conscience and what security they will be able to make their confession before the only begotten Son of God, Jesus Christ, into whose hands the Father has given all things, if, in this matter which so peculiarly concerns them, they refuse to obey him who was crucified for sinners, by whose favor and goodness they live and are sustained, nay, more, by whose blood they are redeemed.

7. Lest we should seem to put on other men's shoulders burdens so heavy that we would not so much as put a finger to them, like those who say, but do not, we give £30,000 out of our savings for this work, and beside the passage-money which we give all crusaders from Rome and the surrounding country, we also give 3,000 silver marks which are left in our hands from the gifts of certain Christians, the rest having been spent for the benefit of the Holy Land by the patriarchs of Jerusalem and the masters of the Templars and the Hospitallers.

8. Since we wish all other prelates and clergy to have a share in this meritorious work and its reward, we, with the approval of the council, decree that all the clergy of whatever rank shall, for three years, give one twentieth of the income of their churches to the aid of the Holy Land, and for the collection of it we shall appoint certain persons. We except from this tax certain monks and also those who shall take the cross and go in person on the crusade.

9. Moreover, we and our brethren, the cardinals of the holy Roman church, will pay a tenth of our incomes; and let all know that they must faithfully do

this. For any cardinal who shall knowingly commit any fraud in this matter shall incur the sentence of excommunication.

10. Now, because it is only just that those who devote themselves to the service of the heavenly ruler should enjoy some special prerogative, and since it is a little more than a year until the time set for going, we decree that all who have taken the cross shall be free from all collections, taxes, and other burdens. As soon as they take the cross we receive them and their possessions under the protection of St. Peter and of ourselves, so that archbishops, bishops, and other prelates are entrusted with their defense, and besides, other protectors shall be specially appointed to defend them. And until they return or their death shall be certainly known, their possessions shall not be molested. And if anyone shall act contrary to this he shall be restrained by ecclesiastical censure.

11. If any of those who go on the crusade are bound by oath to pay interest, their creditors, under threat of ecclesiastical censure, shall be compelled to free them from their oath and from the payment of the interest. If anyone compels them to pay the interest, he shall be forced to pay it back to them. We order the secular authorities to compel the Jews to remit the interest to all crusaders, and until they do remit it they shall have no intercourse with Christians. If any are not able for the present to pay their debts to Jews, the secular authorities shall secure an extension of time for them, so that after they have set out on the journey until their return or their death is certainly known, they shall not be disturbed about the interest. The Jews shall be compelled, after deducting the necessary expenses, to apply the income which they receive in the meantime from the property which they hold in pawn, toward the payment of the debt; since a favor of this kind, which defers the payment but does not cancel the debt, does not seem to cause much loss. Moreover, all prelates must know that they will be severely punished if they are lax in securing justice for crusaders or their families.

12. Since corsairs and pirates greatly impede the work by taking and robbing those who are going to, or returning from, the Holy Land, we excommunicate all who aid and protect them. Under the threat of anathema we forbid anyone knowingly to have anything to do with them in buying or selling, and we command all rulers of cities and other places to prevent them from practicing this iniquity. Otherwise, since not to interfere with the wicked is the same as to aid them, and since he who does not prevent a manifest crime is suspected of having a secret share in it, we command all prelates to exercise ecclesiastical severity against their persons and lands.

13. Besides, we excommunicate and anathematize those false and impious Christians who, against Christ and the Christian people, furnish the Saracens with arms, irons, and timbers for their galleys. If any who sell galleys or ships to the Saracens, or accept positions on their piratical craft, or give them aid,

counsel, or support with regard to their [war] machines to the disadvantages of the Holy Land, we decree that they shall be punished with the loss of all their goods, and they shall be the slaves of those who capture them. We command that this decree be published anew every Sunday and Christian feast day in all the maritime cities, and the bosom of the church shall not be opened to offenders against it unless, for the support of the Holy Land, they give all that they have gained from such a damnable business, and as much more from their possessions, so that they shall be justly punished for their crimes. But if they cannot pay, they shall be punished in some other way, in order that by their punishment others may be prevented from impudently attempting things of the same sort.

14. We forbid all Christians for the next four years to send their ships, or permit them to be set, to lands inhabited by Saracens, in order that a larger supply of vessels may be on hand for those who wish to go to the aid of the Holy Land, and also that the Saracens may be deprived of that aid which they have been accustomed to get from this.

15. Although tournaments have been prohibited by many councils under the general threat of punishment, we forbid them for three years under the threat of excommunication because the crusade is hindered by them.

16. Since, for the accomplishment of this work, it is necessary that Christian princes and peoples live in peace, and in order that the clergy may be able to make peace between all who are quarreling, or persuade them to make an inviolable truce, with the approval of the holy universal council we decree that a general peace shall be observed in the whole world for at least four years. And those who refuse to observe this peace shall be compelled to do so by excommunication of their persons and interdict on their lands, unless they have been so malicious in inflicting injuries on others that they themselves do not deserve the protection of such a peace. If they disregard the censure of the church, the ecclesiastical authorities shall invoke the secular power against them as disturbers of the business of Christ.

17. Trusting, therefore, in the mercy of omnipotent God and the authority of Saints Peter and Paul, and by the authority to bind and loose, which God has given us, to all who shall personally and at their own expense go on this crusade we grant full pardon of their sins, which they shall repent and confess, and, besides, when the just shall receive their reward we promise them eternal salvation. And to those who shall not go in person, but nevertheless at their own expense and in proportion to their wealth and rank shall send suitable men, and likewise to those who go in person but at the expense of others, we grant the full pardon of their sins. All who shall give a fitting part of their wealth to the aid of the Holy Land shall, in proportion to their gifts and according to the degree of their devotion, have a share in this forgiveness. This

universal council wishes to aid in the salvation of all who piously set out on this work, and therefore grants them in common the benefit of all its merits. Amen.

Questions: What does this text tell us about the difficulties of planning a successful crusade? How did the council address the problems of recruitment and of making certain that crusaders carried out their vows? How was the crusade to be financed? What financial incentives were offered to those who took the cross? What problems were posed by the Italian cities and their trade with the East? How did the council deal with them? What elements of this legislation, if any, were new?

63. OLIVER OF PADERBORN ON THE FIFTH CRUSADE

With the mistakes of the Fourth Crusade in mind, Innocent III had been determined that his next crusading venture would be firmly under ecclesiastical control. Honorius III, who became pope after Innocent's death, continued preparations for the crusade. Austrian, Hungarian and other smaller forces converged on the Holy Land in 1217 and engaged in a number of small battles. They were not far into this campaign when the large Hungarian army decided to returned home, leaving the rest of the crusading force with no choice but to wait for the arrival of the Frisians and Germans, who came in the spring of 1218. It was then agreed to attack Egypt, as this region was considered to be the source of Muslim wealth and power. The crusaders headed for Damietta on the Nile Delta, making camp outside the city on May 27, 1218, and settling in for a long siege. In September the cardinal legate, Pelagius of Albano, arrived and quickly assumed a leading role in the command of the crusade. This was indeed the ecclesiastical control advocated by Innocent III and the Fourth Lateran Council, but Pelagius's arrogance won many enemies among the already divided crusading force. The siege dragged on until November 9, 1219, when the city suddenly fell without resistance. The account below picks up at this point. Oliver of Paderborn was a cleric who had assisted Innocent III in preaching the Fifth Crusade. He accompanied the Frisian and German forces to Egypt and was both a secretary to Pelagius and a papal legate himself.

Source: trans. J.J. Gavigan, *The Capture of Damietta by Oliver of Paderborn* (Philadelphia: University of Pennsylvania Press, 1948), pp. 46-48, 53-54, 63-66, 82-84, 88-90, 92.

Chapter 37

... As we were entering [Damietta], there met us an intolerable odor, a wretched sight. The dead killed the living. Man and wife, father and son, master and slave, killed each other by their odor. Not only were the streets full of the dead, but in the houses, in the bedrooms, and on the beds lay the corpses. When a husband had perished, a woman, powerless to rise and lacking the help of one to support her, died, not being able to bear the odor; a son near his father or vice versa, a handmaid beside her mistress or vice versa, wasted away with illness and lay dead. "Little ones asked for bread and there was none to break it for them," infants hanging at the breasts of their mothers opened their mouths in the embrace of one dead. Fastidious rich men died of hunger amid piles of wheat, those foods being lacking by which they had been raised; in vain did they desire melons and garlic, onions, fish and fowl, fruits of the tree and herbs. In them was fulfilled the prophecy of the prophet: "Instead of a sweet smell there shall be stench, as rotten carcass shall not have company in burial." Almost 80,000, as we learned from the report of captives, perished in the city from the beginning of the siege to its end: all except those whom we found, healthy or ill, about 3,000 in number. Three hundred of these, the more notable ones of both sexes, were kept for the ransom of our captives; some died after the victory, others were sold for a great price, and others were baptized and given to Christ.

Chapter 46

The legate, after frequent public and private admonitions, grieved that so numerous an army was stationary, and not progressing, and would be going back in the next passage; finally by his example of action, he began to urge others to join the retinue, causing his tents to be pitched in a flat place. However, the opposition of the leaders prevailed to such a degree that even some Gallic and German mercenaries, who had accepted his money, hindered his plan of advancing. Certain of them were excommunicated, and others who were to be excommunicated afterwards were disturbed, and were compelled to return the pay that they accepted according to proportion of time. The Italian soldiers by vain hope cheated the religious zeal of the legate, promising assistance for the advance, "but the sons of Ephraim, bending and shooting the bow, have turned back in the day of battle." For while they were clearly regarding the persistence of the legate and the boldness of the march against the sultan, they agreed with the dissenters mentioned above, and opposed the advance, although the Christians did not lack an abundance of soldiers or attendants. Galleys were in abundance, barbots [that is, armored boats] were prepared, a numerous multitude of archers was present, there was a plentiful supply of provisions, there was a suitable place between the river on the right and the lake on the left, as if the Lord were saying to us: "What is there I ought to do more to my vineyard and I have not done it?…" For besides the other things which were provided by the Lord for the setting out of the expedition, as we learned from our scouts, the king of Babylon [that is, the sultan of Cairo] then had little aid, and a great multitude of Bedouins had joined us and would have given their wives and children as hostages if they had known that the Christians had undertaken the attempt manfully, as we learned through their letters and messengers. And this seemed probable because they are subject under tribute to the sultan; indeed they formerly ruled in the land of Egypt until they were powerfully oppressed by Saladin and were scattered through the wilderness of the desert.

Chapter 47

The legate, after much weariness, because he had an unwilling retinue and especially because the river overflowed at that time, withdrew to the previous camp, strongly urging the authors of the delay, in a public sermon, that the work of God, being happily begun, should not be ended and that they should judge themselves, lest they be grievously condemned by the Judge of secret things.

Chapter 48

No one can describe the corruption of our army after Damietta was given us by God, and the fortress of Tanis was added. Lazy and effeminate, the people were contaminated with chamberings and drunkenness, fornications and adulteries, thefts and wicked gains. Afterwards, certain of our men set out for a day's march into hostile territory, bringing back captives, oxen, and horses. Then the Templars, with their own special following, advanced in a swift march to a town on the seacoast, which is called Broil, and brought back many spoils—about 100 camels, the same number of captives, horses, mules, oxen, and asses and goats, clothing and much household furniture, returning unharmed after two days. However, on account of a lack of water, many horses and mules died on the way, although the men themselves returned safe. The Teutonic House, with many others, met them for joy, but when they delayed behind the Templars (it is not fully known for what reason), the swift horsemen of the Turks made an attack on them at the sea. Terrified men from other nations fled from them, but the English, the Flemish, the Teutons, and Robert of Belmont sustained the attack as they came upon them. The preceptor and the marshal of the same house, with many other brothers and about twenty secular knights, were captured. Many horses of those who fled to defend themselves were killed because our men went out, not for battle, but to meet the Templars, and therefore were without crossbowmen and archers.

Chapter 49

In the month of August there reached Damietta fourteen galleys equipped and sent at the same time by the doge of Venice, which brought some help to the Christians. At the same time the king of Babylon armed thirty-three galleys which caused us inestimable loss. For they captured the merchant ships, along with the men themselves, which were bringing supplies to Damietta; they even took the pilgrims captive, plundering and burning the ships. Besides, they attacked a large ship which was bringing Count Henry of Schwerin, and other Teutonic nobles who were coming to us. They, however, defended themselves manfully; and having killed and wounded many pirates they fortunately escaped, although they lost one vessel from the Teutonic House, with barley which Greek fire destroyed.

Chapter 73

From the day when we lost the river our men frequently assembled to consult together, and to ponder what would be more expedient: to wait in camp for the galleys promised by the emperor, or to go out, no matter what the loss, because of our dwindling supply of food. The greater number counseled going out, which was more dangerous because of the arrival of the enemy and the decided hindrance of the waters. But a certain one of the lesser members, who saw and heard these things and described them with a crude but truthful pen, proposed David as an example, who having choice among three things, any one of which was hard, chose not a famine of seven years, nor to be conquered by an enemy for three months, but what was the common wish of the king and the poor people: a pestilence of three days. Wherefore he answered, when he was consulted, as did the weak and infirm whom there were not sufficient ships nor animals to carry, that help should be awaited in a fortified place, since the provisions, if they were carefully distributed, could last even for twenty days. Nevertheless this plan was not accepted, but a departure, and that by night, was more favored. In this, the opinion of the bishop of Passau and that of the Bavarians prevailed.

[After sustaining heavy losses in withdrawing from the camp, the crusaders were ready to negotiate with the sultan.]

Chapter 77

On the very day of the Beheading of St. John the Baptist [that is, Aug. 29], at about the twelfth hour, our side, urged on by the lack of food and fodder, but especially by the great size of the waters, decided that it was more honorable to live happily or to die bravely in war, than to perish infamously in the flood. So when all the Franks had been roused to combat, battle lines were drawn up here and there looking upon each other fiercely and dreadfully. But the Turks realized that he who provokes an enemy is by his own fault bound by a yoke; they retreated a little upon receiving a command from their king, and the arrival of nightfall prevented a battle. Besides, while the treaty of peace was pending, a display of treachery was feared by wise men, if the common good were to be destroyed by a dangerous attack.

Chapter 79

And so when the conditions had been laid down according to the decisions of the sultan, the documents of the contracts were completed by both sides, oaths were sworn, and hostages were named. The sultan, therefore, placing his right hand on a paper which he had signed, swore in this way: "I, Kamil, king of Babylon, from a pure heart and a good will, and without interruption, do swear by the Lord, by the Lord, by the Lord and my law, that I will in good faith observe all the things that this written paper contains which is placed under my hand; if I shall not do this, may I be separated from future judgment and the society of Mohammed, and may I acknowledge the Father, the Son, and the Holy Ghost." In this manner swore Scraphus and Coradin, and their more eminent emirs. Behold under how many mistakes and contradictions is that blind nation laboring; three times they name God, but not knowing the mystery of the Trinity, they are unwilling to distinguish the name of the Father, of the Son, and of the Holy Ghost, to the increase of their own damnation. If they swear in bad faith or with any interruption of the form of the ritual, they say that they are not under obligation. Now this writing contained an agreement of this kind: that they would restore the true cross, along with all captives taken any time at all in the kingdom of Babylon, or all Christians held in the power of Coradin; and that when they had received Damietta with all its belongings, they would send us all away free, as well as all our movable goods, and would faithfully keep a truce of eight years. Our leaders swore that they would free all Saracen captives, whom they were holding in the two kingdoms of Egypt and Jerusalem; that they would restore Damietta and would observe the treaty, unless our crowned king who was coming should wish to break it. Besides, twenty-four hostages were given, whom the sultan chose: the legate, the king of Jerusalem, the duke of Bavaria, and three masters of [military orders], along with eighteen others. On the other hand, the son of the sultan, heir of the kingdom, and one of his brothers of whom there are many, and sons of nobles were given to us until our return to Turo and the port of Damietta.

Chapter 82

"The beast has gone into his covert, and abides in his den." If it is asked why Damietta returned so quickly to the unbelievers, the reason is clear: it was luxury-loving, it was ambitious, it was mutinous; besides, it was exceedingly ungrateful to God and to men. For to pass over other things, when that city had been given to us from on high by heaven in the distribution of the riches that were found in her, not an old woman nor a boy of ten years and over was excluded; to Christ alone, the bestower of the goods, was a share denied, not even a tenth being paid to him....

In the distribution of towers and dwellings most praise was deservedly given to that obedient and energetic nation, who from the beginning attacked Damietta with great courage, and considered no position either humble or lowly; by the fleet of ships which it brought, the camp of the faithful was supplied with food and weapons, the tower of the river was captured, the crossing to the opposite bank was organized, the upper and lower bridges were built, the watchtower of Turo was constructed, the walls of the rampart were fortified. It has consolation in the face of such ingratitude since "God will render the inestimable reward" of his slaves "and will conduct them in a wonderful way."

Questions: Why had Damietta fallen so suddenly to the crusaders? Why did the crusaders ultimately lose the city? How did the Fifth Crusade differ from earlier campaigns with regard to the role of church officials? In what ways did the Fifth Crusade live up to the ideal framework laid out by the Fourth Lateran Council? In what ways did it fall short?

CHAPTER SEVEN:

CRUSADES OF THE HOLY ROMAN EMPIRE

Fig. 22: Pagans being baptized in central Europe. This nineteenth-century engraving of a fifteenth-century manuscript illustration represents forced conversions in the time of Charlemagne, though the clothing and buildings are those of the late Middle Ages. From P. Lacroix, *Military and Religious Life in the Middle Ages* (London, Chapman and Hall, 1874).

64. CHARTER TO GERMAN SETTLERS

The Christian Germans of central Europe had been pushing eastward since the eighth century. Under the emperor Charlemagne (768-814), the border of Christian Germany had been established at the Elbe River; east of this informal boundary lay lands inhabited by non-Christian Slavic peoples, troubled by occasional invasion from the west. In the early twelfth century, a period of sustained German expansion eastward began. German aggression against the pagan East had usually combined religious conversion efforts with colonization, so this movement was well suited to the ideology and rhetoric of crusading, as will be seen in this chapter. The early twelfth-century movement, however, was one of mainly peaceful settlement. In the following charter, dating from 1106, Bishop Frederick of Hamburg sets down the regulations for and obligations of German colonists wishing to settle in Slavic lands.

Source: O.J. Thatcher and E.H. McNeal, *A Sourcebook for Medieval History: Selected Documents Illustrating the History of Europe in the Middle Ages* (New York: Charles Scribner's Sons, 1905), pp. 572-73; revised.

1. In the name of the holy and undivided Trinity, Frederick, by the grace of God bishop of Hamburg, to all the faithful in Christ, gives a perpetual benediction. We wish to make known to all the agreement which certain people living this side of the Rhine, who are called Hollanders, have made with us.

2. These men came to us and earnestly begged us to grant them certain lands in our bishopric, which are uncultivated, swampy, and useless to our people. We have consulted our subjects about this and, considering that this would be profitable to us and to our successors, have granted their request.

3. The agreement was made that they should pay us every year one penny for every hide of land. We have thought it necessary to determine the dimensions of the hide, in order that no quarrel may hereafter arise about it. The hide shall be 720 royal rods long and thirty royal rods wide. We also grant them the streams which flow through this land.

4. They agree to give the tithe according to our decree, that is, every eleventh sheaf of grain, every tenth lamb, every tenth pig, every tenth goat, every tenth goose, and a tenth of the honey and of the flax. For every colt they shall pay a penny on St. Martin's day [that is, Nov. 11], and for every calf a half-penny.

5. They promise to obey me in all ecclesiastical matters according to the decrees of the holy fathers, the canonical law, and the practice in the diocese of Utrecht.

6. They agree to pay every year two marks for every 100 hides, for the privilege of holding their own courts for the settlement of all their differences about secular matters. They did this because they feared they would suffer

Fig. 23: The activities of war, science, commerce, and farming, as shown in a nineteenth-century reproduction of a thirteenth-century illuminated manuscript. Western Europeans fought in eastern Europe, introduced new agricultural techniques, and increased commercial activity there. From P. Lacroix, *The Arts in the Middle Ages* (London: Chapman and Hall, 1870).

from the injustice of foreign judges. If they cannot settle the more important cases they shall refer them to the bishop. And if they take the bishop with them [that is, from Hamburg to the colony] for the purpose of deciding one of their trials, they shall provide for his support as long as he remains there by granting him one third of all the fees arising from the trial; and they shall keep the other two thirds.

7. We have given them permission to found churches wherever they may wish on these lands. For the support of the priests who shall serve God in these churches we grant a tithe of our tithes from these parish churches. They promised that the congregation of each of these churches should endow their church with a hide for the support of their priest. The names of the men who made this agreement with us are: Henry, the priest, to whom we have granted the aforesaid churches for life; and the others are laymen, Helikin, Arnold, Hiko, Fordolt and Referie. To them and to their heirs after them we have granted the aforesaid land according to the secular laws and to the terms of the agreement.

Questions: What did the bishop of Hamburg gain from this charter? What did the settlers gain? How was the colony to be regulated and governed, by both the secular authorities and the church?

65. POEM DESCRIBING CISTERCIAN SETTLEMENT

The establishment of Christianity was often seen as an important prerequisite to settlement, as the placement of churches and monasteries helped to ease the subjugation of the native population while providing justification for the defense of the newly acquired territory. Cistercian monks were known for land reclamation on the frontier and, however deserved this reputation might have been, it was one that they themselves promoted. Below is a Cistercian poem of the late fourteenth century which praises the earlier work of twelfth-century monks who settled in Poland.

Source: trans. E. Amt; Latin text in *Monumenta Polonaise Historica: Pomniki Dziejowe Polski*, ed. A. Bielowski (Lwow: Nakladem Akademii Umiejetnosci w Krakowie, 1878), Vol. III, pp. 709-10.

...In the year 1131, [the king of Silesia]
Brought in worthy [Cistercians] to praise God forever.
Throwing the statues of Mars and Julius into ditches,
He established peaceful dwellings for Christ and the saints.
There was no monastery there for the first twenty years,
But only a few brothers cultivating the wilderness....
Then [in 1151] a convent of monks was first founded here,
And the same year Abbot Florence died
Of poverty and nakedness.
So another abbot, Father Ticelin, was sent hither.
The monks were scarcely surviving and were very poor,
For the country was wooded and without farmers,
And Poland's poor people were not industrious;
They plowed the sandy soil with wooden plows, not iron,
And with no more than two oxen at a time.
Throughout the land there were no cities or towns,
But only castles, country markets, swamps, and chapels.
They had no salt, no iron, no coins,
No metal, no good clothing, and no shoes.
They simply herded their animals.
Such were the delights the first monks encountered.
And yet the monks brought in all these amenities,
And filled the land with them, making everything possible.
Living by the toil of these things, without exertion on our part,
Let us never believe we have won all this by our own efforts,
Or that we ourselves have granted our own wishes.

Questions: What picture of the pre-Cistercian landscape does this poem paint? Why?

What benefits are said to have been introduced by the Cistercians? How is Cistercian expansion justified in the text?

66. PROCLAMATIONS OF NORTHERN EUROPEAN CRUSADES

In the spring of 1147, a group of German nobles sought permission to wage a crusade against the pagan Wends, a Slavic people living east of the Elbe. The motivation for this initiative was clearly political and economic, and the planners conveniently overlooked the fact that diplomacy and mission work were under way among the Wends. But the would-be crusaders attracted the attention of Bernard of Clairvaux (see docs. 35, 49), who persuaded Pope Eugenius III to support the campaign. Bernard's letter below is addressed to a council of churchmen and nobles at Frankfurt. The second document shows the expansion of crusading in northeastern Europe to Estonia in the later twelfth century.

Sources: Bernard's letter: trans. B.S. James, *The Letters of St. Bernard of Clairvaux* (Chicago: Henry Regnery Company, 1953), pp. 466–68; bull: trans. E. Amt from *Diplomaticum Danicum Udgivet af det Danske Sprog-og Litteraturselskab Bekostet af Carlsberfondet, 1. Raekke 3. Bind*, ed. C.A. Christensen, H. Nielsen, and L. Weibull (Copenhagen: C.A. Reitzels Boghandel, 1976–77), pp. 37–38.

Letter of Bernard of Clairvaux, 1147

To his lords and reverend fathers, the archbishops, bishops, and princes, and to all the faithful of God, the spirit of strength and deliverance, from Bernard, styled abbot of Clairvaux.

Without doubt it has been heard in your land, without doubt the news has gone forth in oft repeated words that God has stirred up the spirit of kings and princes to take vengeance on the pagans and to wipe out [paganism] from Christian lands.... How good and great is the bounty of God's mercy! But the evil one sees this and resents it, he gnashes his teeth and withers away in fury, for he is losing many of those whom he held bound by various crimes and enormities. Abandoned men are now being converted, turning aside from evil, and making ready to do good. But the evil one feared far more the damage he would incur from the conversion of the pagans, when he heard that their tale was to be completed, and that the whole of Israel was to find salvation. This is what he believes to be threatening him now at this very time, and with all his evil cunning he is endeavoring to see how he can best oppose such a great good. He has raised up evil seed, wicked pagan sons, whom, if I may say so, the might of Christendom has endured too long, shutting its eyes to those who with evil intent lie in wait, without crushing their poisoned heads under its heel. But the scriptures say: "Presumption comes first, and ruin close behind it." And so God grant that the pride of these peoples may be speedily humbled and the road to Jerusalem not closed on their account. Because the Lord has committed to our insignificance the preaching of this crusade, we make known to you that at the council of the king, bishops, and princes who had come together at Frankfurt, the might of Christians was armed against them, and that for the complete wiping out or, at any rate, the conversion of these peoples, they have put on the cross, the sign of our salvation; and we, by virtue of our authority, promised them the same spiritual privileges as those enjoy who set out towards Jerusalem. Many took the cross on the spot, the rest we encouraged to do so, so that all Christians who have not yet taken the cross for Jerusalem may know that they will obtain the same spiritual privileges by undertaking this expedition, if they do so according to the advice of the bishops and princes. We utterly forbid that for any reason whatsoever a truce should be made with these peoples, either for the sake of money or for the sake of tribute, until such a time as, by God's help, they shall be either converted or wiped out. We speak to you, archbishops and bishops, and urge you to oppose any such plan for a truce with all your strength, and to watch with the greatest care this matter, and to apply all the zeal of which you are capable to seeing that it is carried through manfully. You are the ministers of Christ, and therefore it is demanded of you with all the more confidence that you should watch faithfully over God's work, which, because it is his work, should be especially your concern. And this is what we too pray for from God with our whole heart. The uniform of this army, in clothes, in arms, and in all else, will be the same as the uniform of the other, for it is fortified with the same privileges. It has pleased all those who were gathered together at Frankfurt to decree that a copy of this letter should be carried everywhere and that the bishops and priests should proclaim it to the people of God, and arm them with the holy cross against the enemies of the cross of Christ, and that they should all meet at Magdeburg on [June 29,] the feast of the apostles Peter and Paul.

Bull of Pope Alexander III, 1171

Our mind is distressed not a little, and tortured with no small bitterness and sorrow, when we hear that the wildness of the Estonians and other pagans of those parts rises up violently and rages furiously and savagely against God's faithful people and the upholders of the Christian faith. Nevertheless we praise and bless the Lord that with unmovable steadfastness you persist in the catholic faith and in devotion to the holy Roman church, which is the head of all churches and, established by our Lord as their mistress, holds first place over all other churches by heavenly privilege, and that you preserve the bond and unity of the Christian religion. Wherefore, since it is proper for our office to supply to you by careful urging, and eagerly to recommend, those things which are known to lead to the strengthening of the faith and to the health of your souls, we advise all of you and exhort you in the Lord, to turn to godly worship; to love mercy, justice, and judgment; to hold back from pillaging and evil works; to devote yourselves to proper obedience given to God; to display due honor and reverence to the aforesaid holy Roman church, as your mother and mistress; to humbly obey your bishops, priests, and other prelates; to render to them their tithes, first fruits, offerings, and other rights; to honor those men in every way as the fathers and pastors of your souls; and to defend, support, and willingly preserve their rights. Fortified with heavenly arms and weapons and strengthened with apostolic encouragement, may you be girded with the spirit of courage to defend the truth of the Christian faith, so aiming to spread the Christian religion with a strong arm, that you will be able to snatch the victory from your enemies and, with the Lord's help, attain the crown of justice which is laid up for you. Wherefore we, trusting in God's mercy and the merits of the apostles Peter and Paul, grant to those persons who fight powerfully and bravely against the aforesaid pagans one year's remission of their sins, for which they have confessed and received penance, in the same way that we are accustomed to grant it to those who visit the Holy Sepulcher. Moreover, we extend the remission of all their sins to those who die in that fight, if they have received penance. Given at Tusculum on September 11.

Questions: According to Bernard, what was the objective of the crusade against the Wends? How did it compare with the aims of the Second Crusade? What did Alexander III hope to accomplish by his letter to the Scandinavians? How did he attempt to strengthen papal authority over the crusaders and the region they were to conquer? How could crusades be justified when they were not aimed at restoring the Holy Land?

67. HELMOLD'S *CHRONICLE OF THE SLAVS*

The campaign against the Wends was notoriously brutal, and contemporary observers recognized its political and economic (rather than religious) focus. For Helmold, writing between 1167 and 1172, conversion was the primary goal of the northern crusades. Because of this, he was often frustrated by the political ambitions of the princes of the Holy Roman Empire and, as detailed here, the king of Denmark.

Source: trans. F.J. Tschan, *The Chronicle of the Slavs by Helmold, Priest of Bosau* (New York: Octagon Books Inc., 1966), pp. 170-72, 175-76 and 180-81.

In those days [that is, the 1140s] there took place events which were strange and which amazed the whole world. For while the most holy pope Eugenius was in authority and the third Conrad was at the helm of the state [that is, the Holy Roman Empire], there flourished Bernard, the abbot of Clairvaux, whose name had been made so famous by reports of miracles that crowds of people flocked to him from everywhere out of their desire to witness the wonders that were done through him. Bernard also came into Germany and appeared at the celebrated diet at Frankfurt where King Conrad then chanced to have come in festive mood, with his whole retinue of princes.... The holy man began, by what divine order instructed I do not know, to exhort the princes and the other faithful fold to set out for Jerusalem to conquer the barbarous nations of the east and to reduce them to Christian rule, saying that the time was at hand in which the fullness of the gentiles should come in and so all Israel would be saved. At the word of the preacher an incredibly great mass of people devoted itself forthwith to this very course; among them the first and foremost were King Conrad, Duke Frederick of Swabia, who afterwards was king, Duke Guelph, along with bishops and princes, an army of the noble and the common and the vulgar, exceeding estimation in number.... They were signed with the sign of the cross on their garments and arms. The initiators of the expedition, however, deemed it advisable to design one part of the army for the eastern regions [that is, the Holy Land], another for Spain, and a third against the Slavs who lived hard by us....

The third army of crusaders was directed against the Slavic peoples, the Abodrites and the Lutici, namely on our frontier, in order to avenge the death and destruction which they had inflicted upon the worshippers of Christ, especially upon the Danes. The leaders of this expedition were Adalbero of Hamburg and all the bishops of Saxony, besides the young duke Henry ["the Lion," of Saxony], Conrad, duke of Zähringen, Albert, margrave of Salzwedel, and Conrad of Wettin....

In the meantime the news spread though all Saxony and Westphalia that the Slavs had broken forth and had been the first to engage in war. All that army, signed with the sign of the cross, hastened to descend upon the land of the Slavs and to punish their iniquity. They divided the army and invested two fortresses Dobin and Demmin, and they "made many engines of war against" them. There came also an army of Danes, and it joined those who were investing Dobin, and the siege waxed. One day, however, those who were shut up noticed that the army of the Danes acted dilatorily — for they are pugnacious at home, unwarlike abroad. Making a sudden sally, they slew many of the Danes and laid them as a thickness for the ground. The Danes, also, could not be aided on account of intervening water. Moved to anger thereat, the army pressed the siege more obstinately. The vassals of our duke and of the margrave

Albert, however, said to one another: "Is not the land we are devastating our land, and the people we are fighting our people? Why are we, then, found to be our own enemies and the destroyers of our own incomes? Does not this loss fall back on our lords?"

From that day, then, uncertainty of purpose began to seize the army and repeated truces to lighten the investment. As often as the Slavs were beaten in an engagement, the army was held back from pursuing the fugitives and from seizing the stronghold. Finally, when our men were weary, an agreement was made to the effect that the Slavs were to embrace Christianity and to release the Danes whom they held in captivity. Many of them, therefore, falsely received baptism, and they released from captivity all the Danes that were old or not serviceable, retaining the others whom more robust years fitted for work. Thus, that grand expedition broke up with slight gain. The Slavs immediately afterwards became worse: they neither respected their baptism nor kept their hands from ravaging the Danes.

Questions: What threat did the Slavs pose to the Holy Roman Empire and the Danes, according to Helmold? What accounts for the failure of the campaign described above?

68. THE CHRONICLE OF HENRY OF LIVONIA

Henry of Livonia was a cleric under Bishop Albert of Uexküll, the first bishop in the Baltic region of Livonia (modern Estonia and northern Latvia). Henry wrote his chronicle in 1225-26. The excerpt below covers the early attempts by Bishop Meinhard of Uexküll to convert the Livonians in the 1180s and 1190s, and later efforts by Henry's patron, Bishop Albert, to strengthen the Livonian church. These included the founding (here credited to Brother Theodoric) of a military order, the Brothers of the Militia of Christ (also known as the Livonian Brothers of the Sword) in 1202.

Source: trans. J.A. Brundage, *The Chronicle of Henry of Livonia* (Madison: University of Wisconsin Press, 1961), pp. 25-30, 35-36, 40.

Book I

... In the monastery of Segeberg there was a man of worthy life, and with venerable gray hair, Meinhard by name, a priest of the order of St. Augustine. He came to Livonia with a band of merchants simply for the sake of Christ and only to preach. For German merchants, bound together through familiarity with the Livonians, were accustomed to go to Livonia, frequently sailing up the Dvina River. After receiving, therefore, the permission of King Vladimir of Polozk [a Russian prince], to whom the Livonians, while still pagan, paid tribute, and at the same time, after receiving gifts from him, this priest boldly set out upon the divine work, preaching to the Livonians and building a church in the village of Uexküll. And in the same village, Ylo, the father of Kulewene, and Viezo, the father of Alo, were the first to be baptized, while the others followed in their turn.

The next winter, the Lithuanians, after having laid waste Livonia, took many into captivity. The same preacher, together with the people of Uexküll, avoided the wrath of the Lithuanians and took to the forests. When the Lithuanians had withdrawn, Meinhard accused the Livonians of foolishness, because they had no fortifications; he promised them that forts would be built if they decided to become and to be considered sons of God. This pleased them and they promised and confirmed by an oath that they would receive baptism. Therefore, stonemasons were brought from Gothland the next summer. The Livonians, meanwhile, confirmed the sincerity of their intentions a second time. Part of the people were baptized before the beginning of the fort of Uexküll, and, after the fort was completed, all promised, though deceitfully, to be baptized. The walls, therefore, arose from their foundations. Because Meinhard paid for the building of a fifth part of the fort, this part was his property. Meinhard had first bought the land upon which the church at Uexküll stood. When the fort had at last been finished, those who had been baptized relapsed; those who had not yet been reborn refused to accept the faith. Meinhard, himself, nevertheless, did not desist from the enterprise. At the time the Semgalls, pagans of the neighborhood, hearing of the building made of stones, and not knowing that the stones were held together with cement, came with large ship's ropes, foolishly believing they could pull the fort into the Dvina. But they were wounded by the *ballistarii* [that is, large, wheeled cross-bows] instead and went away after having suffered losses.

The neighboring people of Holm cheated Meinhard by making a similar promise. After a fort had been built for them, they profited from their fraud. But at first some were baptized, with whatever sort of intentions, and their names are: Viliendi, Uldenago, Wade, Waldeko, Gerverder, and Vietzo. Between the construction of the above-mentioned forts, Meinhard was consecrated bishop [in 1186] by the metropolitan of Bremen. After the second fort had been completed, in their iniquity they forgot their oath and perjured themselves, for there was not even one of them who accepted the faith. Truly the soul of the preacher was disturbed, inasmuch as, by gradually plundering his possessions and beating his household, they decided to drive him outside their borders. They thought that since they had been baptized with water, they could remove their baptism by washing themselves in the Dvina and thus send it back to Germany. As a coworker in the Gospel the bishop had Brother Theodoric of the Cistercian order, subsequently a bishop in Estonia. Because the crops in his fields were quite abundant and in their own fields dying because of a flooding rain, the Livonians of Treiden prepared to sacrifice him to their gods. The people were collected and the will of the gods regarding the sacrifice was sought after by lot. A lance was placed in position and the horse came up and, at the signal of God, put out the foot thought to be the foot of life. Brother Theodoric prayed aloud and gave blessings with his hand. The pagan priest asserted that the Christian God was sitting on the back of the horse and was moving the horse's foot forward; that for this reason the back of the horse had to be wiped off so that the God might slide off. When this was done, the horse again put forth the foot of life, as before, and Brother Theodoric's life was saved. When Brother Theodoric was sent in to Estonia, he likewise endured from the pagans a great many dangers to his life....

Now that the aforementioned bishop had observed the stubbornness of the Livonians and had, accordingly, seen his labors falling to the ground, he abandoned his project, collected the monks and brothers, and, resolving to return, set out for the merchants' ships which were now preparing to go to Gothland at Easter. The tricky Livonians thus feared and suspected that a Christian army would come upon them. They therefore sought deceitfully with guile and tears and in many other ways to call back the bishop. They said to him...: "Why do you desert us, father? And to whom are you leaving us desolate creatures? Does a shepherd boy going away dangerously expose his sheep to the jaws of wolves?" And these very Livonians again promised that they would fully receive the faith. The innocent bishop believed every word, and upon the advice of the merchants and upon the promise of an army, went back with the Livonians. For some of the Germans and certain of the Danes and Norwegians and each of the trading groups had promised that if necessary they would bring an army. After the departure of the merchants, certain of the people of Holm greeted the bishop on his return like Judas, and said: "Hail Rabbi! At what price can salt and *watmal* [that is, a coarse cloth] be bought in Gothland?" And with bitterness in his heart he wept and crossed over to Uexküll and was received in his home. He appointed a day on which the people were to assemble in order that he might admonish them concerning their promise. The day was not observed and they did not fulfill their promise. After taking council with his men he proposed to go into Estonia in order to go on to Gothland with the merchants who were wintering in that place. The Livonians, in the meantime, prepared to kill him on the road, but he was forewarned by Anno of Treiden and advised to go back. Much perplexed and unable to get out of the country, he, therefore, went back to Uexküll.

Then he secretly sent away his messenger, Brother Theodoric of Treiden, to take counsel with the lord pope [Celestine II]. Brother Theodoric saw that he could not get out of the country, unless by a pious fraud he escaped the trap which the Livonians had set. Clad in a stole and carrying a book and holy water, he rode away on his horse, pretending that he was going to visit a sick man. When travelers questioned him, he insisted that this was the cause of his journey, and thus he escaped from the country and came at last to the supreme pontiff [that is, the pope]. When the supreme pontiff heard how many had been baptized, he thought that they should not be deserted and decreed that they ought to be forced to observe the faith which they had freely promised. He granted, indeed, the remission of all sins to all those who would take the cross and go to restore that newly founded church.

By this time the bishop, with the duke of Sweden, Germans, and inhabitants of Gothland, had already attacked the Kurs [that is, peoples to the south and west of the Livonians]. They were, however, thrown back by a storm and landed in Wierland, a province of Estonia, and devastated its territory for three days. But while the people of Wierland were negotiating about receiving the faith, the duke, preferring to accept tribute from them, put sail and to the annoyance of the Germans turned away.

Bishop Meinhard of pious memory, after many labors and sorrows, meanwhile took to his bed. Seeing that he was at the point of death, he called together all of the elders of Livonia and Treiden and asked them if after his death they would rather do without a bishop. They jointly declared that they preferred to rejoice in a bishop and father. After a short time the bishop died [in 1196]....

Book III

In the year of the Lord [1199], the venerable Albert, a canon of Bremen, was consecrated bishop.

In the summer following his consecration he went to Gothland and there signed about five hundred men with the cross to go to Livonia.... [He then traveled to Denmark.] Going back to Germany, he signed many in Magdeburg at Christmas. There King Philip [of Swabia, the Holy Roman emperor,] and his wife were crowned. In the presence of the king an opinion was asked for as to whether the goods of the pilgrims [that is, crusaders] to Livonia were to be placed under the protection of the pope, as is the case of those who journey to Jerusalem. It was answered, indeed, that they were included under the protection of the pope, who, in enjoining the Livonian pilgrimage for the plenary remission of sins, made it equal with that of Jerusalem.

Book VI

...Albert, the bishop of Uexküll, in the third year of his consecration moved the convent of regulars and the episcopal see from Uexküll to Riga and dedicated the episcopal cathedral with all of Livonia to Mary, the blessed mother of God. He constructed a monastery for Cistercian monks at the mouth of the

Dvina, which he called Dünamünde Cloister or Mount St. Nicholas. He consecrated his co-worker in the gospel, Brother Theodoric of Treiden, abbot of the monastery.

At the same time Brother Theodoric, foreseeing the treachery of the Livonians and fearing he would be unable to resist the multitude of pagans, and moreover, to multiply the number of the faithful and to preserve the church among the pagans, founded certain Brothers of the Militia of Christ. The lord pope Innocent gave them the rule of the Templars and also an insignia to be worn on their clothing, a sword and a cross. He commanded that they be under the obedience of their bishop.

Questions: How did Meinhard go about converting the Livonians? How did the Livonians respond to his efforts? Did the pope's solution amount to a crusade? Given that forced conversion was forbidden by canon law, how was the treatment of the Livonians justified by church authorities? What role did merchants play in the region? Were they a hindrance or a help to the church? How did Bishop Albert consolidate the church's position in Livonia?

69. THE RULE OF THE TEUTONIC KNIGHTS

The Teutonic Knights were a German military order, similar to the Templars, that emerged at the time of the Third Crusade. Although initially based in the Holy Land, the order ceased to exist there in 1268, when the Mamluk leader Baybars (see doc. 87) captured its main stronghold, the castle of Montfort in western Galilee. Greater and more lasting success came from the order's campaigns in eastern Europe. Hungary, Prussia and Livonia each felt the influence of this powerful order. The regulations below date from 1264.

Source: trans. I. Sterns, "The Statutes of the Teutonic Knights: A Study of Religious Chivalry" (Philadelphia: University of Pennsylvania, unpublished Ph.D. dissertation, 1969), *http://orb.rhodes. edu/encyclop/religion/monastic/tk_rule.html.*

This is how the order of the German House was established.

1. In the name of the Holy Trinity we inform all who now are or who are to come by whom, when and how the order of the Hospital of St. Mary of the German House of Jerusalem was established. In the year 1190 from the birth of our Lord, at the time when Acre was being besieged by the Christians and, with God's help, was won back again from the hands of the infidels, at that very time there was in the army a band of good people from Bremen and from

Lübeck, who, through the charity of our Lord, took pity on the manifold needs of the sick in the army and started the aforementioned hospital under a sail of a ship, called "a cog," under which they brought the sick with great devotion and cared for them with zeal. This small beginning moved the hearts of Duke Frederick of Swabia and other noble lords, whose names are written hereafter: the honorable patriarch of Jerusalem and Henry, king of the same realm, and Duke Henry of Brabant, who was head of the army there, and the master of the Hospital of St. John and the master of the Temple, the archbishop and the great men of the same realm, by whose counsel, the aforementioned duke of Swabia sent his messengers overseas to his brother King Henry, who was the holy emperor, to get the pope, Celestine, to confirm the aforesaid hospital and grant to the sick the rule of the Hospital of St. John and to the knights, the order of the Templars. It thus came about that both these ways of life and their liberties, by the grace of our Lord and by the liberality of the pope, were confirmed and given to the hospital. Yet this way of life itself is granted not just by men on earth, but it is likewise granted by God in heaven.... Thus arose the knightly order of the faithful to fight the infidels.

3. This order, signifying both the heavenly and the earthly knighthood, is the foremost, for it has promised to avenge the dishonoring of God and his cross and to fight so that the Holy Land, which the infidels subjected to their rule, shall belong to the Christians....

This is the rule of the brethren who serve the German House of Saint Mary

To the praise of the almighty Trinity. Here begins the rule of the brethren of the Hospital of Saint Mary of the German House of Jerusalem, and it is divided into three parts. The first part speaks of chastity, of obedience, and of living without property. The second part speaks of the hospitals, how and where they shall be established. The third part speaks of the rules which the brethren are bound to observe....

30. How children shall be received into the order

We will likewise that no child be given the habit or received into this order before he has reached his fourteenth year. But should it happen that fathers or mothers or guardians bring a child to this order before his fourteenth year, or the child come of his own accord, he, if the brethren wish to receive him, shall be well brought up until the prescribed age, and then, if he and the brethren consent, he may be received into the order in the customary manner.

31. How women shall be received into the service of the house

Furthermore we decree that no women shall be admitted in full service and fellowship to this order, for it often happens that manly courage is most harmfully softened by familiarity with women. And yet, since there are some services for the sick in the hospitals and also for the livestock which are better performed by women than by men, therefore, it is permitted to receive women as sister aids for such services. However, they shall be received only with the permission of the provincial commander, and, after they are received, they shall be housed apart from the quarters of the brethren, for the chastity of professed brethren, who dwell with women, although a light is kept on, still is not safe, and also may not last long without scandal.

32. How to receive those who are married as domestics of the house

Since this order may have need of more people, we permit the reception, as domestics [that is, servants], into this order, of lay people, married or single, who submit their bodies and property to the direction of the brethren; furthermore, their life, as is seemly, shall be honest, and they shall not only avoid manifest sin, but also shall not pursue illicit profit and trade. They shall wear garments of a religious hue, but not with the full cross. And if they are married and one dies, half of the estate of the deceased falls to the order, but the other half to the survivor until his death; and after his death the entire estate falls to the use of the order. In addition, whatever they acquire after reception into the order shall all fall to the house. It is also decreed that, at the will and discretion of the provincial commander, some persons may be received on other terms, if he deems it useful.

33. How to receive those who serve for charity or for wages

If anyone wishes to serve the brethren for charity or for wages, since it is difficult to make a special rule how each shall be received, we decree that it be left to the discretion of the official in charge of receiving applicants at the particular time and place; and further that no brother beat any servant, who serves the house for charity or for wages, except the officeholders, who, in order to correct their subordinates, may chastise them from time to time, as is customary. Whenever it happens that a knight or a man worthy of knighthood joins the brethren to serve in arms for charity and then dies, each brother present shall recite thirty paternosters for his soul, and give to the poor for seven days such food as it is customary to give to one brother.

34. Of the master's care for the brethren

In the ark were placed both the rod and the manna, which signify to us that for judges there should be both: the one mildly calling for mercy and the other justly calling for severity. Therefore, the master who is over all the others and shall, himself, give to all the brethren an example of good works, shall both reprove the turbulent and receive the sick, and shall comfort the downhearted and be gentle and patient to all, and shall carry in his hand the rod and the staff, according to the words of the prophet, the rod of watchfulness, with which, keeping nightly watch over his flock, he graciously frees the slothful from the deadly sleep of sloth and of neglect of the sacred observances, diligently and justly, chastises all disobedience; the staff shall be the fatherly care and compassion with which he shall support frailty and strengthen those who are faint of heart and broken by sorrow so that they, uncomforted, are not destroyed by despair....

37. Of the heedful discretion of the master

The master has the power to dispense with all the above regulations laid down in the Rule, except for three — chastity, living without property, and obedience — and, with due regard to the time, the place, the person and the needs of the case, to give dispensations, but yet in such a way that in all instances he act to the honor of God with due regard to piety and practical considerations.

Here ends the Rule.

Questions: What led to the founding of the Teutonic Knights? What was their primary purpose in the Holy Land? What was the role of children, women and lay men within the workings of this order? What were the responsibilities of the master of the order? What ideals govern the specifics of the Rule?

70. NIKOLAUS VON JEROSCHIN ON THE PRUSSIAN CRUSADES

The Teutonic Knights fought their main series of campaigns along the Baltic coast, beginning in the early thirteenth century. Here they struggled mainly against the Prussians (in what is now Poland) and the Livonians. In Livonia they eventually absorbed the Brothers of the Sword. In the 1330s, in an effort to make the history of the Teutonic Knights and their achievements more accessible to the order's members, Nikolaus von Jeroschin, a chaplain of the order, wrote a chronicle that was largely a German translation of an earlier Latin work by another Teutonic Knight. The extracts below focus on the early thirteenth-century prelude to the Prussian and Livonian crusades. The work incorporates a decree by Emperor Frederick II.

Source: trans. H.F. Schwarz, *The Portable Medieval Reader*, ed. J.B. Ross and M.M. McLaughlin (Harmondsworth: Penguin Books, 1977), pp. 421-29.

Concerning Brother Hermann von Salza, fourth master of the German house

This powerful hero received God's blessing in many manifestations of grace. In all his actions he was eloquent, wise, far-seeing, just, honorable, and kind. When he saw the order, as master of which the brothers had elected him, in such a miserable condition, he said with a sigh: "Oh, heavenly God, I would gladly lose an eye if only the order, in my time, would increase enough so that it could equip ten knightly brothers." Thus he prayed fervently. And you, most gentle Christ, who are always willing to fulfill the wishes of the just who beseech you, what did you do? Did you let his prayer go unheard? No, your sweet kindness gave him all he prayed for: while he was master, the order increased in wealth and power so greatly that after his death it numbered two thousand brothers of German origin and of excellent manly strength....

Master Hermann also acquired for his order the most useful and best papal and imperial privileges. Also the order was given many a territory in Apulia, Greece, Cilicia, and Germany, Transylvania, Livonia, and Prussia....

God loved Master Hermann because he obeyed his orders, and he therefore helped him to rise high. All people loved him; pope and emperor, kings, dukes, famous princes, and other courageous lords were drawn to Master Hermann to such an extent that all his wishes were fulfilled to the benefit, honor, and advantage of the order.

How the Prussians devastated the lands of Duke Conrad of Masovia and Kujavia

The Prussians often did much harm to these lands. They burned, destroyed, murdered men and drove women and children into eternal slavery. And if a pregnant woman could not keep up with their army, they killed her, together with the unborn child. They tore children from their mothers' arms and impaled them on fence poles where the little ones died in great misery, kicking and screaming. They devastated the duke's lands to such an extent that, of all the weaker and stronger fortresses of his territory, only Plock on the Vistula was left to him.

The heathen also destroyed about two hundred and fifty parish houses and many beautiful monasteries in which monks, nuns, and the secular clergy had served God. The heathen stormed about everywhere like madmen. They killed the priests before their altars while the body and blood of our Lord Jesus Christ were devoutly being consecrated. The heathen threw God upon the ground to the outrage and infamy of the sacred object, and stamped upon the sacred body of Christ and his blood in their fury. One could further see the unclean heathen stealing in their hate chalices, lamps, and all sorts of sacred vessels. It was pitiful to see how they treated not only the worldly virgins but also those devoted to God. The devilish crowd dragged them out of the cloisters by force and, to their great distress of heart, used them for their disgusting lust.

The Brothers of the Sword

When Duke Conrad saw his land so miserably destroyed, and he was not able to protect it, he conferred with Bishop Christian of Prussia and the great nobles of his court about what would help him and them most. He thus created for the protection of his country the Brotherhood of the Knights of Christ. They wore white tunics with red swords and stars on them. (The duke gave the order the castle of Dobrin on the Vistula.)

How the lands of Prussia and Kulm were given to the brothers of the order of the German house

The fame of the heroic deeds of the Teutonic order spread so far that Conrad of Masovia heard of it. Then the idea came to him—and the spirit of God moved him so that he did not relinquish it again—to invite these brothers for the protection of his country; to ask them whether they could not, with their force, free the Christians from their heathen oppressors since the Brothers of the Sword were unable to do so.

Imperial confirmation of the gift of land of Kulm to the Teutonic order (1226)

In the name of the holy and undivided Trinity, Amen. Frederick II, by the grace of God, emperor of the Romans, Augustus, king of Jerusalem and Sicily. God has raised our emperorship over all kings of the earth, and expanded the sphere of our power over different zones that his name may be magnified in this world and the faith be spread among the heathen peoples. Just as he created the Holy Roman Empire for the preaching of the Gospel, so likewise we must turn our care and attention to the conquest and conversion of the heathen....

For this reason we make known to and inform with this proclamation all living and future members of our empire: Brother Hermann, the worthy master of the Holy German Hospital of St. Mary at Jerusalem and our trustworthy servant, has informed us in all submissiveness that our dear Conrad, duke of Masovia and Kujavia, intends to make provision for him and his brothers in the land of Kulm and the land between his march and the territories of the Prussians. Therefore the brothers shall take upon themselves the trouble and, on a suitable occasion, to the honor and glory of the true God, enter into the Prussian land and occupy it. Hermann postponed the acceptance of this offer and approached our majesty first with his submissive application; if we should deign to agree, he would begin the great task, trusting in our authorization. Our majesty should then confirm to him and his house all the land which the duke gave him, as well as all the land they would gain in Prussia through their efforts; also we should grant his house through a charter all rights and liberties for this area. Then he would accept the gift of said duke and use the goods and men of his house for the invasion and conquest of the county in tireless, unremitting effort.

Considering the attitude of active Christianity of this master, and how he eagerly desires to acquire these lands for his house in the name of God, and since this land belongs to our empire; trusting also in the wisdom of this master, a man mighty in word and deed, who will take up the matter forcefully with his brothers and carry through the conquest manfully, not abandoning it as many did before him, who wasted so much energy in this undertaking for nothing, we give this master the authority to invade the land of Prussia with the forces of his house, and with all means at his disposal.

We also permit and confirm to this master, his successors and his house for all time that they shall hold the said land which they will get from Duke Conrad according to his promise, any other lands which he may give them in the future, finally, all they conquer in Prussia with the grace of God, with rights to the mountains, the flat country, rivers, forests, and lakes as if it were an ancient imperial right, freely and unencumbered by any services or taxes, without any ordinary burdens, and no one shall have to give account for this, their land. They also shall be allowed in the land they conquer now or in the future, for the benefit of their house to erect road and other toll stations, hold fairs and markets, coin money, collect taxes and other tributes, set up traffic laws for their rivers and the sea as it seems good to them; they also shall always have the right of mining gold, silver, and other metals, and salt if such are at present found in their territories, or should be found there in the future. We also give them the right to set up judges and administrators, thus to govern and lead justly the people subject to them, both those who have been converted to the true faith as well as those who live in their delusion; to punish crimes of evildoers wisely, to examine civil and criminal matters and to make decisions according to the dictates of reason. To this we add, out of our especial grace, that this master and his successors shall have and exercise sovereign rights in all their lands in the same manner as they are enjoyed by princes of the empire exercising the fullest rights in their lands, so that they may introduce good customs and promulgate regulations through which the faith of the Christians may be strengthened and their subjects enjoy peace and quiet.

Through this charter we prohibit any prince, duke, margrave, count, court official, magistrate, bailiff, every person of high or low estate, whether temporal or spiritual, to infringe on these privileges and authorizations. Should anyone dare to do so, let him know that he will have to pay a fine of one thousand pounds of gold, one half to our treasury, the other to the ones that were injured....

Of the images, disbeliefs, and customs of the Prussians

[The Prussians knew neither writing nor books,] and they were very much surprised at first when they saw the letters of the knights. And thus God was unknown to them; and thence came their error that they, in their foolishness, worshipped any creature as a god: thunder, sun, moon, stars, birds, animals, and even toads. They also had fields, woods, and waters which were holy to them, so that they neither plowed nor fished nor cut wood in them....

The Prussians also believed in a resurrection, but not correctly. They believed that as he is on earth, noble or common, poor or rich, powerful or not, just so would he be after the resurrection. Therefore it was customary after the death of a noble to burn with him his weapons and horse, servants and maids, beautiful clothes, hunting dogs, falcons, and whatever else belongs to the equipment of a noble. Also with the common people everything they owned was burned, because they believed it all would rise with them and continue to serve them.

Also there was a devilish fraud connected with such a death, for the relatives of the dead came to the priest and asked if he had seen somebody go or drive by his house at such and such a time of the day or night. The priest then generally described to them exactly the figure of the dead man, his gestures, his weapons and dress, servants and horses. And to make them believe him more readily, he often showed them some mark which the dead man cut or scratched into his door while driving by.

After a victory, the heathen, for their salvation, usually sacrificed to their idols one-third of their booty which they gave to the priest, who burned it for the gods. [They also sacrificed horses and cast lots.]...

Wealth and good-looking clothes they value very slightly; as they take off their furs today, they put them on tomorrow. They are ignorant of soft beds and fine food. They drink, since ancient times, only three things: water, mead, and mares' milk....

[Their greatest virtue is hospitality.] They freely and willingly share food and drink. They think they have not treated their guests politely and well if they are not so full of drink that they vomit. Usually they urge each other mutually to take an innumerable number of drinks of equal measure. When they sit down to drink, every member of the household brings a measure to his host, drinks to him out of it, and the host then gladly finishes the drink. Thus they drink to each other, and let the cup go round without rest, and it runs to and fro, now full, now empty. They do this until man and woman, host and friends, big and small, all are drunk; that is pastime to them and a great honor—to me that does not seem honorable at all.

According to an old custom, they buy their women with money. The husband keeps his wife like a maid; she is not allowed to eat at his table, and daily has to wash the feet of the members of the household and the guests.

Nobody has to beg, because the poor man can go from house to house and eat wherever he likes.

If there is a murder, there is no reconciliation until the friends of the dead have killed the guilty person or one of his close relatives.

If a Prussian is met suddenly by a great calamity, he usually kills himself in his distress....

Some Prussians, in honor of their gods, bathe daily; others never. Man and woman spin thread; some wool, the others linen, whichever they think the gods like most. Some never mount a black horse; some never a white one, or one of some other color.

Questions: According to Nikolaus, what made for a successful military order? What did Frederick II have to gain from lending his support to the Tuetonic Knights and Duke Conrad? What role did he see the order playing in Prussian territory? Compare Niko-

laus's description of pagan Prussian society with Henry of Livonia's description of the pagan Livonians. What does each writer find most reprehensible in pagan society? What, if anything, do they admire or accept?

71. PHILIP OF NOVARA ON FREDERICK II'S CRUSADE

Frederick II (1197-1250), king of Sicily and Holy Roman emperor, grew up in the sophisticated and cosmopolitan Sicilian royal court. He was familiar with Sicilian Muslims, practiced rudimentary experimental science, and held many views that were unconventional by European standards. He took a crusading vow in 1215 but put off his departure for a decade, despite continued papal pressure. In 1225 he married Isabella (or Yolanda) of Brienne, heiress to the throne of Jerusalem, thus establishing a personal claim to the crusader kingdom. The following year he began negotiating with the Egyptian sultan al-Kamel, and in 1227 he sent his troops ahead to the Holy Land. Meanwhile, conflict with Pope Gregory IX led to Frederick's excommunication just before his own departure on crusade. The following account of Frederick's expedition is by Philip of Novara, a supporter of John of Ibelin, the "lord of Beirut" and a member of an active family of Europeans in the Middle East. Hence it focuses on the internal politics of the island of Cyprus, which at this time had a child king, Henry, a great-nephew of John of Ibelin.

Source: trans. J. Brundage, *The Crusades: A Documentary History* (Milwaukee: Marquette University Press, 1962), pp. 231-32.

In the year [1228] the emperor came to Syria with his whole navy. The [infant] king [of Jerusalem] and all the Cypriots, together with [John d'Ibelin,] the lord of Beirut, accompanied him. The lord of Beirut went to Beirut, where he was joyfully received, for never was a lord more warmly loved by his men. He remained there but one day and then followed the emperor to Tyre. The emperor was very well received in Syria where all did homage to him as regent, because he had a little son called King Conrad, who was the rightful heir of the kingdom of Jerusalem through his mother who was dead. The emperor and his men and all the Syrians left Acre to go to Jaffa. There they held truce conferences with al-Kamel, who was then sultan of [Egypt] and who held Jerusalem and the whole country. As a result of their agreement Jerusalem, Nazareth, and Lydda were thereby turned over to the emperor.

In [1229], amidst these events, the emperor ordered Count Stephen of Gotron and other Longobards [that is, southern Italians] as well, to come to Cyprus. He had all the fortresses and the royal revenues seized for his use. He claimed that he was regent and that this was his right. The Cypriots were much perplexed and had their wives and children placed in religious houses wherever they could. Some of them ... fled in the midst of the winter. It was a bad season and they barely escaped drowning, but, as it so pleased God, they finally arrived at Tortosa. The emperor held Cyprus. The Cypriots who were in his army were very uncomfortable and, had the lord of Beirut sanctioned it, they would have carried off and kidnapped the young King Henry and would have fled from the emperor's camp.

The emperor was now disliked by all the people of Acre. He was the object of the Templars' special disfavor.... The people of the lowlands also had little use for the emperor. The emperor seemed to be delaying. Every day, even in winter, he kept his galleys armed, with the oars in the locks. Many people said that he wished to seize the lord of Beirut and his children, ... and his other friends, the master of the Temple and other persons and have them shipped to Apulia. Another said that he wished to have them killed at a council to which he had called and summoned them but that they had been aware of this and went to the council with such forces that he dared not do it.

He made his truce with the Saracens in all particulars as they wished it. He went to Jerusalem [where he was crowned king] and then to Acre. The lord of Beirut never left him and, though he was often advised to leave, he did not wish to do so. The emperor assembled his people at Acre and had all the people of the city come and there were many who thought well of him....

The emperor secretly prepared to depart. At daybreak on the first of May, he boarded a galley before the Butchers' Street, without notifying anyone. Thus it happened that the butchers and the old people who lived on the street and who were very unfriendly saw his party and pelted him most abusively with tripe and scraps of meat....

Thus the emperor left Acre, cursed, hated, and despised.

Questions: What is this author's view of Frederick? Why? What does this text reveal about crusader and settler politics in the Middle East? What seem to be the sources of conflict between Frederick and the Franks of the Middle East? What were Frederick's concerns and motivations? How well did he accomplish his goals?

72. FREDERICK II ON HIS TAKING OF JERUSALEM

Frederick had won Jerusalem not by force of arms but by negotiations with the Egyptian sultan al-Kamel, who had granted him Jerusalem (except for the Dome of the Rock and some other mosques, which remained in Muslim hands), some other territories in the Holy Land, and a ten-year truce. Although Frederick's triumphal entry into Jerusalem is barely mentioned in Philip of Novara's history (above), it was in fact a major event and the climax of his controversial crusade. Here Frederick gives his own account.

Source: trans. J.A. Giles, *Roger of Wendover's Flowers of History* (London: Henry G. Bohn, 1849), pp. 522-24; revised.

Frederick, by the grace of God, the august emperor of the Romans, king of Jerusalem and Sicily, to his well-beloved friend Henry [III], king of the English, health and sincere affection.

Let all rejoice and exult in the Lord, and let those who are correct in heart glorify him, who, to make known his power, does not make boast of horses and chariots, but has now gained glory for himself in the scarcity of his soldiers, that all may know and understand that he is glorious in his majesty, terrible in his magnificences, and wonderful in his plans on the sons of men, changing seasons at will, and bringing the hearts of different nations together; for in these few days, by a miracle rather than by strength, that business has been brought to a conclusion, which for a length of time past many chiefs and rulers of the world amongst the multitude of nations, have never been able till now to accomplish by force, however great, nor by fear.

Not, therefore, to keep you in suspense by a long account, we wish to inform your holiness, that we, firmly putting our trust in God, and believing that Jesus Christ, his Son, in whose service we have so devotedly exposed our bodies and lives, would not abandon us in these unknown and distant countries, but would at least give us wholesome advice and assistance for his honor, praise, and glory, boldly in the name set forth from Acre on the fifteenth day of November last past and arrived safely at Jaffa, intending to rebuild the castle at that place with proper strength, that afterwards the approach to the holy city of Jerusalem might be not only easier, but also shorter and more safe for us as well as for all Christians. When, therefore, we were, in the confidence of our trust in God, engaged at Jaffa, and superintending the building of the castle and the cause of Christ, as necessity required and as was our duty, and whilst all our pilgrims were busily engaged in these matters, several messengers often passed to and fro between us and the sultan of Babylon [that is, Egypt]; for he and another sultan, called Xaphat, his brother, were with a large army at the city of Gaza, distant about one day's journey from us; in another direction, in the city

Fig. 24: Frankish merchants on the wharf in a crusader state seaport, in a fifteenth-century miniature copied by a nineteenth-century engraver. From P. Lacroix, *Manners, Customs, and Dress during the Middle Ages* (London: Chapman and Hall, 1874).

of Sichen, which is commonly called Neapolis, and situated in the plains, the sultan of Damascus, his nephew, was staying with an immense number of knights and soldiers also about a day's journey from us and the Christians.

And whilst the treaty was in progress between the parties on either side of the restoration of the Holy Land, at length Jesus Christ, the Son of God, beholding from on high our devoted endurance and patient devotion to his cause, in his merciful compassion of us at length brought it about that the sultan of Babylon restored to us the holy city, the place where the feet of Christ trod, and where the true worshippers adore the Father in spirit and in truth. But that we may inform you of the particulars of this surrender each as they happened, be it known to you that not only is the body of the aforesaid city restored to us, but also the whole of the country extending from thence to the seacoast near the castle of Jaffa, so that for the future pilgrims will have free passage and a safe return to and from the sepulcher; provided, however, that the Saracens of that part of the country, since they hold the Temple in great veneration, may come there as often as they choose in the character of pilgrims, to worship according to their custom, and that we shall henceforth permit them to come, however, only as many as we may choose to allow, and without arms, nor are they to dwell in the city, but outside, and as soon as they have paid their devotions they are to depart.

Moreover, the city of Bethlehem is restored to us, and all the country between Jerusalem and that city; as also the city of Nazareth, and all the country between Acre and that city; the whole of the district of Turon, which is very extensive, and very advantageous to the Christians; the city of Sidon, too, is given up to us with the whole plain and its appurtenances, which will be the more acceptable to the Christians the more advantageous it has till now appeared to be to the Saracens, especially as there is a good harbor there, and from there great quantities of arms and necessaries might be carried to the city of Damascus, and often from Damascus to Babylon. And although, according to our treaty we are allowed to rebuild the city of Jerusalem in as good a state as it has ever been, and also the castles of Jaffa, Cesarea, Sidon, and that of St. Mary of the Teutonic order, which the brothers of that order have begun to build in the mountainous district of Acre, and which it has never been allowed the Christians to do during any former truce; nevertheless the sultan is not allowed, till the end of the truce between him and us, which is agreed on for ten years, to repair or rebuild any fortresses or castles.

And so on Sunday, February 18, ... this treaty of peace was confirmed by oath between us. Truly then on us and on all does that day seem to have shone favorably, in which the angels sing in praise of God, "Glory to God on high, and on earth peace, and good-will toward men." And in acknowledgment of such great kindness and of such an honor, which, beyond our deserts and contrary to the opinion of many, God has mercifully conferred on us, to the lasting renown of his compassion, and that in his holy place we might personally offer to him the burnt offering of our lips, be it known to you that on March 17 ..., we, in company with all the pilgrims who had with us faithfully followed Christ, the Son of God, entered the holy city of Jerusalem, and after worshipping at the Holy Sepulcher, we, as being a Catholic emperor, on the following day, wore the crown, which almighty God provided for us from the throne of his majesty, when of his especial grace, he exalted us on high amongst the princes of the world; so that whilst we have supported the honor of this high dignity, which belongs to us by right of sovereignty, it is more and more evident to all that the hand of the Lord has done all this; and since his mercies are over all his works, let the worshippers of the orthodox faith henceforth know and relate it far and wide throughout the world, that he, who is blessed for ever, has visited and redeemed his people, and has raised up the horn of salvation for us in the house of his servant David.

And before we leave the city of Jerusalem, we have determined magnificently to rebuild it, and its towers and walls, and we intend so to arrange matters that, during our absence, there shall be no less care and diligence used in the business than if we were present in person. In order that this our present letter may be full of exultation throughout, and so a happy end correspond with its happy beginning, and rejoice your royal mind, we wish it to be known to you, our ally, that the said sultan is bound to restore to us all those captives whom he did not in accordance with the treaty made between him and the Christians deliver up at the time when he lost Damietta some time since, and also the others who have been since taken.

Given at the holy city of Jerusalem, on March 17, in the year of our Lord 1229.

Questions: What were the conditions of the treaty between Frederick and al-Kamel? What did Frederick gain for Christians in Jerusalem and the surrendered territory? How did Muslims fare under the treaty?

73. RESPONSES TO FREDERICK II'S CRUSADE

Although his repossession of Jerusalem was initially met with praise, Frederick's conces-
sions to the Muslims were soon made known, and joy quickly turned to anger. Below is
a hostile reaction to Frederick's crusade, written just after the event by the patriarch of
Jerusalem. While Frederick sought to consolidate Jerusalem, Pope Gregory IX embarked
upon a campaign to undermine the emperor's European holdings. Frederick was forced to
return to Europe, leaving Jerusalem undefended and in the hands of bickering Christian
factions. In 1240, Gregory again excommunicated Frederick as the emperor was advanc-
ing with an army on the city of Rome. Although Gregory died in 1241, papal hostilities
against Frederick were continued by his successor, Innocent IV, and in 1248, Innocent
called a crusade (which did not materialize) against the emperor. Frederick died in 1250.

Source: trans. D.C. Munro, *Translations and Reprints from the Original Sources of European History*,
Series 1, Vol. I (Philadelphia: University of Pennsylvania Department of History, 1902), no. 2, pp.
18-19; no. 4, pp. 27-31.

Letter of Patriarch Gerold

Gerold, patriarch of Jerusalem, to all the faithful—greeting.

If it should be fully known how astonishing, nay rather, deplorable, the conduct of the emperor [Frederick] has been in the eastern lands from beginning
to end, to the great detriment of the cause of Jesus Christ and to the great
injury of the Christian faith, from the sole of his foot to the top of his head no
common sense would be found in him. For he came, excommunicated, without money and followed by scarcely forty knights, and hoped to maintain
himself by spoiling the inhabitants of Syria. He first came to Cyprus and there
most discourteously seized that nobleman John of Ibelin and his sons, whom
he had invited to his table under pretext of speaking of the affairs of the Holy
Land. Next the king, whom he had invited to meet him, he retained almost as
a captive. He thus by violence and fraud got possession of the kingdom.

After these achievements he passed over into Syria. Although in the beginning he promised to do marvels, and although in the presence of the foolish he
boasted loudly, he immediately sent to the sultan of Babylon to demand peace.
This conduct rendered him despicable in the eyes of the sultan and his subjects, especially after they had discovered that he was not at the head of a
numerous army, which might have to some extent added weight to his words.
Under the pretext of defending Jaffa, he marched with the Christian army
towards that city, in order to be nearer the sultan and in order to be able more
easily to treat of peace or obtain a truce. What more shall I say? After long and

mysterious conferences, and without having consulted anyone who lived in the country, he suddenly announced one day that he had made peace with the sultan. No one saw the text of the peace or truce when the emperor took the oath to observe the articles which were agreed upon. Moreover, you will be able to see clearly how great the malice was and how fraudulent the tenor of certain articles of the truce which we have decided to send to you. The emperor, for giving credit to his word, wished as a guarantee only the word of the sultan which he obtained. For he said, among other things, that the holy city was surrendered to him.

He went thither with the Christian army on the eve of the Sunday when "Oculi mei" is sung [that is, the third Sunday in Lent]. The Sunday following, without any fitting ceremony and although excommunicated, in the chapel of the Sepulcher of our Lord, to the manifest prejudice of his honor and of the imperial dignity, he put the diadem upon his forehead, although the Saracens still held the Temple of the Lord and Solomon's Temple, and although they proclaimed publicly, as before, the law of Mohammed—to the great confusion and chagrin of the pilgrims.

This same prince, who had previously very often promised to fortify Jerusalem, departed in secrecy from the city at dawn on the following Monday. The Hospitallers and the Templars promised solemnly and earnestly to aid him with all their forces and their advice, if he wanted to fortify the city, as he had promised. But the emperor, who did not care to set affairs right, and who saw that there was no certainty in what had been done, and that the city in the state in which it had been surrendered to him could be neither defended nor fortified, was content with the name of surrender, and on the same day hastened with his family to Jaffa. The pilgrims who had entered Jerusalem with the emperor, witnessing his departure, were unwilling to remain behind.

The following Sunday when "Laetare Jerusalem" is sung [that is, the fourth Sunday in Lent], he arrived at Acre. There in order to seduce the people and to obtain their favor, he granted them a certain privilege. God knows the motive which made him act thus, and his subsequent conduct will make it known. As, moreover, the passage was near, and as all pilgrims, humble and great, after having visited the Holy Sepulcher, were preparing to withdraw, as if they had accomplished their pilgrimage, because no truce had been concluded with the sultan of Damascus, we, seeing that the holy land was already deserted and abandoned by the pilgrims, in our council formed the plan of retaining soldiers, for the common good, by means of the alms given by the king of France of holy memory.

When the emperor heard of this, he said to us that he was astonished at this, since he had concluded a truce with the sultan of Babylon. We replied to him that the knife was still in the wound, since there was not a truce or peace with the sultan of Damascus, nephew of the aforesaid sultan and opposed to him, adding that even if the sultan of Babylon was unwilling, the former could still do us much harm. The emperor replied, saying that no soldiers ought to be retained in his kingdom without his advice and consent, as he was now king of Jerusalem. We answered to that, that in the matter in question, as well as in all of a similar nature, we were very sorry not to be able, without endangering the salvation of our souls, to obey his wishes, because he was excommunicated. The emperor made no response to us, but on the following day he caused the pilgrims who inhabited the city to be assembled outside by the public crier, and by special messengers he also convoked the prelates and the monks.

Addressing them in person, he began to complain bitterly of us, by heaping up false accusations. Then turning his remarks to the venerable master of the Templars he publicly attempted to severely tarnish the reputation of the latter, by various vain speeches, seeking thus to throw upon others the responsibility for his own faults which were now manifest, and adding at last that we were maintaining troops with the purpose of injuring him. After that he ordered all foreign soldiers, of all nations, if they valued their lives and property, not to remain in the land from that day on, and ordered Count Thomas, whom he intended to leave as bailiff of the country, to punish with stripes [that is, with whipping] anyone who was found lingering, in order that the punishment of one might serve as an example to many. After doing all this he withdrew, and would listen to no excuse or answers to the charges which he had so shamefully made. He determined immediately to post some crossbowmen at the gates of the city, ordering them to allow the Templars to go out but not to return. Next he fortified with crossbows the churches and other elevated positions, and especially those which commanded the communications between the Templars and ourselves. And you may be sure that he never showed as much animosity and hatred against Saracens.

For our part, seeing his manifest wickedness, we assembled all the prelates and all the pilgrims, and menaced with excommunication all those who should aid the emperor with their advice or their services against the church, the Templars, the other monks of the holy land, or the pilgrims.

The emperor was more and more irritated, and immediately caused all the passages to be guarded more strictly, refused to allow any kind of provisions to be brought to us or to the members of our party, and placed everywhere crossbowmen and archers, who severely attacked us, the Templars and the pilgrims. Finally to fill the measure of his malice, he caused some Dominicans and Minorites who had come on Palm Sunday to the proper places to announce the word of God, to be torn from the pulpit, to be thrown down and dragged along the ground and whipped throughout the city, as if they had been robbers. Then seeing that he did not obtain what he had hoped from the above-mentioned siege, he treated of peace. We replied to him that we would not hear of peace until he sent away the crossbowmen and other troops, until he had returned our property to us, until finally he had restored all things to the condition and freedom in which they were on that day when he entered Jerusalem. He finally ordered what we wanted to be done, but it was not executed. Therefore we placed the city under interdict.

The emperor, realizing that his wickedness could have no success, was unwilling to remain any longer in the country. And, as if he would have liked to ruin everything, he ordered the crossbows and engines of war, which for a long time had been kept at Acre for the defense of the Holy Land, to be secretly carried onto his vessels. He also sent away several of them to the sultan of Babylon, as his dear friend. He sent a troop of soldiers to Cyprus to levy heavy contributions of money there, and, what appeared to us more astonishing, he destroyed the galleys which he was not able to take with him. Having learned this, we resolved to reproach him with it, but shunning the remonstrance and the correction, he entered a galley secretly, by an obscure way, on the day of the apostles St. Philip and St. James, and hastened to reach the island of Cyprus, without saying adieu to anyone, leaving Jaffa destitute; and may he never return! Very soon the bailiffs of the above-mentioned sultan shut off all departure from Jerusalem for the Christian poor and the Syrians, and many pilgrims died thus on the road. This is what the emperor did, to the detriment of the Holy Land and of his own soul, as well as many other things which are known and which we leave to others to relate. May the merciful God deign to soften the results! Farewell.

Innocent IV's Call for a Crusade, 1248

Wherefore we advise that publicly in Rome, Campania, and Maratima, you preach a crusade against the aforesaid Frederick; and that you also cause suitable men to preach the crusade frequently and solemnly. And by our authority grant the remission of sins—which was granted in the general council to those who went to the succor of the Holy Land—to all those who with fervent zeal choose to undertake a crusade against the same Frederick, in order to aid the church in rooting out, from the aforesaid kingdom, the perfidy which flows from its diseased head to the adjacent members, and in restoring there the faith formerly cherished. And also publish solemnly, and cause others to publish, that the same Frederick and all who aid him by counsel, succor, or favor, in person or property, openly or secretly, are excommunicated by us; and also that the whole kingdom of Sicily is placed under an ecclesiastical interdict, as long as it shall adhere to him.

Questions: Compare Frederick's version of his taking of Jerusalem with Gerold's. According to Gerold, how did Frederick fail in his crusade? How did Frederick work to maintain his hold over the city and its territories? What did Gregory hope to achieve by excommunicating Frederick? How does Innocent justify a crusade against the emperor?

CHAPTER EIGHT:

CONFLICT AND COEXISTENCE IN SPAIN

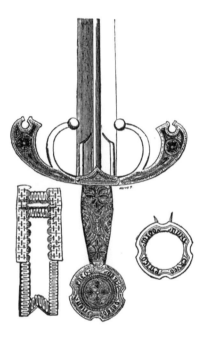

Fig. 25: The ceremonial sword of Queen Isabella, fifteenth century. From P. Lacroix, *Military and Religious Life in the Middle Ages* (London, Chapman and Hall, 1874).

74. CHRONICLE OF THE CID

From the time of the Muslim conquest in the early eighth century, the Iberian peninsula was both a land of great ethnic diversity and a site of Christian-Muslim warfare (see doc. 7). In 1002, the caliphate of Cordova (the Muslim state) broke up, creating an opportunity for the remaining small Christian kingdoms (the most important of which were Navarre, Aragon, and Castile) to begin to expand at Muslim expense. By 1064, French knights were traveling to Spain to help in the effort, and by the 1170s such participants had been offered a papal indulgence. One of the major figures of the early Spanish "Reconquista" (Reconquest) was Rodrigo de Bivar (d. 1199), better known as the Cid (that is, "lord" or "master"). Although he was portrayed as an exemplary Christian holy warrior in later legend, his efforts were mainly directed toward protecting and extending his own power, and at times he fought alongside Muslims. The following composite text incorporates medieval accounts of the Cid by both Christian and Muslim writers. The final episode printed here, concerning Valencia, is from a Muslim source.

Source: trans. R. Southey, *Chronicle of the Cid* (London: George Routledge and Sons, 1885), pp. 9-12, 17-18, 175-80; revised.

And the Moors entered Castile, in great power, for there came with them five kings, and they ... plundered Carrion, and Vilforado, ... and Logroño, and Najara, and all that land; and they carried away many captives both male and female, and brood mares, and flocks of all kinds. But as they were returning with all speed, Rodrigo of Bivar raised the country, and came up with them in the mountains of Oca, and fell upon them and defeated them, and won back all their booty, and took all the five kings prisoners. Then he went back to his mother, taking the kings with him, and there he divided the whole spoil with his gentlemen and other companions, both the Moorish captives and all the spoil of whatever kind, so that they departed joyfully, being very pleased with what he had done. And he gave thanks to God for the grace which had been vouchsafed to him, and said to his mother that he did not think it good to keep the kings in captivity, but to let them go freely; and he set them at liberty and bade them depart. So they returned each to his own country, blessing him for their deliverance, and magnifying his great bounty; and forthwith they sent him tribute and acknowledged themselves to be his vassals....

But when the [Christian] counts of Castile saw how Rodrigo increased day by day in honor, they took counsel together that they should plot with the Moors, and fix a day of battle with them..., and that they should invite Rodrigo to this battle, and contrive with the Moors that they should slay him; by which means they should be revenged upon him, and remain masters of Castile, which now because of him they could not be. This counsel they sent to communicate to the Moors and to the Moorish kings who were Rodrigo's vassals, being those whom he had made prisoners and set at liberty. But [the Moorish kings], when they saw this counsel and the falsehood which was devised, took the letters of the counts, and sent them to Rodrigo their lord, and sent to tell him all the secret of the treason. And Rodrigo thanked them greatly for their good faith, and took the letters and carried them to the king, and showed him all the enmity of the counts, and especially of the count Don Garcia, who was afterwards called of Cabra. When the king saw this as it was, he was astonished at their great falsehood, and he issued his letters in which he ordered them to leave his dominions; then he went to Santiago on a pilgrimage, and ordered Rodrigo to cast these counts out of the land; and Rodrigo did as the king commanded him. Then Doña Elvira his kinswoman, the wife of the count Don Garcia, came and fell upon her knees before him; but Rodrigo took her by the hand and raised her up, and would not hear her till she was arisen. And when he raised her up she said, "I beseech you, cousin, since you have banished me and my husband, that you would give us a letter to some king who is one of your vassals, enjoining him to befriend us, and give us something for your sake whereon we may live." So he gave her a letter to the king of Cordova, who received her and her husband well for the love of Rodrigo, and gave Cabra to him, that he and his people might dwell therein. This count was afterwards so ungrateful to the king of Cordova that he made war upon him from Cabra which the king had given him, till Rodrigo came and took it....

On the ... day after the Christians had taken possession of the town [of Valencia], the Cid entered it with a great company, and he ascended the highest tower of the wall, and beheld all the city; and the Moors came unto him, and kissed his hand, saying he was welcome. And the Cid did great honor unto them. And then he gave orders that all the windows of the towers which looked in upon the town should be closed up, that the Christians might not see what the Moors did in their houses; and the Moors thanked him for this greatly. And he commanded and requested the Christians that they should show great honor to the Moors, and respect them, and greet them when they met: and the Moors thanked the Cid greatly for the honor which the Christians did them, saying that they had never seen so good a man, nor one so honorable, nor one who had his people under such obedience.

... And the Cid ... made them take their seats before him with full honor, and began to speak unto them, saying, "I am a man who has never possessed a kingdom, neither I nor any man of my lineage. But the day when I first beheld this city I was pleased with it, and coveted it that I might be its lord; and I besought the lord our God that he would give it to me. See now what his power is, for the day when I sat down before Juballa I had no more than four loaves of bread, and now by God's mercy I have won Valencia. And if I administer right and justice here God will let me enjoy it, but if I do evil, and demean myself proudly and wrongfully, I know that he will take it away. Now then let everyone go to his own lands, and possess them even as he was accustomed to have and to hold them [before the siege and fall of the city]. He who shall find his field, or his vineyard, or his garden, deserted, let him immediately enter into it; and he who shall find his land being farmed, let him pay the one who has cultivated it the cost of his labor, and of the seed which he has sown therein, and remain on his inherited lands, according to the law of the Moors.... And I have resolved in my heart to hear your complaints two days in the week, on Mondays and Thursdays; but if causes should arise which require haste, come to me when you will and I will give judgment, for I do not retire with women to sing and to drink, as your [previous] lords have done, so that you could obtain no justice, but will myself see to these things, and I will watch over you as friend over his friend, and kinsman over his kinsman...." When he had said these things they all replied that they prayed to God to preserve him through long and happy years, ... and he bade them go their way.

Well pleased were the Moors when they departed from him, and they marveled at the greatness of his promises, and they set their hearts at rest, and put away the fear which they had had, thinking all their troubles were over; for in all the promises which the Cid had made unto them, they believed that he spoke the truth; but he said these things only to quiet them, and to make them come to what he wished, even as came to pass. And when he had finished [speaking], he sent his [official], Abdalla Adiz, to the custom house, and made him appoint men to collect the rents of the town for him, which was done accordingly. And ... the Moors wished to enter again into possession of their inherited lands as he had told them; but they found it otherwise, for of all the fields which the Christians had farmed, they would not yield up one.... So the Moors, seeing this, waited till Thursday, when the Cid was to hear complaints, as he had said unto them. When Thursday came all the honorable men went to the garden, but the Cid sent to say unto them that he could not come out that day, because of other causes which he had to determine; and he desired that they would go their way for that time, and come again on the Monday: this was to show mastery. And when it was Monday they assembled again in the garden, and the Cid came out to them, ... and the Moors made their complaint. And when he had heard them, he began to make similitudes, and offer reasons which were not like those which he had spoken the first day, for he said to them, "I ask you, whether it is well that I should be left without men? ... The first thing which I have to look to is the well-being of my people, that they may live in wealth and honor, so that they may be able to serve me, and defend my honor: for since it has pleased God to give me the city of Valencia,

I do not wish that there be any other lord here than me. Therefore I say unto you and command, if you would be well with me, and wish that I should show favor unto you, that you see how to deliver that traitor Abeniaf [that is, the previous ruler of Valencia] into my hands. You all know the great treason which he committed upon King Yahia, his lord and yours, how he slew him, and the misery which he brought upon you in the siege; and since it is not fitting that a traitor who has slain his lord should live among you, and that his treason should be confounded with your loyalty, see to the obeying of my command."

When the honorable Moors heard this they were dismayed; verily they knew that he spoke truth touching the death of the king, but it troubled them that he departed from the promise which he had made; and they answered that they would take counsel concerning what he had said, and then reply. Then five of the best and most honorable among them withdrew, and went to Abdalla Adiz, and said unto him, "Advise us now the best and truest that you can, for you are of our religion.... The Cid promised us many things, and now behold he says nothing to us of what he said before, but puts forward other new reasons, at which great dismay has seized us. And because you know his ways better, tell us now what his pleasure is, for although we might wish to do otherwise, this is not a time when anything but what he shall command can be done."

When [Abdalla Adiz] heard this he answered, "Good men, it is easy to understand what he wants, and to do what should be done. We all know the great treason which Abeniaf committed against you all in killing your lord the king.... And since God has brought [Abeniaf] to this state, see now by all means how you may deliver him into the hands of the Cid. And fear not, neither take thought for the rest; for though the Cid may do his pleasure in some things, it is better to have him for a lord than this traitor who brought so much evil upon you. Moreover the things of this world soon pass away, and my heart tells me that before long we shall come out of the bondage of the Cid, and of the Christians, for the Cid is nearly at the end of his life, and we who remain alive after his death shall then be masters of our city." When the good men heard what he said, they thanked him much, and held themselves to be well advised, and said that they would do willingly what he bade them; and they returned forthwith to the Cid, and said unto him that they would fulfill his commandment.

Questions: How are the ideals of honor and chivalry in Spanish society apparent in this text? What relationship exists between the Christians and the Moors? What role does religious motivation play in the wars described here? How does the author's view of the Cid change in the account of the Cid in Valencia, which is based on Moorish sources?

75. ACCOUNTS OF ARAB LEARNING

From the time of their initial conquests in the Middle East, Muslims respected and contributed greatly to the traditions of learning and scholarship that they encountered. Much ancient learning was preserved in Muslim lands while it was lost in early medieval Europe. One of the milestones in European intellectual history was the capture of the Muslim city of Toledo by the Christian army of Castile in 1085; Toledo became one of the magnets drawing European Christian scholars to southern Europe. In the twelfth century, European Christian scholars traveled to Sicily, with its lively Muslim presence, as well as to Spain, where Christians were gaining territory from the Moors, to study ancient books as well as those written by Muslim scholars. The following extracts from Muslim histories describe the libraries and learning of al-Hakem, a tenth-century Moorish ruler of Cordova.

Source: trans. P. de Gayangos, *The History of the Mohammedan Dynasties in Spain* (London: The Oriental Translation Fund, 1843), vol. II, pp. 169-70; revised.

Anonymous historian:

Al-Hakem was the most virtuous and liberal of men; and he treated all those who came to his court with the utmost kindness. He amassed such a collection of books that it is impossible to estimate even approximately either their value or their number, some writers stating that they amounted to 400,000 volumes; and that when they were removed [from the palace] six months were expended in the operation. Al-Hakem was a man of irreproachable conduct; he was learned, and had a quick understanding: his tutors in the various sciences were Kasim Ibn Asbagh, Ahmed Ibn Dahim, Mohammed Ibn 'Abdi-s-sellan Al-khoshani, Zakkariyya Ibn Khattab, and Thabit Ibn Kasim. He caused works on all subjects to be conveyed to Cordova from every country, however remote, lavishing his treasures in the acquisition of them, until the number of books thus collected was such that they could no longer be contained in his libraries. He was, moreover, so fond of reading that he preferred the pleasure of perusing his books to all the enjoyments which royalty can afford; by which means he considerably increased his learning, doubled his information, and improved his taste. In the knowledge of history, biography, and genealogy, he was surpassed by no living author of his days. He wrote a voluminous history of Andalus [that is, Spain], filled with precious information; and so sound was the criticism which he displayed in it, that whatever he related [as borrowed from more ancient sources] might be confidently believed to be a fact.

Ibnu-l-abbar:

Abu Mohammed Ibn Hazm says: "I was told by Talid, the eunuch, who was the keeper of the library and repository of the sciences in the palace of [al-Hakem], that the catalogue only of the books consisted of forty-four volumes, each volume having twenty sheets of paper, which contained nothing else but the titles and descriptions of the books."...

To give an idea of al-Hakem's immense erudition, it will only be necessary to record here a well-ascertained fact..., namely, that not one book was to be found in al-Hakem's library, whatever might be its contents, which the caliph had not perused, writing on the fly-leaf the name, surname, and patronymic of the author; that of the tribe or family to which he belonged; and the year of his birth and death; after which followed such interesting anecdotes about the author or his work as he had derived from other writers through his immense reading.

Questions: What points do the authors make about al-Hakem and his library? What values are expressed here? What advantages did learning confer on a society in the Mediterranean world? What knowledge of Christian culture was a ruler such as al-Hakem likely to have?

76. THE CONQUEST OF LISBON

The Spanish Reconquista was a long and incremental process, full of setbacks and limited advances. One such campaign was the siege of Lisbon. In 1147, as part of the Second Crusade, a group of crusaders left England for the Holy Land, perhaps intending to stop in Portugal (as they in fact did) on their way. There they helped King Alfonso VII of Leon and Castile in his campaign to take the city of Lisbon from the Moors. Excerpts from the surviving anonymous account of this expedition are printed here.

Sources: sections 1, 3, and 5: trans. C.W. David, *De Expugnatione Lyxboniensi: The Conquest of Lisbon* (New York: Columbia University Press, 2001), pp. 53-59, 101-05, 137-39; sections 2, 4, and 6: trans. J.A. Brundage, *The Crusades: A Documentary Survey* (Milwaukee: Marquette University Press, 1962), pp. 97-98, 100-03.

[1.] To begin, then, men of diverse nations, customs, and speech assembled in the port of Dartmouth [on the south coast of England] in about one hundred and sixty-four vessels. The whole expedition was divided into three parts. Under Count Arnold of Aerschot, nephew of Duke Godfrey [of Lower Lotharingia] were the forces from the territories of the [Holy] Roman Empire; under Christian of Ghistelles, the Flemings and the men of Boulogne. All the others were under four constables: the ships of Norfolk and Suffolk under Hervey de Glanvill, those of Kent under Simon of Dover, those of London under Andrew, and all the rest under Saher of Archelle.

Among these people of so many different tongues the firmest guarantees of peace and friendship were taken; and, furthermore, they sanctioned very strict laws, as, for example, a life for a life and a tooth for a tooth. They forbade all display of costly garments. Also they ordained that women should not go out in public; that the peace must be kept by all, unless they should suffer injuries recognized by the proclamation; that weekly chapters [that is, meetings] be held by the laity and the clergy separately, unless perchance some great emergency should require their meeting together; that each ship have its own priest and keep the same observances as are prescribed for parishes; that no one retain the seaman or the servant of another in his employ; that everyone make weekly confession and communicate on Sunday; and so on through the rest of the obligatory articles with separate sanctions for each. Furthermore, they constituted for every thousand of the forces two elected members who were to be called judges..., through whom the cases of the constables were to be settled in accordance with the proclamation and by whom the distribution of moneys was to be carried out.

These ordinances having been thus established, we began to make sail on the Friday before Ascension [that is, on May 23. In late June the fleet arrived in Portugal.]...

[2.] The city of Lisbon at the time of our arrival consisted of sixty thousand families paying taxes... The city was populous beyond belief, for, as we learned from its alcayde, or governor, after the capture of the city, it had one hundred fifty-four thousand men, not counting women and children.... The reason for such a dense population was that there was no established religion there. Each man was a law unto himself. As a result the basest element from every part of the world had gathered there, like the bilge water of a ship, a breeding ground for every kind of lust and impurity....

[3. King Alfonso now asked the crusaders to delay going to Jerusalem and to help him capture Lisbon.] To frame a reply to this we all assembled in council ... [where] William Viel, yet breathing out threatenings and piratical slaughter, and his brother Ralph and almost all the men of Southampton and Hastings, together with those who had come to besiege Lisbon five years before this, all with one voice declared that they took the king's promise [of rewards and plunder] to be nothing but treachery; and, bringing up many points against it which were either false or, if in any respect true, to be imputed to their own foolishness rather than the king's baseness, or things which were even more obvious, [they said] that they were unwilling to bear the expense of a long labor in the siege. Moreover, it would be more profitable if they should sail quickly past the coast of Spain and then extort much easy money from the merchant vessels of Africa and Spain. And, besides, they recalled that the wind at that season was very favorable for voyagers to Jerusalem. And they said that they would not wait for anyone, if only they should have eight or ten ships associated with them, and many other similar things which depend upon the turn of fate rather than upon virtue. But the greater part of our force, setting aside every objection, agreed to remain....

[4. After an unsuccessful attempt to persuade the Muslims to surrender the city, the crusaders besieged Lisbon.] The Moors, meanwhile, made frequent sorties against our men by day because they held three gates against us. With two of these gates on the side of the city and one on the sea, they had an easy way to get in and out. On the other hand, it was difficult for our men to organize themselves. The sorties caused casualties on both sides, but theirs were always greater than ours. While we kept watch, meanwhile, under their walls through the days and nights, they heaped derision and many insults upon us.... They also continuously attacked blessed Mary, the mother of God, with insults and with vile and abusive words, which infuriated us. They said that we venerated the son of a poor woman with a worship equal to that due to God, for we held that he was a God and the Son of God, when it is apparent that there is only one God who began all things that have begun and that he has no one coeval with him and no partaker in his divinity.... They attacked us with these and similar calumnies. They showed to us, moreover, with much derision the symbol of the cross. They spat upon it and wiped the feces from their posteriors with it. At last they urinated on it, as on some despicable thing, and threw our cross at us....

[5. Meanwhile,] the men of Cologne five times began to dig mines for the purpose of overturning the [city] wall and were as many times overwhelmed. Hence our forces again had cause for deep discouragement, and, murmuring much among themselves, they were making such complaints as that they might have been better employed elsewhere, when, after some days, there came to us by the determination of divine mercy no small consolation.

For in the evening ten Moors entered a skiff beneath the wall and rowed away in the direction of the castle of Palmela. But our men pursued them so closely that they abandoned the skiff in desperation, and everything they were carrying in it. Letters were found in it, directed to several parties and written in the Arabic language. An example of one, as I got it from an interpreter, is as follows:

"To Abu Muhammed, king of Évora, [from] the unfortunate people of Lisbon: may he maintain his kingdom in safety. What great and terrible and unexpected disasters have come upon us, the desolate ruin of our city and the great effusion of noble blood—memorials, alas, of our everlasting grief—proclaim. Already the second moon has almost passed since the fleet of the

Franks, which has been borne hither to our borders with the aid of heaven and earth and sea, has kept us shut within the circuit of this close-drawn wall. And what is to be hoped for amid this sum of woes is more than doubtful, except only to look for succor by means of ransom. But with our cooperation we doubt not that you will liberate the city and the country from the barbarians. For they are not so very numerous or warlike, as their tower and engines which we have burned with force and arms bear witness. Otherwise, let your prudence beware, for the same outcome of events and evils awaits you."

And the other letters besought the same things from parents and other relatives and friends, and from debtors; and … also gave information concerning their supply of bread and other foodstuffs. When our men learned of these things, their spirits were greatly encouraged to continue the attack against the enemy for some days longer. After a short time the corpse of a man who had been drowned was found beneath our ships; and on an arm a letter was tied, of which the tenor was as follows:

"The king of Évora to the men of Lisbon…. Having long since entered into a truce with the king of the Portuguese, I cannot break faith and wage war upon him and his people. For the rest, take heed in good time. Buy safety with your money, lest that prove a cause of your hurt which ought to be a cause of your well-being. Farewell. Give something worthwhile to this our messenger."

So, finally, as the Moors' last hope of relief was destroyed, our men kept watch the more vigilantly… [and the siege continued until the Moors agreed to surrender].

[6.] When these matters had been agreed upon by both sides, the arrangements which the Moors had proposed on the previous day for the delivery of the city, were accepted. It was decided among us that one hundred and forty of our armed men and one hundred and sixty of the Flemish and the Cologne contingents should enter the city before everyone else and peacefully take over the fortifications of the upper fortress so that the enemy might bring all of their money and possessions there and give a guarantee by swearing before our men. When all these things had been collected, the city was then to be searched by our men. If any further possessions were found, the man in whose house they were discovered was to pay for it with his head. When everyone had thus been despoiled, they were to be let go in peace outside of the city. When the gates had been opened and those who were chosen were allowed to enter, the men of Cologne and the Flemings thought up a sly method of deceiving us: they requested our men to allow them to enter first for the sake of their honor. When they had received permission and got a chance to enter first, they slipped in more than two hundred of their men, in addition to those who had been selected. These were also in addition to others who had already slipped through the ruined places in the walls which lay open to them, while none of our men, except those selected, had presumed to enter.

The archbishop and the other bishops went in front of us with the Lord's cross and then our leaders entered together with the king and those who had been selected. How everyone rejoiced! What special glory for all! What great joy and what a great abundance there was of pious tears when, to the praise and honor of God and of the most Holy Virgin Mary the saving cross was placed atop the highest tower to be seen by all as a symbol of the city's subjection, while the Archbishop and bishops, together with the clergy and everyone, intoned with wonderful rejoicing the *Te Deum Laudamus* and the *Asperge me*, together with devout prayers.

The king, meanwhile, went around the strong walls of the fortress on foot. The men of Cologne and the Flemings, when they saw in the city so many spurs to their greed, did not observe their oaths or their religious guarantees. They ran hither and yon. They plundered. They broke down doors. They rummaged through the interior of every house. They drove the citizens away and harassed them improperly and unjustly. They destroyed clothes and utensils. They treated virgins shamefully. They acted as if right and wrong were the same. They secretly took away everything which should have been common property. They even cut the throat of the elderly Bishop of the city, slaying him against all right and justice.... The Normans and the English, however, for whom faith and religion were of the greatest importance, contemplating what such actions might lead to, remained quietly in their assigned position, preferring to stay their hands from looting rather than to violate the obligations of their faith and their oathbound association.... Finally [the men of Cologne and the Flemings] came to themselves and besought our men with earnest prayers that we should occupy the remaining sections of the city together with them so that, after the loot had been divided, all the injuries and thefts might be discussed peacefully and they would be prepared to make amends for the evils they had presumed to commit. The enemy, when they had been despoiled in the city, left the town through three gates continuously from Saturday morning until the following Wednesday. There was such a multitude of people that it seemed as if all of Spain were mingled in the crowd....

Questions: What motivations for the expedition are evident in the text? How did the expeditionary force make decisions? On what level did the two sides understand and criticize each other's religion? Why did no neighboring Muslim power come to the assistance of Lisbon during the siege? What moral standards does the author adopt in describing the sack of the city?

77. ALFONSO VIII'S REPORT ON LAS NAVAS DE TOLOSA

The battle of Las Navas de Tolosa in 1212 was one of the most decisive of the entire Reconquista. Here the combined armies of Castile, Navarre, and Aragon defeated the forces of the Almohad dynasty, one of the major Moorish powers remaining in Spain, and before the end of the century only the kingdom of Granada would be left in Muslim hands on the Iberian peninsula. In the letter below, King Alfonso VIII of Leon and Castile, who led the Christian forces, reports the victory to Pope Innocent III. In this account he minimizes Christian losses, exaggerates Muslim numbers and casualties, and glosses over problems between the Spanish and non-Spanish elements in the Christian army.

Source: trans. C. Smith, *Christians and Moors in Spain, Volume II: 1195-1614* (Warminster: Aris & Phillips Ltd., 1989), pp. 15-25.

To the most holy father Innocent, pope by grace of God, Alfonso, king of Castile and Toledo by the same, sends greetings, kissing your hands and feet. We know that your holiness has not forgotten that we planned to do battle against the perfidy of the Saracens, and we reported to you humbly and devotedly by our messengers, begging your help in all things pertaining to a father and a lord, which help we recognize we have obtained in kindly and compassionate fashion from our loving father.

For this reason we did not delay in sending our heralds (whom we thought most suitable for carrying this forward) out with our letters to certain parts of France, adding that we would provide, to the extent that could reasonably be sustained, the necessary costs of provisioning all those knights coming to join the campaign, and for all their serving-men to the degree that was fitting. Hence it was that, when people heard of the remission of sins which you granted to those coming to join us, there arrived a vast number of knights from the regions beyond the Pyrenees, including the archbishops of Narbonne and Bordeaux and the bishop of Nantes. Those who came numbered up to 2,000 knights with their squires, and up to 10,000 of their serving-men on horseback, with up to 50,000 serving-men on foot, for all of whom we had to provide the food. There came also our illustrious friends and relatives the kings of Aragon and of Navarre in support of the Catholic cause, with all their forces. We did not fail to provide for all of them, as we had promised through our heralds, while delaying for a time at Toledo as we waited for some of our men who were due to present themselves for the campaign, and it must be said that the costs for us and for our kingdom were extremely heavy on account of the huge numbers involved. We had to provide not only what we had promised, but also money and clothing, for almost everybody, both knights and serving-men, was in need. However, God, who gives increase to the fruits of justice, provided abundantly for us in accordance with the generosity of his grace, and gave us all that could be desired equitably and richly.

When both hosts were assembled, we set out on the road God had chosen for us, and coming to a certain fort named Malagón, amply defended, the French, who got there one day ahead of us, at once stormed and took it with God's help.

Even though it had fallen to us to provide them generously with all necessities, they [that is, the French] became too concerned with the difficulties of the terrain, which was empty and rather hot, and they wished to turn back and go home. At length, after much pressure from us and the king of Aragon, they continued as far as Calatrava, which was only some two leagues from the aforementioned fort, and we all—Castilians and Aragonese and French, each from his own side—began to attack in God's name. The Saracens inside, realizing that they would not be able to hold off this army of God, negotiated about surrendering the place to us, on condition that they should be allowed to leave unharmed, although without their belongings. We were unwilling to accept any such arrangement. The king of Aragon and the French held a council about it, and knew that the place was strongly fortified with walls and outer defenses, deep ditches and loftier towers, so that it could not be taken unless the walls were undermined and made to collapse; but this would be much to the detriment of the friars of Salvatierra, to whom it had earlier belonged, and by whom it would not be tenable (the walls being razed) in case of need. For this reason they most earnestly urged that the place should be handed over to us whole and undamaged with the weapons and all the great stores of food that were in it, and that the Saracens should be allowed to leave empty-handed and without weapons. So we, paying heed to their firm wishes in this matter, assented to their proposals, the conditions being that a half of all that there was inside should go to the king of Aragon and the other half to the French, no part of it being retained by ourselves or our men. The French— still keen on the idea of going home, even though the Lord God was showing us grace and favor, and even though we were willing to go on providing them all with necessities in a generous way—driven as they were by the urge to go home, all together abandoned the cross, together with the archbishop of Bordeaux and the bishop of Nantes, even though there was certainly going to be a battle with the Saracens; and they went off, except a very few who stayed on with the archbishop of Narbonne and Tibaldo de Blazon, who was one of our liegemen, and also his men and certain other knights of Poitou. Those who remained, knights and serving-men, amounted to scarcely 150; and of their foot-soldiers, none at all remained.

Since the king of Aragon was waiting at Calatrava for certain knights of his and the king of Navarre, who had still not joined us, we set out with our men and arrived at a certain enemy castle called Alarcos. We took this castle, well defended though it was, together with three others, Caracuel, Benavente, and Piedrabuena.

Going forward from there we reached Salvatierra, where the king of Aragon joined us, he having brought only a small number of noble knights in his army; and the king of Navarre, who similarly was accompanied by a force of scarcely 200 knights.

Since the sultan of the Saracens was close to us, we resolved not to attack Salvatierra, but, advancing towards the Saracen host, we reached a mountain range which was impossible to cross except in certain places. Since on our side we were at the foot of the range, the Saracens advancing from the other side were able to occupy the crest, seeking to bar our passage. But our men went up bravely, because up to that time only a few Saracens had reached the area, and our men vigorously drove them off, with God's help; and they took a fort called Reffal, which the Saracen ruler had built on in order to bar our way. Once this was taken, the army of the Lord was able to go on up to the mountain peaks in safety, but it was hard going because of the lack of water and the barrenness of the place. The Saracens, seeing that they could not block that pass, occupied another passage on the downward slope, exceptionally narrow and difficult; it was such, indeed, that a thousand men could readily defend it against the greatest army on earth. At the far end of it lay the whole Saracen army with their tents already pitched.

Since we could not stay there because of the lack of water, nor advance because of the difficulty of the pass, certain of our men advised that we should go back down the mountain and look for another pass some distance away. But we, concerned for the danger to the faith and disgrace to our person, refused to accept this advice, preferring to die for the faith on the difficult terrain of the pass rather than to seek an easier way, or to back down from an affair which concerned the faith, in whatsoever fashion it might be.

When we had thus strengthened our resolve, our barons—who were to strike the first blows in the battle—heard of the suggestion of a certain shepherd, whom God by his command sent to us, that in that very spot another relatively easy passage existed. In a certain place close to the enemy camp, although barren and dry, they pitched camp, since the Saracens did not know of this pass. When the Saracen army realized what was happening, they advanced in order to stop the camp being established. Our men, even though few, defended themselves bravely.

We and the kings of Aragon and Navarre waited, fully armed, with our men in the place where we had first halted, which was on the crest of the mountain, until the whole army of the Lord safely reached the spot where our advance patrols had marked out the camp. Thanks be to God, it happened that although the way was difficult and waterless, also rocky and wooded, we lost none of our men. This was Saturday, 14 July. Late that day the Saracens, observing that we had safely erected all our tents, drew up their battle-lines and approached our camp, indulging in skirmishing rather as in a tournament, as a prelude to battle.

Very early next day, Sunday, the Saracens came up with their huge army arrayed in battle-lines. We, wishing to study the numbers of their men and their disposition and attitude, and to find out how they behaved in all circumstances, took advice from our expert and seasoned men, and resolved to wait until the following day, Monday. In these circumstances, we posted cavalrymen and footsoldiers so that the enemy should not in any way be able to attack the ends of our line, and this, thanks to God's grace, did not happen.

The following day, Monday, we all armed and set out in God's name, in full array, to do battle with them for the Catholic faith. The enemy occupied certain eminences, very steep places and difficult to climb by reason of the woods which lay between us and them, and by reason of some very deep gorges cut by streams, all of which formed a major impediment to us and was a great help to the enemy. Then indeed he by whom, and in whom, and through whom, all things are miraculously done, directed his army against his enemies; and our front ranks, and some of the middle ranks, by virtue of the cross of the Lord, cut down many lines of the enemy who were stationed on the lower eminences. When our men reached the last of their lines, consisting of a huge number of soldiers, among whom was the king of Carthage, there began desperate fighting among the cavalrymen, infantrymen, and archers, our people being in terrible danger and scarcely able to resist any longer. Then we, realizing that the fighting was becoming altogether impossible for them, started a cavalry charge, the cross of the Lord going before and our banner with its image of the holy Virgin and her Son imposed upon our device. Since we had already resolved to die for the faith of Christ, as soon as we witnessed the same being suffered by the cross of Christ and the image of his mother when the Saracens assailed them with stones and arrows, we broke their line with its vast numbers of men, even though the Saracens resisted bravely in the battle, and stood solidly around their lord.

Our Lord slew a great multitude of them with the sword of the cross. Then the sultan with a few of his men turned in flight. Others of the enemy for a time bore the thrust of our attacks, but soon, after heavy loss of life, the rest turned and fled. We followed up the pursuit till nightfall, and killed more in that rout than we had in the battle.

In this way the battle of the Lord was triumphantly won, by God alone and through God alone. To God be the honor and the glory, who granted the victory of his cross though Jesus Christ, our Lord.

The Saracen horsemen had numbered 185,000, as we afterwards learned in a true account from certain servants of the sultan, whom we took prisoner; the footsoldiers were uncountable.

On their side there fell in the battle 100,000 armed men, perhaps more, according to the estimates of Saracens we captured later. Of the army of the Lord—a fact not to be mentioned without the most fervent thanksgiving, and one scarcely to be believed, unless it be thought a miracle—only some twenty or thirty Christians in our whole host fell. What cause for joy and thanksgiving! Yet there is one cause for regret here: that so few in such a vast army went to Christ as martyrs.

In order to show how immense were the numbers of the enemy, when our army rested after the battle for two days in the enemy camp, for all the fires which were needed to cook food and make bread and other things, no other wood was needed than that of the enemy arrows and spears which were lying about, and even then we burned scarcely half of them. Even though our army was running short of food and other supplies, because we had spent so long in bare and barren countryside, we found such an abundance of food and weapons, as also of warhorses and beasts of burden, that our men, by taking as many of them as they wished, still left more out of the huge number of animals than those they took.

On the third day we advanced to certain enemy fortresses, Vilches, Baños, and Tolosa, and at once captured them.

Eventually we reached two towns, Baeza and Ubeda, the largest there are on this side of the sea except for Cordova and Seville. We found Baeza already destroyed. A great number of people had fled from all the nearby settlements to Ubeda, because it was exceptionally strong both on account of its situation and on account of its defenses. Since the people knew that no other city of that size had been stormed or taken by the emperor or by any other Hispanic ruler, they thought they would be safe there. However, by God's grace we captured Ubeda in a short time, and, since we did not have enough people to settle it, we razed it to the ground. Some 60,000 Saracens perished there: some we killed, others were taken as captives into the service of the Christians and of the monasteries which needed to be repaired in the border regions.

We ordered all this to be set down in writing for you, most holy father, earnestly offering all the thanks we can for the aid of all Christendom, and humbly asking you whom God has chosen for the highest rank among his priests, with all praise to him, to offer up a sacrifice for the salvation of our people.

Questions: What difficulties did the Christian forces encounter on this campaign? What tensions existed within the Christian army? What role does religion play in this account? How well did the various sides know each other in this situation, compared with the level of knowledge in the Middle East?

78. MUSLIM-CHRISTIAN TREATY

In 1245, the Moorish leader Abu 'Abd Allah Ibn Hudhayl, known as al-Azraq, surrendered to Alfonso, the son of James the Conqueror, king of Aragon and Catalonia in northeastern Spain. The unusual documents printed below are two versions of the treaty drawn up on this occasion. It came at the end of James's fifteen-year campaign to take the territory of Valencia on Spain's east coast; the treaty dealt with one small territory within Valencia.

Source: trans. R.I. Burns and P.E. Chevedden, *Negotiating Cultures: Bilingual Surrender Treaties in Muslim-Crusader Spain under James the Conqueror* (Leiden: Brill, 1999), pp. 36-37, 49-50.

Castilian Spanish version of the treaty:

Let it be known to all present and future: that I Abu 'Abd Allah Ibn Hudhayl, vizier and lord of Alcalá, make myself your vassal, lord Don Alfonso the elder son of the king of Aragon, and I give you eight castles—the one called Pop and the other Tárbena, and Margarida, Cheroles, Castell, Alcalá, Gallinera, and Perpunchent.

These aforesaid castles I give you with their villages, and with districts, and with pastures, and with as much as belongs to them. And of the aforesaid castles, I give you lord Don Alfonso two castles immediately, Pop and Tárbena; and I retain for myself Alcalá and Perpunchent, as an estate for me and for my children and for my family-line, to do with them entirely according to my will. And the other four castles—Margarida, Cheroles, Castell, and Gallinera—these I keep for three years in such accord that you lord Don Alfonso have half the revenues and I the other half; and those three years having passed, that I give you the castles free and quit, without any litigation, with all their districts and with all their rights just as is said above.

And besides, I make this agreement with you, lord: that of as many castles as I can win from here on through the three years, I give you half the revenues; and the three years having passed, that I give you the castles that I will gain, along with the other four, just as is said above.

And I Don Alfonso by the grace of God prince, elder son of the king of Aragon, receive you Abu 'Abd Allah Ibn Hudhayl vizier and lord of Alcalá as my cherished and much esteemed and very honored and loyal vassal. And I grant and give two castles, Alcalá and Perpunchent, as an estate for you and all your family-line, to give, sell, pledge, or use entirely according to your will.

And I give you the revenues of the two villages Ebo and Tollos for those three years, and after the three years that you release to me those two villages, with the other castles.

Furthermore I swear and contract and grant that all these agreements hold, just as is written above, but in such wise that you be my vassal for the castle of Alcalá and for that which I give you.

Given at Pouet, the sixteenth day of April....

Arabic version of the treaty:

In the name of God, the merciful, the compassionate. May God bless our lord Mohammed and his family!

This is a noble decree, enjoined by the exalted prince, the heroic, the most fortunate, ...the infante [that is, prince] Don Alfonso, son of the exalted king, the divinely assisted, the ruler of Aragon, upon the most illustrious wazir, the noble, the highest, the most eminent, the most exalted Abu 'Abd Allah b. Hudhayl—may God honor him! [Wherefore] the abovementioned exalted prince makes an agreement with him for three years from the present date, which is stated at the end of the decree, that his [the wazir's] property and retainer[s] shall remain in his castles, and that the abovementioned wazir shall give to the abovementioned exalted prince two castles, namely Pop and Tárbena, which he shall now hand over to him. The rest of the castles shall remain in the possession of the abovementioned wazir, namely Castell, Cheroles, Margarida, Alcalá, Perpunchent, and Gallinera, until the end of the three years. But the abovementioned wazir shall hand them over to the abovementioned prince when the three years have expired, except for the castle of Alcalá with its revenues and the revenues of the villages of Perpunchent, which shall remain henceforth in the perpetual possession of the abovementioned wazir and his descendant for the duration of the reign of the exalted prince. [Furthermore,] the exalted prince shall give to the abovementioned wazir the revenues of Ebo and Tollos for the duration of the three years. When he [the wazir] hands over to him [the prince] the abovementioned castles, namely Margarida, Castell, Cheroles, and Gallinera, he [the wazir] shall [also] hand over to him [the prince] Ebo and Tollos. The exalted prince [also agrees] to give to the qa'id [that is, lord] Abu Yahyá b. Abu Ishaq, the ruler of Castell, the village[s] of Espel-la and Petracos to be his perpetually for the duration of the reign of the prince, [both] for himself and his descendant.

[It is further agreed] that the wazir shall give to the exalted prince from the four castles, which he shall hand over to him when three years have elapsed [that is, Margarida, Castell, Cheroles, and Gallinera], half the tithe; and whatever castles the wazir obtains [for] the ruler of Aragon, either by force or by capitulation, the wazir shall have half of the revenue [from these castles] for the duration of the three years. But when the three years expire, he [the wazir] shall hand them over to him [the prince] along with the four other castles. Written on [15 April 1245].

Questions: Compare the two versions. Is one a translation of the other? How do they differ in tone, implications, and details? What light is shed on the treaty by the knowledge that the Muslim leader rebelled against the Christian king two years after the treaty was written?

79. MOORISH LAWS

Throughout Spain, when Moors and Christians were not fighting each other, they lived side by side under either Muslim or Christian rule. The following laws are excerpted from collections of mainly commerical regulations drawn up in Muslim Spain in different periods. The first selection comes from the city of Seville around the year 1100. The second is from a general compendium relying mainly on ninth-century authorities.

Source: trans. C. Melville and A. Ubaydli, *Christians and Moors in Spain*, vol. III (Warminster: Aris & Phillips, Ltd., 1992), pp.111-15.

Ibn 'Abdun (11th-12th century)

A Muslim should not rub down a Jew, nor a Christian [in the baths], neither should he throw out their refuse nor cleanse their lavatories; the Jews and Christians are more suitable for such a job, which is a task for the meanest. A Muslim should not work with the animals of a Jew, nor of a Christian, neither should he ride in their company, nor grasp their stirrup [that is, serve as their squire]. If the *mutasib* [that is, the market inspector], gets to know of this, the perpetrator will be censured.

Muslim women must be prevented from entering disgusting churches, for the priests are fornicators, adulterers and pederasts. Frankish women [too] should be forbidden to enter churches except on days of particular merit or festivals, for they eat and drink and fornicate with the priests: there is not one of them who does not keep two or more of these women, spending the night with them. This has become a regular custom with them, for they have made what is lawful unlawful, and made what is unlawful lawful. The priests must be made to marry, as they do in the East; if they wanted to, they would.

No woman, old or otherwise, should be left in the house of a priest if he has refused to marry. They [that is, the priests] should be forced into circumcision, as al-Mu'tamid 'Abbad made them do. According to their assertions, they follow the path of Jesus (God bless him and grant him salvation!), and Jesus was circumcised; with them, the day of his circumcision is a festival which they hold in great regard, [but] they themselves abandon [this practice]!

One must not sell a scientific book to the Jews, nor to the Christians, unless it deals with their own law; for they translate books of sciences, and attribute them to their own people and to their bishops, when they are [really] the works of the Muslims. It would be best if no Jewish or Christian doctor were left to treat the Muslims; for they have no concern for the welfare of a Muslim, but only for the medical treatment of their co-religionists. How could one trust his lifeblood with someone who has no concern for what is best for a Muslim?

Ibn 'Abd al-Ra'uf (9th century or later)

Muslims are forbidden to buy meat intentionally from the butcheries of the *dhimmis* [that is, Christians and Jews]. [The legal writer] Malik abhorred this and [the caliph] 'Umar [b. al-Khattab]—may God be pleased with him—ordered them to be expelled from the Muslims' markets. Ibn Habib said, "There is no objection to them having a butchery isolated from the others, and being forbidden to sell to Muslims. Any Muslim who buys from them will not have his purchase invalidated, but he will be a bad man." [Another authority said] that if the meat [the Muslim] buys from them is the sort they do not eat themselves, such as *tarif* [that is, non-kosher meat] and suchlike, the purchase is invalidated, and the same for fat. God Almighty said, "We have made unlawful for them [the Jews] the fat of cattle and sheep" (Qu'ran 6:147); such are the undiluted and pure fats such as the intestines, the fat of the kidneys and that which attaches to the stomach and suchlike. God says, "except what their backs carry, or the entrails, or what is mixed with the bone" (Qu'ran, 6:147). All fat that is in this category becomes an exception. It is specifically not lawful for us either to eat or to trade in any of these fats that are forbidden to them from the animals they have slaughtered....

If a Muslim buys wine from a Christian, whatever wine is found in his possession will be destroyed. If the Christian has already received the price, this will be left to him, but if he has not received it, it will not be settled in his favor. If the wine is no longer in the Muslim's hands, and he has not paid for it, the price will be taken from him and given as alms, and both of them will be punished. If a Muslim destroys wine belonging to a *dhimmi*, he will be punished. Malik has conflicting opinions on the question of the payment of damages for its value: in one place he says, no fine is imposed on him, and none is lawful, because God has made its price unlawful; elsewhere, he says the price is incumbent on him.

He [that is, Malik] abhorred traveling with them [*dhimmis*] on ships, because of the fear of divine wrath descending on them.

'Umar al-Jarsifi (late Middle Ages)

The *dhimmis* must be prevented from having houses that overlook Muslims, and from spying on them, and from exhibiting wine and pork in the Muslims' markets, from riding horses with saddles and wearing the costumes of Muslims or anything ostentatious. They must be made to display a sign that will distinguish them from Muslims, such as the shakla [that is, a piece of yellow cloth] in the case of men and a bell in the case of women. Muslims must be forbidden from undertaking everything that entails baseness and humiliation for the Muslims, such as removing garbage, transporting equipment connected with wine, looking after pigs, and suchlike, because this involves the elevation of unbelief above Islam; whoever does such things will be punished.

Questions: Compare these regulations with the provisions of the Pact of Omar (doc. 5). How are the Christians viewed by the Muslims here? How restrictive were these laws? What does the restriction on bookselling imply?

80. CHRISTIAN LAWS

The following laws are part of the Siete Partidas, *a long and elaborate legal code compiled by King Alfonso X of Castile in the late thirteenth century. Alfonso was an energetic crusader against his Muslim neighbors as well as an active patron of cultural and intellectual life. Although the code as a whole attempted to incorporate Roman law and to be as widely useful as possible rather than locally focused, the passages reproduced here reveal some of the special conditions of Reconquista Spain.*

Source: trans. S.P. Scott, *Las Siete Partidas*, ed. R.I. Burns (Philadelphia: University of Pennsylvania Press, 2001), Vol. 2, pp. 410-11, 516-18, 520; Vol. 5, pp. 1433-42, 1450.

Partida 2, Title 20

1. The People Should Endeavor to Beget Offspring, in Order to Provide Inhabitants for the Country

Increase, and multiply, and replenish the earth was the first command which God issued to the first man and woman after he had created them. He did this because he knew that it was the first principle of nature, and the most powerful one by which men can be influenced in the land where they are obliged to live...; for this is, as it were, their mother, by means of whom they come into the world, and grow to be men. Wherefore, the people should sustain all these relations to the country in which they wish to live, and it is especially desirable that the progeny which springs from them should be born there, for this will cause them to love her....

In order to create this offspring many things should be observed that it may be born and multiply. The first is, that those who have arrived at a proper age should marry early, for many advantages result from this, since they obey the commandment of God, as we have explained, and are also enabled to live without sin, through which they will obtain the love of God and he will increase their offspring. Moreover, they will take pleasure in their lives, and obtain the assistance of the descendants, from which they will experience great comfort, for the reason that they leave others in their places who are, as it were, one person with them, to whom their property should be left, and who may accomplish after their death what they were bound to do. In addition to all this, there is still another great advantage, for when persons marry early, and one of them dies, the survivor can marry subsequently, and thus have children at a fit time, which those who marry late cannot do so well.

2. What Things Persons Should Avoid in Order Not to Be Prevented from Having Offspring

Persons should exercise care in their marriages, and be sure to marry under such circumstances that they can have children, in order to people the country, as stated in the preceding law. In order to be able to accomplish this, they must avoid the things mentioned in this law which may hinder them. An instance of this would be where the husband and wife are very young, or very old.... Moreover, they should be very careful that the marriage be not very unequal, as, for instance, where a boy marries an old woman, or an old man a very young girl. For, without taking into consideration the bad appearance which they will make, two evils will result; first, no love can exist between them; second, they can have no children on account of the difference in their ages. The same rule was established with regard to those suffering from a [physical] defect, or some disease which would prevent them from having children....

Partida 2, Title 29. Concerning Captives and Their Property...

1. What the Word Captive Means...

...Those are properly called captives who come under the control of men embracing another belief, for these have the power to put them to death after they have taken them prisoners, on account of the contempt which they have for their religion, or they can subject them to cruel punishments, or make use

Fig. 26: The great mosque of Codova, dating from the eighth century, as depicted in a nineteenth-century engraving. From P. Lacroix, *Military and Religious Life in the Middle Ages* (London, Chapman and Hall, 1874).

of them as slaves, compelling them to perform such arduous tasks that they will prefer death to life. And, in addition to this, they are not allowed to possess their own property, but must surrender it to those who inflict all these evils upon them, or have a right to sell them whenever they desire to do so. [The captors] have also the power to commit a still greater act of cruelty, for they can separate what God united, as, for instance, a husband from his wife, who became so according to law and by marriage. They have, moreover, a right to violate the ties of nature, as for instance to separate children from fathers and mothers, or brothers from one another, or persons from other relatives of the same blood....

3. What Men Are Bound to Rescue Those Held in Captivity

Liberation of persons from captivity is something very pleasing to God, for the reason that it is a work of piety and mercy, and in this world is very becoming to those who accomplish it, as we explained in another law..... For this reason we declare that whenever a son maliciously delays to rescue from captivity his father, or any near relative, or any other relative, or any other kinsman, the said captive, when he is liberated, has the power to disinherit any of those who hesitated to set him free.... We decree that this also shall apply to such as are under obligations on account of an agreement, as for instance, husband and wife; for, although they are in reality two persons, they become one, just as is the case in a union by nature....

7. What Rights Children, Born to Men While They Are in Captivity, Have in the Property of Their Parents

Where a woman was pregnant when taken captive, although she may be delivered in the enemy's country, and when a son or daughter born there is liberated, he or she should be put in possession of the property belonging to his or her father or mother, and enjoy in security all its rights to the same, just as if the said child had been born in the house of its parents. But where a husband and wife are captured together and, while in captivity, the wife becomes impregnated by her husband, and both together are afterwards freed from the power of the enemy, and their son or daughter along with them, the latter shall have their rights in all their property, just as if they had been begotten or born in the country of the Christians. When a child is liberated from captivity with its father or mother, it is to be considered the heir of the property of the one with whom it was set free, and all its rights to the same shall remain unimpaired. It has, however, no claim to the property of the parent remaining in captivity, except where the latter subsequently is freed from the hands of the enemy, and acknowledges the child....

Partida 7, Title 24. Concerning the Jews...

2. In What Ways Jews Should Pass Their Lives among Christians...

Jews should pass their lives among Christians quietly without disorder, practicing their own religious rites, and not speaking ill of the faith of our Lord Jesus Christ, which Christians acknowledge. Moreover, a Jew should be very careful to avoid preaching to, or converting any Christian, to the end that he may become a Jew, by exalting his own belief and disparaging ours. Whoever violates this law shall be put to death and lose all his property....

4. How Jews Can Have a Synagogue Among Christians

A synagogue is a place where the Jews pray, and a new building of this kind cannot be erected in any part of our dominions, except by our order. Where, however, those which formerly existed there are torn down, they can be built in the same spot where they originally stood; but they cannot be made any larger or raised to any greater height, or be painted. A synagogue constructed in any other manner shall be lost by the Jews, and shall belong to the principal church of the locality where it is built. And for the reason that a synagogue is a place where the name of God is praised, we forbid any Christian to deface it, or remove anything from it, or take anything out of it by force, except where some malefactor takes refuge there; for they have a right to remove him by force in order to bring him before the judge....

5. No Compulsion Shall Be Brought to Bear upon the Jews on Saturday...

Saturday is the day on which Jews perform their devotions, and remain quiet in their lodgings, and do not make contracts or transact any business; and for the reason that they are obliged by their religion to keep it, no one should on that day summon them or bring them into court. Wherefore we order that no judge shall employ force or any constraint upon Jews on Saturday, in order to bring them into court on account of their debts; or arrest them; or cause them any other annoyance; for the remaining days of the week are sufficient for the purpose of employing compulsion against them, and for making demands for things which can be demanded of them, according to law....

6. Jews Who Become Christians Shall Not Be Subject to Compulsion...

No force or compulsion shall be employed in any way against a Jew to induce him to become a Christian; but the Christians should convert him to the faith of our Lord Jesus Christ by means of the texts of the holy scriptures, and by kind words, for no one can love or appreciate a service which is done him by compulsion. We also decree that if any Jew or Jewess should voluntarily desire to become a Christian, the other Jews shall not interfere with this in any way, ... [nor] stone, wound, or kill any such person, because they wish to become Christians ... and we also order that, after any Jews become Christians, all persons in our dominions shall honor them; and that no one shall dare to reproach them or their descendants, by way of insult, with having been Jews; ... and that they can hold all offices and dignities which other Christians can do.

7. What Penalty a Christian Deserves Who Becomes a Jew

Where a Christian is so unfortunate as to become a Jew, we order that he shall be put to death just as if he had become a heretic; and we decree that his property shall be disposed of in the same way that we stated should de done with that of heretics.

8. No Christian, Man or Woman, Shall Live with a Jew

We forbid any Jew to keep Christian men or women in his house, to be served by them, although he may have them to cultivate and take care of his lands, or protect him on the way when he is compelled to go to some dangerous place. Moreover, we forbid any Christian man or woman to invite a Jew or a Jewess, or accept any invitation from them, to eat or drink together, or to drink any wine made by their hands. We also order that no Jews shall dare to bathe in company with Christians, and that no Christian shall take any medicine or cathartic made by a Jew; but that he can take it by the advice of some intelligent person, only where it is made by a Christian, who knows and is familiar with its ingredients.

9. What Penalty a Jew Deserves Who Has Intercourse with a Christian Woman

Jews who live with Christian women are guilty of great insolence and boldness, for which reason we decree that all Jews who, hereafter, may be convicted of having done such a thing shall be put to death. For if Christians who commit adultery with married women deserve death on that account, much more do Jews who have sexual intercourse with Christian women, who are spiritually the wives of our Lord Jesus Christ because of the faith and the baptism which they receive in his name; nor do we consider it proper that a Christian woman who commits an offense of this kind shall escape without punishment. Wherefore we order that, whether she be a virgin, a married woman, a widow, or a common prostitute who gives herself to all men, she shall suffer the same penalty which we mentioned in the last law in the title [below] concerning Moors, to which a Christian woman is liable who has carnal intercourse with a Moor.

10. What Penalty Jews Deserve Who Hold Christians as Slaves

A Jew shall not purchase, or keep as a slave a Christian man or woman, and if anyone violates this law the Christian shall be restored to freedom and shall

THE CRUSADES: A READER

not pay any portion of the price given for him, although the Jew may not have been aware, when he bought him, that he was a Christian; but if he knew that he was such when he purchased him, and makes use of him afterwards as a slave, he shall be put to death for doing so. Moreover, we forbid any Jew to convert a captive to his religion, even though said captive may be a Moor, or belong to some other barbarous race. If anyone violates this law we order that the said slave who has become a Jew shall be set at liberty.... If any Moors who are captives of Jews become Christians, they shall at once be freed....

11. Jews Shall Bear Certain Marks in Order That They May Be Known

Many crimes and outrageous things occur between Christians and Jews because they live together in cities, and dress alike; and in order to avoid the offenses and evils which take place for this reason, we deem it proper, and we order that all Jews male and female living in our dominions shall bear some distinguishing mark upon their heads so that people may plainly recognize a Jew or a Jewess....

Partida 7, Title 25. Concerning the Moors

2. Christians Should Convert the Moors by Kind Words, and Not by Compulsion

Christians should endeavor to convert the Moors by causing them to believe in our religion, and bring them into it by kind words and suitable discourses, and not by violence or compulsion; for if it should be the will of our Lord to bring them into it and to make them believe by force, he can use compulsion against them if he so desires, since he [that is, God] has full power to do so; but he is not pleased with the service which men perform through fear, but with that which they do voluntarily and without coercion....

4. What Punishment a Christian Deserves Who Becomes a Moor

Men sometimes become insane and lose their prudence and understanding, as, for instance, where unfortunate persons, and those who despair of everything, renounce the faith of our Lord Jesus Christ, and become Moors; and there are some of them who are induced to do this through the desire to live according to their customs, or on account of the loss of relatives who have been killed or died; or because they have lost their property and become poor; or because of unlawful acts which they commit, dreading the punishment which they deserve on account of them.... Wherefore we order that all those who are guilty of this wickedness shall lose all their possessions, and have no right to any portion of them…; and, in addition to this, we order that if any person who has committed such an offense shall be found in any part of our dominions he shall be put to death.

9. Moors Who Come on a Mission from Other Kingdoms to the Court of the King Should, with Their Property, Be Safe and Secure

Envoys frequently come from the land of the Moors and other countries to the court of the king, and although they may come from the enemy's country and by his order, we consider it proper and we direct that every envoy who comes to our country, whether he be Christian, Moor, or Jew, shall come and go in safety and security through all our dominions, and we forbid anyone to do him violence, wrong, or harm, or to injure his property….

10. What Penalty a Moor and a Christian Woman Deserve Who Have Intercourse with One Another

If a Moor has sexual intercourse with a Christian virgin [or widow], we order that he shall be stoned, and that she, for the first offense, shall lose half her property, and that her father, mother, or grandfather shall have it, and if she has no such relatives, that it shall belong to the king. For the second offense, she shall lose all her property, and the heirs aforesaid, if she has any, shall obtain it, and if she has none, the king shall be entitled to it, and she shall be put to death…. If a Moor has sexual intercourse with a Christian married woman, he shall be stoned to death, and she shall be placed in the power of her husband who may burn her to death, or release her, or do what he pleases with her. If a Moor has intercourse with a common woman [that is, a prostitute] who abandons herself to everyone, for the first offense, they shall both be scourged together through the town, and for the second, they shall be put to death.

Partida 7, Title 26

6. What Punishment Jews and Moors Deserve Who Offer Insults to God…

Although neither Jews nor Moors should be compelled to believe in the Christian religion, nevertheless, we do not consider it proper that any of them should be permitted to offer insults to God or holy Mary, or to any of the saints accepted by the church of Rome. For if the Moors in all places where they have authority forbid Christians to insult Mohammed or to speak ill of their belief, and scourge them, do them harm in many ways, and even decapitate them, for this reason, [then] it is much more proper that we should forbid them, and others who do not believe in our religion, to speak ill of it, or insult it. Wherefore we forbid all the Jews and Moors in our dominions to dare to vilify our Lord Jesus Christ in any way whatever, or holy Mary, his mother, or any of the other saints; or to insult them by any act, ... and anyone who does so we shall cause to be punished in person and property, as we think he deserves for the offense he has committed. For it is but proper and just that the Jews and Moors, who do not believe in our religion, and whom we permit to live in our country, should not remain unpunished if they offer any insult to, or publicly commit any act against our Lord Jesus Christ or holy Mary, his mother, or against our Catholic religion, which is so holy, excellent, and true.

Questions: In what ways is it apparent from the laws that this is a frontier society frequently at war? How are minorities treated? Identify the elements of discrimination and the elements of protection in the laws about Jews. Compare the treatment of Jews with the treatment of Moors. How are converts treated differently from those born into the same religion? Compare this law code's treatment of religious minorities with that mandated by Muslims in the Pact of Omar (doc. 5) and the Moorish laws (doc. 79).

81. CONSTITUTIONS OF THE ORDER OF MERCED

The Spanish holy wars gave birth to several Spanish religious and military orders. One of these was the Order of Merced, whose mission was the ransoming of Christian captives taken by the Muslims. Excerpts from the regulations of this order, drawn up in the Catalan language in 1272, are printed here.

Source: trans. J.W. Brodman, *Ransoming Captives in Crusader Spain: The Order of Merced on the Christian-Islamic Frontier* (Philadelphia: University of Pennsylvania Press, 1986), pp. 127-34, 137-38.

Prologue

God, the father of mercy and the source of all consolation, the provider of courage for every tribulation, out of his own great compassion sent his son, Jesus Christ, into this world to visit the entire human race, which at that time was like a captive in prison, under the power of the devil and of hell. [He came] to visit and deliver all of those friends who were in that prison, under the power of that named enemy, and to bring them to his glory with those others who have climbed up to that place through [God's] mercy to claim and gain the positions of those angels who because of pride fell from heaven and became devils. So also, the Father, Son, and Holy Spirit, in whose works there is no division, ordered through their mercy and pity the foundation and establishment of this order, called the order of the Virgin Mary of the Ransom of Captives of St. Eulàlia of Barcelona. By that command, they ordained Brother Pere Nolasc as their servant, delegate, founder, and executor. The virtue and intention of this man, and of all the other masters who have followed him, have established for all time as the work and labor of the brothers and of the entire order that the master and brothers…, as a good work, will labor willingly and visit and deliver those Christians who are in captivity and in the power of Saracens or of other enemies of our law, this according to the proper commandment and wishes of the master of this order…. For this specifically God has established this order.

2. Of the Chapter General and Its Form

We establish and ordain that each year on the feast of the Holy Cross, at the beginning of the month of May, a chapter general be assembled and held at a place and in a manner ordained by the master. All the commanders, each with a brother from the place that he commands, are to come prepared to act and to follow the commandment of the order. And he who is unable to come is to send letters to the chapter giving precise and accurate reasons why he is unable to attend.

3. What Must Be Done on the First Day of the Chapter

On the first day of the chapter, all of the commanders and officials are to come to the chapter and give to the master the purses and keys, and give account of the alms that have been received. Let each one give one *dobla* [that is, a gold coin] to pay for the expenses of the chapter. And let them then give a written account to the aforesaid master of any item or amount of money that was lent or borrowed, taken in or paid out, for reason of any captive. This is to be handed over to that brother who, with the advice of the chapter, will be sent to that land whence these things ought to be delivered….

The prior is to excommunicate all those brothers who are embezzlers, thieves, conspirators, fugitives, disobedient or violent, and all those who consciously go against the edicts of the chapter general.

Likewise, let there be read at this chapter all the names of the brothers and sisters and familiars of the order who died during the year. Let them be absolved by the prior according to the form of the order. And let them [that is, the brothers present] leave the chapter and let the mass of St. Mary be solemnly sung.

5. Concerning the Profession of Novices

[On the second day], novices can be received for profession. The poverty and hardships of the order must be explained to these [candidates] and they must be asked and questioned whether they are bound by a vow, or to any order, or if there are debts or obligations for which they must render account to any person for reason of a bailiwick or for a charge held from anyone. And if they swear the truth about this, that there are no impediments, and promise for the love of Jesus Christ to assume all these hardships for all their life, then let them make a solemn vow in the hands of the master and promise obedience, chastity and poverty and to observe the constitutions of the chapter general. And then let them be vested by the said brothers of the order.

6. What Ought to Be Done on the Third Day

On the third day of the chapter general, the master and the prior together with the four aforesaid brothers, two clerics and two laymen, according to the grace with which Jesus Christ will endow them, are to divide the commanderies. This should not be done out of any earthly considerations, nor from anger or ill-will but only for God and the good of the order and the benefit of the captives. And with that done, let them make their appointments and let the mass of the Trinity be sung. With all of those matters fittingly accomplished, each of the commanders and brothers joyfully, and with the grace of the Father, the Son, and the Holy Spirit, is to travel to the land and place that he has been assigned.

7. Concerning the Clothing of the Brothers

The clothing of the brothers is to be of wool and white. Let them display on the cloak and scapular the insignia of the order. The tunic should be round and the breeches without stockings; let underclothes be of linen. The brothers are to wear the shoes of the Templars. They should not wear gloves of leather or carry pointed knives. Let them sleep clothed and girded, each in his own bed if he can do so. Likewise, the master or any commander or conventual brother is not to wear any mantle or overcoat or habit made of Narbonnese cloth or of anything better or worse than rough wool. Let the same clothing serve for commanders as that which novices and brothers first receive. And those who violate this constitution are to spend ten days on the ground without any reprieve and eat bread and water.

10. Concerning the Master and His Companion

The master of the order must never travel without a companion who is to be a brother and, if possible, a priest who can hear the confessions of the brothers when they arrive for a visitation. Likewise, no brother of ours is to travel alone without a particular brother in order to avoid the infamy of laymen.

13. Concerning Bailiwicks and Collectors

Let each collect alms in his own bailiwick that has been assigned to him; no other brother or collector should enter it except him who possesses it. If by chance any brother enter this bailiwick, he cannot stay in this bailiwick, or outside of his own, for more than two days without permission from the master, or if the needs of the entire order should require it. Let the collectors whom the brothers appoint to collect alms be the kind who know how to be on their guard lest the order be defamed through their actions. And when they are appointed and confirmed, they must swear on the four Gospels that they will guard the order with all their power from damage and infamy and that they will faithfully administer all that is given to the order. And let them faithfully report all that they are given to the commander or to his lieutenant. The collectors are to wear white clothing.

14. Concerning the Property and Income That Come to Us

We command and enjoin by a firm and lasting constitution that no brother of ours be able to sell or alienate or encumber in any way any possession of the order. And if he should do so, let there be no confirmation without special permission from the chapter general. And the one who acts contrary to this constitution is to be put in confinement for a year, and never be able to become a commander. Likewise, by virtue of this constitution, be it ordered that no brother of ours without special permission of the chapter general be able to sell or encumber or alienate or assign alms from any bishopric, archdeaconry or deaconry. And if he should so do, then let there be no confirmation.

16. How Sisters Are to Be Received

No woman henceforth is to be received as our sister unless she has enough of her own goods so that she can live comfortably in her own house, [and] in such manner that her residual property remain with the order without impediment. When she enters the order, she must make a will and draw it up in such a way that no damage or harassment befall the order on account of her friends or parents.

17. Concerning Brothers Who Go Abroad

Our brothers who go abroad must not in any way let their heads or feet be washed by any woman. Let them not eat or drink or recline or sleep in a house with any woman, except with their servants, since this could bring scandal to the order.

19. Concerning the Acceptance of Deposits

The commanders of our houses do not receive deposits from any person except in this way, that the order not be obliged to receive the deposit if it be stolen or in any other way lost.

20. Concerning Those Who Enter the Land of the Saracens

Let no brother of ours dare to enter the land of the Saracens for the redemption of Christian captives without special permission from the master or the chapter general. And those who are chosen by the master or the chapter general and sent there to redeem Christian captives are to be temperate in food and drink, and wise and prudent in the buying of captives.

21. Concerning Redeemed Captives

Captives ransomed by the brothers are immediately to swear an oath and do homage to the master or to the one or ones who have redeemed them, that they will not leave the service of the order until that time assigned by the master or by those who have redeemed them has passed. During that time assigned to them, let them shave off their beards and let the brother who directs them provide appropriately for their needs without any complaints. When the assigned time is completed, let their beards be shaved and their hair cut. They are to be given new clothing according to the season it is and suitable provision, so that they may return to their lands with cheer and happiness.

38. Concerning Aid for Captives

No commander is to tender any aid to captives without permission from the master or the advice of a bishop. And if it happens by chance that this is done, he must have testimonial letters from that bishop or from his lieutenant that show the amount of aid that was given.

39. Let a Commander Not Absolve an Embezzler

No commander is to be able to absolve anyone who is discovered to be an embezzler from any thing for which he ought to be made to do penance.

40. What a Brother Ought to Do with What He Takes to the Chapter

Let no brother who is going to the chapter dare to entrust what he carries to any secular person, but only to a brother safe in one of our houses. And he who does the contrary is to suffer the punishment of a thief and embezzler.

Questions: What was the theological basis for the mission of the order? How did the organization of the order facilitate its mission? How did the order raise money to fund the ransoms? How was the lifestyle of these brothers and sisters different from that of other monks and nuns? How was it different from that of the military orders? What special problems were anticipated?

82. EXPULSION OF THE JEWS FROM SPAIN

Having united much of Spain under their rule, King Ferdinand and Queen Isabella were determined to Christianize their kingdom by converting or expelling non-Christians. The following account of their treatment of the Jews was written in 1495 by a Jew in Italy. (For the capture of Granada mentioned at the beginning, see doc. 83.)

Source: trans. J.R. Marcus, *The Jew in the Medieval World, A Source Book: 315-1791* (Cincinnati: Union of American Hebrew Congregations, 1938), pp. 51-55.

And in the year [1492], in the days of King Ferdinand, the Lord visited the remnant of his people … and exiled them. After the king had captured the city of Granada from the Moors, and it had surrendered to him on the [2nd] of January of the year just mentioned, he ordered the expulsion of all the Jews in all parts of his kingdom—in the kingdoms of Castile, Catalonia, Aragon, Galicia, Majorca, Minorca, the Basque provinces, the islands of Sardinia and Sicily, and the kingdom of Valencia. Even before that the queen [that is, Isabella] had expelled them from the kingdom of Andalusia [in 1483].

The king gave them three months' time in which to leave. It was announced in public in every city on the first of May, which happened to be the 19th day of the *Omer* [that is, the period following the Passover], and the term ended on the day before the 9th of Ab.

About their number there is no agreement, but, after many inquiries, I found that the most generally accepted estimate is 50,000 families, or, as others say, 53,000. They had houses, fields, vineyards, and cattle, and most of them were artisans. At that time there existed many [Talmudic] academies in Spain, and at the head of the greatest of them were Rabbi Isaac Aboab in Guadala-jara, Rabbi Isaac Veçudó in Leon, and Rabbi Jacob Habib in Salamanca. In the last named city there was a great expert in mathematics, and whenever there was any doubt on mathematical questions in the Christian academy of that city they referred them to him. His name was Abraham Zacuto.

In the course of the three months' respite granted them they endeavored to effect an arrangement permitting them to stay on in the country, and they felt confident of success. Their representatives were the rabbi, Don Abraham Seneor, the leader of the Spanish congregations, who was attended by a retinue on thirty mules, and Rabbi Meïr Melamed, who was secretary to the king, and Don Isaac Abravanel, who had fled to Castile from the king of Portugal, and then occupied an equally prominent position at the Spanish royal court. He, too, was later expelled, went to Naples, and was highly esteemed by the king of Naples. The aforementioned great rabbi, Rabbi Isaac of Leon, used to call this Don Abraham Seneor "*Soné Or*" [that is, "Hater of Light," a Hebrew pun on *Seneor*], because he was a heretic, and the end proved that he was right, as he converted to Christianity [rather than leave Spain] at the age of eighty, he and all his family, and Rabbi Meïr Melamed with him. Don Abraham had arranged the nuptials between the king and queen. The queen was the heiress to the throne, and the king one of the Spanish nobility. On account of this, Don Abraham was appointed leader of the Jews, but not with their consent.

The agreement permitting them to remain in the country on the payment of a large sum of money was almost completed when it was frustrated by the interference of a prior who was called the Prior of Santa Cruz [that is, Torque-mada, head of the Inquisition]. Then the queen gave an answer to the representatives of the Jews, similar to the saying of King Solomon [Proverbs 21:1]: "The king's heart is in the hand of the Lord, as the rivers of water. God tur-neth it whithersoever he will." She said furthermore: "Do you believe that this comes upon you from us? The Lord hath put this thing into the heart of the king."

Then they saw that there was evil determined against them by the king, and they gave up the hope of remaining. But the time had become short, and they had to hasten their exodus from Spain. They sold their houses, their landed estates, and their cattle for very small prices, to save themselves. The king did not allow them to carry silver and gold out of his country, so that they were compelled to exchange their silver and gold for merchandise of cloths and skins and other things.

One hundred and twenty thousand of them went to Portugal, according to a compact which a prominent man, Don Vidal bar Benveniste de Cavalleria, had made with the king of Portugal, and they paid one ducat for every soul, and the fourth part of all the merchandise they had carried thither; and he allowed them to stay in his country six months. This king acted much worse toward them than the king of Spain, and after the six months had elapsed he made slaves of all those that remained in his country, and banished seven hundred children to a remote island to settle it, and all of them died. Some say that there were double as many. Upon them the scriptural word was fulfilled [Deut. 28:32]: "Thy sons and thy daughters shall be given unto another people...." He also ordered the [Jewish] congregation of Lisbon, his capital, not to raise their voice in their prayers, that the Lord might not hear their complaining about the violence that was done unto them.

Many of the exiled Spaniards went to [Muslim] countries [in North Africa], to Fez, Tlemçen, and the Berber provinces, under the king of Tunis. On account of their large numbers the Moors did not allow them into their cities, and many of them died in the fields from hunger, thirst, and lack of everything. The lions and bears, which are numerous in this country, killed some of them while they lay starving outside of the cities. A Jew in the kingdom of Tlemçen, named Abraham, the viceroy who ruled the kingdom, made part of them come to this kingdom, and he spent a large amount of money to help them. The Jews of northern Africa were very charitable toward them. A part of those who went to northern Africa, as they found no rest and no place that would receive them, returned to Spain, and became converts [to Christianity], and through them the prophecy of Jeremiah was fulfilled [Lam. 1:13]: "He hath spread a net for my feet; he hath turned me back." For, originally, they had all fled for the sake of the unity of God; only a very few had become converts throughout all the boundaries of Spain; they did not spare their fortunes; yea, parents escaped without having regard to their children.

When the edict of expulsion became known in the other countries, vessels came from Genoa to the Spanish harbors to carry away the Jews. The crews of these vessels, too, acted maliciously and meanly toward the Jews, robbed them, and delivered some of them to the famous pirate of that time who was called the corsair of Genoa. To those who escaped and arrived at Genoa the people of the city showed themselves merciless, and oppressed and robbed them, and the cruelty of their wicked hearts went so far that they took the infants from the mothers' breasts.

Many ships with Jews, especially from Sicily, went to the city of Naples on the coast. The king of this country was friendly to the Jews, received them all, and was merciful towards them, and he helped them with money. The Jews that were at Naples supplied them with food as much as they could, and sent around to the other parts of Italy to collect money to sustain them. The Marranos [that is, Jews who had outwardly converted to Christianity] in this city lent them money on pledges without interest; even the Dominican brother-hood acted mercifully toward them. On account of their very large number, all this was not enough. Some of them died by famine, others sold their children to Christians to sustain their life. Finally, a plague broke out among them, spread to Naples, and very many of them died, so that the living wearied of burying the dead.

Part of the exiled Spaniards went over sea to Turkey. Some of them were thrown into the sea and drowned, but those who arrived there the king of Turkey received kindly, as they were artisans. He lent them money and settled many of them on a island, and gave them fields and estates.

A few of the exiles were dispersed in the countries of Italy, in the city of Ferrar, in the [papal] countries of Romagna, the March, and Patrimonium, and in Rome....

Questions: What was the status of the Jews in Spain before the expulsion? Why were they confident that the expulsion order would be revoked? What were the probable royal motives for expelling the Jews? From whom did the expelled Jews receive the best treatment? Why?

83. ABU ABDILLA MOHAMMED ON THE EXPULSION OF THE MUSLIMS

In his history of the Moors, the seventeenth-century Muslim historian Al-Makkari used the following passage from, or based on, the work of Abu Abdilla Mohammed, a learned near-contemporary historian who described the fall of Granada, the last Muslim state in Spain, to Ferdinand and Isabella in 1492 and the expulsion of the Moors from Spain afterwards.

Source: trans. P. de Gayangos, *The History of the Mohammedan Dynasties in Spain* (London: The Oriental Translation Fund, 1843), vol. II, pp. 386–92; revised.

On [March 22, 1491, Ferdinand] the king of Castile marched his army into the plain of Granada, and began destroying the crops, demolishing the towns and villages, and subduing the whole country. He also laid the foundations of a town with walls and a ditch, the building of which he superintended in person. It had been reported at Granada that the Christians intended to raise the siege of that capital and return to their country, but if they had any such intention they changed their determination, for, instead of raising their tents, they remained encamped in the city which they had built, and pressed the siege with greater vigor than ever. The contest lasted for seven consecutive months, and the Muslims were reduced to great extremities; but still, as the Christians were encamped at some distance from Granada, and the communication between that city and the Alpuxarras was not yet intercepted, the inhabitants received abundant supplies from the district of Sierra Nevada. But when the winter came on, and frost and snow covered the ground, the produce of the earth grew less, its conveyance to Granada became more difficult, and provisions became gradually so scarce that famine began to be felt in that capital. The enemy, too, had purposely taken possession of almost every patch of ground outside of the city, so that it became impossible to gather any crops from the surrounding fields, and the condition of the besieged became every day more distressing and hopeless. This was about [November 1491]. It was evident that the enemy's design was to reduce the city by famine, and not by force of arms. Things being brought to this plight, great numbers of the inhabitants quitted Granada and fled to the Alpuxarras. Provisions grew every day more scarce, and in [December] the privations of the people became almost intolerable. The inhabitants then began to deliberate among themselves as to the expediency of surrendering to the enemy. They therefore sought the advice of their ulema and other learned men, who advised them to look to their own safety, and consult over the matter with the sultan.

Agreeable to this opinion, the sultan convened his officers of state and councilors, when this important affair was discussed in his presence. The people then said, "The Christians are daily receiving reinforcements, while we have none to expect; we all thought and expected that, at the approach of winter, the Christians would have raised the siege and retired to their country, whereas our hopes have completely failed; they have built a town in front of our city, and pressed the siege closer than ever. We ought, therefore, to provide for our safety and that of our children." It was then unanimously agreed to adopt this last determination, and it soon became public that the officers of the army, fearing for their lives and those of the inhabitants, had for some time been treating with the Christians about the surrender of the city. Negotiations then commenced, and a capitulation was drawn up on [standard terms]…, although with some additional articles, such as, for instance, that the pope should be a guarantee for the faithful execution of the treaty and the strict observance of every one of the articles therein contained, before the Christians should be put in possession of the Alhambra and the other forts; and that the [Christian] king should bind himself by oath, after the Christian fashion, to observe the treaty. The deputies sent by the people of Granada insisted upon the insertion of this clause; but it was reported that when they came to discuss the article together, the Christians bribed the Muslim envoys, and gave them considerable sums of money, to have it omitted in the capitulation. The treaty was then read over to the inhabitants, who approved of it and gave it their sanction, some of the principal citizens signing it with their own hands, and pledging their allegiance to the Castilian king, who accepted it. This done, the sultan of Granada left the Alhambra on [Jan. 3, 1492], and the Christian sovereign immediately took possession of it, as well as of the other fortresses in Granada, not without having first received 500 of the principal inhabitants of Granada as hostages, to guard against any treachery on the part of the inhabitants.

The capitulation contained 67 articles, among which were the following: that both great and small should be perfectly secure in their persons, families, and properties. That they should be allowed to continue in their dwellings and residences, whether in the city, the suburbs, or any other part of the country. That their laws should be preserved as they were before, and that no one should judge them except by those same laws. That their mosques, and the religious endowments appertaining to them, should remain as they were in the times of Islam. That no Christian should enter the house of a Muslim or insult him in any way. That no Christian or Jew holding public offices by the appointment of the late sultan should be allowed to exercise his functions or rule over them. That all Muslim captives taken during the siege of Granada, from whatever part of the country they might have come, but especially the nobles and chiefs mentioned in the agreement, should be liberated. That such Muslim captives as might have escaped from their Christian masters, and taken refuge in Granada, should not be surrendered; but that the sultan should be bound to pay the price of such captives to their owners. That all those who might choose to cross over to Africa should be allowed to take their departure within a certain time, and be conveyed thither in the king's ships, and without any pecuniary tax being imposed upon them, beyond the mere charge for passage; and that after the expiration of that time no Muslim should be hindered from departing, provided he paid, in addition to the price of his passage, the tithe of whatever property he might carry along with him. That no one should be prosecuted and punished for the crime of another man. That the Christians who had embraced the Muslim religion should not be compelled to relinquish it and adopt their former creed. That any Muslim wishing to become Christian should be allowed some days to consider the step he is about to take; after which he is to be questioned by both a Muslim and a Christian judge concerning his intended change, and if, after this examination, he still refuse to return to Islam, he should be permitted to follow his own inclination. That no Muslim should be prosecuted for the death of Christian slain during the siege; and that no restitution of property taken during the war should be enforced. That no Muslim should be subject to have Christian soldiers billeted upon him, or be transported to provinces of this kingdom against his will. That no increase should be made to the usual imposts, but that, on the contrary, all oppressive taxes lately imposed should be immediately suppressed.

Fig. 27: The surrender of a Muslim city near Granada in 1486. Ferdinand and Isabella, accepting the surrender, are shown on the right in this sixteenth-century wood carving, as reproduced in a nineteenth-century engraving. From P. Lacroix, *Military and Religious Life in the Middle Ages* (London, Chapman and Hall, 1874).

That no Christian should be allowed to peep over the wall or into the house of a Muslim, or enter a mosque. That any Muslim choosing to travel or reside among the Christians should be perfectly secure in his person and property. That no badge or distinctive mark be put on them, as was done with the Jews and Mudejares [that is, Moors living under Christian rule]. That no muezzin should be interrupted in the act of calling the people to prayer, and no Muslim molested either in the performance of his daily devotions or in the observance of his fast, or in any other religious ceremony; but that if a Christian should be found laughing at them he should be punished for it. That the Muslims should be exempted from all taxation for a certain number of years. That the [pope] should be requested to give his assent to the above conditions, and sign the treaty himself. These, and many others that we omit, were the articles of the treaty.

This matter being settled, and the Christians having taken possession of the Alhambra, and of the city, the king appointed a governor to that fortress, and civil officers and magistrates to govern the inhabitants. On learning the conditions granted to the people of Granada, the inhabitants of the Alpuxarras agreed to the treaty, and made their submission upon the same terms. The king of Castile then ordered the necessary repairs to be made in the Alhambra, as well as in the other fortresses and towers, and applied himself to strengthen its fortifications. Whilst these works were going on, he came daily to the Alhambra, but returned every night to his camp, fearing, no doubt, some treachery on the part of the inhabitants, and he continued to do so until his fears were entirely dissipated. He also entered the city and visited its different quarters, so as to gain exact information of the feeling of the inhabitants towards him, and learn other particulars which he wished to ascertain.

After this the infidel king ordered the sultan of the Muslims to repair to the Alpuxarras, which he said should be his, and to fix his residence at Andarax. In compliance with this order, the [deposed] sultan repaired to that town, and the Christian troops which occupied the Alpuxarras were immediately withdrawn. However, some time after, the king made use of ... stratagems to induce the sultan to leave Andalus [that is, Spain] and cross over to Africa....

Not many years elapsed before the Christians violated the treaty entered into with the Muslims, and began to infringe one by one the settled stipulations. Things even went so far that in [1498] they set about forcing the Muslims to embrace the Christian religion under various pretenses, the most specious of which was that their priests had written [books] on the expediency of compelling such Christians as had become Muslims to embrace their former religion. Notwithstanding the clamor excited among the Muslim community by so revolting an injustice, the people being helpless, the measure was carried into execution. Not satisfied with this breach of the treaty, the Christian tyrants went still farther; they said to a Muslim, "Your ancestor was a Christian, although he made himself a Muslim; you must also become a Christian."

When these proceedings became public, the people of the Albayzin rose up in arms and slew their magistrates; but this was also made an excuse for more rigorous measures, for, soon after, the poor Muslims were told, "The king has promulgated a law by which anyone who revolts against his magistrates is condemned to death, unless he immediately becomes a Christian; so you must either die or be converted to Christianity."

In short, every Muslim, whether residing in Granada or in the neighborhood, was enjoined to embrace the religion of the idolaters within a certain time. A few, however, refused to comply with this order, but it was of no avail to them; seeing which, they had recourse to arms, and rose in several towns and villages, such as Belefique, Andarax, and others. Thither the enemy marched his forces, attacking and pursuing the inhabitants, until they almost exterminated them, killing a great number, and making the rest captives, except such as fortified themselves in Jebal-Balanca, and to whom God almighty was pleased to grant victory over their enemies; for in a battle which took place there they killed a great number of the Christians, and amongst them the lord of Cordova. After this the Muslims obtained terms of capitulation, and were allowed to cross over to Fez [in North Africa] with their families and moveable property, although they were not permitted to take with them more money than that required for the journey.

Such of the Muslims as still remained in Andalus, although Christians in appearance, were not so in their hearts; for they worshipped Allah in secret, and performed their prayers and ablutions at the proper hours. The Christians watched over them with the greatest vigilance, and many were discovered and burnt.

Questions: Why did Ferdinand agree to such generous conditions for the Muslims when they surrendered? What do the terms reveal about relations between Christians and Moors? Why was actual conversion from Islam to Christianity difficult to effect? Why did the Christian authorities force conversions anyway? Compare Ferdinand's treatment of the Moors with his treatment of the Spanish Jews.

CHAPTER NINE:

CRUSADES AT THE CROSSROADS

Fig. 28: In a sixteenth-century woodcut, Louis IX arrives at Carthage in North Africa on his second crusade. From P. Lacroix, *Military and Religious Life in the Middle Ages* (London, Chapman and Hall, 1874).

84. JOINVILLE'S *LIFE OF ST. LOUIS*

King Louis IX of France (1226-1270) took the cross in 1244, the same year that Jerusalem fell once again to Muslim forces. Louis was a devout ruler and a firm believer in the tenets of chivalry and the crusading ideal. His Seventh Crusade was solely a French enterprise and was one of the best organized and financed crusades that had ever been launched. As with some previous crusades, the plan was to strike in Egypt and, like the Fifth Crusade, the first target was Damietta, where the crusaders arrived in June 1249. The fortunes of this crusade and Louis's 1267 expedition to North Africa were chronicled by Jean de Joinville, a knight in the king's service who was present on the Seventh Crusade and wrote a biography of Louis in 1309. Louis was canonized in 1297.

Source: trans. F. Marzials, *Memoirs of the Crusades* (London: J.M. Dent & Sons Ltd., 1908), pp. 172, 174-76, 210-12, 220-21, 224, 239-44; revised.

As soon as we entered into the month of March, by the king's command the king, the barons, and the other pilgrims ordered that the ships should be re-laden with wine and provisions, so as to be ready to move when the king directed. And when the king saw that all had been duly ordered, the king and queen embarked on their ships on the Friday before Pentecost (May 21, 1249), and the king told his barons to follow in their ships straight [from Cyprus] to Egypt. On the Saturday the king set sail and all the others besides, which was a fair thing to look upon, for it seemed as if all the sea, so far as the eye could reach, were covered with the canvas of the ships sails; and the number of the ships, great and small, was reckoned at eighteen hundred....

Then we set ourselves to get to land, and came alongside of the barge belonging to the king's great ship, there where the king himself was. And his people began to cry out to us, because we were going more quickly than they, that I should land by the ensign of St. Denis, which was being borne in anoth-er vessel before the king. But I heeded them not, and caused my people to land in front of a great body of the Turks, at a place where there were full six thousand men on horseback.

As soon as these saw us land, they came toward us, hotly spurring. We, when we saw them coming, fixed the points of our shields into the sand and the handles of our lances in the sand with the points set towards them. But when they were so near that they saw the lances about to enter into their bel-lies, they turned about and fled....

The Saracens sent thrice to the sultan, by carrier-pigeons, to say that the king had landed, but never received any message in return, because the sultan's sickness was upon him. Wherefore they thought that the sultan was dead, and abandoned Damietta. The king sent a knight forward to know if it was true that Damietta was so abandoned. The knight returned to the king and said it was true and that he had been into the houses of the sultan. Then the king sent for the legate and all the prelates of the host, and all chanted with a loud voice *Te Deum laudamus*. Afterwards the king mounted his horse, and we all likewise, and we went and encamped before Damietta.

Very unadvisedly did the Turks leave Damietta, in that they did not cut the bridge of boats, for that would have been a great hindrance to us; but they wrought us very much hurt in setting fire to the bazaar, where all the merchandise is collected, and everything that is sold by weight. The damage that followed from this was as great as if—which God forbid!—someone were, to-morrow, to set fire to the Petit-Pont in Paris....

[After much fighting around the Nile, an epidemic broke out in the crusaders' camp.]

After these things the king's councilors and the councilors of the sultan appointed a set day on which to come to an agreement. The proposed conditions were these: that we should surrender Damietta to the sultan, and the sultan surrender to the king the kingdom of Jerusalem; and that the sultan should take charge of the sick that were at Damietta, and also of the salted meats—because they did not eat pork—and of the king's engines of war, until such time as the king was able to send and fetch all these things.

They asked the king's councilors what security would be given that the sultan should repossess Damietta. The king's councilors offered to deliver over one of the king's brothers, either the count of Anjou or the count of Poitiers, to be kept until such time as Damietta was placed in the sultan's hands. The Saracens said they would consent to nothing unless the person of the king were left with them as a pledge; whereupon my lord Geoffrey of Sargines, the good knight, said he would rather that the Saracens should have them all dead or captive than bear the reproach of having left the king in pledge.

The sickness began to increase in the host, and the dead flesh so to grow upon the gums of our people, so badly that the barber surgeons had to remove the dead flesh in order that the people might chew their food and swallow it. Great pity it was to hear the cry throughout the camp of the people whose dead flesh was being cut away; for they cried like women laboring in childbirth....

When the king saw that he and his people could only remain there to die, he ordered and arranged that they should strike their camp, late on Tuesday [that is, April 5, 1250], at night, after the octave of Easter, to return to Damietta. He caused the mariners who had galleys to be told that they should get together the sick, and take them thither....

Now I will tell you how the king was captured, as he himself related it to me. He told me how he had left his own division and placed himself ... [in] the rearguard.

And the king related to me that he was mounted on a little courser covered with a housing of silk; and he told me that of all his knights and sergeants there only remained behind with him my lord Geoffrey of Sargines, who brought the king to a little village, there where the king was taken [captive]; and as the king related to me, my lord Geoffrey of Sargines defended him from the Saracens as a good servitor defends his lord's drinking-cup from flies; for every time that the Saracens approached, he took his spear, which he had placed between himself and the bow of his saddle, and put it to his shoulder, and ran upon them, and drove them away from the king.

And thus he brought the king to the little village; and they lifted him into a house, and laid him, almost as one dead, in the lap of a burgher-woman of Paris, and thought he would not last till night. Thither came my lord Philip of Montfort, and said to the king that he saw the emir with whom he had treated of the truce, and, if the king so willed, he would go to him and renew the negotiation for a truce in the manner that the Saracens desired. The king begged him to go, and said he was right willing. So my lord Philip went to the Saracen; and the Saracen had taken off his turban from his head, and took off the ring from his finger in token that he would faithfully observe the truce....

Then the sultan caused the chief men [among the captives] to be put into four galleys and taken towards Damietta.... We arrived on the Thursday before Ascension Day [that is, April 28, 1250], at the place where this encampment was set up. The four galleys in which we were all together as prisoners, anchored before the sultan's encampment. The king was taken to a pavilion that stood nearby. Matters had been so ordered by the sultan that on the Saturday before Ascension Day Damietta was to be surrendered to him, and he was to release the king....

[The crusade leaders] agreed with the emirs that, as soon as Damietta was delivered over to them, they would set free the king and the other men of rank who were there. As to the lesser folk, the sultan had caused them to be led away towards Babylon [that is, Cairo], such at least as he had not caused to be put to death. And this thing he had done contrary to the covenant made with the king, whereby it seems likely that he would have put us to death also, as soon as he had come into possession of Damietta.

And the king was to swear to further gratify the Saracens with £200,000 before he left the river, and with £200,000 in Acre. The Saracens, by the covenant they made with the king, were to take charge of the sick in Damietta, and of the crossbows, the arms, the salted meats and the engines of war, until such time as the king sent for them.... [After paying the ransom and being freed, Louis traveled to Acre.]

At the time when we were at Acre, the king sent, one Sunday, for his brother the count of Flanders and the other men of note, and spoke to them thus: "Lords, my lady the queen, my mother, has sent to me, and beseeches me, as urgently as she can, to return to France, because my kingdom is in great peril, seeing that I have neither peace nor truce with the king of England. Those belonging to this land, with whom I have spoken, tell me that, if I depart, this land is all but lost; for all those who are in Acre will follow after me, none daring to remain when the people are so few. So I pray you," said he, "to think well upon this matter; and because it is of great import, I will give you time, and you shall answer me, according as you think right, eight days from today."...

On the Sunday after, we came again before the king; and the king asked his brothers, and the other barons, and the count of Flanders, what advice they wished to give the king. They all replied that they had charged my lord Guy to state this advice accordingly, and he spoke as follows: "Sire, your brothers, and the men of note here present have looked to your estate, and seen that you cannot remain in this land to your own honor, and that of your realm, for of all the knights that came in your company — of whom you led 2,800 into Cyprus — there are not now, in this city, one hundred remaining. So they advise you, sire, that you go to France, and there procure men and money, whereby you may hastily return to this land, and take vengeance upon the enemies of God, who held you in captivity."...

The legate asked Count John of Jaffa, who was behind them, what he thought.... And the count said that if the king could but hold the field for a year, he would do himself great honor by remaining. Then the legate inquired of those who were sitting by the count of Jaffa, and all agreed with my lord Guy Mauvoisin.... [The legate] asked me what I thought, and I replied that I agreed with the count of Jaffa.... Then the king said, "Lords, I have heard you duly, and I will give you my answer as to what it pleases me to do, eight days from today."...

When the tables were set, the king made me sit beside him during the meal, where he was always used to make me sit if his brothers were not present. Never a word did he say to me as long as the meal lasted, which was not according to his custom, for he always took note of me when we were eating. And indeed I thought he was angry with me because I had said he had not yet spent any of his money [on the crusade], and should spend freely.

While the king was hearing grace, I went to a barred window that was in an alcove towards the head of the king's bed, and I passed my arms through the bars of the window, and thought that if the king went back to France, I should go to the prince of Antioch, who held me for his kinsman, and had asked me to come to him and there remain, until such time as another expedition came out to the land overseas, whereby the captives might be delivered....

And while I was there, the king came and leaned upon my shoulders, and placed his two hands upon my head; and I thought it was my lord Philip of

Nemours, who had already tormented me too much that day because of the advice I had given, and I spoke thus: "Leave me in peace, my lord Philip!" By chance, as I was turning my head, the king's hand fell upon my face, and I knew it was the king because of an emerald that he had on his finger. And he said: "Keep quite quiet, for I want to ask how you came to be so bold, you who are but a young man, as to advise me to remain here, against the advice of all the great men and wise of France, who counseled me to depart?"

"Sire," said I, "even if I had so ill a thought in my heart, I should by no means so counsel you."

"Do you mean to say," he replied, "that I should be doing wrong if I deserted?"

"So God help me, sire, yes," said I. And he said to me, "If I remain, will you remain also?" And I told him yes, "if I can, either at my own charges or the charges of another."...

The following Sunday we all came back again before the king; and ... the words which the king spoke were these: "Lords, I greatly thank those who have advised me to return to France, and I thank also those who have advised me to remain here. But I bethink me that if I remain there will be no danger of loss to my realm, for my lady the queen [mother] has people enough to defend it; and I consider also that the barons of this land tell me that if I depart hence, the kingdom of Jerusalem is lost, for none will dare to remain after I have left. I have therefore decided that I will by no means abandon the kingdom of Jerusalem, which I came hither to guard and reconquer. So my conclusion is that for the present I remain here. And I say to you all, you men of note that are here, as also to such other knights as may wish to remain with me, that you come and speak to me boldly, and I will give you so much that the fault will not be mine, but yours, if you be not willing to remain." Many that heard these words were filled with amazement, and many there were that wept.... [Louis remained in the Holy Land, trying to strengthen the crusader states, from May 1250 until April 1254.]

Questions: Compare Louis IX's campaign with the Fifth Crusade. What accounts for the failure of Louis's crusade? What was Louis's attitude toward the Holy Land? Why does Joinville present Louis in such a favorable light in spite of his defeat?

85. MATTHEW PARIS ON THE SHEPHERDS' CRUSADE

After the failure of Louis IX's crusade and while the king was still a prisoner in Egypt, there arose in northern France a popular crusading movement known as the Shepherds' Crusade. The movement was led by a rabble-rouser who preached under the title of the Master of Hungary. He spoke of the arrogance of the noble class and how, as it was humble shepherds who were first to learn of the birth of Christ, so it would be they who would restore the Holy Land to the Christians. The following account of this movement is found in the writings of Matthew Paris, an English monk who heard about the Shepherds' Crusade from Thomas of Sherborne, a fellow monk who had been held prisoner by these "crusaders."

Source: trans. J.A. Giles, *Matthew Paris's English History* (London: Henry G. Bohn, 1853), Vol. II, pp. 451-58; revised.

About this time, the enemy of the human race, conceiving confident hopes that the Jordan would flow into his mouth, as he had already drunk from it by means of the sultan of Babylon, and seeing that even in sweet France the Christian faith was tottering and ready to fall, employed himself in originating a new kind of false doctrine. A certain person, a Hungarian by birth, who was now sixty years old, and had since his early years been an apostate from the Christian religion, who had copiously imbibed the falsehoods and cunning emanating from the sulfurous pit, and was become a servant and disciple of Mohammed, had faithfully promised the sultan of Babylon, whose servant he was, that he would present an immense number of Christians to him as prisoners, so that, France being thus destitute of people and deprived of its king [who was in the Holy Land], the means of entering the country of the Christians would be easier for the Saracens. This said impostor, then, who knew the French, German, and Latin tongues, without any authority from the pope or the patronage of any prelate, wandered hither and thither, preaching, and lyingly asserting that he had received orders from St. Mary, the mother of our Lord, to assemble the shepherds and keepers of other animals, to whom, as he stated, was granted by heaven the power, in their humility and simplicity, to rescue the Holy Land, together with all the prisoners, from the hands of the infidels; for, as he said, the pride of the French soldiery was displeasing to God. His eloquence confirmed his words, as also did the clasping of his inseparable hands, in which he lyingly stated that he held a paper containing the order of the blessed Virgin. He summoned all shepherds to join him, and they, abandoning their flocks, herds, and horses, and without consulting their lords or their relations, followed him on foot, caring naught about food; for this man practiced that chief of devices which was formerly adopted by a beardless youth in France, who about forty years back had infatuated the French people, and convoked an enormous host of boys, who followed his footsteps, singing; and, what was a marvel, could not be restrained by bolts or bars, nor recalled by commands, entreaties, or presents of their fathers and mothers....

The aforesaid lying impostor, as well as all who followed him, bore the sign of the cross; and there were many who showed them favor and gave them assistance, saying, "God frequently chooses the weak portions of the world to confound the stronger ones; neither is the Almighty well pleased with a man's legs, nor are those acceptable to him who presume on their skill and bravery in war." The lady Blanche, too, the queen [mother] and regent of the French, in hopes that they would obtain possession of the Holy Land, and avenge her sons, granted them her favor and showed them kindness. They therefore multiplied to such a degree that they were reckoned to amount to 100,000 and more; and they made standards for themselves to fight under, and on that of their leader was painted the figure of a lamb — this being in token of their humility and innocence, and the standard bearing the cross as a token of victory....The departure of the pope [Innocent IV] and his absence inspired these shepherds, who multiplied in France, with confidence and boldness, and they increased in number and strength.

There now flocked to join their band thieves, exiles, fugitives, and excommunicated persons, ... so that they collected a most numerous army, and had 500 standards similar to that of their master and chief. They carried swords, axes, darts, daggers, and long knives, so that they seemed to cherish the thoughts of war more than of Christ. Madly raving, they contracted unlawful marriages, and their leaders and instructors, who, although laymen, presumed to preach, enormously strayed in their preachings from the articles of the Christian faith and the evident rules of truth; and if anyone contradicted or opposed them, they attacked him with arms, and not by reasoning or force of argument. When their chief leader preached, he was surrounded by armed followers, and condemned all orders excepting their own conventicles, but especially those of the Preachers and Minorites [that is, the Dominicans and Franciscans], whom he called vagrants and hypocrites. The monks of the Cistercian order he declared to be most avaricious lovers of flocks and lands; the Benedictine monks, he affirmed, were gluttonous and proud; the canons, he said, were half-seculars and flesh-devourers; and the bishops and their officials were only money-hunters, and affluent in all kinds of enjoyments. Of the papal court he made many unmentionable statements, so that from his statements they appeared to be heretics and schismatics. The people, out of hatred and contempt of the clergy, applauded these ravings of his and listened favorably to his dangerous doctrines.

On St. Barnabas's Day, these shepherds reached Orléans in great pomp and strength, and against the wishes of the bishop and all the clergy — although the citizens were well pleased with their arrival — they entered the city, and their chief, like a prophet powerful in miracles, by the voice of a herald gave notice, or rather issued an edict like a king, of his intention to preach; whereupon the people flocked to him in endless numbers. The bishop of the city, in great fear at this ruinous peril, forbade any clerk, under penalty of anathema, to listen to their discourses, or to follow in their steps, declaring that all these proceedings were the snares of the devil; for the laymen already despised his threats and commands. Some of the clerical scholars, however, transgressing the bishop's prohibition, could not refrain from lending a longing ear to such extraordinary new doctrines, not planning to follow their errors, but only to witness their insolence. Strange, indeed, it was, and absurd, that a layman, and indeed a plebeian, despising the authority of the pope, should so boldly preach in public in a city where the scholastic community was in its vigor, and should incline the hearts of so many people to his impostures. They carried with them the 500 standards, at which the clerks of sounder understanding firmly bolted and barred their doors, and concealed themselves in perturbation and fear in their houses. Their said master then rose to preach to the people, and, without prefacing his discourse by a text, began to burst forth in loud tones with much unmentionable abuse, when suddenly one of the scholars, who was standing at a distance, boldly forced his way near, and broke forth in the following speech: "Base heretic and enemy to the truth, you lie on your own head; you are deceiving these innocent people by your false and deceitful arguments."

Scarcely, however, had he uttered these words, when one of those vagrants rushed upon him, and raising a beaked axe, clove his head in two parts, so that the wounded man did not speak a word more. A tumult then arose, and the people whom we have called pastors [that is, in Latin, shepherds], but who now deserve the name of impostors and forerunners of Antichrist, armed themselves against the clergy of Orléans in general, and rushed on the unarmed citizens, carried off their beloved children, and broke all the doors and windows of the houses, and set the houses themselves on fire, January 13th. With the connivance or, more properly speaking, the consent of the people of the city (who therefrom deservedly obtained the appellation of a set of hounds), they cut to pieces many of the citizens and drowned many in the Loire, and those who escaped from death were wounded and robbed of their property. Those who had remained concealed in their houses, on seeing these proceedings, fled in crowds from the city by night; the whole community was thrown into confusion, and it was afterwards discovered that about 25 clerks had perished, besides the numbers who were wounded and injured in diverse ways. The bishop and his followers also, who had hidden themselves to avoid being involved in a similar calamity, underwent many insults, and suffered much injury. After this the shepherds took their departure, fearing lest the citizens should rise against and attack them; and the bishop, that he might not appear like a dog unable to bark, laid the city under an interdict, because the inhabitants of it had rendered themselves culpable and infamous by permitting such proceedings, and even consenting to and cooperating in them. The cry of complaint at length reached the ears of the lady Blanche and the nobles and prelates. On hearing it that queen modestly replied, "As the Lord knows, I believed that they in their simplicity and sanctity would gain the Holy Land; but since they are deceivers, let them be excommunicated, seized, and destroyed."

All these villains were therefore excommunicated, and denounced as such; but before the sentence was made public, they went with treacherous designs to Bourges, the gates of which city were thrown open to them by the consent of the citizens, who would not listen to the prohibition of their archbishop; and the greater part of them entered the city, the remainder staying in the vineyards outside the city, for they were so numerous that no city could conveniently receive them all, and their hosts were divided throughout several cities, and even Paris suffered perceptible injury from them. The chief of these deluded men having announced his intention of preaching a sermon in public, and having promised to work some astounding miracles, an immense multitude of people flocked together from all quarters to hear things hitherto unheard of, and to see things which they had never before seen. When this deceiver gave utterance to some raving speeches, and the miracles he had promised were found to be mere trickery, one of the people, a butcher, bearing an axe, struck him on the head, and sent him brainless to hell. His body was thrown on a crossway and left to rot unburied; and as the reports spread abroad that these shepherds and their abettors, and all who listened to them, were excommunicated, they dispersed, and were dispatched like mad dogs. At Bordeaux, also, when some of their assemblages approached that city, the gates were locked by order of Simon [de Montfort], earl of Leicester, and they were not allowed to enter; and on their demanding admission, the earl, in reply, asked them, "By whose authority do you act thus?" To which they answered, "We do not plead the authority of pope or bishop, but that of the omnipotent God, and the blessed Mary, his mother, which is greater than theirs." When the earl heard this reply, considering such a speech as frivolous, he sent back the following message: "Depart, all of you, as speedily as possible, or I will assemble all my troops, as well as the ... inhabitants of this city, and will attack you and cut you to pieces."

These deluded wretches were astounded at hearing these words, and becoming like sand without lime, dispersed in all directions; and as each of them sought his own safety by flight, they were exposed to peril in many shapes.... [Their leaders were captured and executed.]

Then, indeed, many of their followers found that they had been led astray, and discovering their wretched state, accepted the penance enjoined on them, and laid aside the crosses they had received from the hands of these deceivers, and reassuming the sign of the cross from the hands of good men, duly proceeded on their pilgrimage; and setting out for the Holy Land, entered the service of the French king after his release from the power of the Saracens, ... for they said that they had learned from their master that they would liberate the king of the French, wherefore they had all vied with one another in assuming the sign of the cross....

Men of influence and discernment, and prelates of deep reasoning, said that never since the times of Mohammed had such a fearful pestilence crept into the church of Christ, especially as, owing to the misfortune which had happened to the French king, the faith began to totter in the kingdom of France.

Questions: What is the attitude of the writer towards the Shepherds' Crusade? What accounts for this point of view? Compare this popular movement to the Peasants' and Children's Crusade. Who decided the final fate of the Shepherds' Crusade?

86. IBN AL-ATHIR ON THE MONGOL INVASION

The course of thirteenth-century crusades took a very different and unforeseen turn with the arrival in the Middle East of the Mongols. The Mongols (or "Tartars"—many medieval writers used the two terms interchangeably) were an Asiatic tribal people who through brutal conquest had created an empire that spanned from China to the edges of the Islamic world. Under their leader Genghis Khan (d. 1227), the Mongols swept into northern Persia in 1218. The Persian campaign, which raged on until 1224, brought the horrors of Mongol warfare to the Muslim inhabitants, and, for a time, diverted their attention from the crusader states. The Muslim historian Ibn al-Athir (1160-1233) describes below the ferocity of these early Mongol attacks.

Source: trans. E.G. Browne, *A Literary History of Persia* (Cambridge: Cambridge University Press, 1902), Vol. II, pp. 427-31; revised.

For some years I continued averse from mentioning this event, deeming it so horrible that I shrank from recording it, and ever withdrawing one foot as I advanced the other. To whom, indeed, can it be easy to write the announcement of the deathblow of Islam and the Muslims, or who is he on whom the remembrance thereof can weigh lightly? O would that my mother had not borne me or that I had died and become a forgotten thing ere this befell! Yet [nevertheless] a number of my friends urged me to set it down in writing, and I hesitated long; but at last came to the conclusion that to omit this matter [from my history] could serve no useful purpose.

I say, therefore, that this thing involves the description of the greatest catastrophe and the most dire calamity … which befell all men generally, and the
Muslims in particular; so that, should one say that the world, since God
almighty created Adam until now, hath not been afflicted with the like thereof, he would but speak the truth. For indeed history doth not contain aught
which approaches or comes nigh unto it. For [one] of the most grievous
calamities recorded was what Nebuchadnezzar inflicted on the children of
Israel by his slaughter of them and his destruction of Jerusalem; and what was
Jerusalem in comparison to the countries which these accursed miscreants
destroyed, each city of which was double the size of Jerusalem? Or what were
the children of Israel compared to those whom these slew? For verily those
whom they massacred in a single city exceeded all the children of Israel. Nay,
it is unlikely that mankind will see the like of this calamity, until the world
comes to an end and perishes…. For … these [Tartars] spared none, slaying
women and men and children, ripping open pregnant women and killing
unborn babes. Verily to God do we belong, and unto him do we return, and
there is no strength and no power save in God, the high, the almighty, in [the]
face of this catastrophe, whereof the sparks flew far and wide, and the hurt was
universal; and which passed over the lands like clouds driven by the wind. For
these were a people who emerged from the confines of China, and attacked
the cities of Turkestan, like Kashghar and Balasaghun, and thence advanced on
the cities of Transoxiana, such as Samarkand, Bukhara and the like, taking possession of them, and treating their inhabitants in such wise as we shall mention; and of them one division then passed on into Khurasan, until they had
made an end of taking possession, and destroying, and slaying, and plundering,
and thence passing on to Ray, Hamadan and the highlands, and the cities contained therein, even to the limits of Iraq, whence they marched on the towns
of Adharbayjan and Arraniyya, destroying them and slaying most of their
inhabitants, of whom none escaped save a small remnant; and all this in less
than a year; this is a thing whereof the like has not been heard. And when they
had finished with Adharbayjan and Arraniyya, they passed on to Darband-i-
Shirwan, and occupied its cities, none of which escaped save the fortress
wherein was their king; wherefore they passed by it to the countries of the Lan
and the Lakiz and the various nationalities which dwell in that region, and
plundered, slew, and destroyed them to the full. And thence they made their
way to the lands of Qipchaq, who are the most numerous of the Turks, and
slew all such as withstood them, while the survivors fled to the fords and
mountaintops, and abandoned their country, which these Tartars overran. All
this they did in the briefest space of time, remaining only for so long as their
march required and no more.

Another division, distinct from that mentioned above, marched on Ghazna
and its dependencies, and those parts of India, Sistan and Kirman which border

thereon, and wrought therein deeds like unto the other, nay, yet more grievous. Now this is a thing the like of which ear hath not heard; for Alexander
[the Great], concerning whom historians agree that he conquered the world,
did not do so with such swiftness, but only in the space of about ten years; neither did he slay, but was satisfied that men should be subject to him. But these
Tartars conquered most of the habitable globe, and the best, the most flourish-
ing and most populous part thereof, and that whereof the inhabitants were the
most advanced in character and conduct, in about a year; nor did any country
escape their devastations which did not fearfully expect them and dread their
arrival.

Moreover they need no commissariat, nor the conveyance of supplies, for
they have with them sheep, cows, horses, and the like quadrupeds, the flesh of
which they eat, [needing] naught else. As for their beasts which they ride,
these dig into the earth with their hoofs and eat the roots of plants, knowing
naught of barley. And so, when they alight anywhere, they have need of nothing from without. As for their religion, they worship the sun when it rises, and
regard nothing as unlawful, for they eat all beasts, even dogs, pigs, and the like;
nor do they recognize the marriage tie, for several men are in marital relations
with one woman, and if a child is born, it knows not who is its father.

Therefore Islam and the Muslims have been afflicted during this period
with calamities wherewith no people hath been visited. These Tartars (may
God confound them!) came from the East, and wrought deeds which horrify
all who hear of them.... And [one] of these [calamities] was the invasion of
Syria by the Franks (may God curse them!) out of the West, and their attack
on Egypt, and occupation of the port of Damietta therein, so that Egypt and
Syria were [about] to be conquered by them, but for the grace of God and the
help which he vouchsafed us against them.... [Another] of these calamities,
moreover, was that the sword was drawn between those [Muslims] who
escaped from these two foes, and strife was rampant [amongst them].... We ask
God to vouchsafe victory to Islam and the Muslims, for there is none other to
aid, help, or defend the true faith. But if God intends evil to any people,
naught can avert it, nor have they any ruler save him. As for these Tartars, their
achievements were only rendered possible by the absence of any effective
obstacle; and the cause of this absence was that Mohammed Khwarazmshah
had overrun the [Muslim] lands, slaying and destroying their kings, so that he
remained alone ruling over all these countries; wherefore, when he was defeated by the Tartars, none was left in the lands to check those or protect these,
that so God might accomplish a thing which was to be done.

It is now time for us to describe how they first burst forth into the [Mus-
lim] lands.... Stories have been related to me, which the hearer can scarcely
credit, as to the terror of [the Mongols] which God almighty cast into men's
hearts; so that it is said that a single one of them would enter a village or a

quarter wherein were many people, and would continue to slay them one after another, none daring to stretch forth his hand against this horseman. And I have heard that one of them took a man captive, but had not with him any weapon wherewith to kill him; and he said to his prisoner, "Lay your head on the ground and do not move," and he did so, and the Tartar went and fetched his sword and slew him therewith. Another man related to me as follows: "I was going," said he, "with seventeen others along a road, and there met us a Tartar horseman, and bade us bind one another's arms. My companions began to do as he bade them, but I said to them, 'He is but one man; wherefore, then, should we not kill him and flee?' They replied, 'We are afraid.' I said, 'This man intends to kill you immediately; let us therefore rather kill him, that perhaps God may deliver us.' But I swear by God that not one of them dared to do this, so I took a knife and slew him, and we fled and escaped." And such occurrences were many.

Questions: According to Ibn Al-Athir, how did the Mongols go about establishing their empire? What do we learn from him of the Mongols' lifestyle and military tactics? How does he see the Mongols in the context of Middle Eastern history?

87. IBN 'ABD AL-ZAHIR'S BIOGRAPHY OF BAYBARS

While Europe struggled with the failure of Louis IX's crusade, Muslim leaders in the Holy Land were preoccupied with the Mongol threat. This was the prime concern of the sultan known as Baybars (1260-77), one of the greatest heroes of medieval Islam. Born in southern Russia, he was brought to the Middle East as a slave and eventually entered the caste of mamluks, warrior slaves who could rise to any height in the Egyptian government. In the first episode below, which takes place in 1260, another mamluk named al-Malik al-Muzaffar is sultan in Egypt, and Baybars is a high-ranking official of his. Ibn 'Abd al-Zahir, the author of the biography from which these excerpts are taken, was Baybars's confidential secretary.

Source: trans. S.F. Sadeque, *Baybars I of Egypt* (Karachi: Oxford University Press, 1956), pp. 92-94, 96, 117-18, 167-69, 171.

The March against the Mongols (May God defeat them)

When the Syrian army arrived in Egypt, God inspired the heart of [the Mamluk sultan] al-Malik al-Muzaffar to take the field. He began to meet and talk to [Baybars] about it, and the latter gave him advice as to how he should look after the interests of Islam. He then set out with the armies [in 1260]....

[Baybars] entered 'Akka [that is, Acre] in disguise to reconnoiter. I had entered it beforehand ... and heard some of the Franks say: "O Muslim, we wish we had such a person," meaning [Baybars]. When the army was two days' journey out from 'Akka, [Baybars,] with a group of emirs, rode on through the rest of the day and night. [He] then ascended the hill overlooking Ain Jalut. He and those with him stayed on horseback throughout the night, while the Mongols encamped near them. Al-Malik al-Muzaffar and the army marched on ignorant of the nearness of the enemy, till the messengers of [Baybars] arrived and warned them, informing them of the proximity of the enemy; and they also drew their attention to the weakness of the enemy and disparaged the latter, encouraging them to take advantage of the opportunity; and this was one of the causes of the victory....

When the armies reached [Baybars,] he stood before the enemy and bore the first shock of their onslaught. The enemy saw his bravery, the like of which was never heard of before. The Muslims saw that he stood firm among them, and so they ventured against the enemy and drove onward ... and so God had ordained the victory, which was due to [Baybars]. When the enemy, having been put to flight, climbed up the mountain, [Baybars] followed on foot and stood facing the enemy all day long till nightfall. People everywhere heard about his stand on the mountain, and they climbed up to him from every direction, while he was fighting like one who staked his very life. The footsoldiers began to climb up and collect the heads of those whom he killed and who were killed in front of him, and they carried the heads of such persons as Kitbugha Nowin and others to al-Malik al-Muzaffar. Before the day passed, a great number of heads had been gathered before al-Malik al-Muzaffar. When [Baybars] came down he did not heed the fatigue which he had suffered, but rode on and pressed after the enemy, his men following him. He did not cease to ride night and day, without rest, killing or taking captive those who were unwounded, while the enemy was put to flight before him. He did not draw reign until he reached Harim. When he reached Afamiyah the enemy rallied again; and he again inflicted a smashing defeat on them at Afamiyah on Friday, and their wealth, women, children, and horses were plundered....

Al-Malik al-Muzaffar (mercy on him) went [on] with all his army, and they found that our master [Baybars] (may God grant him victory) had put the affairs of the territories in order for them and resettled the rest of the subjects there, and encouraged his men to advance. Al-Malik al-Muzaffar reached Damascus without fatigue or hardship....

The Journey of [Baybars] to Egypt and the Death of al-Malik al-Muzaffar

When al-Malik al-Muzaffar set out accompanied by [Baybars], he became haughty and his attitude changed. [Baybars] noticed this. He wanted to do something in the holy war which would be praised by God and the people, but al-Malik al-Muzaffar prevented him lest [Baybars] should take all the glory for himself, excluding him. On Saturday, the 17th Dhu'l Qa'da [that is, Oct. 26] of the year [1260], [Baybars] went out with al-Malik al-Muzaffar to hunt, while he was near Qusair. [Baybars] had promised that only a few men should come with him, and he rode by [al-Malik al-Muzaffar's] side, talked with him and seized his hand and sword; then, holding him at arm's length, he struck him with his sword, and thus occurred his death as ordained by God. [Baybars] did this himself and attained his object alone, and this was amidst great armies and strong guards; no one was able to speak and none ventured to extend his hand against him.... [After this Baybars was acknowledged as sultan in Egypt.]

Reconstruction of the Forts

When the Mongols (may God defeat them) occupied Syria, they began to destroy the forts and walls. The demolished the walls of the fort of Damascus, and the forts of Salt, 'Ajlun, Sarkhad, Busra, Ba'albek, Subaibah, Shaizar, and Shumaimis. When the sultan [Baybars] took charge of affairs and God established him as the support of the faith, he took an interest in the reconstruction of these forts and the completion of the destroyed buildings, because these were the strongholds of Islam. All these were repaired during his time; their fosses [that is, ditches] were cleared out, the flanks of their walls were broadened, equipment was transported to them, and he sent mamluks and soldiers to them....

The Reasons Why It Was Necessary to Turn against the Franks and to Seize Their Territories

We have told at the beginning of this biography of the peace talks with the Franks. When they saw the kindness of the sultan [Baybars], they began to depart from their work and demand Zar'in; but the sultan replied, "In the reign of al-Malik al-Nasir, you received in exchange for this place ten villages in the district of Marj-'Uyun, and you exchanged that with the ruler of Tibnin." Letters continued to arrive from [the Franks] saying, "Thieves have robbed us, sometimes from the direction of Atrun and sometimes from Banyas," and the sultan gave orders that their wrongs should be redressed. At the same time letters were received from [the sultan's] deputies, who complained of the Franks and said that they were indulging in activities tantamount to a breach of the truce. When the sultan had already reached the middle of their territories, a messenger arrived from them to congratulate him on his safe arrival, through whom the Franks said, "We did not know of the arrival of the sultan." His reply was, "Whoever intends to lead in any matter should keep on the alert, and who is the person that could be unaware of the setting out of these armies, and did not know what was known even to the animals of the desert and the fish in the waters, regarding the huge numbers of soldiers, so that in your houses there remains perhaps not one place in which cannot be swept up the dust raised by the horses of this army; and perhaps the noise of their tread has already deafened the ears of the Franks who live overseas, and the Mongols who dwell in Mughan? If all these troops have reached the door of your houses, without your knowing it, then what do you know?" At this juncture the messengers departed.

... When this was going on the sultan ordered his soldiers not to dismount in the fields of the Franks, and not to let loose any horse or spoil any green leaf, or to seize any of their beasts and peasants. He treated them very kindly, waiting for their conversion from error. Before the approach of the sultan, their letters had expressed their intention of breaking the treaty and regret at having concluded it, but at the approach of the sultan, letters arrived from them stating that they would maintain the peace and keep to the clauses of the treaties.

... [Baybars] summoned the ambassadors of the Franks of the various groups and asked them: "What are your intentions?" They replied: "We shall maintain the truce which has been concluded between us." The sultan replied: "Why then did you not think in this way before our arrival at this place, before we had spent riches which, if they had flowed, would form seas? And yet we have not harmed your harvests, nor any other thing, but you prevented our army from receiving food and provisions...." [He recited a long list of the Franks' misdeeds, concluding:] "Now the kingdom of Syria and other places belong to me, and I do not need your help, nor your succor. Therefore you are to restore the Islamic countries you have taken in this way and set all Muslim prisoners at liberty, for I shall not accept any other conditions." When the infidels heard these words, they were discomfited and said, "We shall not break the truce, and we implore the mercy of the sultan to keep the friendly relation stipulated in the treaty and to maintain it; and we shall desist from occasioning complaints by your governors, and set the prisoners free." The sultan answered: "You should have done these things before we left Egypt in this winter and rainy season, and before our armies had arrived here." At this they departed.

The sultan gave orders that they should not spend the night in the camp. He gave orders that the church of Nazareth should be demolished, this being the most important place of worship for them; it is said that the religion of the Christians had its origin there. He sent there the emir 'Izz al-din Amir-Jandar who razed it to the ground. None of the Franks dared to come out of the gates of 'Akka and they did not utter a single word. Then he dispatched the emir Badr al-din Aidumuri with a body of troops, and they went towards 'Akka and carried out raids as far as its gates. The said emir went again, fell upon the flocks and confiscated a great number of these, and brought them to the Muslims' camp.

Questions: What impression of Baybars's abilities and character does this text give? Why was he such a successful leader? What was the state of relations between the Franks and the Muslims at this time? What does the final episode suggest for the future of those relations?

88. LUDOLPH VON SUCHEM ON THE FALL OF ACRE AND ITS AFTERMATH

The work that Baybars began, with his incremental reduction of the remaining Frankish territories, was brought to completion in 1291, when Acre, the last important mainland city in Frankish hands, fell to Muslim forces in May. Mopping-up operations continued during the summer, as the last Templar castles were taken one by one. The fall of Acre marked the end of an era. Although the idea and even the practice of crusading lived on after this, there was no more Christian-Muslim fighting in Palestine and Syria. The island of Cyprus became the headquarters of the Frankish claimants to the throne of Jerusalem. Rhodes, captured soon afterwards by the Hospitallers, became the center of operations for that military order. Ludolph von Suchem, a German priest, visited the islands during a trip to the Holy Land in 1336-41 and wrote, about ten years later, the work from which the following account is excerpted.

Source: trans. A. Stewart, *Ludolph von Suchem's Description of the Holy Land* (London: Palestine Pilgrims' Text Society, 1895), pp. 34-38, 41-44, 54-60; revised.

After having told of the glories and beauties of Acre, I will now briefly tell you of its fall and ruin, and the cause of its loss, even as I heard the tale told by right truthful men, who well remembered it. While, then, the grand doings of which I have spoken were going on in Acre, at the instigation of the devil there arose a violent and hateful quarrel in Lombardy between the Guelphs and the Ghibellines [that is, between two factions in Italian politics], which brought all evil upon the Christians. Those Lombards who dwelt at Acre took sides in this same quarrel, especially the Pisans and Genoese, both of whom had an exceedingly strong party in Acre. These men made treaties and truces with the Saracens, to the end that they might the better fight against one another within the city. When Pope Urban [IV] heard of this, he grieved for Christendom and for the Holy Land, and sent 12,000 mercenary troops across the sea to help the Holy Land and Christendom. When these men came across the sea to Acre they did no good, but abode by day and by night in taverns and places of ill repute, took and plundered merchants and pilgrims in the public streets, broke the treaty [with the Muslims], and did much evil.

Melot Sapheraph, sultan of Babylon, an exceedingly wise man, most potent in arms and bold in action, when he heard of this, and knew of the hateful quarrels of the people of Acre, called together his counselors and held a parliament in Babylon, wherein he complained that the truces had frequently been broken and violated, to the prejudice of himself and his people. After a debate had been held upon this matter, he gathered together a mighty host, and reached the city of Acre without any resistance, because of their quarrels with one another, cutting down and wasting all the vineyards and fruit trees and all the gardens and orchards, which are most lovely thereabout. When the master of the Templars, a very wise and brave knight, saw this, he feared that the fall of the city was at hand, because of the quarrels of the citizens. He took counsel with his brethren about how peace could be restored, and then went out to meet the sultan, who was his own very especial friend, to ask him whether they could by any means repair the broken truce. He obtained these terms from the sultan, to wit, that because of his love for the sultan and the honor in which the sultan held him, the broken truce might be restored by every man in Acre paying one Venetian penny. So the master of the Templars was glad, and, departing from the sultan, called together all the people and preached a sermon to them in the Church of St. Cross, setting forth how, by his prayers, he had prevailed upon the sultan to grant that the broken treaty might be restored by a payment of one Venetian penny by each man, that therewith everything might be settled and quieted. He advised them by all means to do so, declaring that the quarrels of the citizens might bring a worse evil upon the city than this—as indeed they did. But when the people heard this, they cried out with one voice that he was the betrayer of the city, and was guilty of death. The master, when he heard this, left the church, hardly escaped alive from the hands of the people, and took back their answer to the sultan.

When the sultan heard this, knowing that, owing to the quarrels of the people, none of them would make any resistance, he pitched his tents, set up sixty [siege] machines, dug many mines beneath the city walls, and for forty days and nights, without any respite, assailed the city with fire, stones, and arrows, so that [the air] seemed to be stiff with arrows. I have heard a very honorable knight say that a lance which he was about to hurl from a tower among the Saracens was all notched with arrows before it left his hand. There were at that time in the Sultan's army 600,000 armed men, divided into three companies; so that 100,000 continually besieged the city, and when they were weary another 100,000 took their place ..., [and] 200,000 stood before the gates of the city ready for battle, and the duty of the remaining 200,000 was to supply them with everything that they needed. The gates were never closed, nor was there an hour of the day without some hard fight being fought against the Saracens by the Templars or other brethren dwelling therein. But the numbers of the Saracens grew so fast that after 100,000 of them had been slain 200,000 came back. Yet, even against all this host, they would not have lost the city had they but helped one another faithfully; but when they were fighting outside the city, one party would run away and leave the other to be slain, while within the city one party would not defend the castle or palace belonging to the other, but purposely let the other party's castles, palaces, and strong places be stormed and taken by the enemy, and each one knew and believed his own castle and place to be so strong that he cared not for any other's castle or strong place. During this confusion the masters and brethren of the [military] orders alone defended themselves, and fought unceasingly against the Saracens, until they were nearly all slain; indeed, the master and brethren of the house of the Teutonic Order, together with their followers and friends, all fell dead at one and the same time.

As this went on with many battles and thousands slain on either side, at last the fulfillment of their sins and the time of the fall of the city drew near; when the fortieth day of its siege was come, in the year of our Lord 1292, on the twelfth day of the month of May, the most noble and glorious city of Acre, the flower, chief and pride of all the cities of the East, was taken. The [Frankish] people of the other cities, to wit, Jaffa, Tyre, Sidon and Ascalon, when they heard this, left all their property behind and fled to Cyprus. When first the Saracens took Acre they got in through a breach in the wall near the king of Jerusalem's castle, and when they were among the people of the city within, one party still would not help the other, but each defended his own castle and palace, and the Saracens had a much longer siege, and fought at much less advantage when they were within the city than when they were outside, for it was wondrously fortified....

Nevertheless, more than 100,000 men escaped to Cyprus. I have heard from a most honorable lord, and from other truthful men who were present, that more than 500 most noble ladies and maidens, the daughters of kings and princes, came down to the seashore, when the city was about to fall, carrying with them all their jewels and ornaments of gold and precious stones, of priceless value, in their bosoms, and cried aloud, [asking] whether there were any sailor there who would take all their jewels, and take whichever of them he chose to wife, if only he would take them, even naked, to some safe land or island. A sailor received them all into his ship, took them across to Cyprus, with all their goods, for nothing, and went his way. But who he was, whence he came, or whither he went, no man knows to this day. Very many other noble ladies and damsels were drowned or slain. It would take long to tell what grief and anguish was there.

While the Saracens were within the city, but before they had taken it, fighting from castle to castle, from one palace and strong place to another, so many men perished on either side that they walked over their corpses as it were over a bridge. When all the inner city was lost, all who still remained alive fled into the exceedingly strong castle of the Templars, which was immediately besieged on all sides by the Saracens; yet the Christians bravely defended it for two months, and before it almost all the nobles and chiefs of the sultan's army fell dead. For when the city inside the walls was burned, yet the towers of the city, and the Templars' castle, which was in the city, remained, and with these the people of the city kept the Saracens within the city from getting out, as before they had hindered their coming in, until of all the Saracens who had entered the city not one remained alive, but all fell by fire or by the sword. When the Saracen nobles saw the others lying dead, and themselves unable to escape from the city, they fled for refuge into the mines which they had dug under the great tower, that they might make their way through the wall and so get out. But the Templars and others who were in the castle, seeing that they could not hurt the Saracens with stones and the like, because of the mines wherein they were, undermined the great tower of the castle, and flung it down upon the mines and the Saracens therein, and all perished alike.

When the other Saracens outside the city saw that they had thus, as it were, failed utterly, they treacherously made a truce with the Templars and Christians on the condition that they should yield up the castle, taking all their goods with them, and should destroy it, but should rebuild the city on certain terms, and dwell therein in peace as before. The Templars and Christians, believing this, gave up the castle and marched out of it, and came down from the city towers. When the Saracens had by this means got possession both of the castle and of the city towers, they slew all the Christians alike, and led away the captives to Babylon. Thus Acre has remained empty and deserted even to this day.... When the glorious city of Acre thus fell, all the eastern people sang of its fall in hymns of lamentation, such as they are wont to sing over the tombs of their dead, bewailing the beauty, the grandeur, and the glory of Acre even to this day....

The Different Isles of the Sea and, First of All, Rhodes

...This isle of Rhodes is an exceeding precious one, being mountainous, and standing in a very healthy air, abounding in the wild animals called fallow deer. Furthermore, from whatever part of the sea you sail you must pass by or near Rhodes. In this isle there is a city named Rhodes, exceeding beauteous and strong, with high walls and impregnable towers built of such great stones that it is a wonder how human hands can have laid them in their place. When Acre was lost, the master and brethren of St. John of Jerusalem took this isle by force from the Greeks [in 1310]. They besieged it for years, but they never would have taken the city had they not won over the inhabitants by bribes, so that they delivered up the isle of their own accord. Thereupon the brethren of the order made it their headquarters, and there they dwell to this day. There are 350 brethren and the master of the order, who in my time was Elyonus, a very old and very stingy man, who has amassed countless treasure, and built much in Rhodes, and has set the order free from vast debts.

This isle lies within the sound of a man's voice from Turkey, from which it is separated by an arm of the sea, and takes tribute from all the country round about, and from Turkey a third part of the produce of the land. It has also a small and exceedingly strong castle in Turkey. These brethren have a truce with the rest of the Turks on land, but not at sea, nor yet in places where they are harming the Christians. These same brethren of the Hospital hold also another island hard by, named Lango [that is, Cos], abounding in corn, wine, oil, and many fruits, and therein dwell fifty brethren from Rhodes. The brethren have yet another small isle, a good and fertile one, named Castleroys, which once was laid waste by the Turks, but now is well inhabited by the brethren and their mercenaries. In it there is an exceedingly strong and lofty castle, from which all ships sailing to whatsoever part of the sea can be seen for a distance of almost fifty miles, and then they make signals to the brethren in Rhodes and Lango and to the other Christians round about, with smoke by day and with flames by night, telling them how many ships there are at sea, whereupon the brethren and Christians make preparations for battle and defense according to the number of ships signaled. This island is exceedingly useful to the Christians, for since the brethren have held the island and castle, the Turks have done the Christians no harm with their ships. Moreover, before the time of the brethren, the islands of Rhodes and Lango, and all the isles and country of the Christians round about, used to pay tribute to the Turks, but now by the grace of God the brethren have turned this the other way....

At Rhodes there are also many venerable relics, among which is a brass cross, which is believed to be made out of the basin in which Christ washed the disciples' feet. Wax molds of this cross have great power in quelling storms at sea. This cross and some other venerable relics of the brethren of St. John once belonged to the Templars, all of whose goods and castles are now owned by the aforesaid brethren. It would take too long to tell of the other glories of Rhodes, and of all the many victories of the aforesaid brethren. From Rhodes one sails to Cyprus.

Cyprus

Cyprus is an exceedingly noble and famous and also an exceedingly rich isle, beyond all comparison with all the other isles of the sea, and is fertile in all good things beyond the rest.... This glorious island once belonged to the Templars, who sold it to the king of Jerusalem. Then, when Acre and the Holy Land were lost and ruined [in 1291], the king of Jerusalem and the princes, nobles, and barons of the kingdom of Jerusalem removed to Cyprus and dwelt there, and there they abide to this day, and thus Cyprus became a kingdom.

In Cyprus there are three bishoprics — to wit, Paphos, Limasol, and Famagusta, and one metropolitan [that is, an archbishop], the bishop of Nicosia, who in my day was a Minorite friar named Elias, who was made a cardinal by Pope Clement VI. The oldest city in Cyprus is Paphos, once a very noble and great place, but now it is almost ruined by continual earthquakes. It stands on the seashore directly over against Alexandria. Paul and Barnabas converted this city to faith in Christ, and from thence the whole earth has been converted to the faith, as is set forth in the Acts of the Apostles....

The City of Famagusta

The third city of Cyprus is called Famagusta. It stands on the seashore, and the harbor for the whole sea and the whole kingdom is now there, and thither merchants and pilgrims must flock together. This city stands directly over against Armenia, Turkey, and Acre. This is the richest of all the cities in Cyprus, and its citizens are exceedingly wealthy. Once one of the citizens of Famagusta was betrothing his daughter, and the French knights who were sailing with us reckoned that the jewels she wore on her head were better than all the jewels of the king of France. There was a merchant of this city who sold a royal golden orb to the sultan for sixty thousand florins.... Moreover, the constable of Jerusalem had four pearls which his wife wore as a brooch, which whenever and wherever he pleased he could pawn for three thousand florins. In a warehouse in this city there is more aloeswood than five carts can carry; I say nothing about spices, for they are as common there as bread is here, and are just as commonly mixed and sold. Neither dare I say any more about precious stones, cloth-of-gold, and other kinds of wealth, because in those parts there is an unheard-of and incredible store of them. In this city dwell numberless exceedingly rich courtesans, some of them possessing more than a hundred thousand florins, about whose riches I dare say no more.

Salamina and Nicosia

Near Famagusta there is another city on the seashore named Constantia or Salamina, which once was an exceedingly noble, famous, and beauteous city, as its ruins bear witness....

Also in Cyprus there is another exceedingly great city named Nicosia. This is the metropolis of Cyprus, and stands in the midst thereof in a plain at the foot of the mountains, and in an exceedingly healthy air. The king of Cyprus and all the bishops and other prelates of the kingdom dwell in this city because of the healthiness of the air, and also the greater part of all the other princes, counts, barons, and knights live there, and every day they amuse themselves with joustings, tournaments, and especially with hunting. In Cyprus there are wild rams, which are not found anywhere else in the world, and they are taken [that is, hunted] with leopards; they can be taken in no other way. The princes, nobles, barons, knights, and citizens of Cyprus are the richest in the world, for one who has a revenue of three thousand florins is thought less of there than a man who had a revenue of three marks would be in these parts. But they spend it all in hunting. I knew a count of Jaffa who kept more than five hundred hounds, every pair of which dogs, according to the custom of those parts, had a servant of their own, to keep them clean, bathe them, and anoint them, which must be done to hunting dogs in those parts. Also another noble keeps at least ten or twelve falconers, with special wages and their expenses. I have known many nobles and knights in Cyprus who could have kept and maintained two hundred armed men for less than they paid for their huntsmen and falconers; for when they go forth to hunt they dwell sometimes for a whole month in the woods and mountains, wandering with their tents from place to place, taking their pleasure with their hounds and falcons, sleeping in the woods and fields in their tents, and carrying all that they need and all their provisions with them on camels and beasts of burden.

You must know that all the princes, nobles, barons, knights, and citizens in Cyprus are the best and richest in the world, and now they dwell there with their children, but once they used to dwell on the mainland, in the cities of Syria and Judea, and in the noble city of Acre; but now that the mainland and its cities are lost they have fled to Cyprus, and abide there even to this day. There are also in Cyprus exceedingly rich citizens and merchants, and no wonder, seeing that Cyprus is the furthest [east] of all Christian lands, wherefore all ships both great and small, and all merchandise of whatever kind and from whatever country, must come first of all to Cyprus, and can in no way pass by it. Moreover, all pilgrims from all parts of the world whatsoever, when bound for the parts beyond the sea [that is, the Middle East], must come to Cyprus, and every day from sunrise to sunset one hears rumors and news here.

In Cyprus also all the languages of the world are heard and spoken, and are taught in special schools; and in Cyprus excellent wine grows on lofty mountains exposed to the rays of the sun.... [And] it is exceedingly wholesome to take some of the wine unmixed upon an empty stomach, and nowhere are there better winedrinkers or more of them than in Cyprus. In Cyprus all trees and herbs grow as they grow in the Holy Land.

Questions: What, according to Ludolph, were the reasons for the fall of Acre? What role did the military orders play in the defense of the city? What was the significance of the fall of Acre to the crusading cause? What were relations like between the islands of Cyprus and Rhodes and the Muslim territories? Compare the Frankish society of Rhodes and Cyprus with that of the former crusader states on the mainland. What were the concerns of the Franks living here? How important was crusading to them?

89. PIERRE DUBOIS'S *THE RECOVERY OF THE HOLY LAND*

The loss of Acre in May of 1291 was followed by the surrender of the remaining Christian strongholds and cities along the coast. All crusader fortifications in this region were destroyed to prevent the Christians from returning. This final expulsion from the Holy Land was a devastating blow to Europe and prompted many to devise schemes by which Jerusalem and its territories might be recovered. Below are excerpts from one such plan, written in 1306 by French lawyer and royal advisor Pierre Dubois, who addressed the treatise to King Philip IV.

Source: trans. W.I. Brandt, *The Recovery of the Holy Land*, by Pierre Dubois (New York: Columbia University Press, 1956), pp. 117-20 and 124.

In every province, according to the local facilities available for this purpose and the size of the population, on the property of such priories of the Templars and Hospitallers there should be established what would be better suited to the purpose, namely two or more schools for boys and about the same number for girls. The pupils should be selected for instruction there at the age of four or five years, being chosen by some wise philosopher who would recognize their probable natural aptitude for making progress in philosophical studies. To these schools should be admitted children of noble birth of either sex, if and in so far as they shall be found; afterwards other children [may be admitted], who should be taught continuously after the manner set forth below, which may be changed, perfected, and augmented by wiser heads. These children shall be accepted with the proviso that they shall never be returned to their parents unless they refund all expenses incurred in their behalf. Some will be sent from school to school, and finally to the Holy Land and to such other lands as the holy Roman church may determine through those assigned to this task. The students and their teachers shall subsist from the property of the said priories and from the holdings of the above mentioned foundation for the Holy Land, as the directors of the foundation, appointed by the local archbishops with the advice of experienced suffragans [that is, bishops], shall see fit to arrange.

All these children are to be instructed first in the Latin language, up to the point where they have a good, or at least a fair, grasp of it. Afterwards some of them should be given more thorough training in the Greek language, others in Arabic, and so in the case of other literary idioms, especially [in those spoken by eastern] Catholic peoples, so that eventually with the help of these youths, trained to speak and write the languages of all peoples, the Roman church, and the Catholic princes as well, may through them communicate with all men and draw them to the Catholic faith and into unity with its head.

Now let youths already instructed in grammar be enrolled, with preference given to the younger; if there be some trained in logic, so much the better. Of these, some should be rapidly instructed in the articles of faith, the sacraments, and the Old and New Testaments so that, as soon as they have completed this course of study, they may be sent to the Holy Land to be advanced to the priesthood and thus have the care of souls. From among them provision may be made for the churches and the people. Some should be trained in medicine, others in both human and veterinary surgery; by them the army and the whole populace of either sex may be helped.

Girls should be instructed in medicine and surgery, and the subjects necessary as a preliminary to this. With such training and a knowledge of writing, these girls—namely, those of noble birth and others of exceptional skill who are attractive in face and figure—will be adopted as daughters and granddaughters by the greater princes of their own countries, of the Holy Land, and of other lands adjacent thereto. They will be so adorned at the expense of the said foundation that they will be taken for daughters of princes, and may then conveniently be married off to the greater princes, clergy, and other wealthy easterners. They must promise that when married to leading men or to those of other rank they will, during their lifetime if possible, repay to the said foundation the sum expended on them. If unable to do so [they must agree to make provision for repaying it] or any part left unpaid at their death, so the foundation may in this way be increased beyond measure. It would be an excellent thing for the eastern prelates and clergy to have such wives; it is their custom to marry, and they have been most unwilling to follow the Roman and other western clergy in renouncing the privilege of marriage.

Wives with such education, who held the articles of faith and the sacraments according to Roman usage, would teach their children and husbands to adhere to the Roman faith and to believe and sacrifice in accordance with it.

They would employ arguments and opportunities far more effective than those which by the wiles of his wives led Solomon, the wisest of men, into idolatry. Such women, through love of their native land, would arrange to have many girls from these schools married to their sons and other leading men of the land, especially to clerics who eventually are to be elevated to prelacies. They would have chaplains celebrating [mass] and chanting according to the Roman ritual, and would gradually by this means draw the inhabitants of those districts to the Roman ritual. Especially [would they influence] the women, whom they would aid through the practice of medicine and surgery, and particularly in their secret infirmities and needs. It could scarcely happen otherwise than that they, nobler and richer than other matrons and recognized everywhere as having a knowledge of medicine, surgery, and experimental science, would attract matrons in need of their counsel, who admired their skills so advantageous to them and loved them on that account: would attract them, I say, to communicate with them and be glad to unite with them in the articles of faith and the sacraments....

While others are pursuing a policy of inflicting injury on the Saracens, making war upon them, seizing their lands, and plundering their other property, perhaps girls trained in the proposed schools may be given as wives to the Saracen chiefs, although preserving their faith lest they participate in their husbands' idolatry. By their efforts, with the help of God and the preaching disciples so they may have assistance from Catholics—for they cannot rely on the Saracens—their husbands might be persuaded and led to the Catholic faith. Little by little our faith might be made known among them. Their wives would strive the more zealously for this because each of them has many wives. All the wealthy and powerful among them lead a voluptuous life to the disadvantage of their wives, any one of whom would rather have a man to herself (nor is it to be wondered at) than that seven or more wives should share one husband. It is on that account, as I have generally heard from merchants who frequent their lands, that the women of that sect would easily be strongly influenced toward our manner of life, so that each man would have only one wife.

Questions: According to Dubois, what is the secret to a successful crusade and the retention of the Holy Land? Compare his plan for the Holy Land with that of earlier crusades. What is Dubois's education policy and how does it fit in with his notion of crusading? How realistic was his plan?

90. HUMBERT OF ROMANS ON CRITICISMS OF CRUSADING

Even before the loss of the Holy Land, the crusades in the East had drawn criticism from both secular and ecclesiastical quarters. Although this was not the dominant view, Pope Gregory X felt compelled to call upon Humbert of Romans to produce a defense of the crusading movement, in which he repeated—and then refuted—various criticisms of crusading; only the criticisms are reprinted below. Humbert, a crusade preacher and a former master general of the Dominican order, wrote this work sometime before 1274.

Source: trans. L. and J. Riley-Smith, *The Crusades: Ideal and Reality* (London: Edward Arnold, 1981), pp. 104, 106-10, 112-13, 115.

[1] There are some of these critics who say that it is not in accordance with the Christian religion to shed blood in this way, even that of wicked infidels. For Christ did not act thus; rather, "When he suffered, he threatened not, but delivered himself to him that judged him unjustly," as Peter says. Nor did Christ teach this, but he said to Peter when the latter wanted to defend him, "Put up thy sword into the scabbard."... One should conclude, therefore, that the Christian religion, which ought to adhere to the example and teaching of Christ and the saints, ought not to initiate wars of any kind whatsoever, through which so much blood may be shed....

[2] There are others who say that although one ought not to spare Saracen blood one must, however, be sparing of Christian blood and deaths. It is true that on this sort of pilgrimage against the Saracens countless people die, sometimes from sickness at sea, sometimes in battle, sometimes from a lack or excess of food; not only the common people, but also kings and princes and persons who do great service to Christianity. How much harm was done through the death of King Louis [IX], whose life was so beneficial to the church of God, and through the deaths of many others! Is it wisdom to put at risk in this way so many and such great men of ours, to expose so many to death for the sake of killing Saracens and thus to empty Christendom of so many and such good people? ...

[3] There are others who say that when our men go overseas to fight the Saracens the conditions of war are much worse for our side, for we are very few in comparison to their great numbers. We are, moreover, on alien territory, while they are on their own ground; we are in a climate foreign to us, while they are in one to which they are accustomed; we must eat many kinds of food strange to us, while they are used to their diet; they are familiar with dangerous passes and hiding-places, while we are not; we are often short of supplies there, while they have plenty. And so it looks as though we are putting God to the test or we are showing a great lack of faith when we enter into such a contest.

Therefore, since discretion is the most necessary attribute in wars, it seems that Christians ought never to undertake wars of this kind....

[4] There are others who say that, although we have a duty to defend ourselves against the Saracens when they attack us, it does not seem that we ought to attack their lands or their persons when they leave us in peace. It does not seem, moreover, that this can be done without committing an injury....

[5] There are others who say that, if we ought to rid the world of the Saracens, why do we not do the same to the Jews and why do we not treat the Saracens who are our subjects in the same way? Why do we not proceed with the same zeal against any other idolaters who still exist in the world? Why do we not mete out similar treatment to the Tartars and barbarian nations of this kind who are all infidels?...

[6] Other people are asking, what is the point of this attack on the Saracens? For they are not roused to conversion by it but rather are stirred up against the Christian faith. When we are victorious and have killed them, moreover, we send them to hell, which seems to be against the law of charity. Also when we gain their lands we do not occupy them like colonists, because our countrymen do not want to stay in those regions, and so there seem to be no spiritual, corporeal or temporal fruits from this sort of attack....

[7] Others say that it does not appear to be God's will that Christians should proceed against Saracens in this way, because of the misfortunes which God has allowed and is still allowing to happen to the Christians engaged in this business. For how could God have allowed Saladin to retake from us almost at a blow nearly all the land which had been won with so much Christian blood and toil; and the emperor Frederick [Barbarossa] to perish in shallow water as he hurried to bring it aid; and King Louis [IX] of happy memory to be captured in Egypt with his brothers and almost the entire nobility of France; and, when he had started out afresh on this business, to die with his son when he had reached Tunis; and then when their remaining ships were withdrawing, so many of them to be wrecked in a storm off Sicily; and so great an army to have achieved nothing, and countless other such events, if this kind of proceeding had been pleasing to him?...

Questions: What sort of criticism can we tell was being leveled against the crusading movement? How do the reasons differ from each other? Which would hold water today? How might a medieval supporter of the Crusades have responded to these criticisms?

91. RAMON LULL'S PLAN TO CONVERT THE MUSLIMS

The notion that large-scale conversion could play an important role in the success of a crusade to the Holy Land was not widely held until the loss of the crusader states in the late thirteenth century. Although missions had always been a part of the northern and eastern European crusades, the crusaders to Palestine had not promoted mass conversion, even among the various Christian sects of that region. Forced conversion was forbidden by canon law, but there arose at this time support for peaceful missions alongside military endeavors. Ramon Lull (1232-1316) was a Franciscan friar who traveled as far afield as North Africa and Asia in order to convert Muslims to Christianity. The treatise excerpted below combines his instruction on missions with his thoughts on the organization of a military crusade.

Source: trans. N. Housley, *Documents on the Later Crusades, 1274-1580* (London: Macmillan, 1996), pp. 35-38.

The First Section: On Discussions with the Infidels

The following procedure is needed in order to bring about the conversion of the infidels. The lord pope and their lords the cardinals should entrust the matter to one of the latter; he should be very holy and devout, and learned in scripture, and should be released from all other consistorial business. Using the church's resources, he would see to the building of four monasteries in suitable and pleasant locations outside the lands of the pagans. He should endow these in perpetuity with revenues adequate for the support of men learning languages, and to provide them with sufficient books, and with the people to teach those books. The costs involved would be small in comparison with the resources of the church. For there are many bishops and prelates, any one of whom could meet the bill with a fifth of his income.

It is required and shown in this treatise that the lord cardinal who is appointed by the high pontiff for this matter should have trustworthy and law-worthy messengers, who would faithfully conduct an inquiry amongst the clergy everywhere. They would know how to pick the right men, devout and learned, who show themselves to be eager to add those languages to their knowledge, who are willing to bear with great charity and patience the distasteful work involved, and finally to die on behalf of that most benign Son of God, our Lord Jesus Christ, who did not fear to suffer death for them. The men who are tracked down in this way, whether they are religious or outside the orders, should immediately receive a papal license to depart and take up residence in the said monasteries. It seems sufficient to me that in each of the

Fig. 29: A scholar at work in late medieval Europe, as depicted in a fifteenth-century manuscript copied in a nineteenth-century engraving. From P. Lacroix, *The Arts in the Middle Ages* (London: Chapman and Hall, 1870).

[monasteries] there should be a convent of twelve, with a thirteenth member as superior. And things should be so arranged that when two men had completed their linguistic training and were being dispatched to preach, two others would be newly admitted.

These four monasteries should be established in such a way, that in one the Saracen language [that is, Arabic] would be taught, in another Jewish [that is, Hebrew], in the third schismatic [that is, Greek], and in the fourth Tartar or pagan. And to procure teachers knowing these, the lord cardinal would send [a messenger] to those regions, where he would find poor people willing to come for the sake of money, and they would instruct these worthy men in the aforesaid languages....

The apostles said to Jesus Christ: "Look, here are two swords." And he replied: "It is enough." By this he meant that you should fight against the unbelievers both with preaching and with weapons. . . .

The Second Section: On the Way to Fight

It is desirable that the Holy Land, and the other territories which the unbelievers keep from the Latins, should be recovered, through the angels who are
in paradise, through the saints, and through the Latins themselves. It is the lord
pope and cardinals who are principally charged with bringing about this great
benefit, as well as honoring our Lord Jesus Christ and effecting the salvation of
men. To this end they should choose a cardinal, most holy and devout, to
whom may be entrusted everything which will be touched on in this section,
just as was the case in the first section with the other cardinal.

The lord pope and the cardinals should select and establish a single noble
[religious] order, to be called the order of knighthood. The head of this order
would be termed both master and warrior-king. "Warrior," on the grounds
that the subject matter of this section requires it; "king" because of his magis-
tracy of the knighthood. A kingdom should be granted to him; if at all possible, the kingdom of Jerusalem should be assigned to him. This is just, since this
king will have a more noble office than any other king of this world, and
because the principal aim of this warrior-king must be to conquer Jerusalem.
If it may not be given to him at present, at all events he should be temporarily
given another kingdom, which it proves possible to get hold of. It follows that
this warrior[-king] must be a king's son, both because of the honor or the
office which is given to him, and in order that all the [religious] orders of
knighthood should be the more willing to submit themselves to his order.
When one warrior[-king], the son of a king, passes away, another man, also a
king's son, would be chosen in his place. And so the succession would proceed.

Further: the lord pope, together with the cardinals, should decree that this
single [military] order, [the order of] knighthood, be created from the union of
the order of the Temple and the knighthood of the Hospital, the Teutons,
Uclés, and Calatrava, and all the other orders of knights without exception,
whoever and wherever they are. And all the orders of knighthood should welcome this step because of the name of the king of the knighthood; and above
all because of its goal of honoring our Lord Jesus Christ, and [bringing about]
the gentiles' salvation. And should anyone oppose it, he would be seen to be
neither faithful nor devout, and he should consider the judgment on the Last
Day, when the Lord Jesus Christ says: "Depart into the everlasting fire, you
accursed ones."...

If this appointment proves unacceptable, a very great danger follows... for
some Christian princes have their eye on the church's tenth, and as we know
from experience, they use it to promote their secular affairs. But if the warrior-king has the tenth, and is constantly engaged in hard combat in order to

exalt the Christian faith and conquer the Holy Land, then the lord pope and cardinals have an excuse for not granting the tenth to anybody else. So the church's goods are deployed towards the end for which they are given. And if the warrior-king is chosen in the manner described, many secular knights, and many townspeople or other lay or common folk would voluntarily, and at their own costs or expenses, proceed to join the army thus established, and would all submit themselves to the command of the warrior-king, to undertake penance for their sins. For there are many who desire to die for our Lord Jesus Christ....

It will be good if jurists, doctors, and surgeons are in the order of the warrior[-king], so that they can together judge cases, cure the sick and heal the wounded. Books which I wrote, [called] *The book of law* and *The book of medicine*, will be useful for this purpose; with these they will be able to offer advice to many, in accordance with nature.

It would also be a good idea if some of the religious clerics in the order of the warrior[-king] possessed the knowledge to speak, read, and understand the Arabic language and various other barbarian languages. They should know how to read, write, and understand the warrior[-king]'s correspondence, and to look after confidential material, which would be assigned to each in turn. They could also enter into discussions with captive princes, in order to win them over to the holy Catholic faith. If they could not convert them, at least they could teach them our faith, and the problematic aspects of our dispute with them. They could prove to them that Mohammed was not a true prophet. Should they wish to concentrate on this, it can easily be proved by a book called *Alquindi*, and by another, called *Telif*, and by another which I wrote called *De gentili*. And those captured would have to learn those books whether they wanted to or not. Afterwards the lord warrior-king would set them free, and give them expenses in a friendly and pleasant way. He would send them to the Saracen kings and the other princes, from whose regions they originate, to show and prove to them what we believe about the most blessed Trinity, and in what manner we believe in the incarnation of our Lord Jesus Christ.... Thus they will be the means of converting the infidel and spreading our sacrosanct faith.

Again: some of the aforesaid brothers who know Arabic should be sent to the Saracen princes and others of the infidel, as I said, by the lord warrior-king. And they should tell them that the lord warrior-king will give them castles and towns, should they return [*sic*] of their own free will to our sacrosanct Catholic faith. And they would show them the reasons for our faith; and should they refuse, they would inform them of the steps which have been taken against them in perpetuity, and that the warrior[-king]'s sword will be put into motion, slashing and destroying them.

Further: the warrior-king should send out his religious [with a knowledge of] Arabic, in Saracen clothing, to act as spies so that the warrior-king can build up information on the conditions facing the Saracens, in order the better to prepare to fight them....

Questions: How does Lull's plan compare with that of Pierre Dubois? How do the two differ in their view of the role of church and state authorities with regards to crusading? How does Lull suggest converting non-Christians?

92. MARSILIUS OF PADUA'S *THE DEFENDER OF PEACE*

Marsilius of Padua (c. 1275-1343) was an Italian political philosopher who developed an anti-papal stance due, in part, to his reaction against contemporary papal politics. His views on government and the place of the church were recorded in his most famous work, Defensor Pacis *(1324). The selection below sets forth Marsilius's opinion of Pope John XXII and his crusades against his political enemies.*

Source: trans. A. Gewirth, *Defensor Pacis*, by Marsilius of Padua (New York: Columbia University Press, 2001), pp. 357-59.

But now we come to what is the most vicious and most gravely harmful of all the acts of this present Roman bishop: an iniquitous practice which we have briefly mentioned above, and which no one who desires to cling to the law of love can pass over in silence. I refer to those acts of his whereby he brings about the eternal confusion and destruction of "all Christ's sheep," who he says were entrusted to him that he might feed them with salutary doctrine. For again putting "good for evil and light for darkness," he has issued oral and written pronouncements "absolving from all guilt and punishment" every soldier, in cavalry or in infantry, that has waged war at a certain time against those Christian believers who maintain steadfast and resolute subjection and obedience to the Roman ruler; and by himself or through others this Roman bishop has issued oral and written proclamations making it lawful to attack in any way, to rob and even to kill these faithful subjects, as being "heretics" and "rebels" against the cross of Christ. And, what is horrible to hear, this bishop declares that such action is just as pleasing in God's sight as is fighting the heathen overseas, and he has this declaration published far and wide by false pseudo-brethren who thirst for ecclesiastic office. To those whom physical disability prevents from participating in such criminal action, he grants a similar fallacious pardon if they have up to that same time gotten others to perpetrate these outrages in their place or if they have paid to his vicious collectors a

Fig. 30: Middle Eastern peoples, as portrayed in a late medieval European woodcut.

sufficient sum for this purpose. But no one should doubt that, according to the catholic religion, this empty and ridiculous pardon is utterly worthless, nay, harmful, to men who fight in such a cause. Nevertheless, by vocally granting something that is not in his power, the bishop dupes simple men into carrying out his impious desires, or rather he seduces and misleads them to the eternal perdition of their souls. For when men, unjustly invading and attacking a foreign land, disturb the peace and quiet of innocent believers, and, even though they well know that their victims are true catholics, nevertheless rob and kill them because they are defenders of their own country and loyal to their true and legitimate ruler, then such aggressors are fighters not for Christ but for the devil. For they commit rapine, arson, theft, homicide, fornication, adultery, and practically every other kind of crime. And hence it is indubitably certain that the proper desert of such men is not pardon but rather prosecution and punishment by eternal damnation. And yet they are misled into perpetrating these crimes by the words and writings of the very man who calls himself (although he is not) Christ's vicar on earth.

Not content with these horrible crimes committed by laymen at his command and incitement, this "bloody and deceitful man" [Ps. 5:6] chose a priest from among his brethren or accomplices (who are called cardinals) and sent him with a large body of cavalry and infantry into the province of Lombardy, for the purpose of attacking and killing Christian believers; and a monk, the abbot of the march of Ancona in Italy, was sent by him on a similar expedition. Those believers who refuse to obey his vicious and impious commands against their ruler he relentlessly attacks with all sorts of persecution; and because their pious ruler [the Holy Roman emperor] Ludwig sympathizes with them and supports them as much as he can, this man has with his usual insolence gone so far as to call him, in speeches and writings, a "supporter of heretics."

Such are the purposes for which this bishop wastes the ecclesiastic temporal goods that devout believers, both rulers and subjects, communities and individuals, have put aside for the aid and support of Gospel ministers and of the helpless poor; and he tries to make similar vicious use of the temporal funds which have been bequeathed for the cause of religion, such as for crossing overseas, ransom of men captured by the infidels, and other such ends — to all such funds he unjustly lays claim as being subject to his own power. But to draw weapons, or to order weapons drawn, among Christian believers, especially for an unjust cause, is not an apostolic or priestly deed, nor does it befit a priest, or a man dedicated to God, to do such things. Rather, if disagreement or discord arises among Christians, the priest should by suitable exhortations recall them to harmony, as has been sufficiently shown [earlier in my work]....

No bishop, therefore, should be permitted to have or be entrusted with such general, absolute, and far-reaching power to bestow and distribute temporal goods; but rather the rulers and legislators must either revoke such power entirely, or else so moderate it that goods which are set aside for the present and future welfare of the believers do not yield them continued temporal tribulations and finally eternal torment.

Questions: How does Marsilius view crusades against fellow Christians? How does he view crusades against Muslims? What, in Marsilius's opinion, is the proper duty of the pope in relation to the politics and governments of Europe?

93. ORDER FOR THE ARREST OF THE TEMPLARS

The late thirteenth and early fourteenth century was a turning point for the military orders. The loss of the Holy Land meant the loss of their reason for existence. While the Teutonic Knights would be able to remain active in eastern Europe until the fifteenth century, and the Hospitallers found a home first on Rhodes and then on Malta, the Templars had no choice but to return to Europe. Here they did not find a hearty welcome. As has been seen in the previous documents, the mood of Europe was changing with regard to crusades and the role of church and state. Moreover, many in Europe blamed the military orders for the loss of the Holy Land. With no Holy Land to defend, many debated what should be the fate of these orders. Some, such as Ramon Lull (doc. 91), argued for the union of all the military orders, while others felt their time had passed with the fall of Acre. In particular, the Templars' rich holdings, their association with banking, and the fact that they owed political allegiance to no secular ruler meant that they acquired many powerful enemies. One of these was the French King Philip IV, who was determined to make the Templar riches his own. In this letter of September 1307, Philip laid the groundwork for the later suppression of the order. The letter, addressed to his provincial administrators in Normandy, was one of many sent out by Philip at this time.

Source: trans. E. Hallam, *Chronicles of the Crusades: Eyewitness Accounts of the Wars between Christianity and Islam* (London: Salamander Books, 2000), pp. 286, 288.

There has been sounded in our ears a report of a matter exciting bitterness and grief, whose very thought arouses horror and terror on hearing it. It is a hateful crime, a damnable sin, an abominable deed, an abhorrent disgrace, deeply inhuman—or rather, completely lacking in all human feeling. And we can now believe the report owing to its substantiation from many sources. It cannot be doubted that such great sins in their enormity have burst their banks, to become an offense to the divine majesty and the whole of Christendom, a sham on mankind, a pernicious demonstration of evil and a scandal of universal proportions.

By the testimony of a great number of reliable witnesses, the brothers of the order of Knights Templar have been behaving as though they were wolves under sheep's clothing, and villainously trampling on the religion of our faith under the dress of religion.

They are again crucifying in these days our Lord Jesus Christ, by bringing him wounds more grievous than those he bore on the cross. For on initiation into their order, his image is presented to them, and they deny him three times with wretched and miserable blows, and with horrific cruelty spit three times in his face.

Then, taking off their everyday clothes, they line up in the presence of the visitor or deputy who is receiving them for initiation. Next he kisses them; first at the bottom of the spine, secondly on the navel, and finally on the mouth, in accordance with the profane rite of their Order—but for shame on human dignity. Not fearing to break human law, they bind themselves with a vow of initiation to give themselves over, one to another, to that disgusting and terrifying vice of sexual intercourse—when asked and without excuse.

That treacherous, mad race, given over as it is to the worship of idols, does not fear to commit these and other sins. It is not just their deeds and detestable acts but also their terrifying words that taint the earth with their repulsiveness.

We were hardly able to give the matter our attention earlier, since we were well aware of the sort of informers who would broadcast so awful a rumor. However, the number of them multiplied and the rumor grew stronger.

Accordingly, we established an investigation designed to uncover the truth. We then held conference on the matter with our most holy father in the Lord, Pope Clement V, and a fuller council with our prelates and barons, in which we dealt carefully with the charges; and the more fully we investigated the matter, the graver were the abominations that we found.

You know that to defend the freedom of the church's faith the Lord has set kings apart, as observers from our royal heights, and that before all the desires of our heart we strive for the advancement of the catholic faith. Accordingly, we held a thorough inquiry through the offices of our beloved brother in Christ, William of Paris, an inquisitor into heretical perversion authorized by papal authority. Here, at least, the Templars gave in to the just entreaties of the aforesaid inquisitor, who later called in the help of our strong arm. We acknowledged it was possible that some were guilty and some innocent, but it was expedient to try them, and, if necessary, to acquit them after the correct judicial examination.

Thus we decreed that every single member of the aforesaid order in our kingdom be, without exception, taken into custody to await trial in the ecclesiastical court, and that all their goods, both moveable and immovable, be seized by our hand and be faithfully kept.

Therefore we command that you, singly or together, personally see to the matter as far as concerns the district of Rouen, and take every single brother of the order, without exception, into custody to await trial at the ecclesiastical court. We command, through the content of this present document, all our judges and faithful subjects to obey you promptly and strenuously in all the above.

Written in the royal abbey of St. Mary, near Pontoise, on 14 September 1307.

Questions: What accusations does Philip bring against the Templars? What is his evidence? How does he propose to verify the charges?

94. PAPAL BULL SUPPRESSING THE TEMPLARS

Many of the Templar leaders confessed, under torture, to a range of blasphemous crimes, such as spitting on the cross and participating in obscene initiation rites. The pope at this time was Clement V, and while he initially resisted Philip's campaign against the Templars, he eventually gave in and issued the following papal bull on March 22, 1312.

Source: trans. N.P. Tanner, *Decrees of the Ecumenical Councils* (London and Washington: Sheed & Ward and Georgetown University Press, 1990), Vol. I, pp. 336-43.

Clement, bishop, servant of the servants of God, for an everlasting record. A voice was heard from on high, of lamentation and bitter weeping [Jer. 31:15], for the time is coming, indeed has come, when the Lord shall complain through his prophet: "This house has aroused my anger and wrath, so that I will remove it from my sight because of the evil of its sons, for they have provoked me to anger, turning their backs to me, not their faces, and setting up their idols in the house in which my name is invoked, to defile it [Jer. 32: 32-34]...."

...Indeed a little while ago, about the time of our election as supreme pontiff, before we came to Lyons for our coronation, and afterwards, both there and elsewhere, we received secret intimations against the master, preceptors, and other brothers of the order of Knights Templar of Jerusalem and also against the order itself. These men had been posted in lands overseas for the defense of the patrimony of our lord Jesus Christ, and as special warriors of the catholic faith and outstanding defenders of the Holy Land seemed to carry the chief burden of the said Holy Land. For this reason the holy Roman church honored these brothers and the order with her special support, armed them with the sign of the cross against Christ's enemies, paid them the highest tributes of her respect, and strengthened them with various exemptions and privileges; and they experienced in many and various ways her help and that of all faithful Christians with repeated gifts of property.... The order, moreover, had a good and holy beginning; it won the approval of the apostolic see. The rule, which is holy, reasonable and just, had the deserved sanction of this see. For all these reasons we were unwilling to lend our ears to insinuation and accusation against the Templars; we had been taught by our Lord's example and the words of canonical scripture.

Then came the intervention of our dear son in Christ, Philip [IV], the illustrious king of France. The same crimes had been reported to him. He was not moved by greed. He had no intention of claiming or appropriating for himself anything from the Templars' property; rather, in his own kingdom he abandoned such claim and thereafter released entirely his hold on their goods. He was on fire with zeal for the orthodox faith, following in the well marked footsteps of his ancestors. He obtained as much information as he lawfully could. Then, in order to give us greater light on the subject, he sent us much valuable information through his envoys and letters. The scandal against the Templars themselves and their order in reference to the crimes already mentioned increased. There was even one of the knights, a man of noble blood and of no small reputation in the order, who testified secretly under oath in our presence, that at his reception the knight who received him suggested that he deny Christ, which he did, in the presence of certain other knights of the Temple; he furthermore spat on the cross held out to him by this knight who received him. He also said that he had seen the grand master, who is still alive, receive a certain knight in a chapter of the order held overseas. The reception took place in the same way, namely with the denial of Christ and the spitting on the cross, with quite two hundred brothers of the order being present. The witness also affirmed that he heard it said that this was the customary manner of receiving new members: at the suggestion of the person receiving the profession or his delegate, the person making profession denied Jesus Christ, and in abuse of Christ crucified spat upon the cross held out to him, and the two committed other unlawful acts contrary to Christian morality, as the witness himself then confessed in our presence.

We were duty-bound by our office to pay heed to the din of such grave and repeated accusations. When at last there came a general hue and cry with the clamorous denunciations of the said king and of the dukes, counts, barons, other nobles, clergy, and people of the kingdom of France, reaching us both directly and through agents and officials, we heard a doleful tale: that the master, preceptors, and other brothers of the order as well as the order itself had been involved in these and other crimes.... Since we, though unworthy, represent Christ on earth, we considered that we ought, following in his footsteps, to hold an inquiry. We called to our presence many of the preceptors, priests, knights and other brothers of the order who were of no small reputation. They took an oath, they were adjured urgently by the Father, Son and Holy Spirit; we demanded, in virtue of holy obedience, invoking the divine judgment with the menace of an eternal malediction, that they tell the pure and simple truth. We pointed out that they were now in a safe and suitable place where they had nothing to fear in spite of the confessions they had made before others. We wished those confessions to be without prejudice to them. In this way we made our interrogation and examined as many as seventy-two, many of our brothers being present and following the proceedings attentively. We had the confessions taken down by a notary and recorded as authentic documents in our presence and that of our brothers. After some days we had these confessions read in consistory in the presence of the knights concerned. Each was read a version in his own language; they stood by their confessions, expressly and spontaneously approving them as they had been read out.

After this, ... [we] empowered and commanded our beloved sons Berengar, cardinal..., and Stephen, cardinal priest..., and Landulf, cardinal deacon..., in whose prudence, experience and loyalty we have the fullest confidence, to make a careful investigation with the grand master, visitor, and preceptors, concerning the truth of the accusations against them and individual persons of the order and against the order itself.... On their return to our presence, the cardinals presented to us the confessions and depositions of the master, visitor and preceptors in the form of a public document, as has been said. They also gave us a report on their dealings with these knights.

From these confessions, depositions and report we find that the master, the visitor and the preceptors of Outremer, Normandy, Aquitaine, and Poitou have often committed grave offenses, although some have erred less frequently than others. We considered that such dreadful crimes could not and should not go unpunished without insult to almighty God and to every Catholic. We decided on the advice of our brothers to hold an enquiry into the above crimes and transgressions. This would be carried out through the local ordinaries and other wise, trustworthy men delegated by us in the case of individual members of the order; and through certain prudent persons of our considered choice in the case of the order as a whole. After this, investigations were made both by the ordinaries and by our delegates into the allegations against individual members, and by the inquisitors appointed by us into those against the order itself, in every part of the world where the brothers of the order have usually lived. Once made and sent to us for examination, these investigations were very carefully read and examined, some by us and our brothers, cardinals of the holy Roman church, others by many very learned, prudent, trustworthy and God-fearing men, zealous for and well-trained in the catholic faith, some being prelates and others not. This took place at Malaucène in the diocese of Vaison.

Later we came to Vienne where there were assembled already very many patriarchs, archbishops, selected bishops, ... abbots, other prelates of churches, and procurators of absent prelates and of chapters, all present for the council we had summoned ... to consider this affair, and we asked them, in the course of a secret consultation in our presence, how we should proceed, taking special account of the fact that certain Templars were presenting themselves in defense of their order. The greater part of the cardinals and nearly the whole council, that is those who were elected by the whole council and were representing the whole council on this question, in short the great majority, indeed four-fifths among every nation taking part, were firmly convinced, and the said prelates and procurators advised accordingly, that the order should be given an opportunity to defend itself and that it could not be condemned, on the basis of the proof provided thus far, for the heresies that had been the subject of the inquiry, without offense to God and injustice. Certain others on the contrary said that the brothers should not be allowed to make a defense of their order and that we should not give permission for such a defense, for if a defense were allowed or given there would be danger to a settlement of the affair and no small prejudice to the interests of the Holy Land. There would be dispute, delay and putting off a decision; many different reasons were mentioned. Indeed although legal process against the order up to now does not permit its canonical condemnation as heretical by definitive sentence, the good name of the order has been largely taken away by the heresies attributed to it. Moreover, an almost indefinite number of individual members, among whom are the grand master the visitor of France and the chief preceptors, have been convicted of such heresies, errors and crimes through their spontaneous confessions. These confessions render the order very suspect, and the infamy and suspicion render it detestable to the holy church of God, to her prelates, to kings and other rulers, and to Catholics in general. It is also believed in all probability that from now on there will be found no good person who wishes to enter the order, and so it will be made useless to the church of God and the carrying on of the undertaking to the Holy Land, for which service the knights had been destined. Furthermore, the putting off of a settlement or arrangement of this affair of the Templars, for which we had set ourselves a final decision or sentence to be promulgated in the present council, would lead in all probability to the total loss, destruction, and dilapidation of the Templars' property. This has for long been given, bequeathed and granted by the faithful for the aid of the Holy Land and to oppose the enemies of the Christian faith.

There were therefore two opinions: some said that sentence should immediately be pronounced, condemning the order for the alleged crimes, and others objected that from the proceedings taken up to now the sentence of condemnation against the order could not justly be passed. After long and mature deliberation, having in mind God alone and the good of the Holy Land, without turning aside to right or to left, we elected to proceed by way of provision and ordinance; in this way scandal will be removed, perils avoided, and property saved for the help of the Holy Land. We have taken into account the disgrace, suspicion, vociferous reports, and other attacks mentioned above against the order, also the secret reception into the order, and the divergence of many of the brothers from the general behavior, way of life and morals of other Christians. We have noted here especially that when new members are received, they are made to swear not to reveal the manner of their reception to anyone and not to leave the order; this creates an unfavorable presumption. We observe in addition that the above have given rise to grave scandal against the order, scandal impossible to allay as long as the order continues to exist. We note also the danger to faith and to souls, the many horrible misdeeds of so many brothers of the order, and many other just reasons and causes, moving us to the following decision.

The majority of the cardinals and of those elected by the council, a proportion of more than four-fifths, have thought it better, more expedient and advantageous for God's honor and for the preservation of the Christian faith, also for the aid of the Holy Land and many other valid reasons, to suppress the order by way of ordinance and provision of the apostolic see, assigning the property to the use for which it was intended. Provision is also to be made for the members of the order who are still alive. This way has been found preferable to that of safeguarding the right of defense with the consequent postponement of judgment on the order. We observe also that in other cases the Roman church has suppressed other important orders for reasons of far less gravity than those mentioned above, with no fault on the part of the brethren. Therefore, with a sad heart, not by definitive sentence, but by apostolic provision or ordinance, we suppress, with the approval of the sacred council, the order of Templars, and its rule, habit and name, by an inviolable and perpetual decree, and we entirely forbid that anyone from now on enter the order, or receive or wear its habit, or presume to behave as a Templar. If anyone acts otherwise, he incurs automatic excommunication. Furthermore, we reserve the persons and property for our disposition and that of the apostolic see. We intend with divine grace, before the end of the present sacred council, to make this disposition to the honor of God, the exaltation of the Christian faith, and the welfare of the Holy Land. We strictly forbid anyone, of whatever state or condition, to interfere in any way in this matter of the persons and property of the Templars. We forbid any action concerning them which would prejudice our arrangements and dispositions, or any innovation or tampering. We decree that from now on any attempt of this kind is null and void, whether it be made knowingly or in ignorance. Through this decree, however, we do not wish to derogate from any processes made or to be made concerning individual Templars by diocesan bishops and provincial councils, in conformity with what we have ordained at other times....

Given at Vienne on 22 March in the seventh year of our pontificate.

Questions: Compare this bull with the previous document? Does the bull offer any more evidence than Philip's order? What decisions does it announce? How did the pope manage the investigation and decision-making process? What was to become of surviving ex-Templars and their property?

CHAPTER TEN:

FROM CRUSADES TO COLONIZATION

Fig. 31: One of Christopher Columbus's ships, in a late fifteenth-century woodcut said to be based on a drawing by Columbus himself. The islands known as the Antilles are shown in the background. From P. Lacroix, *Military and Religious Life in the Middle Ages* (London, Chapman and Hall, 1874).

95. JOHN MANDEVILLE ON PRESTER JOHN

Prester John was long believed to be a Christian king ruling an empire of vast wealth somewhere in the East. The origin of the legend is not known, but its popularity in Europe grew during the crusading period. The idea of a faraway Christian kingdom may be linked to the actual presence in Asia of the Nestorians, a Christian sect which had sent out missionaries as far as China and had even converted a small number of Mongols under the rule of Genghis Khan. Below is an account of Prester John from the pen of John Mandeville. His book of travels covers the years 1322 to 1356 (1366 in some versions) and tells of his time spent with the sultan of Egypt and the great khan of the Mongols. The Travels of John Mandeville became one of the most widely read books of the later Middle Ages, and while its accuracy is questioned, it does demonstrate the European view of the world at this time.

Source: trans. T. Wright, *Early Travels in Palestine* (London: Henry G. Bohn, 1848), pp. 262–66; revised.

This emperor, Prester John, possesses very extensive territory, and has many very noble cities and good towns in his realm, and many great and large islands. For all the country of India is divided into islands, by the great floods that come from paradise, that separate all the land into many parts. And also in the sea he has full many islands. And the best city in the island of Pentexoir is Nyse, a very royal city, noble and very rich. This Prester John has under him many kings, and many islands, and many diverse people of diverse conditions. And this land is full good and rich, but not so rich as the land of the great khan. For the merchants come not thither so commonly to buy merchandise, as they do in the land of the great khan, for it is too far. And on the other side, in the island of Cathay, men find all things needful to human life, cloth of gold, of silk, and spicery. And therefore, although men have them cheap in the island of Prester John, they dread the long way and the great perils of the sea...

This emperor, Prester John, takes always to wife the daughter of the great khan; and the great khan also in the same way marries the daughter of Prester John. For those two are the greatest lords under the firmament. In the land of Prester John are many diverse things and many precious stones, so great and so large, that men make of them plates, dishes, cups, and so on. And many other marvels are there, that it would be too long to put in a book. But I will tell you of his principal islands, and of his estate, and of his law. This emperor Prester John is a Christian, and a great part of his country also; but they have not all the articles of our faith. They believe in the Father, Son, and Holy Ghost, and they are very devout and true to one another. And he has under him seventy-two provinces, and in every province is a king, all which kings are tributary to Prester John....

Fig. 32: Prester John and his servant, as represented in a sixteenth-century Venetian printed book. From P. Lacroix, *Military and Religious Life in the Middle Ages* (London, Chapman and Hall, 1874).

This emperor Prester John, when he goes to battle against any other lord, has no banners borne before him; but he has three large crosses of gold full of precious stones; and each cross is set in a chariot full richly arrayed. And to keep each cross are appointed 10,000 men of arms, and more than 100,000 footmen. And this number of people is independent of the chief army. And when he has no war, but rides with a private company, he has before him but one plain cross of wood, in remembrance that Jesus Christ suffered death upon a wooden cross. And they carry before him also a platter of gold full of earth, in token that his nobleness, and his might, and his flesh, shall turn to earth. And he has borne before him also a vessel of silver, full of noble jewels of gold and precious stones, in token of his lordship, nobility, and power. He dwells commonly in the city of Susa, and there is his principal palace, which is so rich and noble that no man can conceive it without seeing it. And above the chief tower of the palace are two round pommels of gold, in each of which are two large carbuncles, which shine bright in the night. And the principal gates of his palace are of the precious stones called sardonyx; and the border and bars are of ivory; and the windows of the halls and chambers are of crystal; and the tables, on which men eat, some are of emeralds, some of amethyst, and some of gold, full of precious stones; and the pillars that support the tables are of the same precious stones. Of the steps approaching his throne, where he sits at meat, one is of onyx, another crystal, another green jasper, another amethyst, another sardonyx, another cornelian, and the seventh, on which he sets his feet, is of crysolite. All these steps are bordered with fine gold, with the other precious stones, set with great oriental pearls. The sides of the seat of his throne are of emeralds, and bordered full nobly with gold, and dubbed with other precious stones and great pearls. All the pillars in his chamber are of fine gold with precious stones, and with many carbuncles, which give great light by night to all people. And although the carbuncle gives light enough, nevertheless at all times a vessel of crystal, full of balm, is burning to give good smell and odor to the emperor, and to expel all wicked airs and corruptions. The frame of his bed is of fine sapphires blended with gold, to make him sleep well, and to restrain him from lechery. For he will not lie with his wives but four times in the year, after the four seasons. He has also a very fair and noble palace in the city of Nyse, where he dwells when he likes; but the air is not so temperate as it is at the city of Susa. And you shall understand that in his country, and in the countries surrounding, men eat but once in the day, as they do in the court of the great khan. And more than 30,000 persons eat every day in his court, besides goers and comers, but these 30,000 persons spend not so much as 12,000 of our country. This emperor Prester John always has seven kings with him, to serve him, who share their service by certain months; and with these kings serve always 72 dukes and 360 earls. And all the days of the year, twelve archbishops and twenty bishops eat in his household and in his court. And the patriarch of St. Thomas is there what the pope is here. And the archbishops, and the bishops, and the abbots in that country, are all kings. And each of these great lords knows well the attendance of his service. One is master of his household, another is his chamberlain, another serves him with a dish, another with a cup, another is steward, another is marshal, another is prince of his arms; and thus is he very nobly and royally served. And his land extends in extreme breadth four months' journey, and in length out of measure, including all the islands under earth, that we suppose to be under us.

Questions: What explains the popularity of the Prester John legend? What perhaps did the Christian West expect from Prester John? What part did the Mongols play in the legend? How did Europeans see the world beyond their doorstep? How might this have influenced their dealings with foreign peoples?

96. LETTERS BETWEEN POPE INNOCENT IV AND GUYUK KHAN

When news of the Mongol invasion of Islamic lands reached Europe, there was a general belief that here was an ally who would help rid the West of a long-standing enemy. As John Mandeville's description (doc. 95) shows, many linked the Mongols to Prester John and believed them to be Christian (albeit of a heretical sect). It was perhaps this mistaken notion that led Pope Innocent IV to open negotiations with Guyuk, the great khan or ruler of the Mongols. The pope's letters and the khan's response are printed below.

Source: trans. anonymous nun of Stanbrook Abbey, *The Mongol Mission: Narratives and Letters of the Franciscan Missionaries...*, ed. C. Dawson (London and New York: Sheed and Ward, 1955), pp. 73-76, 85-86.

First Letter of Innocent IV to Guyuk Khan, 1245

God the Father, of his graciousness regarding with unutterable loving-kindness the unhappy lot of the human race, brought low by the first man, and desiring of his exceeding great charity mercifully to restore him whom the devil's envy overthrew by a crafty suggestion, sent from the lofty throne of heaven down to the lowly region of the world his only-begotten Son....

He therefore offered himself as a victim for the redemption of mankind and, ... rising from the dead and ascending into heaven, he left his vicar on earth [that is, St. Peter], and to him ... he committed the care of souls, that he should with watchfulness pay heed to and with heed watch over their salvation.... Wherefore we, though unworthy, having become, by the Lord's disposition, the successor of this vicar [that is, pope], do turn our keen attention, before all else incumbent on us in virtue of our office, to your salvation and that of other men, and on this matter especially do we fix our mind, sedulously keeping watch over it with diligent zeal and zealous diligence, so that we may be able, with the help of God's grace, to lead those in error into the way of truth and gain all men for him. But since we are unable to be present in person in different places at one and the same time—for the nature of our human condition does not allow this—in order that we may not appear to neglect in any way those absent from us we send to them in our stead prudent and discreet men by whose ministry we carry out the obligation of our apostolic mission to them. It is for this reason that we have thought fit to send to you our beloved son Friar Laurence of Portugal and his companions of the Order of Friars Minor, the bearers of this letter, men remarkable for their religious spirit, comely in their virtue and gifted with a knowledge of holy scripture, so that following their salutary instructions you may acknowledge Jesus

Christ the very Son of God and worship his glorious name by practicing the Christian religion. We therefore admonish you all, beg and earnestly entreat you to receive these friars kindly and to treat them in considerate fashion out of reverence for God and for us, indeed as if receiving us in their persons, and to employ unfeigned honesty towards them in respect of those matters of which they will speak to you on our behalf; we also ask that, having treated with them concerning the aforesaid matters to your profit, you will furnish them with a safe-conduct and other necessities on both their outward and return journey, so that they can safely make their way back to our presence when they wish. We have thought fit to send to you the above-mentioned friars, whom we specially chose out from among others as being men proved by years of regular observance and well versed in holy scripture, for we believed they would be of great help to you, seeing that they follow the humility of our Savior: if we had thought that ecclesiastical prelates or other powerful men would be more profitable and more acceptable to you we would have sent them.

Second Letter of Innocent IV to Guyuk Khan, 1245

Seeing that not only learned men but even irrational animals, nay, the very elements which go to make up the world machine, are united by a certain innate law after the manner of the celestial spirits, … it is not without cause that we are driven to express in strong terms our amazement that you, as we have heard, have invaded many countries belonging both to the Christians and to others and are laying waste in a horrible desolation, and with a fury still unabated you do not cease from stretching out your destroying hand to more distant lands, but, breaking the bond of natural ties, sparing neither sex nor age, you rage against all indiscriminately with the sword of chastisement. We, therefore, following the example of the king of peace, and desiring that all men should live united in concord in the fear of God, do admonish, beg, and earnestly beseech all of you that for the future you desist entirely from assaults of this kind and especially from the persecution of Christians, and that after so many and such grievous offenses you conciliate by a fitting penance the wrath of divine majesty, which without doubt you have seriously aroused by such provocation; nor should you be emboldened to commit further savagery by the fact that when the sword of your might has raged against other men almighty God has up to the present allowed various nations to fall before your face; for sometimes he refrains from chastising the proud in this world for the moment, for this reason, that if they neglect to humble themselves of their own accord he may not only no longer put off the punishment of their wickedness in this life but may also take greater vengeance in the world to come. On this account we have thought fit to send to you our beloved son [John of Plano Carpini] and his companions the bearers of this letter, men remarkable for their religious spirit, comely in their virtue and gifted with a knowledge of holy scripture; receive them kindly and treat them with honor out of reverence for God, indeed as if receiving us in their persons, and deal honestly with them in those matters of which they will speak to you on our behalf, and when you have had profitable discussions with them concerning the aforesaid affairs, especially those pertaining to peace, make fully known to us through these same friars what moved you to destroy other nations and what your intentions are for the future, furnishing them with a safe-conduct and other necessities on both their outward and return journey, so that they can safely make their way back to our presence when they wish.

Letter of Guyuk Khan to Innocent IV, 1246

We, by the power of the eternal heaven, khan of the great *ulus* [that is, community]....

This is a version sent to the great pope, that he may know and understand in the [Persian] tongue, what has been written. The petition of the assembly held in the lands of the emperor [for our support] has been heard from your emissaries.

If he reaches [you] with his own report, thou, who art the great pope, together with all the princes, come in person to serve us. At that time I shall make known all the commands of the *Yasa* [that is, the Mongol laws and statutes].

You have also said that supplication and prayer have been offered to you, that I might find a good entry into baptism. This prayer of thine I have not understood. Other words which thou hast sent me: "I am surprised that thou hast seized all the lands of the Magyar and the Christians. Tell us what their fault is." These words of thine I have also not understood. The eternal God has slain and annihilated these lands and peoples, because they have neither adhered to Genghis Khan, nor to the khagan [that is, supreme ruler], both of whom have been sent to make known God's command, nor to the command of God. Like thy words, they also were impudent, they were proud and they slew our messenger-emissaries. How could anybody seize or kill by his own power contrary to the command of God?

Though thou likewise sayest that I should become a trembling Nestorian Christian, worship God and be an ascetic, how knowest thou whom God absolves, in truth to whom he shows mercy? How dost thou know that such words as thou speakest are with God's sanction? From the rising of the sun to its setting, all the lands have been made subject to me. Who could do this contrary to the command of God?

Now you should say with a sincere heart: "I will submit and serve you."

Thou thyself, at the head of all the princes, come at once to serve and wait upon us! At that time I shall recognize your submission.

If you do not observe God's command, and if you ignore my command, I shall know you as my enemy. Likewise I shall make you understand. If you do otherwise, God knows what I know.

Questions: What assumptions does the pope make concerning his relationship with the great khan and the Mongol people? What did the pope hope to achieve by his letters? How did the khan view the pope and the people of the West? What is his attitude towards Christianity? Compare the aims and purpose of the pope with those of the khan.

97. WILLIAM OF RUBRUCK ON THE MONGOLS

William of Rubruck, a Franciscan friar, traveled into Mongol territories in 1253 as part of the ongoing Christian missionary effort to convert the Mongols to Christianity. He was probably in the service of the French king Louis IX, to whom his account of his journey, excerpted below, is addressed. William's writings are important for their detailed (albeit western) view of Mongol life.

Source: trans. W.W. Rockhill, *The Journey of William of Rubruck to the Eastern Parts of the World, 1253-55...* (London: The Hakluyt Society, 1900), second series, vol. 4, pp. 52-55, 75-84, 95-96, 103-05, 107, 116, 281-82; revised.

After having left Sodaia we came on the third day across the Tartars, and when I found myself among them it truly seemed to me that I had been transported into another century. I will describe to you as well as I can their mode of living and manners.

Nowhere do they have fixed dwelling-places, nor do they know where their next will be. They have divided Scythia among themselves, which extends from the Danube to the rising of the sun; and every captain, depending on the number of men under him, knows the limits of his pasture lands and where to graze in winter and in summer, spring and autumn. For in winter they go down to warmer regions in the south: in summer they go up to cooler regions towards the north. The pasture lands without water they graze over in winter when there is snow there, for the snow serves them as water.

They set up the dwelling in which they sleep on a circular frame of interlaced sticks converging into a little round hoop on the top, from which projects above a collar as a chimney, and this framework they cover over with white felt.... And they make these houses so large that they are sometimes 30 feet in width. I myself once measured the width between the wheel-tracks of a cart 20 feet, and when the house was on the cart it projected beyond the wheels on either side five feet at least....

It is the duty of the women to drive the carts, get the dwellings on and off them, milk the cows, make butter and sour curds, and dress and sew skins, which they do with a thread made of tendons. They divide the tendons into fine shreds, and then twist them into one long thread. They also sew boots, the socks and the clothing. They never wash clothes, for they say that God would be angered at this, and that it would thunder if they hung them up to dry. They will even beat those they find washing them.... Furthermore, they never wash their bowls, but when the meat is cooked they rinse out the dish in which they are about to put it with some of the boiling broth from the kettle, which they pour back into it. The women also make the felt and cover the houses.

The men make bows and arrows, manufacture stirrups and bits, make saddles, do the carpentering on [the framework] of their dwellings and the carts; they take care of the horses, milk the mares, churn the *cosmos* or mare's milk, make the skins in which it is put; they also look after the camels and load them. Both sexes look after the sheep and goats, sometimes the men, other times the women milking them....

As to their marriages, you must know that no one among them has a wife unless he buys her; so it sometimes happens that girls are well past marriageable age before they marry, for their parents always keep them until they sell them. They observe the first and second degrees of consanguinity, but no degree of affinity; thus one [man] will have at the same time or successively two sisters [as his wives]. Among them no widow marries, for the following reason: they believe that all who serve them in this life shall serve them in the next, so they believe that a widow will always return to her first husband after death. Hence this shameful custom prevails among them: that sometimes a son marries all his father's wives, except his own mother; for the dwellings of the father and mother always belong to the youngest son, so it is he who must provide for all his father's wives who come to him with the paternal household, and if he wishes it he uses them as wives, for he does not think himself injured if they return to his father after death. So when anyone has made a bargain with a man to marry his daughter, the father of the girl gives a feast, and the girl flees to her relatives and hides there. Then the father says: "Here, my daughter is yours: take her wherever you find her." Then [the bridegroom] searches for her with his friends till he finds her, and must take her by force and carry her off with a semblance of violence to his house....

When anyone dies, they lament with loud wailing, and then they are free, for they pay no taxes for the year. And if anyone is present at the death of an adult, he may not enter the dwelling even of Mangu Khan [the emperor] for the year. If it is a child who dies, the person who was present may not enter it for a month. Beside the tomb of the dead they always leave a tent if he is one of the nobles, that is, of the family of Genghis Khan, who was their first father and lord. Of him who is dead, the burying place is not known. And around these places where they bury their nobles there is always a camp with men watching the tombs. I did not understand that they bury treasures with their dead....

When therefore we found ourselves among these barbarians, it seemed to me, as I said before, that I had been transported into another world. They surrounded us on their horses, after having made us wait for a long while seated in the shade under our carts. The first question [they asked] was whether we had ever been among them before.... Then they asked where we came from and where we wanted to go. I told them ... that we had heard that Sartach was a Christian, and that I wanted to go to him, for I had your letters to deliver to him....

There were five of us [Europeans], and the three [Mongols] who were conducting us, two driving the carts and one going with us to Sartach. The meat they had given us was insufficient, and we could find nothing to buy with money. To add to this, when we were seated in the shade under our carts, [the people of the neighborhood] pushed in most importunately among us, to the point of crushing us, in their eagerness to see all our things.... Above all this, however, I was distressed because I could do no preaching to them; the interpreter would say to me, "You cannot make me preach, I do not know the proper words to use." And he spoke the truth; for after a while, when I had learned something of the language, I saw that when I said one thing, he said a totally different one, according to what came uppermost in his mind. So, seeing the danger of speaking through him, I made up my mind to keep silence....

And so we came to Sartach's dwelling, and they raised the felt which hung before the entry, so that he could see us. Then they made the clerk and the interpreter bow [to him]; of us they did not demand it. Then they enjoined us earnestly to be most careful in going in and coming out not to touch the threshhold of the dwelling, and also to chant some blessing for him. So we went in chanting, "*Salve, regina!*" ... Then Coiac [a Nestorian priest who served Sartach] handed [Sartach] the censer with the incense, and he examined it, holding it in his hand most carefully. After that he handed him the psalter [we had brought], at which he took a good look, as did the wife who was seated beside him. Then he handed him the Bible, and he asked if the Gospels were in it. I said that it contained all the sacred writings. He also took in his hand the cross, and asked if the image on it were that of Christ. I replied that it was. Those Nestorians and Hermenian [Christians] never make the figure of Christ on their crosses; they would thus appear to entertain some doubt of the Passion, or to be ashamed of it. Then I presented to him your letter, with translations in Arabic and Syriac, for I had had them both translated and written in these languages at Acon....

Before we left Sartach, the above-mentioned Coiac and a number of scribes of the court said to us, "You must not say that our lord is a Christian. He is not a Christian, but a Moal" [or Mongol]. For the name of Christian seems to them that of a nation. They have risen so much in their pride, that though they may believe somewhat in Christ, yet they do not wish to be called Christians, wishing to exalt their own name of Moal above all others, nor do they wish to be called Tartars. The Tartars were another people....

Of Sartach I know not whether he believes in Christ or not. This I do know, that he will not be called a Christian, and it even seemed to me that he mocked the Christians. For he is on the road of the [local] Christians, ... all of whom pass by him when going to his father's household carrying presents to him, so he shows himself most attentive to them. Should, however, Saracens come along carrying more presents than they, they are sent along more expeditiously. He has Nestorian priests around him who [conduct their worship services]....

... [I]f the army of the church were to come to the Holy Land, it would be very easy to conquer or to pass through [the lands on the way]. The king of Hungary has at most 30,000 soldiers. From Cologne to Constantinople it is no more than forty days in a cart. From Constantinople it is not so far as that to the country of the king of Hermenia. In times past valiant men passed through these countries, and succeeded, though they had most powerful adversaries, whom God has since removed from the earth. Nor should we (if we followed this road) be exposed to the dangers of the sea or to the mercies of the sailor men, and the price which would have to be given for a fleet would be enough for the expenses of the land journey. I state it with confidence, that if your peasants — to say nothing of the princes and noblemen — would only travel like the Tartar princes, and be content with similar provisions, they would conquer the whole world.

It seems to me inexpedient to send another friar to the Tartars as I went, or as the preaching friars go; but if the lord pope, who is head of all Christians, wishes to send with proper state a bishop, and reply to the foolishness [the Mongols] have already written three times to the Franks (once to Innocent IV of blessed memory [from Guyuk Khan], and twice to you...); he would be able to tell them whatever he pleased, and also make them reply in writing. They listen to whatever an ambassador [as opposed to a lower-level envoy like a friar] has to say, and always ask if he has more to say; but he must have a good interpreter — nay, several interpreters — abundant travelling funds, and so on.

Questions: What western, Christian attitudes are evident in William's account of the Mongols? What do we learn about their customs? What problems did the Europeans encounter in their religious mission? How did William apply what he had learned on his travels to the problem of crusading? What would be the best plan for creating an alliance between the Mongols and the West?

98. JOHANN SCHILTBERGER ON THE NICOPOLIS CRUSADE

The empire of the Ottoman Turks emerged in the early fourteenth century under its founding leader Osman. By the mid-fourteenth century, this dynasty had reduced the territory of the Byzantine Empire to the city of Constantinople and its outskirts and was moving into eastern Europe. To Europeans, a Muslim army on the offensive beyond the Middle East was a new and disturbing trend, and it prompted one of the last great crusades of the Middle Ages. In 1395 King Sigismund of Hungary sought aid against the Ottomans from the French king, Charles VI. Charles and other western leaders sent money and fighting men. Although there were two rival popes at the time, both support-ed the crusade. The armies met near the city of Nicopolis on the border with Wallachia, and here the Christian forces suffered a devastating defeat. The following account is by a participant, Johann Schiltberger, a German traveler who fought in the crusade, was cap-tured, but later escaped and wrote about his experiences.

Source: trans. J.B. Telfer, *The Bondage and Travels of Johann Schiltberger* (London: The Hakluyt Society, 1879), pp. 1-4, revised.

From the first, King Sigmund [of Hungary] appealed in the above-named year, 1394, to Christendom for assistance, at the time that the infidels were doing great injury to Hungary. There came many people from all countries to help him; then he took the people and led them to the iron gate, which separates [the province of] Ungern from Pulgary and Walachy, and he crossed the Tunow into Pulgary, and made for a city called Pudem. It is the capital of Pulgary. Then came the ruler of the country and of the city, and gave himself up to the king; then the king took possession of the city with 300 men, good horsemen and footsoldiers, and then went to another city where were many Turks. There he remained five days, but the Turks would not give up the city; but the fighting men expelled them by force, and delivered the city to the king. Many Turks were killed and others made prisoners. The king took pos-session of this city also, with 200 men, and continued his march towards anoth-er city called Schiltaw, but called in the infidel tongue "Nicopoly." He besieged

Fig. 33: Travelers and merchants in the Middle East, as shown in a sixteenth-century woodcut. From P. Lacroix, *Manners, Customs, and Dress during the Middle Ages* (London: Chapman and Hall, 1874).

it by water and by land for sixteen days; then came the Turkish king, called Wyasit, with 200,000 men. Then came the duke of Walachy, called Wererway-wod, who asked the king to allow him to look at the winds [that is, to recon-noiter]. This the king allowed, and he took with him 1,000 men for the purpose of looking at the winds, and returned to the king and told him that he had looked at the winds, and had seen twenty banners, and that there were 10,000 men under each banner, and each banner was separate from the other. When the king heard this, he wanted to arrange the order of battle. The duke of Walachy asked that he might be the first to attack, to which the king would willingly have consented. When the duke of Burgundy heard this, he refused to cede this honor to any other person, for the just reason that he had come a great distance with his 6,000 men, and had expended much money in the expedition, and he begged the king that he should be the first to attack. The king asked him to allow the Hungarians to begin, as they had already fought with the Turks, and knew better than others how they were armed. This [the duke of Burgundy] would not allow to the Hungarians, and assembled his men, attacked the enemy, and fought his way through two corps; and when he came to the third, he turned and would have retreated, but found himself surrounded, and more than half his horsemen were unhorsed, for the Turks aimed at the horses only, so that he could not get away, and was taken prisoner. When the king heard that the duke of Burgundy was forced to surrender, he took the rest of the people and defeated a body of 12,000 footsoldiers that had been sent to oppose him. They [that is, the Turks] were all trampled upon and destroyed, and in this engagement a shot killed the horse of my lord Lienhart Richartinger; and I, Hanns Schiltberger his runner, when I saw this, rode up to him in the crowd and assisted him to mount my own horse, and then I mounted another which belonged to the Turks, and rode back to the other runners. And when all the [Turkish] footsoldiers were killed, the king advanced upon another corps which was of horsemen. When the Turkish king saw the king advancing, he was about to fly, but the duke of Iriseh, known as the despot, seeing this, went to the assistance of the Turkish king, with 15,000 chosen men and many other bannerets [that is, knights], and the despot threw himself with his people on the king's banner and overturned it; and when the king saw that the banner was overturned and that he could not remain, he took to flight. Then came [Herman] of Cily, and Hanns, burgrave of Nuremberg, who took the king and conducted him to a galley on board of which he went to Constantinople. When the horsemen and footsoldiers saw that the king had fled, many escaped to the Tunow and went on board the ships; but the vessels were so full that they could not all remain, and when they tried to get on board they struck them on the hands, so that they were drowned in the river; many were killed on the mountain as they were going to the Tunow. My lord Lienhart Richartinger, Werner Pentznawer, Ulrich Kuchler, and little Stainer, all bannerets, were killed in the fight, along with many other brave knights and soldiers. Of those who could not cross the water and reach the vessels, a portion were killed; but the larger number were made prisoners. Among the prisoners were the duke of Burgundy and Hanns Putzokardo [that is, the Frenchman John Boucicaut], and a lord named Centumaranto [that is, St. Omer]. These were two lords of France, and the great count of the Hungarians. And other mighty lords, horsemen, and footsoldiers were made prisoners, and I also was made a prisoner.

Questions: According to Schiltberger, what mistakes were made by the Christian forces at the battle of Nicopolis? Why did European nobles go on this crusade? How well informed is the narrator? Why? What role did military honor play in the events described here? What role did religion play?

99. KRITOVOULOS ON THE FALL OF CONSTANTINOPLE

The Byzantine Empire was in deep trouble by the 1440s. Hemmed in on all sides by the Ottoman Turks, the emperor appealed for help from the West, but none was forthcoming. The Ottoman ruler Mehmed II (the Conqueror) came to power in 1451 and was eager to expand his holdings. On May 29, 1453, he took possession of Constantinople and thus brought the Byzantine Empire to an end. Kritovoulos was a Greek writer, who, although he was not present at the siege and capture of Constantinople, did visit the city soon after this event. He became an administrator for Mehmed II and wrote a biography of the sultan which covers the first seventeen years of his reign.

Source: trans. C.T. Riggs, *History of Mehmed the Conqueror by Kritovoulos* (Princeton: Princeton University Press, 1954), pp. 66-72, 76-77.

Position and orders given to the generals

...The hour was already advanced, the day was declining and near evening, and the sun was at the Ottomans' backs but shining in the faces of their enemies. This was just as the sultan had wished; accordingly he gave the order first for the trumpets to sound the battle-signal, and the other instruments, the pipes and flutes and cymbals too, as loud as they could. All the trumpets of the other divisions, with the other instruments in turn, sounded all together, a great and fearsome sound. Everything shook and quivered at the noise. After that, the standards were displayed.

To begin, the archers and slingers and those in charge of the cannon and the muskets, in accord with the commands given them, advanced against the wall slowly and gradually. When they got within bowshot, they halted to fight. And first they exchanged fire with the heavier weapons, with arrows from the archers, stones from the slingers, and iron and leaden balls from the cannon and muskets. Then, ... they closed with battleaxes and javelins and spears, hurling them at each other and being hurled at pitilessly in rage and fierce anger. On both sides there was loud shouting and blasphemy and cursing. Many on each side were wounded, and not a few died. This kept up till sunset, a space of about two or three hours.

Then, with fine insight, the sultan summoned the shield-bearers, heavy infantry and other troops and said: "Go to it, friends and children mine! It is time now to show yourselves good fighters!" They immediately crossed the moat, with shouts and fearful yells, and attacked the outer wall. All of it, however, had been demolished by the cannon. There were only stockades of great beams instead of a wall, and bundles of vine-branches, and jars full of earth. At that point a fierce battle ensued close in and with the weapons of hand-to-hand fighting. The heavy infantry and shield-bearers fought to overcome the defenders and get over the stockade, while the Romans and Italians tried to fight these off and to guard the stockade. At times the infantry did get over the wall and the stockade, pressing forward bravely and unhesitatingly. And at times they were stoutly forced back and driven off.

The sultan followed them up, as they struggled bravely, and encouraged them. He ordered those in charge of the cannon to put the match to the cannon. And these, being set off, fired their stone balls against the defenders and worked no little destruction on both sides, among those in the near vicinity.

So, then, the two sides struggled and fought bravely and vigorously. Most of the night passed, and the Romans [that is, the Byzantine Greeks] were successful and prevailed not a little. Also, Giustinianni [a Genoese nobleman who had come to the aid of the Byzantine emperor] and his men kept their positions stubbornly, and guarded the stockade and defended themselves bravely against the aggressors.

And the other generals and officers with their own troops, and particularly the admiral of the fleet, also attacked the wall by land and sea and fought vigorously. The archers shot arrows from their bows, others fired cannon, and others brought up ladders and bridges and wooden towers and all sorts of machines to the walls. Some of them tried to climb up the wall by main force, especially where Zaganos and Karaja [Mehmed's officers] were in command.

Zaganos had crossed the bridge in safety, and brought ladders and bridges up to the wall. He then tried to force the heavy infantry to climb up, leaving with him the archers and musketeers from the ships inside the harbor. These fired from the decks fiercely, attacking the left flank of those who were on the fortifications as the ships sailed by.

Karaja crossed the moat and bravely attacked, attempting to get through inside the demolished wall.

But the Romans on their part met them stubbornly and repulsed them brilliantly. They fought bravely and proved superior to the Ottomans in battle. Indeed they showed that they were heroes, for not a one of all the things that occurred could deter them: neither the hunger attacking them, nor sleeplessness, nor continuous and ceaseless fighting, nor wounds and slaughter, nor the death of relatives before their very eyes, nor any of the other fearful things could make them give in, or diminish their previous zeal and determination. They valiantly kept on resisting as before, through everything, until evil and pitiless fortune betrayed them.

Sultan Mehmed saw that the attacking divisions were very much worn out by the battle and had not made any progress worth mentioning, and that the Romans and Italians were not only fighting stoutly but were prevailing in the battle. He was very indignant at this, considering that it ought not to be endured any longer. Immediately he brought up the divisions which he had been reserving for later on, men who were extremely well armed, daring and brave, and far in advance of the rest in experience and valor. They were the elite of the army: heavy infantry, bowmen, and lancers, and his own body-guard, and along with them those of the division called *yenitsari* [that is, janis-saries].

Calling to them and urging them to prove themselves now as heroes, he led the attack against the wall, himself at the head until they reached the moat. There he ordered the bowmen, slingers, and musketeers to stand at a distance and fire to the right, against the defenders on the palisade and on the battered wall. They were to keep up so heavy a fire that those defenders would be unable to fight, or to expose themselves because of the cloud of arrows and other projectiles falling like snowflakes.

To all the rest, the heavy infantry and the shield-bearers, the sultan gave orders to cross the moat swiftly and attack the palisade. With a loud and terri-fying war-cry and with fierce impetuosity and wrath, they advanced as if mad. Being young and strong and full of daring, and especially because they were fighting in the sultan's presence, their valor exceeded every expectation. They attacked the palisade and fought bravely without any hesitation. Needing no further orders, they knocked down the turrets which had been built out in front, broke the yardarms, scattered the materials that had been gathered, and forced the defenders back inside the palisade.

Giustinianni with his men and the Romans in that section fought bravely with lances, axes, pikes, javelins, and other weapons of offense. It was a hand-to-hand encounter, and they stopped the attackers and prevented them from getting inside the palisade. There was much shouting on both sides — the mingled sounds of blasphemy, insults, threats, attackers, defenders, shooters, those shot at, killers and dying, of those who in anger and wrath did all sorts of terrible things. And it was a sight to see there: a hard fight going on hand-to-hand with great determination and for the greatest rewards, heroes fighting valiantly, the one party struggling with all their might to force back the defenders, get possession of the wall, enter the city, and fall upon the children and women and the treasures, the other party bravely agonizing to drive them off and guard their possessions, even if they were not to succeed in prevailing and in keeping them.

Instead, the hapless Romans were destined finally to be brought under the yoke of servitude and to suffer its horrors. For although they battled bravely, and though they lacked nothing of willingness and daring in the contest, Gius-tinianni received a mortal wound in the breast from an arrow fired by a cross-bow. It passed clear through his breastplate, and he fell where he was and was carried to his tent in a hopeless condition. All who were with him were scattered, being upset by their loss. They abandoned the palisade and wall where they had been fighting, and thought of only one thing—how they could carry him on to the galleons and get away safe themselves.

But the emperor Constantine besought them earnestly, and made promises to them if they would wait a little while, till the fighting should subside. They would not consent, however, but taking up their leader and all their armor, they boarded the galleons in haste and with all speed, giving no consideration to the other defenders.

The emperor Constantine forbade the others to follow. Then, though he had no idea what to do next—for he had no other reserves to fill the places thus left vacant, the ranks of those who had so suddenly deserted, and meantime the battle raged fiercely and all had to see to their own ranks and places and fight there—still, with his remaining Romans and his bodyguard, which was so few as to be easily counted, he took his stand in front of the palisade and fought bravely.

Sultan Mehmed, who happened to be fighting quite near by, saw that the palisade and the other part of the wall that had been destroyed were now empty of men and deserted by the defenders. He noted that men were slipping away secretly and that those who remained were fighting feebly because they were so few. Realizing from this that the defenders had fled and that the wall was deserted, he shouted out: "Friends, we have the city! We have it! They are already fleeing from us! They can't stand it any longer! The wall is bare of defenders! It needs just a little more effort and the city is taken! Don't weaken, but on with the work with all your might, and be men and I am with you!"

Capture of the City

So saying, he led them himself. And they, with a shout on the run and with a fearsome yell, went on ahead of the sultan, pressing on up to the palisade. After a long and bitter struggle they hurled back the Romans from there and climbed by force up the palisade. They dashed some of their foe down into the ditch between the great wall and the palisade, which was deep and hard to get out of, and they killed them there. The rest they drove back to the gate.

Death of Emperor Constantine

He had opened this gate in the great wall, so as to go easily over to the palisade. Now there was a great struggle there and great slaughter among those stationed there, for they were attacked by the heavy infantry and not a few others in irregular formation, who had been attracted from many points by the shouting. There the emperor Constantine, with all who were with him, fell in gallant combat.

The heavy infantry were already streaming through the little gate into the city, and others had rushed in through the breach in the great wall. Then all the rest of the army, with a rush and a roar, poured in brilliantly and scattered all over the city. And the sultan stood before the great wall, where the standard also was and the ensigns, and watched the proceedings. The day was already breaking.

Great Rush, and Many Killed

Then a great slaughter occurred of those who happened to be there: some of them were on the streets, for they had already left the houses and were running toward the tumult when they fell unexpectedly on the swords of the soldiers; others were in their own homes and fell victims to the violence of the janissaries and other soldiers, without any rhyme or reason; others were resisting, relying on their own courage; still others were fleeing to the churches and making supplication—men, women, and children, everyone, for there was no quarter given.

The soldiers fell on them with anger and great wrath. For one thing, they were actuated by the hardships of the siege. For another, some foolish people had hurled taunts and curses at them from the battlements all through the siege. Now, in general they killed so as to frighten all the city, and to terrorize and enslave all by the slaughter.

Plunder of the City

When they had had enough of murder, and the city was reduced to slavery, some of the troops turned to the mansions of the mighty, by bands and companies and divisions, for plunder and spoil. Others went to the robbing of churches, and others dispersed to the simple homes of the common people, stealing, robbing, plundering, killing, insulting, taking and enslaving men, women, and children, old and young, priests, monks—in short, every age and class....

Entry of the Sultan into the City, and His Seeing of It All, and His Grief

After this the sultan entered the city and looked about to see its great size, its situation, its grandeur and beauty, its teeming population, its loveliness, and the costliness of its churches and public buildings and of the private houses and community houses and of those of the officials. He also saw the setting of the harbor and of the arsenals, and how skillfully and ingeniously they had everything arranged in the city — in a word, all the construction and adornment of it. When he saw what a large number had been killed, and the ruin of the buildings, and the wholesale ruin and destruction of the city, he was filled with compassion and repented not a little at the destruction and plundering. Tears fell from his eyes as he groaned deeply and passionately: "What a city we have given over to plunder and destruction!"...

Questions: What military tactics did the Ottomans use to take Constantinople? How does Kritovoulos view the defending Byzantines and their emperor? What is Kritovoulos's opinion of Mehmed II?

100. GIANFRANCESCO MOROSINI ON THE JANISSARIES

The success of the Ottoman empire was due to the organization of its administrative and military institutions. The janissaries were an Ottoman army corps made up of Christian slaves who had been captured or conscripted from an early age. This system of recruitment came to be known as devshirme. *Like the mamluks of thirteenth-century Egypt, the janissaries were divided into an elite few, who became part of the sultan's personal guard, and the rest who served as soldiers. Their intensive training and lack of family ties meant that they were well suited to the job and could be trusted to serve the sultan faithfully. Below is a sixteenth-century description of the janissaries by Gianfrancesco Morosini, an Italian diplomat. Although the janissaries are believed to have been established in the fourteenth century, they did not become an official part of the empire until the rule of Murad II (1421-51).*

Source: trans. J.C. Davis, *Pursuit of Power: Venetian Ambassadors' Reports on Spain, Turkey, and France in the Age of Philip II, 1560-1600* (New York: Harper & Row, 1970), pp. 135-38.

There are two types of [Ottoman] Turks. One is composed of people native-born of Turkish parents, while the other is made up of renegades who are sons of Christians. The latter group were taken by force in the raids their fleets and pirates make on Christian lands, or else harshly levied in their villages from the sultan's non-Muslim subjects and taxpayers. They are taken while still boys, and either persuaded or forced to be circumcised and made Muslims. It is the custom of the Porte [that is, the Turkish government] to send men throughout the country every fourth or fifth year to levy one-tenth of the boys, just as if they were so many sheep, and after they have made Turks of these boys they train each one according to his abilities and what fate has in store for him.

Not only is most of the Turkish army made up of these renegades, but at one time they used to win all the chief positions in the government, up to the first vizierate, and the highest commands in the armed forces, because ancient custom forbids that the sons of Turks should hold these jobs. But the present grand signor ignores this custom and chooses whatever men he wants and believes can serve him best, without regard for their status.

After they have been taken away as young boys the renegades are sent to different places to be trained according to the jobs they will be given. The handsomest, most wide-awake ones are placed in the seraglio [that is, palace] of the grand signor, or in one of two others used only for this purpose, and there they are all prepared for the same end, which is to rise to the highest government offices. The Turks care not at all whether these boys are the children of noblemen or of fishermen and shepherds. All of this explains why their major officials are all good-looking and impressive, even when their manners are uncouth.

The other boys, who are not so handsome but are strong and healthy, are made *adjemi-oghlani*, which means they are in a kind of seminary for the janissary corps. In order to accustom them to hard work and physical suffering they are made to tend the sultan's gardens, look after horses, sail on ships, transport lumber, building stone, and other goods, or work in the mills. They make them drudge day and night, and they give them no beds to sleep on and very little food. When these boys begin to shave they make them janissaries [that is, soldiers].

The first group, the ones destined for the higher positions, presently number about six thousand. They are trained under discipline which is stricter than that of our monasteries, they never leave the seraglios, nor even their own rooms, and they speak to each other only when it is urgently necessary. Eunuchs, most of them Negroes, have charge of them, and for any little offense they beat them cruelly with sticks, rarely hitting them less than a hundred times, and often as much as a thousand. After punishments the boys have to come to them and kiss their clothing and thank them for the cudgelings they have received. You can see, then, that moral degradation and humiliation are part of the training system.

The first thing they are made to learn is the Turks' false religion, which they know so well as to put us to shame. They pray together without fail at four prescribed times every day. They also learn to read and write in Turkish, but except for that they have no instruction in things pertaining to gentlemen and soldiers—no horsemanship, no training with arms. Far from that, they do such tasks as sweeping the place where they live, and cooking.

Four of these young men are assigned when they are at least eighteen or twenty to serve continually with the sultan. Each of these is almost sure to end in such an important position as aga of the janissaries, admiral, beglerbeg in Greece and Anatolia, and finally pasha in the Porte. These four have the task of dressing and undressing the grand signor, and guarding him at night while he sleeps. When he rides on horseback through the city or in battle or while hunting, one of them carries his arms, another his rain clothes, the third a pitcher full of an iced drink, and the fourth something else.

Every three years the grand signor allows those of the young men who have reached an age where they can serve in battle to leave the seraglios if they wish. He gives them either the position of cesimir, with forty aspers a day, or that of spahi, with twenty-five or thirty, according to how well they are thought of at the time they leave.

Perhaps I have discussed these young men a little longer than I should have, but [you] will understand why the matter is important. It is these young renegades who will provide the future army officers of all grades, the governors of the provinces, and even the pashas themselves. They are usually the sons of the commonest peasants and other people and they have been taught nothing of any significance about the world, trained in no military matters except the use of bows and arrows, and treated vilely and cruelly. It is amazing that any of them turn out well, and yet it is these who end up governing that enormous empire.

Questions: Why was the institution of the janissaries of concern to the Ottomans' enemies? What specific criticisms does this author make of the practice? What do his criticisms reveal of his world view? How important is religion in this text?

101. CHRISTINE DE PISAN'S *SONG OF JOAN OF ARC*

In 1429 the writer Christine de Pisan composed a poem praising the French heroine Joan of Arc, who was at this time at the height of her success in France's war against England. Joan (c. 1412-1431) was a young girl when she heard voices telling her to fight for France. Although successful in her early campaigns, she became a captive of the English in 1430 and was executed for witchcraft in 1431. The poem, written before Joan's capture, is unusual not only for its female writer and subject, but because it demonstrates an interesting slant on the crusading ideal.

Source: trans. Angus J. Kennedy and Kenneth Varty, *Ditié de Jehanne D'Arc* (Oxford: Society for the Study of Medieval Languages and Literature, 1977), pp. 41-48.

28. I have heard of Esther, Judith and Deborah, who were women of great worth, through whom God delivered his people from oppression, and I have

heard of many other worthy women as well, champions every one; through them he performed many miracles, but he has accomplished more through this maid.

29. She was miraculously sent by divine command and conducted by the angel of the Lord to the king, in order to help him. Her achievement is no illusion for she was carefully put to the test in council (in short, a thing is proved by its effect)

30. and well examined, before people were prepared to believe her; before it became common knowledge that God had sent her to the king, she was brought before clerks and wise men so that they could find out if she was telling the truth. But it was found in history-records that she was destined to accomplish her mission....

33. Oh, how clear this was at the siege of Orléans where her power was first made manifest! It is my belief that no miracle was ever more evident, for God so came to the help of his people that our enemies were unable to help each other any more than would dead dogs. It was there that they were captured and put to death.

34. Oh! What honor for the female sex! It is perfectly obvious that God has special regard for it when all these wretched people who destroyed the whole kingdom—now recovered and made safe by a woman, something that 5000 men could not have done—and the traitors [have been] exterminated. Before the event they would scarcely have believed this possible.

35. A little girl of sixteen (isn't this something quite supernatural?) who does not even notice the weight of the arms she bears—indeed her whole upbringing seems to have prepared her for this, so strong and resolute is she! And her enemies go fleeing before her, not one of them can stand up to her. She does all this in full view of everyone,

36. and drives her enemies out of France, recapturing castles and towns. Never did anyone see greater strength, even in hundreds or thousands of men! And she is the supreme captain of our brave and able men. Neither Hector nor Achilles had such strength! This is God's doing: it is he who leads her.

37. And you trusty men-at-arms who carry out the cask and prove yourselves to be good and loyal, one must certainly make mention of you (you will be praised in every nation!) and not fail to speak of you and your valor in preference to everything else,

38. you who, in pain and suffering, expose life and limb in defense of what is right and dare to risk confronting every danger. Be constant, for this, I promise, will win you glory and praise in heaven. For whoever fights for justice wins a place in paradise—this I do venture to say....

42. She will restore harmony in Christendom and the church. She will destroy the unbelievers people talk about, and the heretics and their vile ways,

for this is the substance of a prophecy that has been made. Nor will she have mercy on any place which treats faith in God with disrespect.

43. She will destroy the Saracens, by conquering the Holy Land. She will lead Charles there, whom God preserve! Before he dies he will make such a journey. He is the one who is to conquer it. It is there that she is to end her days and that both of them are to win glory. It is there that the whole enterprise will be brought to completion.

44. Therefore, in preference to all the brave men of times past, this woman must wear the crown, for her deeds show clearly enough already that God bestows more courage upon her than upon all those men about whom people speak. And she has not yet accomplished her whole mission! I believe that God bestows her here below so that peace may be brought about through her deeds.

45. And yet destroying the English race is not her main concern for her aspirations lie more elsewhere: it is her concern to ensure the survival of the faith. As for the English, whether it be a matter for joy or sorrow, they are done for. In days to come scorn will be heaped on them. They have been cast down!...

47. Oh, all you blind people, can't you detect God's hand in this? If you can't, you are truly stupid, for how else could the maid who strikes you all down dead have been sent to us? — And you don't have sufficient strength? Do you want to fight against God?

Questions: Why does Christine believe that France is especially favored by God, and what is its destiny because of this? In what way does she merge religious convictions with nationalistic sentiments? What part is Joan to play in the future of France and in the wider scheme of things? How does Christine justify the fact that Joan is a female soldier? What is her concept of crusading? Is this a traditional view?

102. PIUS II'S *COMMENTARIES*

Pope Pius II (1458-64) is regarded by many historians as the last crusading pope. In 1459 he convened a congress with the purpose of launching a crusade against the Ottoman Turks, but it failed to obtain the support of many European rulers, and even those who had pledged arms, money and supplies did not, in the end, fulfill their promises. Undaunted, Pius set out in 1464 to lead the crusade himself, but having arrived at the Italian port of Ancona, he contracted the plague and died. The extract below is from Pius's autobiography, The Commentaries, *published in 1584.*

Source: trans. F.A. Gragg, "The Commentaries of Pius II, Books II and III," *Smith College Studies in History* 25:1-4 (1939-1940), pp. 191-92, 277-79.

On June 1 [1459], the day fixed for the opening of the congress, the pope descended from his palace to the church accompanied by the cardinals, bishops, and all the clergy. The monks of every order in the city [of Mantua] had also been bidden to assemble, and mass was celebrated with solemn pomp and with profound reverence on the part of all present. Then the bishop of Coron, a man distinguished for his learning as well as for his probity, delivered a speech in which he explained the pope's purpose, the reason for the congress, and the need for action and exhorted all who had gathered there to further the pope's desire with ready and willing hearts. When all were on the point of rising, Pius made a gesture for silence and from his throne spoke as follows:

"Our brethren and our sons, we hoped on arriving in this city to find a throng of royal ambassadors had preceded us. We see that only a few are here. We have been mistaken. Christians are not so concerned about religion as we believed. We fixed the day of the congress very far ahead. None can say that the time was too short; no one can plead the difficulties of travel. We who are old and ill have defied the Apennines and winter. Not even mother Rome could delay us, although beset as she is with brigands, she sorely needed our presence. Not without danger we left the patrimony of the church to come to the rescue of the Catholic faith which the Turks are doing their utmost to destroy. We saw their power increasing every day, their armies, which had already occupied Greece and Illyricum, overrunning Hungary, and the loyal Hungarians suffering many disasters. We feared (and this will surely happen if we do not take care) that once the Hungarians were conquered, the Germans, Italians, and indeed all Europe would be subdued, a calamity that must bring with it the destruction of our faith. We took thought to avert this evil: we called a congress in this place; we summoned princes and peoples that we might together take counsel to defend Christendom. We came full of hope and we grieve to find it vain. We are ashamed that Christians are so indifferent. Some are given over to luxury and pleasure; others are kept away by avarice. The Turks do not hesitate to die for their most vile faith, but we cannot incur the least expense nor endure the smallest hardship for the sake of Christ's Gospel. If we continue thus, it will be all over with us. We shall soon perish unless we can summon up a different spirit. Therefore, we urge you, who are holy men, to pray God without ceasing that he may change the temper of the Christian kings, rouse the spirit of his people, and kindle the hearts of the faithful, so that now at least we may take arms and avenge the wrongs which the Turks day after day are inflicting on our religion. Up, brethren! Up, sons! Turn to God with all your hearts. Watch and pray; atone for your sins by fasting and giving alms; bring forth works meet for repentance; for thus God will be appeased and have mercy on us, and if we show ourselves brave, he will deliver our enemies into our hands. We shall remain here till we have learned the disposition of the princes. If they intend to come, we will together take counsel for our state. If not, we must go home again and endure the lot God has given us. But so long as life and strength last we shall never abandon the purpose of defending our religion, nor shall we think it hard, if need be, to risk our life for our sheep."

The cardinal and bishops listened with rapt attention to the pope's words and praised his purpose to the skies....

[In January, 1460,] in the church of St. Andrew before the senators and all the ambassadors of princes, after mass had been celebrated the pope commanded silence and from his throne spoke as follows: "My brothers and sons, we have for eight months awaited those who have been summoned to the congress. You know who have come. To hope longer for the arrival of anyone who could contribute anything to our cause is vain and therefore we may now disperse. We have done what had to be done here. We pray that God's cause has been well pleaded. Though we dreamed of more than we have found, nevertheless we cannot think that nothing has been accomplished, nor is all our hope gone. We must now expound the present situation, that all may know what prospects we have and what kings and peoples have been ready to protect the faith or indifferent. If the Hungarians receive aid, they will attack the Turks energetically with all their forces. The Germans promise an army of 42,000 fighting men, Burgundy 6,000. The Italian clergy, with the exception of the Venetians and the Genoese, will contribute a tenth and the laity a thirtieth of their income, [and] the Jews a twentieth of their possessions. With this sum naval forces can be maintained. John, king of Aragon, promises like aid. The Rugusans will furnish two galleys, the Rhodians four. So much has been promised by princes and ambassadors in solemn and explicit agreement. The Venetians, although they have promised nothing publicly, when they see the crusade actually ready will surely not fail us nor endure to seem inferior to their ancestors. We can say the same of the French, the Castilians, and the Portuguese. England, now racked with civil war, holds out no hope, nor does

Scotland, remote as it is at ocean's farthest bounds. Denmark, Sweden, and Norway also are too far away to be able to send soldiers, and they have no money to contribute, as they are content with fish alone. The Poles, who border the Turks along Moldavia, will not dare to desert their own cause. The Bohemians we shall be able to hire; they will not fight outside their country at their own expense. Such is the situation of the Christian cause. Italian money will equip a fleet, if not at Venice then at Genoa or in Aragon, and it will not be smaller than the occasion requires. The Hungarians will arm 20,000 cavalry and as many infantry. These with the Germans and Burgundians will make 88,000 soldiers in the field. Does anyone think the Turks will not be conquered with these forces? They will be joined by [the Albanian leader] Georg Skanderbeg and a very strong force of Albanians, and many all over Greece will desert from the enemy. In Asia Charamanus and the Armenians will attack the Turks in the rear. We have no reason to despair if only God himself will favor our undertaking. Go and tell those at home what has been done here; admonish your masters to fulfil their promises promptly; and by your words and works strove that the divine mercy may be propitious to us."

At these words all present confirmed their promises; those who had offered nothing sat silent and confused. Borso [d'Este]'s ambassadors [from Ferrara], that they might seem to have done somewhat more than the rest, promised 300,000 ducats for the crusade—to the derision of their hearers "who knew how empty were the promises of a man whose mean soul would do least when it promised most."

After everyone had spoken the pope bade all the cardinals, bishops, abbots, and priests present don their sacred robes. He himself came down from his throne and knelt at the steps of the high altar. There with sighs and tears for a long time he intoned in a voice of supplication verses of the Psalms appropriate to the occasion, while the prelates and all the clergy made the responses. Then he spoke to the people and blessed them. Thus he brought to an end the congress of Mantua.

Questions: What reasons did Pius give for the lack of enthusiasm for a crusade against the Ottomans? How did he work to persuade the rulers of Europe to participate? Was Pius being realistic in his crusading plans? Why or why not? What does this episode tell us about European attitudes toward crusading in the late fifteenth century?

103. ERASMUS'S *ON THE WAR AGAINST THE TURKS*

The Ottoman Turks continued to menace Europe in the sixteenth century. Although they failed in their attempt to move into western Europe via Vienna in 1529, there remained a high sense of unease among the Christians of this region, and many sought to address the problem of holy war in an age of religious division. The Protestant leader Martin Luther had earlier preached against an Ottoman crusade, believing that it was a Catholic cause, and therefore wrong in the eyes of God. Luther changed his mind after Vienna, when the threat moved close to home, but he advocated a secular rather than a religious war. The great Catholic scholar Erasmus's treatise on the subject, excerpted below, was written in 1530 in light of Luther's views and in the context of the difficulties in reconciling issues of church and state.

Source: trans. M.J. Heath, *The Erasmus Reader*, ed. E. Rummel (Toronto: University of Toronto Press, 1990), pp. 316-22, 325-26, 333.

It is easy to see how profitable their false religion has been to them, as long as we have neglected the duties of true piety. While we have been endlessly fighting among ourselves over some useless plot of ground in what are worse than civil wars, the Turks have vastly extended their empire or, rather, their reign of terror....

Can we attribute these successes to the Turks' piety? Of course not. To their valor? They are a race softened by debauchery and fearsome only as brigands. What, then, is the answer? They owe their victories to our sins; we have opposed them but, as the results plainly show, God has been angered against us. We assail the Turks with the selfsame eagerness with which they invade the lands of others. We are betrayed by our lust for power; we covet riches; in short, we fight the Turks like Turks. For the chronicle of these events shows clearly enough that it was our treachery, our ambition, our inherent faithlessness which provoked all these dreadful disasters.... Now, if we had undertaken this legitimate war against the Turks in harmony among ourselves, with purer hearts, beneath the banners of Christ, and relying on his aid alone, Christendom would never have been reduced to its present straits. But I shall say more of this in its proper place.

Before that I must briefly take issue with two sets of opponents, those who are eager for a Turkish war for the wrong reasons, and those who, also wrongly, argue against making war on the Turks. Both groups seem to me equally wrong, though for different reasons. Of course, not all wars against the Turks are legitimate and holy, yet there are times when failure to resist the Turks simply means the surrender of part of Christendom to these barbaric enemies, and the abandonment of those of our brethren who are already enslaved beneath their foul yoke.

On the other hand, whenever the ignorant mob hear the name "Turk," they immediately fly into a rage and clamor for blood, calling them dogs and enemies to the name of Christian; it does not occur to them that, in the first place, the Turks are men, and, what is more, half-Christian; they never stop to consider whether the occasion of the war is just, nor whether it is practical to take up arms and thereby to provoke an enemy who will strike back with redoubled fury. They do not realize that the church has no more dangerous enemies than sinners in high places, especially if they are in holy orders; finally, they do not understand that God, offended by our wickedness, from time to time uses the outrages committed by these barbarians to reform us. For instance, pictures are painted showing examples of Turkish cruelty, but these ought in fact to remind us how reluctant we should be to make war against anyone at all, since similar "amusements" have been common in all the wars in which, over so many years, Christian has wickedly fought against Christian. These paintings condemn their cruelty, yet worse crimes were perpetrated at Asperen, not by the Turks, but by my own countrymen, many of them even my friends. The memory of that calamity is too fresh; I need not reopen the wound. If the subjects of these paintings truly shock us, we should curb our own impetuosity, which so easily leads us headlong into war. For however cruel the deeds of the Turks, the same deeds committed against his fellow by a Christian are still more cruel. What a sight it would be if men were confronted with paintings of the atrocities which Christians have committed against Christians in the last forty years! This is all I have to say to those who do no more than scream "War on the Turks! War on the Turks!"

Now I shall deal with the errors of those whose arguments for the opposite point of view, though perhaps more plausible, are no less dangerous; for there are those who claim that the right to make war is totally denied to Christians. I find this idea too absurd to need refutation, although there has been no lack of people ready to contrive accusations against me because of this, in that in my writings I am lavish in my praise of peace and fierce in my hatred of war. But honest men reading my works will recognize, without any prompting from me, the obvious impertinence of these slanders. My message is that war must never be undertaken unless, as a last resort, it cannot be avoided; war is by its nature such a plague to man that even if it is undertaken by a just prince in a totally just cause, the wickedness of captains and soldiers results in almost more evil than good. St. Bernard [of Clairvaux] goes further, in calling "malicious" the "militia" of this world; he designates it "of this world" because so often the call to arms is provoked by ambition, anger, or the hope of plunder; the man who falls in wars of this kind, he says, is dead for all eternity, while he who kills and conquers lives on — as a murderer.

Now I come to those who agree with Luther's contention that those who make war on the Turks rebel against God, who is punishing our sins through them. The theologians of Paris have censured this opinion in the following sentence: this proposition is universally understood to be false, and does not conform to holy writ. They attack it as false, not as heretical, and they do not simply condemn it but declare that it is universally false. Their meaning is, I believe, that sometimes war against the Turks is rightly undertaken, sometimes not, according to the circumstances....

As far as Luther's argument is concerned, I may add that if it is not lawful to resist the Turks, because God is punishing the sins of his people through them, it is no more lawful to call in a doctor during illness, because God also sends diseases to purge his people of their sins. He uses the wiles of Satan for the same purpose, and yet we are commanded to resist them. It is therefore lawful to fight off the Turks, unless God manifestly prohibits it.

However, it is clear that this war will be fought in the face of God's anger if we are moved by the desire for greater power, the lust for wealth, or any similar reason, rather than by concern for the peace of Christendom; or if, on meeting the enemy, we rely on our own strength rather than on God's protection, or fight without regard for our Christian principles. What is more, since God sends the Turks so frequently against us to call us to reform our lives, all the omens will be against us in this war if we take up arms without correcting the errors which have provoked God to punish us through their barbaric cruelty. It is obvious that this has been the case up to now; I am afraid that in the future things will get worse unless we turn wholeheartedly towards the Lord, and offer to him the sacrifice which the psalm suggested.

Someone will intervene here to say that it is lawful for Christian to fight Christian, but that it is not lawful to fight the Turks, since Paul declares that it is not his business to judge outsiders, and that he has enough to judge those within the community; the Turks are outsiders, and do not belong to the church; if we are permitted to kill Turks, why did not the church arm herself long ago against the gentiles who cruelly persecuted all who confessed the name of Christ? But Augustine refused to authorize this, even at a time when our numbers and our wealth were greater than theirs; in fact, he appealed to the emperor not to execute certain men who had murdered some Christians, his reason being that in this way the glory of the martyrs would not be sullied....

The mass of Christians are wrong, on the other hand, in thinking that anyone is allowed to kill a Turk, as one would a mad dog, for no better reason than that he is a Turk. If this were true then anyone would be allowed to kill a Jew; but if he dared to do so he would not escape punishment by the civil authorities. The Christian magistrate punishes Jews who break the state's laws, to which they are subject, but they are not put to death because of their religion; Christianity is spread by persuasion, not by force; by careful cultivation, not by destruction....

But to take away the power of the sword from secular princes and magistrates is simply to undermine the whole foundation of the state, and to expose the lives and property of the citizens to the violence of criminals. There is, on the one hand, no good precedent for priests becoming involved in the business of war, to say nothing of actually fighting themselves. Their fight is for the Lord, and they must not be involved in the struggles of this world. War is such a soulless business that it should really be called pagan. If it is right for priests to make war, it is equally right for them to play the executioner. Now, when papal decrees forbid the priest to practice medicine, on what grounds is he permitted to turn to war, since all the energies and skill of the doctor go to preserving life, and those of the warrior to taking it? But this analogy of curing sickness does not entirely fit the present case, for the use of drugs does not entail loss or injury to anyone, whereas anyone using war as a cure applies it in such a way that he contrives the death of others. Anyone who makes war with too little justice on his side, or who conducts the campaign improperly, is no more acceptable than a man trying hard to ward off illness by witchcraft....

Someone will perhaps deduce from all this that I have undertaken the task of arguing *against* a Turkish war. Not at all; on the contrary, my purpose is to ensure that we make war against them successfully and win truly splendid victories for Christ. Merely to clamor for war against the Turks, calling them inhuman monsters, traitors to the church and a race tainted with all kinds of crime and villainy, is simply to betray the ignorant mob to the enemy.

We have been hearing from close at hand of the recurrent misfortunes of Hungary, and most recently of the wretched death of Louis, the pitiable fate of Queen Mary, and now, besides the occupation of the kingdom of Hungary, the merciless devastation of Austria; during all these events, I have more than once been astonished by the nonchalance of other Christian lands, and especially of Germany herself, as if these things in no way affected the rest of us. We become tight-fisted, and spend on pleasures and trivialities what we do not wish to spend on rescuing Christians. I am well aware of the excuses that some apologists for this attitude put forward. This charade, they say, has been played too often by the various popes, and the outcome has always been farcical. Either nothing gets done at all, or the situation takes a turn for the worse. The money collected has stuck fast in the hands of the popes, cardinals, monks, princes, and dukes, and the common soldiers are given permission to plunder, instead of receiving pay. We have heard so often, they say, of crusading expeditions, of recovering the Holy Land; we have seen so often the red cross adorned with the triple crown, together with the red wallet [that is, papal emblems]; we have heard so often the holy sermons promising us the earth; we have heard so often of valiant deeds and boundless hopes—but the only thing that has triumphed has been money. How can we, who have been misled thirty times over, believe any more promises, however splendid? We have been plainly tricked so often, and as the proverb says: once bitten, twice shy....

Someone may press me here and say: why such a long speech? Tell us plainly, do you think we should make war or not? Now, if the Lord had spoken to me, I should readily speak out; it is very easy now to say what I should like to see done, but what will actually happen is a different matter. I cannot predict the outcome nor do I know enough details about the enterprise; I am merely giving our rulers a warning to consider this undertaking with greater care. I am not against such a war, but I am doing my best to show how it may be successfully begun and continued. For when we finally set about this most dangerous of all tasks, it must result either in complete success for Christendom, or in total disaster. "What?" you may say; "must we therefore endure all the evils which Turkish cruelty has inflicted upon us for centuries past, the evils which continue to afflict us and threaten us in the future, without striking back?" I agree that it is hard, but it is better to endure this hardship, if it be God's will, than to invite utter ruin. The best solution of all would be to conquer the Turkish empire in the way in which the apostles conquered all the peoples of the earth for their master, Christ; but the best alternative must be to have as the chief object of an armed campaign that the Turks will be glad to have been defeated. This task will be made easier if, firstly, they see that Christianity is not mere words, and can observe that our deeds are worthy of the Gospel; secondly, if honest preachers are sent in to reap the harvest, men will further Christ's interests, not their own. Thirdly, if any infidel cannot so quickly be persuaded, he should be allowed for a time to live under his own laws, until gradually he comes to agree with us. Long ago, Christian emperors used this method to abolish paganism by degrees. At first they allowed the pagans to live on equal terms with our Christians, in such a way that neither interfered with the other. Then they deprived the idolaters' temples of their privileges, and finally, after forbidding the sacrifice of victims in public, they abolished the worship of idols completely. In this way our religion gradually grew stronger, paganism was stamped out, and the signs of Christ's triumph filled the world.

Questions: How does Erasmus see warfare? How does he see the Turks? When does he believe it is justifiable to make war on them? What, according to Erasmus, is the role of the state in this affair? How does he propose that Europe should bring the Turks into the Christian fold? Were his views backward-looking or innovative?

104. NARRATIVES OF EXPLORATION

Europe on the eve of the sixteenth century was in the twilight of its crusading era. The Protestant Reformation would divide the Christian community, while emerging notions of secular sovereignty would work to subordinate church authority to the state. The beginning of European exploration, however, had interesting connections with the crusading movement. In some cases the rhetoric of crusading and its ideals were merely transferred to new theaters of conquest: Africa, Asia and the Americas. Below are three accounts of the exploration and exploitation of these new lands.

Sources: Gomes: trans. C.R. Beazley and E. Prestage, *The Chronicle of the Discovery and Conquest of Guinea written by Gomes Eannes de Azurara* (London: The Hakluyt Society, 1896), vol. I, pp. 27-30, revised; Columbus: trans. C. Jane, *Select Documents Illustrating the Four Voyages of Columbus* (London: The Hakluyt Society, 1930), vol. I, pp. 2, 6, 8, 10; Manuel: trans. E.G. Ravenstein, *A Journal of the First Voyage of Vasco de Gama, 1497-1499* (London: Hakluyt Society, 1898), pp. 113-14, revised.

Gomes Eannes de Azurara's Biography of Prince Henry the Navigator, 1453

In which five reasons appear why the lord infante [that is, Prince Henry the Navigator] was moved to command the search for the lands of Guinea [in Africa].

We imagine that we know a matter when we are acquainted with the doer of it and the end for which he did it. And since in former chapters we have set forth the lord infante as the chief actor in these things, giving as clear an understanding of him as we could, it is meet that in this present chapter we should know his purpose in doing them. And you should note well that the noble spirit of this prince, by a sort of natural constraint, was ever urging him both to begin and to carry out very great deeds. For which reason, after the taking of Ceuta he always kept ships well armed against the infidel, both for war, and because he had also a wish to know the land that lay beyond the isles of Canary and that cape called Bojador, for that up to his time, neither by writings, nor by the memory of man, was the nature of the land beyond that cape known with any certainty. Some said indeed that St. Brendan had passed that way [in the early Middle Ages]; and there was another tale of two galleys rounding the cape, which never returned. But this does not appear at all likely to be true, for it is not to be presumed that if the said galleys went there, some other ships would not have endeavored to learn what voyage they had made. And because the said lord infante wished to know the truth of this, since it seemed to him that if he or some other lord did not endeavor to gain that knowledge, no mariners or merchants would ever dare to attempt it (for it is clear that none of them ever trouble themselves to sail to a place where there is not a sure and certain hope of profit)—and seeing also that no other prince took any pains in this matter, he sent out his own ships against those parts, to have manifest certainty of them all. And to this he was stirred up by his zeal for the service of God and of King Edward his lord and brother, who then reigned. And this was the first reason of his action.

The second reason was that if there chanced to be in those lands some population of Christians, or some ports into which it would be possible to sail without peril, many kinds of merchandise might be brought to this realm, which would find a ready market, and reasonably so, because no other people of these parts traded with them, nor yet people of any other that were known; and also the products of this realm might be taken there, which traffic would bring great profit to our countrymen.

The third reason was that, as it was said that the power of the Moors in that land of Africa was very much greater than was commonly supposed, and that there were no Christians among them, nor any other race of men, and because every wise man is obliged by natural prudence to wish for a knowledge of the power of his enemy, therefore the said lord infante exerted himself to cause this to be fully discovered, and to make it known for certain how far the power of those infidels extended.

The fourth reason was because during the one and thirty years that he had warred against the Moors, he had never found a Christian king, nor a lord outside this land, who for the love of our Lord Jesus Christ would aid him in the said war. Therefore he sought to know if there were in those parts any Christian princes, in whom the charity and the love of Christ was so ingrained that they would aid him against those enemies of the faith.

The fifth reason was his great desire to make increase in the faith of our Lord Jesus Christ and to bring to him all the souls that should be saved, understanding that all the mystery of the incarnation, death, and passion of our Lord Jesus Christ was for this sole end—namely the salvation of lost souls—whom the said lord infante by his travail and spending would fain bring into the true path. For he perceived that no better offering could be made unto the Lord than this; for if God promised to return one hundred goods for one, we may justly believe that for such great benefits, that is to say for so many souls as were saved by the efforts of this Lord, he will have so many hundreds of rewards in the kingdom of God, by which his spirit may be glorified after this life in the celestial realm. For I that wrote this history saw so many men and women of those parts turned to the holy faith, that even if the infante had been a heathen, their prayers would have been enough to have obtained his salvation. And not only did I see the first captives, but their children and grandchildren as true Christians as if the divine grace breathed in them and imparted to them a clear knowledge of itself.

Letter of Christopher Columbus to Luis de Santángel, 1492-93

Sir, as I know that you will be pleased at the great victory with which our Lord has crowned my voyage, I write this to you, from which you will learn how in thirty-three days, I passed from the Canary Islands to the Indies with the fleet which the most illustrious king and queen, our sovereigns, gave to me. And there I found very many islands filled with people innumerable, and of them all I have taken possession for their highnesses, by proclamation made and with the royal standard unfurled, and no opposition was offered to me. To the first island which I found, I gave the name *San Salvador*, in remembrance of the divine majesty, who has marvelously bestowed all this; the Indians call it "Guanahani." To the second, I gave the name *Isla de Santa Maria de Concepción*; to the third, *Fernandina*; to the fourth, *Isabella*; to the fifth, *Isla Juana*, and so to each one I gave a new name....

The people of this island, and of all the other islands which I have found and of which I have information, all go naked, men and women, as their mothers bore them, although some women cover a single place with the leaf of a plant or with a net of cotton which they make for the purpose. They have no iron or steel or weapons, nor are they fitted to use them, not because they are not well built men and of handsome stature, but because they are very marvelously timorous. They have no other arms than weapons made of canes, cut in seeding time, to the ends of which they fix a small sharpened stick. And they do not dare to make use of these, for many times it has happened that I have sent ashore two or three men to some town to have speech, and countless people have come out to them, and as soon as they have seen my men approaching they have fled, even a father not waiting for his son. And this, not because ill has been done to anyone; on the contrary, at every point where I have been and have been able to have speech, I have given to them of all that I had, such as cloth and many other things, without receiving anything for it; but so they are, incurably timid. It is true that, after they have been reassured and have lost their fear, they are so guileless and so generous with all they possess, that no one would believe it who has not seen it. They never refuse anything which they possess, if it be asked of them; on the contrary, they invite anyone to share it, and display as much love as if they would give their hearts, and whether the thing be of value or whether it be of small price, at once with whatever trifle of whatever kind it may be that is given to them, with that they are content. I forbade that they should be given things so worthless as fragments of broken crockery and scraps of broken glass, and ends of straps, although when they were able to get them, they fancied that they possessed the best jewel in the world. So it was found that for a strap a sailor received gold to the weight of two and a half *castellanos*, and others much more for other things which were worth much less. As for new *blancas* [that is, silver coins], for them they would give everything which they had, although it might be two or three *castellanos'* weight of gold or a [measure] or two of spun cotton.... They took even the pieces of the broken hoops of the wine barrels and, like savages, gave what they had, so that it seemed to me to be wrong and I forbade it. And I gave a thousand handsome good things, which I had brought, in order that they might conceive affection, and more than that, might become Christians and be inclined to the love and service of their highnesses and of the whole Castilian nation, and strive to aid us and to give us of the things which they have in abundance and which are necessary to us. And they do not know any creed and are not idolaters; only they all believe that power and good are in the heavens, and they are very firmly convinced that I, with these ships and men, came from the heavens, and in this belief they everywhere received me, after they had overcome their fear. And this does not come because they are ignorant; on the contrary, they are of a very acute intelligence and are men who navigate all those seas, so that it is amazing how good an account they give of everything, but it is because they have never seen people clothed or ships of such a kind.

And as soon as I arrived in the Indies, in the first island which I found, I took by force some of them, in order that they might learn and give me information of that which there is in those parts, and so it was that they soon understood us, and we them, either by speech or signs, and they have been very serviceable....

Letter of King Manuel of Portugal to Ferdinand and Isabella of Spain, 1499

Most high and excellent prince and princess, most potent lord and lady!

Your highnesses already know that we had ordered Vasco da Gama, a nobleman of our household, and his brother Paulo da Gama, with four vessels to make discoveries by sea, and that two years have now elapsed since their departure. And as the principal motive of this enterprise has been with our predecessors, the service of God our Lord, and our own advantage, it pleased him in his mercy to speed them on their route. From a message which has now been brought to this city by one of the captains, we learn that they did reach and discover India and other kingdoms and lordships bordering upon it; that they entered and navigated its sea, finding large cities, large edifices and rivers, and great populations among whom is carried on all the trade in spices and precious stones, which are forwarded in ships (which these same explorers saw and met with in good numbers and of great size) to Mecca, and thence to Cairo, whence they are dispersed throughout the world. Of these [spices] they have brought a quantity including cinnamon, cloves, ginger, nutmeg, and pepper, as well as other kinds, together with the boughs and leaves of the same;

also many fine stones of all sorts such as rubies and others. And they also came to a country in which there are mines of gold, of which [gold], like the spices and precious stones, they did not bring as much as they could have done, for they took no merchandise with them.

As we are aware that your highnesses will hear of these things with much pleasure and satisfaction, we thought well to give this information. And your highnesses may believe, in accordance with what we have learnt concerning the Christian people whom these explorers reached, that it will be possible, although they are not as yet strong in the faith or possessed of a thorough knowledge of it, to do much in the service of God and the exaltation of the holy faith, once they shall have been converted and fully fortified in it. And when they shall have thus been fortified in the faith, there will be an opportunity for destroying the Moors of those parts. Moreover, we hope, with the help of God, that the great trade which now enriches the Moors of those parts, through whose hands it passes without the intervention of other persons or peoples, shall, in consequence of our regulations, be diverted to the natives and ships of our own kingdom, so that henceforth all Christendom, in this part of Europe, shall be able in a large measure to provide itself with these spices and precious stones.

Questions: What role do trade, religion and politics play in the motivations and actions of each of these explorers? How do they justify their actions? Compare these narratives with that of the Cistercian poem on expansion (doc. 65). In what ways do these narratives of the new era of world exploration reflect the mentality, rhetoric, and goals of crusading?

SOURCES

The Authors of the book and the Publisher have made every attempt to locate the authors of the copyrighted material or their heirs or assigns, and would be grateful for any information that would allow them to correct any errors or omissions in a subsequent edition of the work.

"The Quran." *Quran: The Final Testament*. Trans. Rashad Khalifa. Tucson: Islamic Productions, 1989.

"Matthew of Edessa on the Seljuk Conquests." *Armenia and the Crusades, Tenth to Twelfth Centuries: The Chronicle of Matthew of Edessa*. Trans. Ara Edmond Dostourian. Lanham and New York: University Press of America, 1993.

"Abu l-Muzaffar al-Abiwardi on the Fall of Jerusalem," "Ibn al-Athir on the Fall of Edessa," "Imad ad-Din on the Battle of Hattin." *Arab Historians of the Crusades*. Selected and translated from the Arabic sources by Francesco Gabrieli. Translated from the Italian by E.J. Costello. Berkeley: University of California Press, 1969. English translation copyright © Routledge and Kegan Paul, 1969. (Translated from the Italian, *Storici Arabi delle Crociate*. Selected and translated from the Arabic sources by Francesco Gabrieli. Turin, Italy: Giulio Einaudi Editore S.p.A. Copyright © 1957 by Giulio Einaudi Editore.)

"William of Tyre's *History*," "Venetian Treaty." *A History of Deeds Done beyond the Sea, by William Archbishop of Tyre*. Trans. Emily Atwater Babcock and A.C. Krey. New York: Columbia University Press, 1943. Copyright © 1943 Columbia University Press. Reprinted with the permission of the publisher.

"Fulcher of Chartres's *History*." Fulcher of Chartres, *A History of the Expedition to Jerusalem, 1095-1127*. Trans. Frances Rita Ryan. Ed. Harold S. Fink. Knoxville: University of Tennessee Press, 1969. Used by permission of the University of Tennesse Press.

"The Travels of Ibn Jubayr." *The Travels of Ibn Jubayr*. Trans. R.J.C. Broadhurst. London: Jonathan Cape, 1952. Reprinted by permission of The Random House Group Ltd.

"Memoirs of Usamah Ibn Munqidh." *The Autobiography of Ousâma*. Trans. G.R. Potter. London: George Routledge & Sons, Ltd., 1929.

"Odo of Deuil: *The Journey of Louis VII to the East*." *Odo of Deuil: The Journey of Louis VII to the East*. Trans. Virginia Gingerick Berry. New York: Columbia University Press, 1948. Copyright © 1948 Columbia University Press. Reprinted with the permission of the publisher.

"John Kinnamos: *The Deeds of John and Manuel Comnenus*." John Kinnamos, *The Deeds of John and Manuel Comnenus*. Trans. Charles M. Brand.

New York: Columbia University Press, 1976. Copyright © 1976 Columbia University Press. Reprinted with the permission of the publisher.

"Analyses of the Second Crusade," "Documents on the Sack of Constantinople: Letter of Innocent III to Peter," "Chronicle of Henry of Livonia," "Philip of Novara on Frederick II's Crusade," "The Conquest of Lisbon." *The Crusades: A Documentary Survey*. Ed. James A. Brundage. Milwaukee: The Marquette University Press, 1962.

"Personal Arrangements: Contract of Service." Trans. H.G. Richardson and G.O. Sayles, *The Governance of Mediaeval England from the Conquest to Magna Carta*. Edinburgh: Edinburgh University Press, 1963.

"Bernard of Clairvaux: *In Praise of the New Knighthood.*" *In Praise of the New Knighthood*. Trans. Conrad Greenia. Kalamazoo: Cistercian Publications, Inc., 2000.

"The Rule of the Templars." *The Rule of the Templars: The French Text of the Rule of the Order of the Knights Templar*. Trans. J.M. Upton-Ward. Woodbridge, Suffolk: The Boydell Press, 1992.

"Stories of Women Crusaders: Annals of Niketas Choniates." *O City of Byzantium, Annals of Niketas Chonniates*. Trans. Harry J. Magoulias. Detroit: Wayne State University Press, 1984. Reprinted with permission of the Wayne State University Press.

"Crusading Songs": "Pax in Nomine Domini," "Giammi Non Mi Conforto." *Medieval Song: An Anthology of Hymns and Lyrics*. Trans. James J. Wilhelm. New York: E.P. Dutton & Co., Inc., 1971.

"Letter of Innocent III to the Archbishop and Clergy of Magdeburg," "Humbert of Romans on Criticisms of Crusading." *The Crusades: Idea and Reality, 1095-1274*. Trans. Louise and Jonathan Riley-Smith. London: Edward Arnold, 1981. Reproduced by permission of Hodder Arnold.

"William of Tudela's *Song of the Cathar Wars.*" William of Tudela, *The Song of the Cathar Wars: A History of the Albigensian Crusade*. Trans. Janet Shirley. Aldershot: Scolar Press, 1996. Copyright © Janet Shirley, 1996.

"Accounts of the Children's Crusade": "Royal Chronicles of Cologne," "Deeds of Trier." *Medieval Popular Religion, 1000-1500: A Reader*. Ed. John Shinners. Peterborough: Broadview Press, 1997.

"Proclamations of Northern European Crusades: Letter of Bernard of Clairvaux." *The Letters of St. Bernard of Clairvaux*. Trans. Bruno Scott James. Chicago: Henry Regnery Company, 1953.

"Helmold's *Chronicle of the Slavs.*" *The Chronicle of the Slavs by Helmold, Priest of Bosau*. Trans. Francis Joseph Tschan. New York: Octagon Books Inc., 1966. Copyright © 1935 Columbia University Press. Reprinted with the permission of the publisher.

"The Chronicle of Henry of Livonia." *The Chronicle of Henry of Livonia*. Trans. James A. Brundage. Madison: University of Wisconsin Press, 1961. Copyright © 1961. Reprinted by permission of The University of Wisconsin Press.

"Rule of the Teutonic Knights." From "The Statutes of the Teutonic Knights: A Study of Religious Chivalry." Trans. Indrikis Sterns. Philadelphia: University of Pennsylvania, unpublished Ph.D. dissertation, 1969.

"Nikolaus von Jeroschin on the Prussian Crusades." Trans. H.F. Schwarz. *The Portable Medieval Reader*. Ed. J.B. Ross and M.M. McLaughlin. Harmondsworth: Penguin, 1977. Latin text in *Ordensritter und Kirchenfürsten*. Ed. J. Bühler. Leipzig: Insel-Verlag, 1927.

"The Conquest of Lisbon." *De Expugnatione Lyxboniensi: The Conquest of Lisbon*. Trans. Charles Wendell David. New York: Columbia University Press, 2001.

"Alfonso VIII's Report on Las Navas de Tolosa." *Christians and Moors in Spain, Volume II: 1195-1614*. Trans. Colin Smith. Warminster: Aris & Phillips Ltd., 1989.

"Muslim-Christian Treaty." Trans. Robert I. Burns and Paul E. Chevedden. *Negotiating Cultures: Bilingual Surrender Treaties in Muslim-Crusader Spain under James the Conqueror*. Leiden: Brill, 1999. © Koninklijke Brill NV, Leiden, The Netherlands.

"Moorish Laws." *Christians and Moors in Spain*, vol. III. Trans. Charles Melville and Ahmad Ubaydli. Warminster: Aris & Phillips, Ltd., 1992.

"Constitutions of the Order of Merced." *Ransoming Captives in Crusader Spain: The Order of Merced on the Christian-Islamic Frontier*. Trans. James William Brodman. Philadelphia: University of Pennsylvania Press, 1986. Copyright © James William Broadman, 1986.

"Ibn Al-Athir on the Mongol Invasion." Edward Granville Browne, *A Literary History of Persia, Vol II*. Cambridge: Cambridge University Press, 1964. (Originally published by T. Fisher Unwin, 1906). Reprinted with the permission of Cambridge University Press.

"Ibn 'Abd al-Zahir's Biography of Baybars." *Baybars I of Egypt*. Trans. Syedah Fatima Sadeque. Karachi: Oxford University Press, 1956.

"Pierre Dubois's *The Recovery of the Holy Land*." Pierre Dubois, *The Recovery of the Holy Land*. Trans. Walther I. Brandt. New York: Columbia University Press, 1956. Copyright © 1956 Columbia University Press. Reprinted with the permission of the publisher.

"Ramon Lull's Plan to Convert the Muslims." *Documents on the Later Crusades, 1274-1580*. Trans. Norman Housley. London: Macmillan Press Ltd., 1996.

"Marsilius of Padua's *The Defender of Peace*." Marsilius of Padua, *Defensor Pacis*.

INDEX OF TOPICS

Topics are listed by document numbers. In some cases, topics are listed with book, chapter or section numbers within a document. Thus, 2.3 is a reference to document 2 and section, book or chapter 3. If only the document number is listed for a sectioned document, this refers to the document's introduction.

57, 74, 83, 85, 89-92, 95, 100, 103-104 battles 4, 7-8, 10, 12, 15-19, 33, 39, 39.8, 40-41, 54, 63, 63.77, 67, 74, 77, 84, 86-88, 98

siege warfare 4, 7, 9-10, 13, 15, 17-18, 20, 23, 24.III, 29, 33-34, 40-42, 44, 53-54, 57-58, 63.37, 67, 74, 76-77, 83-84, 86, 88, 98-99, 101   spoil and plundering 7, 12-13, 15-16, 19, 24.II, 33-34, 36, 57-58, 63.48-49, 66, 74, 76-77, 86-89, 99, 103

wills 25, 47, 81.16

women 1, 12-14, 17, 20, 22-23, 24.III, 29-30, 32-33, 36, 39.8, 41-43, 45-47, 49.4, 54, 55, 57-58, 60-61, 63.37, 69.31, 70-71, 76, 79-80, 81.16-17, 86, 88-89, 97, 101